DONALD N. FERGUSON

Image and Structure in
CHAMBER MUSIC

UNIVERSITY OF MINNESOTA PRESS
Minneapolis

LIBRARY OF CONGRESS CATALOG CARD NUMBER: 64-18652

PUBLISHED IN GREAT BRITAIN, INDIA, AND PAKISTAN BY THE OXFORD UNIVERSITY PRESS, LONDON, BOMBAY, AND KARACHI, AND IN CANADA BY THOMAS ALLEN, LTD., TORONTO

Preface

As its title will indicate, this book is neither a history of chamber music nor even a comprehensive survey of its literature. It studies only the more important composers and their more important works; yet these are numerous enough to provide the amateur, whether listener or performer, with a fairly broad purview of that literature.

By far the larger portion of the text is devoted to the second item in the title, Structure — to the syntax and the rhetoric of the compositions. This disagreeable exercise in parsing is far more necessary in musical than in verbal structures. For the parts of speech, whose relation is established by the rules of verbal syntax, are not abstract items made to conform to an abstract structural scheme. They are symbols for things and acts, for their qualities and their relations; and their syntactical arrangement is so far dictated by the image of experience to whose projection they are devoted that they appear, to the recipient consciousness, as the parts of experience.

Music, on the other hand, has no words — no parts of speech, directly symbolic of things and acts. Its syntax, therefore, appears as intrinsic to its substance, and wholly independent of that relation to the items — the facts — of external experience in which verbal syntax is rooted. Its basic syntactical principle is doubtless tonality — the governance of a given tonal complex by a single tone, familiarly named tonic or key-note; but the functioning of that central tone has been, and still is, so variable that the idea of tonality is constantly in need of being redefined. What musical syntax yields, however, is an image of structure as essential for the understanding of musical idea as is the image of verbal syntax for the comprehension of verbal idea.

Because the syntactical principle of music is intrinsic, and because the musical substance is wholly lacking in fixed symbolic reference to the facts of external experience, it may be plausibly argued that the image of structure is the only legitimate image evoked by musical art. Whether legitimate or not, however, another sort of image — in essence an image of external, non-musical experience — is commonly evoked by music. This is the Image of my title, and it there precedes Structure because it appears to me to be even more significant.

Since music is not, as language is, directly symbolic of things and acts, the image it evokes is very different from that immediately aroused by words. It is an image, not of the facts from which our minds distil that understanding of fact which we call experience, but an aspect of that understanding itself.

That understanding is primarily an awareness of significance in the confronted circumstance. It is not, however, a merely intellectual understanding. It is also emotional — the emotion being attendant on, and in a sense proportional to, the perceived significance. Being the immediate correlative of understanding, emotion, exhibited, may thus be confidently interpreted as a "sign" of that understanding.

We exhibit our emotion in a thousand subtle ways — through smiles and frowns; through nervous fidgets or bold, belligerent posture; through indifferent or penetrating gaze; through kindly or determined or ironic inflections of our words; and these bodily behaviors are often dependably indicative, not only of our feeling but of the nature of the circumstance that has aroused our feeling. They portray, that is, an aspect of our understanding of experience.

The Image of my title is similarly an image, not of emotion merely, but of emotion interpretable as a sign of its originative and attendant experience. It thus bears the stamp not merely of feeling but of intellection. Contemporary aesthetic will have it that musical intellection is "purely" musical — that its concern is with the tonal structure only and is without reference to the external world of experience. The twentieth century has produced a good deal of music quite in accord with this theorem. But the greatness of that music which the world continues to acknowledge as great extends beyond this narrow frame of reference. Beethoven's *Eroica* speaks — *and intended to speak* — of what we dimly glimpse as the heroic attitude of mind: an attitude concerned with other things than musical structure. The chamber music studied here

speaks similarly of other attitudes — not often as exalted as that portrayed in the *Eroica*, but significant because the experiences that generated them are, in the considered judgment of men, significant. My
Image, then, is the image of a mental attitude, envisaging the experience
out of which it arose, but portraying only the feeling aspect of that
attitude.

But how, you will ask, out of a substance apparently unrelated to
the "things" which are the raw material of experience, is an image related to those things to be constructed? How can experience be envisaged through a medium which can make no tangible reference to the
facts of experience? And will not such an image be too obscure to be
grasped by any but the experienced and erudite listener?

If you abandon the expectation (naturally suggested by the word
image) of a concrete portrayal of fact, and look instead for a portrayal of mental attitude, the answers will become quite simple. The
process will considerably resemble that utterance of attitude given by
our familiar bodily "illustrations" of feeling — posture, gait, facial expression, verbal inflection, and the like. These are the spontaneous out-
lets — the muscular innervations — consequent upon and appropriate to
the inner nervous tensions they illustrate. (They are, to be sure, almost
always controlled — redirected or inhibited; but they betray that conscious effort at control, and are on that account all the more indicative
of their source — the mental attitude toward their exciting experience.)
Their variety is illimitable but their basic structure is simple. There are
but two essential factors: nervous tension and motor impulse.

Music is made of two essential substances: tone and rhythm. The
tonal substance of music can be so constructed as to show an infinity
of tensions (including aspects of calm which, in such excitable creatures as men, is similarly indicative of feeling-attitude). These tensions
may of course be contrived and exhibited as "purely" musical. But they
may also be shaped into recognizable similitudes of our familiar nervous tensions. The resemblance will not be noted as a psychological
datum merely. It will appear as the portrayal of a mental state involving this sort of tension.

The other component of the musical substance is rhythm. Like the
tonal substance, it can be shaped into abstract, purely musical patterns. But so vivid is the motor-suggestion of musical rhythm that it
can hardly be heard without being at least tentatively enacted some-

where in the muscular system of the listener. And it may also be shaped so as to resemble almost any of the myriad muscular responses to nervous excitement roused by actual circumstance, real or imaginal.

Neither will these be noted as mere psychological data. And should the tonal tensions and the rhythmic impulses coincide toward the portrayal of a neuro-muscular response appropriate to a confronted external experience, the percipient listener, although possibly quite unaware of the resemblance as such, will sense in the total impact of the music an unmistakable reference to life as he knows and lives it. For he knows and constantly enacts responses like these, and knows that they are indeed the signs of his participation in experience. Sensing, rather than directly observing, the import of these musical signs, he finds the music to "ring true."

Should he attempt, however, to demonstrate its truth to a perhaps less percipient listener, he will find himself in difficulties. He has indeed derived from the music an image of experience. But this is an image, not of experience as it is factually known, but as it is felt; and for the description of such an image his vocabulary is all but bankrupt. He will picture his image, therefore, in terms of some external circumstance which might plausibly have occasioned such feeling as is actually portrayed by the music. But his friend, who cannot find those circumstances in the music, is more bewildered — and he himself more bankrupt — than ever.

I who write this book am one of these bankrupts. I find in the music I am to study with you images of experience far more compelling in interest than the many ingenuities of structure which — by no means in their whole detail — I have described. I have hoped to make these images visible to you. Warned of the danger of bankruptcy, I have striven to avoid overdrafts of verbal picturization. My intimations of experiential imagery, in consequence, are often conveyed merely by adjectival or adverbial qualifications of structural fact — inconspicuous and, unless interpreted as extrastructural, probably unsuggestive. Yet, having regard to what seems to me the actual means of musical expression — tonal tension and rhythmic impulse — I can find no other justifiable verbal hints of the imagery actually resident in music.

Performances of music — primarily, literal "utterances" of a tonal structure — are capable of similarly adjectival qualification. Warmth, for example, which may be felt in more varied degrees than are marked on our thermometers, is not immediately indicated in our musical notation. It may be strongly implied, however, in the literal contour of a musical phrase; and he who reads this adjectival qualification into the printed notes will begin to evoke an image of experience in the minds of his hearers. For warmth, or its opposite, is of considerable import for the definition of a mental attitude toward experience. A thousand similar qualifications will be seen to be available for the amplification of the literal meaning of musical phrases. Any of them may be so overdrawn by a performer as to distort and falsify the image of experience resident, beneath the surface, in the structure. On the other hand, when they are justly proportioned to that image, the assent of the listeners will be complete and emphatic. But what they then acclaim is not a structure but an image of experience.

Table of Contents

IMAGE AND STRUCTURE
IN CHAMBER MUSIC

The Intimacy of Chamber Music

SEASONED participants in chamber music — and these, to an exceptional degree, are the listeners as well as the performers — are convinced that they enjoy the deepest pleasure that music can offer. The opera can portray more violent passions; the symphony, with its huge volume of sound, its more intricate texture, and its far wider palette of tonal color, can attain to a more imposing grandeur; and the solo literature — especially that for piano — displaying the overwhelming virtuosity of the performer as well as his striking individuality of temperament, may transport an audience to heights of enthusiasm and admiration which chamber music does not even attempt to evoke. But for such displays the audience is more a spectator than a participant; and the peculiar participation of the chamber-music lover arises out of a value which that music somehow possesses in unique measure and which for him transcends all the others. There is no precise name for this virtue. Its nature can perhaps be suggested by the word intimacy; but since that value will be glimpsed in many aspects during our study the meaning of that word, to fit this context, may profitably be explored here.

We enjoy intimacy in many human relations. In any of them it is all but indefinable. Yet some of its essentials can be discerned. We shall probably agree that it is impossible without an implied (even if only momentarily existent) unanimity of perception and feeling among the participants — a unanimity sensed rather than defined, and based upon a common, largely intuitive recognition of spiritual rather than material values.

A similar concern for spiritual values, on a more purely intellectual scale, forms one of the foundations of schools of thought in any field —

politics, science, philosophy, or whatever. It governs also artistic impulse and procedure, so that historians of the arts describe it as unconsciously directing the broad lines of artistic endeavor in those successive periods of effort which they label as Gothic, Renaissance, Baroque, and so on. These broad outlines, however, imply a consensus of perception rather than an intimacy of experience.

For procedure, established, whether in art or science or religion, breeds also method and ritual — coercions of opinion and behavior possibly unfriendly to intimacy, which can hardly be attained unless the participants' assent is free and untrammeled. And since this is so, the most appellant art is that which offers to the individual observer the fullest participation in the artist's vision — the fullest share in that experience which generated his work.

Like the intimacy which its portrayal may stimulate, this experience cannot be precisely defined. It is not visible as mere substantive event or encountered fact. Neither, even though fact may be recognizable in the artist's work, is that work intended to be observed as portraying mere event. Rather, the artist is concerned with the implication of event; and we do not share in his experience unless we catch this implication. In painting, the "thing" portrayed may range from a mere scatter of flowers to a configuration of abstract planes or curves that somehow cohere to suggest another than our familiar three-dimensional space. But unless more than the mere identity of flower or new dimension is presented, we are not interested. We see no implication.

Music also, which almost never portrays any object literally, *can* present a structure wholly lacking in implication. Again, we are not interested. But it can also be profoundly moving; and our emotional response, if we explore it, will be found to arise out of an awareness of something more in the music than its immediate offering of sensuous pleasure or formal interest.

It is the fashion, nowadays, to attribute this emotional compulsion solely to the "objective" facts of sensuous appeal and interesting musical texture. But there are also indubitable suggestions of sadness or gaiety in music which interests us; and these things do not reside intrinsically in tones and tonal structures. They arise in human beings, as the natural response to the impact of external event of some sort — as the *implications* of factual experience; and the portrayal of sadness or gaiety, which may assume a thousand different aspects, is thus by implication the por-

4]

THE INTIMACY OF CHAMBER MUSIC

trayal of the experience that generated our emotion. For emotions of consequence have no other generative source than experience.

Thus the implication of experience, rather than the bare fact of experience, is the starting-point and the real objective of the artist's effort at portrayal. And the musical "language," although it has no nouns or verbs to symbolize directly the thing or act which is the outward manifestation of the experience, is nevertheless capable of wonderful subtlety in the delineation of character and quality in our emotional responses to experience.*

Being an effort to project tangibly not the factual aspect but the character and the quality of experience, all real art is imaginative. Conversely, however it may lack the tangibility which formal structure alone can impart to an imaginative vision, *all imagination is incipient art*, and all men who are in some degree imaginative are to that extent incipient artists. If this were not so, art would have no public and no history, and the intimacy we are trying to explore could not exist. But since the quality of experience — its significance for him who undergoes it — is in question, rather than its factual detail, its depth must be measured by intuition — an imaginative faculty so highly fluctuant as to be suspect to the literal mind.

It is suspect because it operates all but instantaneously, and because it thus evokes a dangerously personal image of experience — an image colored by the observer's concern for his own well-being — and hence an

---

* You will instantly distinguish a funeral march from a military march. The tempo and the tension are not only different. They are *characteristic*. But characteristic of what? Quite obviously, of the mental concepts — the images — of death and war already existent in your mind. Without reference to those images the distinction would be impossible.

While listening to this music, eliminate (if you can) this reference to prior experience. The music will lose half its interest. It will become merely a tonal structure. But even this will be intelligible only in the light of your prior experience of structure.

Your total image of war or of death is much more comprehensive than that which is aroused by the two marches. Many musical compositions which do not march, and whose tensions are quite different from these, may thus also relate to those two images. There are endless other aspects of experience — less clearly discriminable but not less significant — which have been similarly portrayed in the literature of music, and which you may apprehend by a similar imaginative effort. That literature was not addressed to the musically learned. It was addressed to you — whose intuition *may* be keener than that of the learned. Their intuition is often blunted through learned preoccupation with structure.

The process of this inference, involving many remote areas of consciousness, is complex beyond any analysis appropriate to this book. I have set it forth (as I see it) in considerable detail in *Music as Metaphor* (University of Minnesota Press, 1960).

inevitably emotional attitude toward experience. That attitude may be conservative — one of defense against a challenge to cherished ideals. Or it may be liberal — one of challenge to unjustified beliefs or conventions. In either camp emotion may override reason, so that there is almost more truth than fun in Gilbert's delightful verse:

> For every boy and every gal
> That's born into this world alive
> Is either a little liber*al*
> Or a little conserva*tive*.

Similarly opposed attitudes may arise in the field of the plastic and dramatic arts which, at their highest level, are commonly recognized as portraying significant experience. Either attitude, espoused by a large body of followers, will engender an intuited sense of intimacy in the group, since its most cherished tenets are found reflected in the artists' work. The liberal view is commonly called romanticism; the conservative, classicism.

The liberal view is highly suspect in our day, when impersonal, "objective" presentation of artistic idea is widely applauded. Romanticism, indeed, in the current view (strongly espoused by those who have a romantic desire to be counted among the *avant-garde*) is no more than a synonym for sentimentality. It is easy to define sentiment as true feeling, and sentimentality as false. But when we are confronted with an actual expression of feeling, that confident discrimination is of little use. For feeling itself is only excitement — a factual nervous condition; and its trueness or its falsity can be judged only in the light of its appropriateness to the experience that arouses it. To condemn as false the romantic manner, seen merely *as* manner, is thus itself a sentimental judgment; and classicism, merely as manner, is no more defensible.

The chamber music we are to study began to be produced in what is called the classic era. Most of it, however, is romantic. Intimacy is more immediately evoked by romantic music than by classic, but it is also a possible offering of classic music. To explore the foundations of these considerably divergent manners should thus be a useful preliminary to our study.

The two terms are generally applied to the music of the late eighteenth and the early nineteenth centuries; but these opposed manners had revealed themselves in many earlier periods, and are rooted far more deeply in general human experience than is recognized in the current, rather

6]

heedless definitions of them. For their real difference lies, not merely in the contrasted artistic procedures (which are really their surface), but in two contrasting views of experience; and the two manners or styles are only half understood when they are contemplated as "purely" artistic procedures, disassociated from their actual source which, in either case, is intuitively envisioned experience.

Seen in this perspective, classicism and romanticism reflect and illustrate a slow but incessant pendulum-swing not merely of taste but of underlying philosophy. Christianity, as opposed to the pagan religions it superseded, was at first romantic. Becoming highly organized, with an established creed and ritual, it assumed a classic attitude. The Protestant Revolt was a reassertion of the romantic aspect of the earlier belief. The literary "war of the ancients and the moderns," which has its analogue in the twentieth century, pitted the burgeoning culture of the seventeenth century against the established classicism derived from the ancient world, which had itself (e.g., in the opposed methods of such tragic poets as Aeschylus and Euripides) known the same conflict. The French Revolution, like the American, pitted a romantic doctrine of the rights of man against the "classic" notion of the divine right of kings and the political doctrine of absolutism. All these oppositions found interpretation in the work of contemporary artists; these works show similar "drives" to those which differentiate the later classicism from romanticism; and it is evident that the two manners cannot be adequately defined without reference to the two attitudes toward experience which we have roughly called the conservative and the liberal.

What, then, *are* classicism and romanticism, defined not merely as artistic processes, but as ways of portraying that intuition of experience which is the source of both?

Professor Saintsbury managed to compact a definition of each into a single word. Classicism, he said, is Method, romanticism Energy. Each of these words describes a way of attaining an objective; each, in the field of art, *may* be understood as restricted to the objective of structure; but their fullest meaning will appear when their objective is seen, not merely as a search for imposing patterns of structure, but also as the interpretation of experience to which interpretation that pattern is appropriate.

Clearly, a ruling method of artistic structure can be stabilized only when the view of experience which is its source has itself been, however precariously, stabilized: when a view of life enunciated by acknowledged leaders of thought has become the conventional attitude toward life of a great body of followers, and when the artists also, interpreting that attitude, find it accordant with their deepest intuitions.

The classical method in music, which ruled from the 1760's for a considerable period, was just such a conventional procedure. As a manner of communication, it conformed in external elegance and taste to ruling courtly convention.* Yet this rule was not merely arbitrary. It reflected a philosophy — a way of life; and that way, however restricted its vision, acknowledged and interpreted what were called the passions — those same passions which, nowadays somewhat denuded by Freudian terminology, still survive in us. But they had long ago evoked the lyrics of Sappho and of the Troubadours; they had instigated the defiance of John Huss and Martin Luther and the massacre of St. Bartholomew; they had been sung by old Dan Chaucer with a naivety that seems the deepest sort of truth; and they had been analyzed and dissected by La Rochefoucauld and Pascal. Aristocracy tried faithfully to rule these passions — and insisted that the artists interpret them *as* ruled — by its established code. That code forbade undue violence, in behavior or speech or art. But it acknowledged passion and found it in the art it regulated; and we, to whom that code seems a spiritual trammel, too often interpret the classical utterances of Haydn and Mozart as if passion itself, instead of undue violence, had been forbidden by it.

Saintsbury's "method," then, is a pursuit of beauty through restraint. It forbids the gracious contour of ideal art to be marred by excesses or incongruities, whether of idea or design, and gains thereby a high advantage of impersonality and objectivity. Being imbued by approved aristocratic views of life, classicism has no need of the emphasis that strong personal conviction might impart to it. Being the utterance of an accepted philosophy, it would look upon any other than an objective presentation of its tenets as an impertinence. For rightness in the classic artist's method is only a reflection of the indubitable rightness of the theorem of life it interprets.

This will somewhat illuminate the definition of classicism as Method.

---

* It *had* to conform because all secular music was supported — paid for — by aristocracy and its fringe; the artist was essentially the servant (often, to be sure, honored) of his patron; but as Haydn found at Esterház, where he wore livery and ate with the servants, and as Mozart found when he tried with lamentable unsuccess to defy the system of patronage, conformity was the price of life.

8]

The definition of romanticism as Energy will similarly need to be explored. That word, however, will at first seem more obscure than "method," and another of the many phrases the critics have found for description of that artistic manner may be helpful.

Perhaps the most widely quoted definition of romanticism is Pater's "Strangeness added to Beauty." This, indeed, is not self-evident; but on examination it will turn out to be quite in accord with Saintsbury's "Energy."

The beauty to which Pater proposes to add strangeness is quite evidently the beauty of classicism — of method. In the classic art work, every detail will be found essential. Everything that is there must be there, and nothing that ought to be there has been omitted. Yet, to this finished thing, from which nothing can be taken away and to which nothing can be added, Pater proposes to add Strangeness. What, then, can this strangeness be?

It cannot, unless beauty is to be distorted — and so destroyed — be a wholly alien addition. It cannot, then, be a strangeness merely of design or organization; for that could not but appear as a distortion. But the design of classic art was itself not merely a product of "pure" organization. It was a design which, in an appropriately calm and lofty manner, included the passions in its purview and reflected them. And since these same passions — always resurgent and often intractable even for the classicist — will by no means be excluded from the romanticist's originative imagery, it is quite possibly these that will somehow impart the strangeness we are looking for. They will indeed demand, if presented in a new light, a new appropriateness in design; but the romanticist will still continue in his own way the pursuit of beauty, and will accommodate to his new purpose, rather than reject, the canons of beauty he has learned from the classicist. For his imagination will still be rooted, not in another *sort* of experience than that interpreted by the classicist, but in another *view* of that experience.

The classicist's view, considerably dictated by aristocratic convention, was collective and impersonal. The view of the romanticist, questioning that convention and thus dictated by what may be called unauthorized emotion, is individual and personal. For he speaks, not with the calm assurance of one who is the spokesman of an established order, but with the inner perturbation of one who, seeing himself in a new light and finding that his own emotional attitude is shared by other men, seeks to com-

municate more widely, and through awakened understanding to author-
ize, his new vision.

To do this he must persuade. The authority behind the classical artist
— itself originally gained by persuasion — has now wrapped itself in a
pontifical robe and speaks *ex cathedra*; but the romanticist must justify
his new faith, which is not yet reduced to thirty-nine articles. But beneath his fervor, and indeed as its principle of sufficient reason, glow
Pascal's "reasons of the heart, of which reason knows nothing."

These reasons, to be sure, are dangerous. They tend to be vehement;
and vehemence in persuasion is no guarantee that the proposition advo-
cated is sound. (Or that it is false.) But the heart does not operate inde-
pendently of the head; and logic, possibly as much in need of correction
as is sentiment, both aids the heart and is aided by it toward our never
too competent understanding of experience.

Romanticism, then, *is* energy — an energy of understanding and of
persuasion — exerted toward individual rather than impersonal interpre-
tations of experience, and discovering and emphasizing an attitude which
is indeed strange as opposed to the serene authority of classicism. Its
manner must be that of the advocate, for its philosophy is uncertain and
it must plead its convictions rather than assert or assume them apodicti-
cally. But persuasion, argued from the heart, evokes a more immediate
intimacy in the convert than does assertion, even when undisputed, in the
already confessed believer.

Yet the classic and the romantic manners or styles, however different
their surfaces, are more different in manner than in motive. Each reflects
an actual, if unformulated, philosophy. The classicist, striving to accommodate his utterance to that interpretation of experience dictated by his
accepted code, will all too often find his native impulse in conflict with
that interpretation. That is, he becomes for the moment a romanticist.
And the romanticist, similarly, will by no means reduce his understanding of experience to the nebulous state that intuition alone would give it,
but will still be guided by many of the long-approved ideals that underlie the classic attitude.

Thus, no artist is wholly a classic or a romantic. Each shares, according
to the depth of his imagination, the other's purview of experience; and
these labels, devised by critics for neat differentiations of stylistic surface
rather than for more fundamental discriminations of generative impulse,
may become seriously misleading if they are accepted as final criteria.

We shall find many a tinge of romanticism in the music of the classic composers, and a high regard for classic design in that of the romanticists. Through its persuasive tone, romantic utterance offers a more compelling spur to intimacy than does the classic, but neither manner wholly forbids the other. And since the common musical purpose of the composer and the performers of chamber music is less directed toward external effect, and since self-forgetful community of effort is more requisite in chamber music than in any other sort of musical utterance, not only the performers but also the listeners who sense this unity may enjoy the intimacy which this long discussion has tried to illuminate.

The Principal Forms

You will find a great majority of the pieces studied in this book to be in "sonata form." That form is itself not always familiar to players of chamber music, and the way its pattern came to be assumed is much less well known. Such information is not really essential to the enjoyment of the intimacy the music offers, but it is often illuminating. Therefore a brief sketch of its history may well precede our study of the pieces themselves, for some of the conventional jargon of form will have to be used in those studies.

Instrumental music during the middle ages — the jazz of that day — was regarded with contempt by all but a few of the learned composers, who were almost always churchmen. Yet, like jazz, it was alive with a vitality all but unknown to learned vocal music, and (again like jazz) it later came to contribute much to the self-centered learned art. It was of course all but indispensable to the dance (a more meaningful medium of expression in that generally illiterate time than it is now), but it also accompanied popular, and presently learned, song.

Two considerably different species of instrumental music thus grew up side by side — dance-music and a more studied offshoot of learned song. We must glance at each.

Dance-music, as skill in the manufacture and manipulation of instruments expanded, was elaborated so as to be played by more satisfying combinations of instruments than the earlier popular musicians could provide, and came presently to be performed quite apart from the actual activity of dancing. It kept, of course, its appeal to imaginary feet, but it gained a great deal in organization and color, and thus finally yielded what was known as the Suite. This was a succession of dance-measures, so contrasted in speed and character as to form an agreeable succession of movements — short, easily followed, but still interestingly organized.

Naturally, any given dance measure ruled, in its characteristic rhythm, any single movement; but gradually a single pattern evolved in which every one of the dances in the Suite was cast. This was a two-part ("binary") form. Its tune or theme was of course in the characteristic rhythm. This was maintained for some time in the chosen key of the piece. Then new interest was given by modulating — to the Dominant (V) if the main key was major; to the relative major (rel.) if the main key was minor. The tune, in this new key, soon showed signs of coming to an end; and this ending (cadence) took the form of new figures — sometimes derived from the main thought, but sometimes so different from it that they almost assume the character of a Closing Subject (Cl.S.), such as we shall find in the sonata form. This whole section was then repeated.

There followed an excursion of the main theme into more distant keys, giving heightened tension and more vivid color. This went on as long as the composer wished. Then a tentative cadence, often hardly noticeable, brought the relative minor (if the main key had been major) or the Dominant (if it had been minor); and this, with the main idea still predominant, went right past the tonic to the Subdominant (IV), to make unmistakable the main key when the cadence finally was reached. (The simple chord-sequence I–IV–V–I thus becomes the foundation of a passage lasting many bars.) This second part was also repeated.

This is a simple, unassuming design, whose outline could be easily followed even when, as with Bach, the polyphonic texture became of higher interest than the pattern itself. It has also, as we shall see, an unsuspected power of expansion; for the essential features of the later sonata form — exposition, development, and recapitulation — are expansions of the first section (exposition), the modulatory excursion (development) and the return to the main key (recapitulation) of the dance form. It lacks, of course, the second subject or theme of the sonata; for until about 1750 the texture remained polyphonic, and it was a general principle of polyphonic composition that a single piece of music should deal with a single primary theme. Subordinate episodes were allowable, but these remained obviously secondary; and the high contrast presented by the *co-ordinate* second subject of the sonata was not to be attained until the homophonic texture had superseded the polyphonic.

The varied dances in the Suite came gradually to assume a conventional order: Allemande, Courante, Sarabande, Gigue; but between the Sarabande and the Gigue other dances, in indefinite number, were interpolated.* Medieval dances were often paired, slow-fast, slow-fast; and you can see that this alternation (a most obvious way of maintaining interest) governs the order of the main dances in the Suite. When it came to be divorced from the dance itself, the music naturally took on features of ornament displaying the techniques discovered (often through improvisation) by skilled players. Soloists were allowed to emerge from the *tutti* with characteristic but subordinate themes; the main subject often quite abandoned the dance character; the solo subjects, especially in slow movements, even became main themes; and the general result was the Concerto — the most highly developed of Baroque instrumental forms, and the parallel (but not the direct ancestor) of the classic symphony in what might be called its social position.

The word Concerto (from *concertare*) implies a striving. The strife (wholly amiable) was between the soloists (called, as a group, the *concertino*) and the main body of players (by no means reduced, as in later concertos, to the role of accompanists) who might also, as a body, be called the *concerto grosso*. The concerto form was not, as our sketch may have seemed to imply, a direct outcome of the dance. It was primarily designed (as the dance originally was not) for the intimate group of aristocratic listeners who were patrons of composer and performers alike. The emergence of the soloist was, in part, the natural outcome of the fact that in any performing group some people play better than others. But it was also the product of an intuitive search for a greater variety and contrast than strict adherence to polyphonic principle could provide, and was a direct approach to the homophonic texture which, after 1750, rapidly became the ruling method in composition and culminated in the "classical" sonata form.

* The Allemande was a moderately fast measure, usually moving quietly in uninterrupted sixteenths. The Courante was of two types: French and Italian. The French was either in 6-4 or 3-2 time, and took advantage of the six quarter notes that made up either measure to change — often capriciously — the accent of the one rhythm for that of the other. The Italian type was in a simple "running" triple rhythm, faster and more heedlessly gay than in the French. The Sarabande was a sober, exalted measure in 3-4 or 3-2 time, with a characteristic accent on "two" in the first and several later bars. The Gigue was very lively, plebeian in theme and action, and often constructed after the imitative fashion of the Fugue. Minuet, Gavotte, and Bourrée were the most frequently chosen interpolated dances.

The Suite, gradually abandoning immediate suggestion of the dance and idealizing its rhythms, became a favorite type of solo keyboard music; but it also became chamber music by requiring the larger body of players who made up the patron-supported orchestras of that day. The rather diminutive individual dance-movements lacked, however, the impressiveness expected from that larger body, and this lack was compensated for by contriving an imposing introductory movement, borrowed from the most highly regarded of all musical species in that day — the opera.

This was the Overture — the "French" overture — established (but not actually invented) by Jean-Baptiste Lully, court-composer to Louis XIV.* It began with a pompous *Adagio*, went abruptly into an extended, rather fugal *Allegro*, and ended by returning to the (often abbreviated) *Adagio*. The dances followed, but some of these movements (e.g., the *Air* from Bach's Suite in D) abandoned wholly the dance-character. They retained, however, the two-part form. Solo instruments, as with Bach's Suite in B minor, which gives, even in the Overture, large opportunity to a solo flute, frequently added to the variety of the musical scene.

The other progenitor of chamber music was Song which, even before instrumental music had been recognized by learned musicians, had undergone evolutions somewhat similar to those we have just described.

Learned vocal music was at first wholly devoted to religious uses.† But the Motet, the most adventurous of learned forms, came to be set also to secular poems, at first in Latin but later in the vernacular; and popular melody (e.g., the tune of *L'homme armé*) became the thematic basis of countless settings of the Mass. The ferment of the Renaissance fertilized almost every lump of artistic soil, cultivated or fallow, and the learned in art cast off the trammels of tradition to discover that what they once had thought were weeds were blossoms of rare fragrance. Popular mel-

---

* His operas were often given "abstract" performance by presenting the Overture and a succession of the favorite dance movements without the drama itself. This may have been the initiative suggestion for the orchestral Suite. The "Italian" overture of Alessandro Scarlatti, having the movement-sequence fast-slow-fast, is held by some to have suggested the three main movements of the later classical symphony; but this is by no means the only, nor is it even a direct, ancestor of that form.

† Worldly emotions had long found utterance in the songs of the Goliards (the "wandering scholars" so delightfully resurrected by Helen Waddell), the Troubadours, and in the anonymous lyrical outbursts such as may be found in the Lochamer and Glogauer Songbooks where a kind of popular harmony was often provided.

ody, disrespectful of the ecclesiastical Modes, compelled new tricks of harmony to be sought for; and although modal convention still ostensibly ruled, there was a slow but irresistible trend toward tonality.

This trend shows itself most clearly in the Madrigal — a type of composition for unaccompanied voices (three to six) which spread, during the sixteenth century, from Italy to England. Both form and character in the Madrigal were considerably dictated by the texts; and these, ranging over the new world of experience illuminated by the Renaissance, had a variety of impulse and color immensely stimulating to the musical imagination. Madrigal-singing was a favorite after-dinner recreation, host and guests participating with enthusiasm and with a skill which puts the average amateur of our day to shame.

This was indeed chamber music in the best sense. The difficulties of performance were often great, and, to overcome these, instrumentalists were often asked either to play along with a troubled singer or to take over altogether the part of one who was missing. (The lack of words for this part didn't much matter. The words, especially in polyphonic compositions, are seldom intelligible anyway.) Indeed, instrumentalists sometimes took over all the parts; and they found in this way not only a clarification of the musical texture but unsuspected values of color in instrumental combination. And this suggested the possibility of composition for instruments alone in much larger forms than had hitherto been attempted.

Thus the seventeenth century saw a huge expansion of instrumental effort, in the manufacture of instruments, in performing techniques, and in the search for new methods and new forms of composition. For the first time in history it began to appear that instrumental music might become a serious rival of vocal art.

The problems of form were here paramount. Any vocal composition must derive its over-all form, and in no small degree its character, from the text to which it is to be set. Instrumental music has no text. The Dance, to be sure, having an established rhythm and a fairly definite character (slow, fast, calm, excited, graceful, vigorous, or whatever), provided a starting-point for the composer's invention and a certain directive and control for his imagination. But outside this area the instrumental composer's field was largely uncharted.

He borrowed, of course, effective devices already in use. The melodic design appropriate to a word or a phrase could still, in its purely instrumental guise, reflect the character in some measure imparted to it by the words; an instrumental antic, peculiar to a violin or a flute, could appear similarly suggestive; and either of these, in the absence of words, might be repeated or varied (as a text would not permit them to do) so as to form the real core of a musical idea and keep it in focus.

In this way what we know as the theme of an instrumental composition — the "text" of the purely instrumental discourse — gradually evolved. In the Dance, the established rhythm of Allemande or Minuet or Gigue considerably dictated, a priori, the pattern of the theme, and a few distinctive quirks in the melodic pattern gave it enough of definition to make it recognizable as the essential thread of the musical fabric. But just as grace — characteristic of many experiences quite outside the field of the dance — was implied in the Minuet, and abandon similarly implied in the Gigue, so many other types of experience, quite foreign to the dance, might be reflected and portrayed in similarly characteristic tone-patterns, easily distinguishable as tragic or comic. Designed so as to accord with and portray palpable characteristics of our nervous and muscular response to the varied impact of experience, the musical theme became, at its best, a kind of musical epigram.

It was still, to be sure, a "purely" musical design, compounded of fragments that could be separately manipulated and combined, and the musical structure acquired coherence and force accordingly as these manipulations appeared logical and purposive. But the purpose (as in the dance itself, which is addressed to imaginatively excited feet as well as to ears) might involve extramusical imagery, and the syntax of the musical sentence and the rhetoric of the whole musical discourse, while maintaining true musicality, might also be shaped so as to enhance the image of extramusical experience implied in the tensions and rhythms of the notes. The rhetoric of the sonata form, whose essential principle is the contrast of two opposed but expressively cognate themes, is unimaginable as the product of a "purely" musical constructive effort.

Both syntax and rhetoric were immensely clarified by substituting for the old Modes the system of major and minor keys — by substituting tonality for modality. The Final of the Mode was but a feeble counterpart of the key-note or Tonic in a major or minor key. That Final governed so loosely that it often could not be found; the key-note, by comparison, was a most competent and effective ruler. Its base, to be sure, might be shifted by modulation; but, modulation once effected,

16]

this new tonic — or this new residence of the tonic-idea — was as accessible as before. For a given musical phrase, merely transposed to another key, has a new impact on the ear, and even literal repetition is thus made tolerable. The trend toward tonality became irresistible toward the end of the sixteenth century and ruled unquestioned for three hundred years. Indeed, it is doubtful whether the violent attacks on tonality, begun early in the twentieth century, have actually unseated that system.

Tonality, at any rate, provided an indispensable basis for those later expansions of the musical discourse which are found in all the new forms that develop so rapidly after 1750. The most obvious characteristic of these is their homophonic structure — almost continuous song-like melody, supported by harmony either in chord-blocks or in arpeggio figures. This accompaniment might, of course, contain important phrases of counter-melody; but these were incidental and sporadic, and quite unlike the persistent melodic shapes of the voices in a polyphonic texture. Variety in so simple a texture would obviously be essential, but coherence was not less so; and these essentials, over a terrain increasingly widened by modulation, would have been impossibilities without tonality.

By comparison with the simplicity and directness of homophonic structure, not only the Fugue but all polyphonic texture became repugnant to that easily offensible taste with which the court of Louis XIV had infected all Europe. A good deal of the music which delighted the patrons of the 1760's seems animated by a motive similar to that of certain young ladies, chronicled by Dickens, who were taught to compose the lips before entering a drawing-room by saying, "papa, potatoes, poultry, prunes, and prisms." But monophonic structure proved capable of thrusting into the soil of experience vastly deeper roots than were required to nourish these delicate plants; and its chiefest outgrowth — rivaling the Fugue in depth and exceeding it in range of reference — was the classical Sonata.

Its evolution, as to many details, is still obscure, but its main outline clearly appears as an expansion of the dance-pattern just described. A great majority of the chamber works we shall study will be cast in this form. Should this pattern be unfamiliar to the reader, he will find it profitable to learn how to look for its principal features. The skeleton of the form will prove to be quite similar in almost all the examples; but that skeleton, clothed in living musical flesh, is not so easily discernible.

THE INTIMACY OF CHAMBER MUSIC

Let us first recall the Dance form. Its skeleton may be diagramed thus:

|| . S.(Tonic maj.) Cad. figs. dom. . ||. Modulations | Partial cad. (Rel. min.) Final cad. . ||
|| · S.(Tonic min.) Cad. figs. rel. (Cad. figs. dom.) · ||· Modulations in foreign keys | (Dom.) (Rel. maj.) (Tonic) · ||

S stands for its one main "Subject" or theme. (Episodic excursions, not diagramed, may occur.) The key of the piece is first solidly established. A contrasting but closely related key (dominant, if main key is major; relative major or dominant, if minor) is then introduced and established by cadential figures. After repetition, the S is put through a series of modulations, ending, at the single vertical line, with the indefinite cadence noted above. Then the cadential figures from the first section make the final cadence in the original key.

The Sonata form (that of the first movement of the whole four-movement sequence) may be similarly diagramed.

EXPOSITION

|| . S.I (Tonic maj.) tr. S.II (Dom.) tr. Cl.S. . ||
|| · S.I (Tonic min.) tr. S.II (Rel.) tr. Cl.S. · ||

DEVELOPMENT   RECAPITULATION

|| (.) Any matter from Exposition, in (foreign keys | S.I(Tonic) tr. S.II(Tonic) tr. Cl.S.(Tonic) (.) ||
                                      | S.I(Tonic) tr. S.II(Tonic tr. Cl.S.(Tonic) (.) ||
                                      | maj.) |

Clearly, the Exposition is an expansion of the first section of the Dance form — the S.II, in the V or relative key, and approached and quitted by transitions, being the added feature. But it is in the key which closed the exposition of the dance form, so that what was mere key-contrast in the dance becomes subject-contrast in the sonata. The Development, as in the Dance, is largely in foreign keys, on matter from the Exposition. The Recapitulation, since the movement is now much longer, recalls all the matter of the Exposition, with all three subjects in the Tonic. The transitions are readjusted (and often abbreviated or possibly expanded) so that the Tonic does not weary the ear. A Coda may be added. We shall find Beethoven making of the Coda a second, more highly affirmative Development.

The following movements require little description.

Song is the obvious source of most slow movements. The S.II, related and contrasted as in the Sonata form, is frequently introduced, even going on to a Cl.S.; and the whole movement may thus occasionally be cast in the Sonata form. This is rare, however. Mozart is often content with the two main themes and a cadence, and repeats this matter, more highly ornamented, to complete the movement. Sometimes there is but a single theme, relieved by obviously subordinate episodes and intensified when it reappears; also, the theme — often cast in a shape clearly allied to the hymn — may be the basis of a set of Variations.

The third movement (if there are four) is a survival of the interpolated dance in the Suite. With Mozart and Haydn it is almost invariably a Minuet, retaining the general outline of the Dance form, but sometimes acquiring a second theme. Beethoven, as everyone knows (but Haydn also), turned the Minuet into a Scherzo.

The fourth movement (or the third, if the Minuet is omitted) is usually either a Sonata form or a Rondo. The Rondo was originally devised on a single theme which recurred, after an episodic excursion, an indefinite number of times, but always in the Tonic. If the episode became of higher thematic interest, it was treated as a second subject; after its second appearance a third theme appeared — these two (S.I and S.III) being evidently the analogue of the Development in the Sonata form; and if this happened, S.I and S.II reappeared, thereafter, both in the Tonic, with a Coda usually on S.I giving the whole pattern a considerable resemblance to the Sonata form. The outline of the pattern may be seen as A-B-A-C-A-B-Coda (usually on A).

It will be seen that the real innovation in all these forms lies in the introduction of a second subject, co-ordinate with the first. In a mere diagram, this innovation looks very simple. Actually, it was a major problem in design. For the notion — deeply rooted in the tradition of polyphonic composition and in itself wholly rational — that a discourse should stick to one theme, was not easy to overthrow. Encountering a second theme, the traditional hearer would almost certainly ask, "What's this?" And he would hardly be satisfied by the glib answer, "A second theme." For quite obviously anyone who could invent one theme could invent another; but that would not justify the insertion of an incongruous new theme into what was expected by any experienced hearer to be a logical and coherent discourse. Not *a* second theme, then, but *the* second theme — that which is patently appropriate to the first — must be invented; and this is quite another matter.

No purely structural analysis can reveal the secret of this appropriateness, for it is primarily an imaginative rather than a structural feat. It will indeed be discernible on the structural surface, since the S.II may derive from S.I, but its essence lies in the deeps of intuited experience. And no performance, unaware of that essence, can awaken the intimacy which results from participation in that experience. A joyous second theme, interjected into a movement begun on an unmistakable note of tragedy, would doubtless appear at first as a grossly disparate pattern. But it might also, to one not walled in by rigid classical tradition, appear — like the grave-digger scene in *Hamlet* — remotely pertinent to tragedy itself.* We ourselves would have resented, at that moment, the apparition of a Falstaff in a clothes-basket — not merely because it was funny, but because it was wholly inappropriate; and we should resent a similarly incongruous second theme in a sonata. In fact, a good many incongruities of this sort — whether between the themes of a single movement or between the movements themselves — will crop up in the course of our study.

But our rejection, apparent indeed in the design of that theme, cannot but be rooted in the nature of the experience implied in that theme. For neither joyousness nor tragedy nor any other emotion exists in the external things or conditions which excite that emotion. It exists in us. It is our response, as living creatures, to external things — a response primarily cognitive but in its full import intuitive; for that response comprises the awareness, not only of the present "thing" but of a thousand others that have happened to us, actually or imaginatively, and which are associated with this immediate thing; and this thing, interpreted in the light thrown on it by association, is the basis and the real stimulus of our whole intuitive awareness.

That awareness is summed up, not only in our precise cognition of the thing and its visible ramifications, but in an emotional excitement which we cannot but feel as appropriate to the situation confronting us. Inside us, this emotion is perceptible as a characteristic nervous tension and an attendant impulse to motion. The substance of music appears to us as a tonal body, tensed by a thousand variable tonal stresses and actuated thereby to motion — to motion which we cannot but recognize as similar

* Voltaire, contemplating this scene from behind the wall of French classicism, called it the work of a drunken barbarian. But his horror at vulgarity blinded him to the phosphorescent light cast by this episode on the funereal scene to follow.

to that of our own bodies. (Obviously, music can dance or march; less obviously, but not less truly, it can bow its head in grief or wink a naughty eye.) And when music thus simulates our spiritual behavior we recognize ourselves in it.

We do not (although with a considerable effort we might) analyze this portrayal. We do not need to. In a slang phrase perhaps no longer current, it "hits us where we live," and we ask no more from any communication. Such blows, gentle but far-reverberant, chamber music deals with unique force; and this is the source of its persuasive intimacy.

Antecedents

IN BACH'S day and before, virtually all the music for instrumental ensembles — even concertos — was chamber music. The chambers varied in size and appointment, from the palatial music rooms of the aristocracy to the garret above Thomas Britton's (the small coal-man's) shop in Clerkenwell, London — "not much higher than a Canary Pipe, with a window but very little bigger than the Bunghole of a Cask" — where Dr. Pepusch, arranger of the music to *The Beggar's Opera*, John Banister, an eminent violinist and a prolific composer, and even Handel himself provided "many notable Performances in the charming Science of Musick." The Concerto (which word might imply not only the musical form sketched above but the body of players who performed it) was the equivalent of our symphony orchestra; but its concerts were usually offered, not to the public but to the guests of the patron who was wealthy enough to maintain such a group.* Smaller groups were therefore more frequently written for, and the trio-sonata for two violins and bass, with a harpsichord added to fill in and color the harmony, was the standard group.

The musical form best suited to this group and their audience was what (in contrast to the Suite of dances which was often called *Sonata da camera*) was called the Church sonata (*Sonata da chiesa*). It had four movements: a slow, impressive *Adagio* or *Grave,* a more or less fugal *Allegro,* another slow movement, usually lighter than the first, and a final *Allegro,* also often fugal in texture but sometimes a dance. It originated in Italy, with Arcangelo Corelli (1653–1713), Giovanni Batista

* Britton's concerts were probably the first to which admission was offered on payment instead of invitation.

Vitali (1644–1692), and Antonio Vivaldi (1669?–1741); it was adapted to French taste by François Couperin (1668–1733), with later contributions by Rameau (1683–1764) and Jean Marie Leclair (1697–1764); and it became the established sonata form for Bach and Handel and the major composers of the first half of the eighteenth century.

The harpsichord, however, which in the older trio-sonatas had the minor function of doubling the bass and supplying a fuller-sounding harmony than the polyphonically-moving three strings could produce, became a much more integral factor in the structure. Its doubling of the bass, at first largely perfunctory, was stable enough so that the viola da gamba or the 'cello could be dispensed with; and since this task, assumed by the harpsichordist, still left him a few available fingers in the left hand and the same in the right, it was possible to play both the bass and the second violin on the one keyboard instrument. The trio-sonata thus became a duet-sonata with two essential parts and some additional harmonic tones taken by the harpsichord. The loss in sonority and tonal body was compensated for by the economy in the number of performers required. A greater technical skill might also be expected of the performers, with an attendant widening of the range of expression or brilliance.

The duet-sonatas of Bach and Handel display this sort of structure. Handel, occupied with large problems of opera and oratorio, and with no apparent interest in pedagogy, made his sonatas on a relatively undemanding scale. His eye was on his audience and its demand which, since instrumental music was generally regarded as an inferior genre to vocal music, was not extravagant. But he did not write down to his audience. He spoke briefly but to the point; and that point was kept sharply in focus. His six sonatas for violin and piano remain fully in the repertoire, and not merely because of his resounding name along the corridors of music history. The slow movements compress into remarkably small space intimations of spiritual awareness of no low order; and the fast ones, perhaps more perfunctorily constructed, since his invention was unlimited and the rhythmic vitality of a theme could easily be maintained throughout such a design as was conventionally expected, are still models of clarity and compactness. Neither, however, are they wholly in the conventional pattern. They are, indeed, made on one principal theme; but he knows, better than most, the need for contrast and for the timing of contrast in relation to that theme; and in the violin sonatas in A and D the second movements not only provide that contrast but suggest the

[23

possible elevation of the contrasting episode into the co-ordinate second theme which will become the first essential of sonata form.

Handel also specifically varied the instrumentation in the trio-sonata. A set of six trio-sonatas, Op. 2, is mostly for two similar instruments — violins, flutes, or oboes — along with the harpsichord; but the first and the fifth are for flute and violin, very interestingly combined and contrasted. The sixth, for two violins, is however generally regarded as the finest of the set.

There are of course no string quartets, and when larger groups of instruments are demanded the adopted form is that of the concerto. While this form, in Handel's day, was the nearest approach as yet made to the symphony as Haydn and Mozart were to develop it, it was rather the most imposing form of chamber music. With the organ as the solo instrument the chamber characteristics are naturally lost; but with the twelve "Grand" concertos for strings only, the departure is less great, and these may properly be called chamber works. The number of movements is variable (as it is not in the solo or trio-sonatas), and no inconsiderable part of their charm lies in Handel's ingenious alternations of mood. The Ninth of this set (in F) has an almost portentously solemn introductory movement (*Largo*), an *Allegro* of true Handelian vigor, a Siciliana (*Larghetto*, D minor), a Fugue in F — all, thus far, in the conventional order of the Church sonata; but to these four movements two more are added (after the Chamber-sonata fashion) — a Minuet and a Gigue. These concertos can hardly compare with the Brandenburg concertos of Bach, but their interest is greater than the attention they receive. They are all for a *concertino* of two violins and 'cello with the *ripieno* group the conventional body of strings.

Although Henry Purcell (*c.* 1659–1695) had apparently little influence on Handel, or, thereafter, on the course of English music, which Handel continued to dominate, his genius was of the highest order, and his chamber music (relatively slight in volume) ought to be more often performed than it is. His first printed work was a set of twelve *Sonnata's of III parts: two viollins and basse: to the Organ or Harpsechord*, whose preface states that he has "endeavour'd a just imitation of the most fam'd Italian Masters," of whom the most influential was Vitali. The only chamber work of Purcell that is still firmly entrenched in the repertory is the "Golden" sonata, whose musical metal is indeed well described in the title.

Bach's life is in every detail so different from Handel's that although both began their study under the same general auspices Bach's effort is as different as could well be. He had no ambition to write opera, which was Handel's primary interest; he was almost all his life bound to the tedious and often exasperating position of church organist; and he had a consuming interest in the musical education of youth. He was what someone has called a "numerous father" (twenty children were born to him, but only nine survived him) and was able in the later years "to form a concert, vocal and instrumental, with my family, especially as my wife sings a good soprano." Handel never married, and the books are silent as to any romances or rumors thereof. Neither is any interest in the process of musical education recorded, although his harpsichord pieces are often geared to unskilled fingers. Handel was no mean master of counterpoint, but polyphony was for him a device to be employed for its impact on the ear, rather than an underlying principle for the exploration of the last recesses of a musical thought. Hence he never loses himself (or his hearer) in the contriving of strange and often obscure developments, whereas Bach seems unable to dismiss an idea until the last drop of harmonic sap has been squeezed out of it. Handel, enjoying early an extraordinary measure of popularity, had nevertheless to fight his way twice out of bankruptcy and triumphed in the end. Bach, although acclaimed as organist, was understood as composer by pitifully few; he fought the more insidious foe of public indifference out of nothing more than the illumination of his own musical mind, and at last withdrew from the field, undefeated but wearied out.

His chamber music was mostly written at Cöthen, where for six years he was without obligation to serve as church-musician. Many other secular works — such as the first volume of the *Well-tempered Clavier* — were written there, along with the six sonatas (three of which are really suites) for violin alone, so that the number in the category of chamber music as we are thinking of it is relatively small. We need only speak, however, as we did with Handel, of the duet-sonatas and the Brandenburg concertos which, although they are often performed with large orchestras, were conceived as chamber works for a comparatively small number of players.

The six violin sonatas are generally in the same form as those of Handel. But where Handel's are similar in general content, Bach's are as different as could well be within the same framework. The fast movements do not display as much variety as the slow ones, but in each of those a variety of musical experience is portrayed which is far more than the mere elaboration of a theme in tones. The first sonata is in B minor, with a broad *Adagio* in 6-4 time for opening movement, a bold fugue for continuation, an *Andante* in D, quite gentle by comparison with the *Adagio*, and another fugued texture, in two repeated sections, for Finale. It will serve little purpose to describe in such brief terms the remaining five sonatas in this set. But the fifth, in F minor, is surely one of Bach's most imaginative chamber pieces, and an astonishing anticipation of the romanticism which was to flower only after a hundred years. The last sonata is exceptional in having five movements instead of the four which are invariable in the others. Moreover, the first movement is a lively *Allegro*, the second a brief but solemn *Largo*; the third has the superscription (unusually explicit for Bach), *Cantabile, ma un poco Adagio*, and is the expressive core of the work; the fourth is another brief *Adagio*, and the fifth the opening *Allegro* over again. So great a departure from convention must have had some external influence as its source. This must be left, of course, to conjecture, but its actuality can hardly be doubted. Spitta, not irrationally, suspects a wedding which may well have stirred Bach's imagination.

The three sonatas for harpsichord and viola da gamba, playable of course on the piano and 'cello, are not inferior to the violin sonatas. The first was originally written for two flutes and bass; and the perennial question as to the legitimacy of arrangements of Bach's works for other than the original combinations is answered, in favor of that process, not only here but in a hundred similar cases. This sonata is in G, with a gentle *Andante* in E minor. The second, in D, is less interesting, but the third, in G minor, is by common consent the most striking of the set. It has only three movements, but these are developed extensively, after the manner of the concerto. The last movement is particularly rich in subordinate episodes which, in contrast to the main theme, appear as do the varied solo subjects in a concerto and forecast the later emergence of a co-ordinate second theme in the sonata form.

The three sonatas for flute and harpsichord, all in three movements, show the same resemblance to the concerto. The second, in A, has an incomplete first movement. The third is a masterpiece.

Trios for harpsichord and two instruments were for some reason not much favored by Bach. To our taste, that which is one of the "Musical

Offerings" composed on the "right royal theme" which Frederick the Great gave to Bach to improvise upon during his visit to Potsdam in 1747 is the most interesting.

The six "concertos for divers instruments" which Bach composed for the Elector of Brandenburg are of course playable by much larger numbers of performers than are represented in the score by individual parts. Since we almost invariably hear them in orchestral concerts, where the hall is vastly larger than any chamber for music even in a royal palace, this manner of performance has come to seem so appropriate that, when we do hear them with the small number of players which Bach must have envisaged, we find them tonally a little impoverished. Purists will of course vote for the chamber ensemble; but the ideas in many of them are so massive that the weight of the whole string body of the orchestra seems, if not absolutely demanded, at least appropriate. This, to our mind, is particularly true of the third concerto in G. It is for strings alone (with accompanying harpsichord which, if the ensemble is augmented, is quite useless). There are three violins, three violas, three 'celli, and bass. The main or *tutti* theme of the first movement is about the most convincing embodiment of masculine vigor ever represented, whether in tones or any other medium. This weight is of course lifted, in episodes either derived from the main theme or newly invented, and the three instruments of any group emerge, essentially as *concertino*, to effect this end; but the essential vigor never seems to abate. Curiously, there is no slow movement. Two sustained chords make transition (not modulatory, for the last movement is in the same key), and the Finale, in 12-8, ensues. Our inveterate appetite for stimulation is so aroused by the first movement that the second cannot possibly satisfy it, and the two-chord transition, too short to allow that appetite to abate, makes the contrast somewhat disappointing. But it is ourselves, not Bach, who must be blamed.

These concertos represent a summit of structural attainment that, considering the limitations of the concerto form, could not imaginably have been exceeded. They were written before Haydn was born, and at a time when the undercurrent of popular favor in Germany had not yet manifested its dissatisfaction with polyphonic intricacy. But the opera, long since established in Italy and France as the most elegant of musical forms, had begun to intrigue the German courts where, after the devastation of the Thirty Years' War, French taste had artificially undermined the rougher but sturdier conventions of behavior and thought;

and the undercurrent of flimsier musical taste began to rise to the surface. Bach saw it, as the years passed, and took it, apparently without resentment, as a natural manifestation. "People no longer care for the old music," was his only recorded comment. But his disillusionment shows in the last of those works (cantatas) which his position obligated him to compose, and his retreat into himself (momentarily interrupted by his stimulating visit to Potsdam) is similarly indicated by the musical idealism of the *Kunst der Fuge*. He knew he could not stem the tide.

Yet the polyphony which was Bach's natural mode of musical utterance was ultimately to prove the true mode of speech for chamber music. To discover that fact in an era of homophony was the task of Haydn and Mozart. Many other demands of public taste had also to be considered by them — demands more immediate than the obscure problem of an adequate musical style for the utterance of truths obscured by that taste. Composers more sympathetically attuned to the vagaries of convention existed in large number, and their offerings, easy of assimilation, caught the public ear with more attraction than those of Mozart and Haydn.

Their vision, fixed on truths of human sentiment existent in but unperceived by all but a few of their auditors, did not swerve. It could not, of course, penetrate indefinitely into the future. Neither could it always remain fixed on so distant a goal. They were seldom, consciously, reformers, burdened with the artistic salvation of their audiences. They were artists, perceiving with their endowment of artistry that which their hearers did not know about themselves, and trying without offense to sharpen their sensibilities. Their success, in the face of that heedlessness which is inveterate in humans, was really astonishing.

Something of the slow recovery of the abandoned polyphonic principle will be seen in what follows. Students of style would have it that this is the only important matter to be studied. Our disagreement with that view will be evident. We shall, indeed, recognize the vital importance of structure for any convincing clarity of communication; but we shall insist that the thing to be communicated is more fundamental than the manner of its communication.

That "thing" is much more obscure than the manner, which may be discerned and described with almost scientific exactness. So seen, in its high and fascinating intricacy, that manner (which will be called style) is interesting enough to absorb completely the attention of the student. But the musical public, to which after all the effort of the artist is addressed, is not a student body. It sees music in the wider perspective of its whole general interest; and that interest is in matter rather than manner.

The matter of music — its reference to that general interest — is harder to discern, or at any rate to verbalize, than the manner. Yet the incessant changes in taste, sometimes painfully evident in the vagaries of fashion, are really rooted in and reflective of changing visions of matter (which may be called experience); and if this view is just, our effort to keep in view the relation of style to experience will appear justified, even if our manner is annoying.

Joseph Haydn

1732–1809

IF EVER a man was cut out to be the father of a musical form, that man was Joseph Haydn. His paternal experience was ample. His children (for he fathered both the string quartet and the symphony) number somewhere in the 180's. Books on the care and feeding of the infant musical form were less numerous in his day than in our own; but he seems to have grasped clearly the essential aspects of his problem, exerting a discipline neither too strict nor too lax. For musical ideas, like children, are not wholly the property of the parent who engenders them. They have a long genealogy; when they come to birth they are still conditioned by that inheritance (a ruling tradition); they will themselves, if their vital energy is strong, come to mold that tradition; and their vitality is thus more important than their conformity to convention.

This Haydn knew both by instinct and experience. He had been but indifferently taught, and had had to learn for himself the answers to many questions which, if Reutter had troubled to give them, he might have gotten ready-made. But he would have had to test them, in any case, and having (as any genius has) a strong disposition to interpret for himself both the world and the laws of his art, he probably came out at a point not far distant from that to which a more scholastic education would have led him. He came out, in any case, with what Coleridge has percipiently described as the wisdom of love rather than the love of wisdom.

The string quartet grew, under Haydn's tutelage, not precisely out of but rather along with the divertimento — a child with a considerably lower IQ than the quartet. (The quartet's higher capacity could hardly have been attained by the divertimento, which, as its name suggests, was dedicated to idle rather than thoughtful hours.) Yet Haydn's first string quartets, a set of six — labeled Op. 1 although he had already composed voluminously — show few of the characteristics that were later to distinguish them from the divertimento. These date from the 1760's, along with many divertimenti for strings, strings with wind, or winds only, and some sixty trio-sonatas (for two violins and bass) in the pattern we have already mentioned. The trio will later appear as a true piece for three instruments — piano, violin, and violoncello; but with Haydn the 'cello so persistently doubles the bass of the piano that it is all but superfluous. Six quartets, Op. 3, and six, Op. 9, are also of this decade. They show a gradual, perhaps unconscious departure from the *galant* Rococo style. The scheme of four movements (instead of the five, with two Minuets, of the divertimento) is definitely established, and the development is more purposive than the mere excursion into foreign keys which had sufficed for that form. There are imaginative devices, like that of accompanying a melody in pizzicato (in the *Adagio* of Op. 1, No. 6, and in the *Andante cantabile* of Op. 3, No. 5 — the famous "Serenade," in which the plucked strings are all muted); but the first violin is patently the leader, and the other instruments are still far from that equality with it which characterizes the true quartet. The function of the second subject in the sonata-form movements is as yet but dimly grasped — indeed, the parity of the two main themes in that form remained for Mozart to establish. Yet, the classical sonata form is taking shape.

In the quartets of the 1770's (Op. 17 and Op. 20) that fluid pattern begins to "set." In the six of Op. 17 (Haydn, like Bach before him, is fond of doing up his pieces in packages of six, and we shall find him imitated in this preference by both Mozart and Beethoven) — in Op. 17, the developments are much more extended and there is a much sharper definition of character, with a corresponding concern for varied register, in the themes themselves.

Op. 17 dates from 1771. In the following year six more were written (Op. 20), and became known as the "Sun" quartets — for no other reason than that the first edition had a rising sun portrayed on the cover. The emblem, however, was not inappropriate, for there is evident in them something akin to the new spirit in German literature (the "Storm and Stress" movement, initiated at the same time under the leadership of Goethe and Herder) in which strong stirrings of the romantic ferment are evident. These quartets were dedicated to Nikolaus Zmeskall, Baron von Domanovecz, a Hungarian diplomat and a passionate lover (and composer as well) of chamber music. We shall find Beethoven dedicating to him his quartet Op. 95.

The subject itself — the main idea of the musical discourse — now begins to take on a distinctive character. There is seldom any word which can at all adequately define that character; yet something of its effective purport may be sensed if this theme be compared with the sort of musical jingle (itself not without attractiveness) that served as theme in one of the early quartets. The design of this more pregnant theme is of course different, but you cannot account for the difference wholly in terms of design. You can, on the other hand, more adequately account for the design in terms of purpose. The design, that is, will in that light appear appropriate to the purpose — even when your sense of that purpose eludes all attempt at verbal definition.*

* The purpose eludes definition because it is sensed, primarily, not in words but rather as an emotional response to the impact of experience upon our consciousness. The image of response suggested by music, being emotional, is strong. The image of experience is vague, and if it be defined at all, is "constructed" by a sort of inference, drawn from the portrayed response — from what is really a portrayal, not of factual event but of the way we feel when confronted by event.

Thus, even if you can define no more than, let us say, strength or gentleness in a theme, you *know* these things as the qualities or characteristics of human attitude or human activity; you have felt either one or the other in a thousand aspects; and you will find your "definition" of these words to originate in an image, in your mind, of those things as you have both met and enacted them, whether physically or imaginatively. Your image, that is, is extremely complex.

But your word (if you can find one) symbolizing this multiplicity of experience has now become an abstraction — the intellectual summary of a whole category of experiences, in themselves not particularly intellectual. It lacks the vividness of immediate experience, and can regain it only if it can be particularized into a typical image of experience. Consequently, to understand that indubitable quality of gentleness which you found in the theme, you might ask, "what *sort* of gentleness is this?"

Again, you cannot precisely tell, for again you have no word. But you will have made some progress if you can say, merely, this is not the gentleness of mother toward fractious child; of lover toward capricious mate; of judge toward youthful offender. For to the extent that you know what a thing is not, you know what it is; and your theme, thus explored, will begin to take on the character — even if it remain indefinable — of a knowable experience.

You cannot, of course, implicitly trust the images of experience that music thus evokes in your mind. Everyone has grown to dislike music that once enthralled him, and to like music which he at first detested. You are sure of your taste at the moment of judgment; but you cannot be sure that your judgment will survive the moment. You look, therefore, for an impersonal criterion.

Current aesthetic will teach you that it is to be found in structure. If you observe structure to the exclusion of images of non-artistic experience, you may indeed become wholly absorbed. But you are no safer than before. For if you explore the origins rather than the formulated principles of structure you will see that sound structure must originate in and correspond to knowable experience. Sound structure

Something of the new feeling-impulse is suggested in Haydn's now quite frequent use of affective indications for performance. Not only are dynamic contrasts and gradations much more frequent and much more carefully indicated; their purport is amplified by suggestive words, such as the *Affettuoso e sostenuto* of the slow movement of Op. 20, No. 1, or the *Un poco Adagio, affettuoso* of No. 4 and the *Presto scherzando* that follows. These are not mere words. *Their purport is already in the music*, and they caution the players not to ignore that character. You will find it for yourself in such a seven-bar phrase (Haydn's melodies are often cast in irregular rhythm-patterns) as that of the slow movement of Op. 20, No. 1 (Ex. 1), whose seven-bar period is made to feel wholly symmetrical by the simple continuation of the eighth-note flow in the second violin.*

EXAMPLE I. HAYDN QUARTET, OP. 20, NO. I

But not only is there here an adventure into a field of expression foreign to sententious aristocratic utterance. The resources of musical learning are also explored. Op. 20, No. 2 has for Finale a fugue on four subjects — by no means a rival to Bach's, and indeed almost naive in its manipulations, but a serious attempt to explore the value of polyphonic technique, both for its own sake and for the use to which it may be put.

is indeed the counterpart of intelligent thinking; but the object of intelligent thinking can be nothing else than experience, accumulated through the senses, strained and rectified by a higher than merely sensuous faculty, and stored somewhere in the mind as the essence of experience — an essence from which a whole lifetime of thought will not wholly eliminate the dross.

To judge music by structure alone — and particularly by structure as formulated by theory — is thus to repudiate the origin of the primary musical impulse. For the verbal formulation of theory is no more complete than the reduction of other and wider experience to verbal terms. The primary association of music and experience becomes increasingly evident in the Haydn quartets. It can be in only slight measure verbalized, but it *is* primary; and our account of this and later works will attempt to envisage this fact.

* *Affettuoso* means "affectionate(ly)." Ask, in the vein of the previous footnote, what sort of affection is here intended. No one would mistake it for either jubilant or frustrated passion — or indeed for passion at all. Its equilibrium is quiet and assured, but without a trace of insistence, even at the later *sforzandi*. It is the sort of affection that could hardly be uttered otherwise than *mezza voce*. You cannot name it (and neither can I), but you will not doubt its reality nor its high, if wholly undramatic, value as a human experience.

(Op. 20, No. 5 has a fugue on two subjects, more skilled and musically more interesting than the former, but still hardly a masterpiece.) The four voices, of course of equal interest in the fugues, are also more nearly equal in the other movements, and the string quartet as a musical species now definitely exists.

The six quartets of Op. 33 date from 1781. They are called the "Russian" quartets, since they were dedicated to the Grand Duke Paul. No. 2 is chiefly interesting for its second movement, which Haydn labels "Scherzo" (it is indeed a far departure from the Menuetto), and for its *Largo sostenuto*, whose main theme, first announced by viola and 'cello, then answered by the two violins, is distributed effectively thereafter against a sixteenth-note figure derived from a contrasting interlude.

No. 3, called the "Bird" quartet, was a favorite of Joachim's. These titles (none of them Haydn's) are patently the product of some momentary fancy; yet they must have some suggestive basis, and this one — like the "Lark," which we shall later encounter — may be the lyric strain which forms the main theme. It descends two whole octaves from the four high G's with which it begins (a compass far beyond that of any feathered songster), but its descent is as liquid and carefree as any bird-call. When the second violin takes it over (28), the first answers in delightful twitters. The second subject (if it is that) is begun (43) with a diminution of the rhythm of the first, and continues, like it, with descending figures. These, however, are quieter. The brief development is of course all on these figures, and there is a charming, out-of-key beginning of the recapitulation (a *fausse reprise*, 108), in E minor. The *Scherzando* that follows best exemplifies that title in the Trio section (not so marked) where dainty trills on short notes followed by rests continue the hint of bird-song. The *Adagio* is on approved sentiment, neatly worked but not very significant. The Rondo, however, which begins with the suggestion of an uncommonly excited cuckoo, is an unabated delight from beginning to end.

Aside from the really humorous Scherzo in Op. 33, No. 6, which has a definite foretaste of Beethoven's robust vigor, there is nothing particularly striking in the rest of the quartets of this group. And the same is true of the six in Op. 50, dedicated (doubtless for a consideration) to King Wilhelm II of Prussia. This monarch was a skilled 'cellist, and the 'cello parts, especially in the songful slow movements, are often so written as to give that instrument prominence. Haydn, however, does not tax the player's powers as we shall find Mozart doing when he writes three quartets for the same patron. We should not forget, when dismissing works of this sort, that composition was for both these men a means of livelihood, pitifully underpaid by our standards; and the wonder is that so much of real interest was interjected into work which must often have seemed drudgery to the creators.

We have spoken of the sonata form as one in which the contrast between two co-ordinate subjects is the real essence of the structure. Haydn, who was learning for himself what Mozart called "the true way to write string quartets," seems not to have conceived this as a principle. The older idea that a movement should concern itself with one main thought, admitting secondary themes as episodes only, seems for the most part to be his rule; and indeed it is a possible conjecture that Haydn invents a true second subject only when the first has not enough strength or individuality of character to maintain its supremacy throughout the movement. Development, however, which is equally essential to the form even when there are two equal themes, is more requisite when there is one theme than when there are two; and can be more varied when it is not confined to the middle section of the movement but carried over into the recapitulation. This Haydn realizes, and his ingenuity in this effort is striking.

We cannot stop to examine in detail any of the three quartets in Op. 54. These were dedicated to a rich merchant, Johann Tost. Haydn finds here that a fugato section is far more contributory to effective design than were the complete fugues in Op. 20; striking harmony, with remote modulation and occasional harsh dissonance, and even so unusual a feature as an *Adagio* finale, show that consistency in idea is more important to him than the filling out of a conventional design. But all these things are more richly in evidence in the later quartets, to which we must hasten. We can thus merely mention the arrangements for quartet of the seven slow movements written in 1785 for the cathedral of Cadiz on the "Seven Last Words" of Christ on the cross. They are designated as Op. 51, but are hardly quartets in our present perspective, since they were originally scored for two oboes, two bassoons, two horns, and strings. Haydn afterwards added solo voices and choruses, making thus a kind of oratorio, and wrote a *Largo* for winds to be played between the two parts.

Op. 55, again dedicated to Tost, has also only three quartets. The

[35

second of these is known as the "Razor" quartet. An emissary of Salomon's, who had come to Esterház to engage Haydn for a London season, heard the composer execrating a dull razor and saying that he would give his best quartet for a good one. Bland promptly presented him with a pair of his own, and received the quartet in return. It is unusual in form since the sonata-allegro is preceded by a set of variations, but it need not detain us.* The first movement of No. 3, however, begins with a main theme whose sweep (*unisono* for four bars) reveals a musical impulse far more cogent than would have arisen out of the mere problem of designing another quartet movement. The purpose of expression, that is, is here more definite and more conscious than in the earlier works. This is in a sense proved by the second subject (46) in the 'cello, whose upward surge, activated by syncopation and the *sforzandi* on the half notes, is patently akin to the first theme's sweep (Ex. 2). The contrast, however, is one of intensification rather than one of antithesis such as will appear in Mozart and the later composers. The old ideal of unity — which antithesis need not necessarily destroy — is, and will remain, Haydn's guide. Neither, as yet, is there any effort toward a related character in all the movements of a quartet. Incongruity does not, indeed, appear, but the *Adagio non troppo* that follows would not seem out of place in almost any of the earlier quartets, and the Minuet and the Finale might be similarly transplanted.

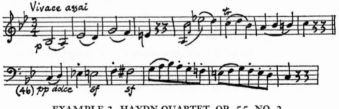

EXAMPLE 2. HAYDN QUARTET, OP. 55, NO. 3

Six more quartets — those in Op. 64 — were dedicated to Tost. Of these, which date from 1790 or possibly 1792, the favorite of the world is No. 5, the "Lark" quartet. The continuous scamper of sixteenths in the Finale has also suggested the title, "Hornpipe." Neither title is distinctively appropriate, since a much richer (if less definite) imagery is suggested by the music. The chief themes of all four movements are shown

* Albert Weir, in his selections from Haydn's chamber music (Longmans, Green, 1940), erroneously attaches the title, "Razor," to the Quartet in A, Op. 55, No. 1.

EXAMPLE 3. HAYDN QUARTET, OP. 64, NO. 5, "LARK"

in Example 3. The opening eight-bar staccato figure forms the accompaniment to the lark's song (which is not in the least "realistic") and that song itself generates (16) the figure which, in the dominant (27) becomes the second subject. In wholly natural sequence follow a passage of somewhat tense suspensions (35) and another of descending scales (50), and the S.II returns to end the exposition. All these features appear in the development. The recapitulation (105) is refreshingly altered, amounting to a second development.

The *Adagio* (like many another) is no more than a gentle poem in the vein of melancholy. Most of its turns of phrases have long since become clichés; but they were not so for Haydn, and imaginative players can still find, if they will, the "truth" which this little piece held for him. The Menuetto, like that in Beethoven's first symphony, has a first section only eight bars long; but the development is fresh and stimulating. The tiny Trio keeps to the motion of running eighths, its contrast being chiefly in its key (D minor). The chuckling gaiety of the Finale is as infectious as the somewhat similar "Gypsy Rondo" in the most famous of Haydn's piano trios.

A similarly easy, conversational manner — with quite different matter — rules in Op. 64, No. 6. The topic, addressed to minds accustomed to leisure, is not portentous. Yet there is here an experience — or if you prefer, an attitude toward an experience — that is of real, if momentary, interest; and that interest is heightened by the comment of a pretty perceptive mind. Note the new angle of vision toward the subject at bar 13; the turning of it into an S.II (25); the lightening of its seriousness by the triplet figures (18 and 36), and the color of the *fausse reprise* (84). You will sense, although you cannot verbally define, the appropriateness of mood in the following movements to that of the first. It is evident that music, for Haydn, has become a language as well as an art.

How much, whether of growing certainty in technical skill or of this expressive insight, may be attributed to the influence of Mozart is a question not likely to be definitively answered. The two great men apparently first met in the winter of 1781–82, since both participated in the festivities attendant upon the visit of the Russian Grand Duke Paul to Vienna. That Mozart admired the older man unreservedly is seen in his oft-quoted reason for the dedication of six quartets to Haydn in 1785: "for it was from him that I first learned the true way to compose quartets." And it was after hearing some of these that Haydn declared to Mozart's father, "I consider your son the greatest composer I have ever heard." But each was by this time so experienced in composition and had attained to such individuality in style that influence such as scholars love to attribute to chance resemblances (and which they often magnify to a point of incredibility) is hardly thinkable. Mozart, as we have said, conceived the second subject in the sonata form as primary in his scheme of that structure. Haydn evidently conceived it as incidental, striving for a unity based on the predominance of the first (and as it is still often called, the main) theme. But he could construct a movement with two themes when he found it desirable to do so; and Mozart, as we shall see, could construct a movement with one. And in each case the individuality of the creator is unmistakable.

This individuality will of course appear, perhaps most conspicuously, in the structure of the music. But that structure is a process necessarily adaptable to the idea itself of the composition, and that idea is the more compelling accordingly as it is rooted in some image of experience. Haydn the composer, that is, will appear as Haydn the man. And the lineaments of his character are revealed with ever greater clarity in the fourteen quartets still to be examined.

Six of these (three in Op. 71 and three in Op. 74) were dedicated to Count Apponyi, an enthusiastic patron of chamber music and a benefactor also of Mozart and Beethoven. They were written in 1793, after Haydn's return from his first, fabulously successful visit to London. No radical departure from his habitual manner is apparent, but the man himself, at home, quietly occupied with unpretentious but engaging thoughts, and welcoming you as listener, is more in evidence than ever.

Of these six we have space to study but one — the so-called "Rider"

38]

quartet in G minor, Op. 74, No. 3. It is perhaps worthy of note, however, that the second quartet of Op. 71 has a slow introduction — a frequent feature in Haydn's symphonies, but found only this once in the quartets. The principal themes of the "Rider" quartet are shown in Example 4.

EXAMPLE 4. HAYDN QUARTET, OP. 74, NO. 3, "RIDER"

Can you imagine a more buoyant jouncing than that portrayed by the opening? The title (of course, not Haydn's) is not inappropriate, but neither is it adequate as a metaphor — unless your imagination is wholly equestrian — for the sheer delight of mind and muscle that was the hidden mainspring of such a theme. There are many gaieties that can start such spiritual bubbling as this, but to name any of them — to attach the music to any single event — is to narrow the range of imaginative response available to any but the most pedestrian mind.

For, unnameable as it is, there is in your mind as you listen a much more complex image of experience — an image to which the sensation of jouncing is only a minor contribution. If there were conveyed no more than that sensation you would weary of it as soon as would the driver of an ailing motor confronted with ten miles of corduroy road. This jouncing, contrariwise, is exhilarating; and if you substitute the notion of exhilaration for that of jouncing, you will find that you have extended the range of your verbal account of the suggested experience. In reality, however, you have only amplified your prior image of jouncing, and you will see that Haydn's music is itself the source of this amplification — is itself the definition of the words you are trying to find, and of the experience you are sharing. For your whole awareness is much larger than any image your words can define.

The tensions and the motion of the music, examined, will account for a part of this awareness. The motion — an unbroken succession of agreeable thumps — does jounce, palpably. But there is also a mounting energy — the rise on the G-minor triad to the active E♭, with the same triad then intensified by the somewhat distorted harmony of the augmented 6th-chord. This energy is by no means wholly muscular. (Hence, "exhilaration," rather than "Rider" or "jouncing.") But all these words are mere illustrations — hints — of the total image of experience and of your participation in it.

The generative source of Haydn's theme was some such image of experience as this. His portrayal is vivid. But the vivid suggestion of an experience, shaped into tones, is still not a piece of music, which must be a kind of discourse on that theme. How to shape this discourse — how to amplify the interest of the theme — how to vary it and sidelight it by inventing and spacing episodes and judicious returns — is the rhetorical and grammatical problem of the composer. How skillfully Haydn solved this problem you can see for yourself if you will parse his musical sentences and study his rhetorical pattern. No more than a hint of that method of study, such as we gave a moment ago, is possible within our space. But do not suppose that such skill as Haydn's can operate without the guiding stimulus of an image of experience.

The slow movement offers a moment of quiet contemplation, far removed from the former "scene." It is in E major — a key very foreign to G minor; the image, which you will form all but unconsciously but which you may intensify by sensing the tensions and the motion of the music, is gentle and retrospective, but not unimpassioned. A hundred verbal "illustrations" could be invented; but the experience itself, in its feeling aspect, is unmistakably real. The Menuetto is so obvious that we did not even quote its theme. The Finale, after these two episodes ("side roads"), reverts to the original image and jounces even more vigorously — to be sure, in quite a different pattern.

The six quartets of Op. 76, appealing again to widely possessed imagery of experience, have acquired verbal titles more often than any earlier set. These are no more adequately suggestive of the content than is the word Rider. But they do suggest a perceptible background of experience as their ultimate source. No. 1 is called "The Farmyard" (an allusion discoverable but hardly worth pursuing); No. 2, from the two descending fifths of its main theme, is called the *Quinten* quartet. Also — probably from its ungraciously vigorous rhythm and its canonic structure (which may have been suggested by the Minuet in Mozart's G minor symphony) — the third movement is often called the *Hexen* (witches') minuet. Possibly from the pattern of the opening fifths, which is nearly that of the bells which chime the third quarter of the hour on Big Ben, the quartet is also called "The Bell"; and since the 'cello has often to bray the descending fifths in its hoarser register, the piece is sometimes called "The Donkey." These associations, it must be said, are pretty idle.

The third quartet is called the "Emperor," since its slow movement is a set of variations on the hymn, *Gott erhalte Franz den Kaiser*, which Haydn, admiring the English *God Save the King*, had written as an Austrian national anthem. This tune is as appropriate to its purpose as the English one; the variations are admirable; but the rest of the quartet, it is generally admitted, is rather perfunctory. The fourth is called "The Sunrise" — a name hardly derivable from any detail, but appropriate to the general impression conveyed by the first movement. The other two have apparently not been christened, although No. 5 has, as slow movement, the "Famous Largo" — a piece as appropriate to indefinable spiritual exaltation as the hymn is to true patriotic sentiment. This theme may be singled out for quotation (Ex. 5), but the rest of the quartet, and especially the Menuetto, with a lively figure of two eighths and a quarter (i.e., two beats against the triple measure) is almost equally interesting. (These six quartets are known as the Erdödy quartets, from their dedication to Count Peter Erdödy, whose countess was later a friend of Beethoven.)

EXAMPLE 5. HAYDN QUARTET, OP. 76, NO. 5

Only two more were to be completed — those in Op. 77 (1799), known as the Lobkowitz quartets. (Op. 103 has only a slow movement and a minuet.) Prince Lobkowitz was a very capable violinist and 'cellist, as well as a trained singer. He was to be "first among the peers" in Vienna whose support made possible Beethoven's hard life as composer during the difficult years of the Napoleonic wars. But he was deeply interested in Haydn also, and had his *Creation* translated into Bohemian for performance at Raudnitz.

Superficially these two works show a considerable departure from that gaiety which so largely rules in the earlier quartets. Beneath the surface, however, there is a fuller revelation of that which the Germans call *genial* — full of genius — a meaning which our English word has lost. We shall try to uncover this quality in Op. 77, No. 2. The main themes are shown in Example 6. It is possible to contemplate these notes objectively. From that aesthetic distance the piece will possess a considerable charm. Neither will a more subjective reading greatly alter the visible surface of the music. For while the music, within, is very sad, there is no windy suspiration of forc'd breath and the forms and modes of grief are hardly denoted. Yet they are there, as a somewhat minute analysis may reveal.

Two details in S.I are highly suggestive. The theme is essentially the descending scale of F major, punctuated at bars 2 and 4 by somewhat hesitant quasi-cadential figures. Persistent melodic descent is generally indicative of depression. (If you go up the scale in the rhythm of this theme you will find that animation replaces depression.) But this barely suggested quality is enhanced, both by the tension of the double-dotted note and by the *forte* of the first phrase. And both these facts are sharply illuminated by the unexpected *piano* of the second phrase with its gentle up-beat. (Play this phrase *f* and the whole suggestion of character will

EXAMPLE 6. HAYDN QUARTET, OP. 77, NO. 2

42]

disappear.) The four sixteenths (4 and 5) that fill the thematic silences are gently but unmistakably ominous, and their implication is now caught by the theme itself which thrice rhythmically diminishes (hastens) the repeated cadential phrase in an intensifying ascent. The downward tripping (7) would be almost trivial in this context were it not contradicted by the double-dotted tension of the half-cadence.

The progress toward S.II consistently maintains these characteristics. A transitional figure in sixteenths begins (14) before the repetition of S.I is completed; the up-beat eighths (20) recall the ominous sixteenths in bars 4 and 5; and the whole modulation, involving the tense chord of the augmented 6th, is so managed that at the pause (36) we expect the key of C minor. Instead, we have C major, and the new theme, whose essence is compacted in the chromatically rising first bar,* is combined with the opening phrase of S.I. The unharmonized bars 2 and 4 of this theme, whose simplicity is packed with implication, will sorely tax the imagination of the first violinist; and the long descending chromatic scale (44) with its incomplete cadence is even more difficult to render justly. The unison sixteenths at the end of the exposition of course signify a conclusion; but in the imaginative light cast on them by what has gone before they signify quite another sense of finality. We could fill pages with description of further detail in the rest of the movement, but if the suggestions already given have awakened the reader's imagination, they will be quite needless.

The Menuetto (*Presto ma non troppo*, F major) follows appropriately the first movement whose moderate speed leaves the hearer desirous of more activity. In character it is really a Scherzo — not a clownish joke, which would have been destructive of the subtleties just heard, but a piece of slightly plebeian banter made of two little motives: a heel-clicking two-beat group and a three-beat hopping on the interval of the 5th. The Trio, brought in on what will become a favorite romantic "change" (to the flat VI key — here, Db in relation to F) flows soulfully in all three upper voices against a pedal Db in the 'cello.

The *Andante* ("going," in the unexpected key of D major, 2-4) is not a march but a stroll — the twilight ambulation of a mind a little weary of the world and musing, not without pleasure, on a long vista of the graying past. Three unrhythmed chords (18) suggest a moment of more

---

* This little pattern (mi-fa-fi-sol) was soon to become a favorite romantic cliché; but it is no cliché here.

painful imagery, but the theme, almost constantly present and enriched with quiet ornament, pursues its appointed course without distortion.

The Finale reasserts the tonality of F with a single chord. (Haydn evidently felt that the theme, in the unprepared key of F, would seem out of perspective.) The *sforzandi* on the up-beats help to portray motion which, without them, would hardly attract attention. But the third *sf*, while it appears to start another four-bar group, does nothing of the sort. It begins a seven-bar period hardly detachable from the four-bar group and delightfully asymmetrical in itself. The wavering on B♮–C (5), the legato approach to the *sf* (6), and the shift of the *sf* (7) to the second half of "two" all combine to make the antic sixteenths (7–9) and the detached eighths of the cadence seem wholly natural. But this is not merely a feat of structure. It is a gleam in the spiritual eye.

The buoyant S.II (23) is a natural outcome, and the bubbling sixteenths (29) which prepare so skillfully for the unexpected return to S.I in the dominant (33) are another stroke of genius. But this is not a rondo-return. There are only four bars of S.I, and more antic sixteenths soon make an end of the sonata-exposition (58). The development begins with imitations in all four voices of the first bar of S.I. Then comes a hustle and bustle of sixteenths against which both main themes are hinted at. Modulation strays as far as B♭ minor, where an augmented 6th chord on D♭ resolves to the 6/4 of F and brings the recapitulation, in which only the conventional deviations from the exposition occur.

Our selections for analysis from the eighty-three string quartets, in comparison with that large number, have been meager enough. In comparison with the whole volume of Haydn's chamber music they would appear microscopic. We did mention in passing the sixty trio-sonatas and the many divertimenti. There are also a great number (one hundred seventy-five) for baryton — an extraordinarily clumsy instrument with 6 bowed strings and as many as 40, vibrating sympathetically but also possibly plucked, underneath the fretted finger-board — written for Prince Esterházy. (Haydn learned to play the instrument, thinking to please his patron; but the Prince "was not amused.") The sonata for violin and piano seems not to have interested Haydn (all but one of his few pieces in this form are piano sonatas with violin accompaniment), and the piano trio, although he wrote many during the nineties, seldom aroused his fullest creative energy. (The trio in G with the "Gypsy

Rondo" for Finale, is the only one to be at all frequently performed.) There are also several early works for larger combinations — e.g., the six *Scherzandi* for flute, 2 oboes, 2 horns, 2 violins, and bass, and a Nonet for 2 oboes, 2 horns, string quartet, and bass. They differ but little in character from the divertimenti, but occasional movements reveal the man himself who, as we have tried to show, emerges in the quartets as both a profoundly human personality and a sincere and accomplished artist.

When Haydn began his long effort the string quartet and the general concept of the sonata form hardly existed. When that effort ended the quartet had emerged (to be sure, also from Mozart's hands) as a highly organized form, rich enough in tonal volume to be wholly satisfying to the ear, so diversified in pattern as to occupy the full attention of the listener both to its texture and to its expressive content, and still so transparent in texture that every note in the score could be seen to be essential. Its musical substance will gain immensely in weight, as we shall see; but that ideal of balance between expression and design which Haydn had sought by instinct and had so largely achieved in his last works will still remain the guiding principle.

Wolfgang Amadeus Mozart

1756-1791

IF EVER a man was cut out to achieve the perfecting of a musical form, that man was Wolfgang Amadeus Mozart. To perfect anything requires the highest degree of skill, and Mozart was surely the most carefully trained, at the earliest age, of all the great composers. But to perfect an art-form requires also both a native imagination and an acquired taste. Mozart possessed the one from the beginning, and he was enabled to attain the other as rapidly as he learned his skill — so rapidly that his amazing equipment must have seemed to him, during the act of creation, perfectly inborn. When he contemplated or exhibited the results of his creative effort, he could not but have seen his superiority; but to feel the surge of creative power is far more satisfying than merely to feel superiority; and even when (as was mostly the case) he was working to order, the delight of creation was the uppermost current in his mind. We shall find Schubert his only rival in spontaneity.

His father, who was his only real teacher, was a skilled violinist and a competent if uninspired composer. He was a man of high principle who recognized his children's gifts and felt that he had a mandate from heaven to make the most of them. His teaching method, which is pretty clearly reflected in his *Versuch einer gründlichen Violinschule* (Toward a fundamental school of violin-playing), was founded on precise observation of the mechanics and sharp analysis of the objectives of performance; and under his tuition both Maria Anna ("Nannerl") and Wolfgang made such rapid progress that in 1762 the first of a long series of concert tours — finally extending to all the principal capitals of Europe — was undertaken.

Here began an acquisition of taste which no formal instruction could impart, but which was essential to his ultimate perfecting of the still inchoate sonata form. With the impressibility of infancy and the perspicacity of genius he absorbed first the externals and more gradually the inner substance of those strivings for the good and the beautiful which animated the courtly behavior and the more considered aspirations of aristocracy. His intuitive repulsion for the ugly was keen; his adjustment of the beauty of music to his expanding vision of life was necessarily gradual, and that adjustment was never allowed to overstep the boundaries of beauty as he saw it; but to suppose that beauty was for him a thing apart from life is, it seems to us, to mistake his whole artistic endeavor.

He presently found that he had to escape certain trammels unconsciously imposed upon both technique and imagination by his father's teaching. He had also to combat many external forces, obstructive of success but probably subtly contributory to his ultimate artistry — e.g., his frustrated passion for Aloysia Weber and his later encumbered marriage with Constanze, her sister; the bitter lessons learned during his fruitless expedition to Paris (1778–79); the violent break with Archbishop Hieronymus and the ensuing fatal attempt, during the ten Vienna years, to defy the system of patronage. But these negations were surmounted by internal forces — by an expanding awareness of the relation of music to life and the attendant necessity for adjusting musical structure to that awareness. Both that adjustment and that awareness are visible in his music. Mozart would never have attempted a "Critique of Pure Musical Reason," but his musical creativity springs from the most lucid artistic philosophy ever attained.

Any great artist's work, revealing his maturing attitude toward the world, thus becomes an unconscious autobiography — not a chronicle of event, but the gradual evolution of a developing personality shaped by event. Mozart's personality — a little aloof, since it necessarily reflected aristocratic traditions and reserves foreign to our democratic notions — is less frankly revealed in his music than Haydn's. Yet it is there, and is probably more evident in his chamber music than in any other works. We shall note some of the evidences of it in our study.

Every chamber-music combination seems to have interested him (as, in contrast, several did not interest Haydn), and we may therefore establish the plan, hereafter to be followed, of beginning with works for two instruments (chiefly sonatas for piano and violin), going on thereafter to trios, quartets, and larger combinations.*

The Violin Sonatas

Three sets of violin sonatas (K.6–15, K.26–31, and K.55–61) — twenty-three in all — belong to Mozart's earliest years and were composed in Paris, in Holland, and at Salzburg in 1767 after returning from the first long tour. As source material for a study of Mozart's technical growth they are of high interest; for our present purpose they are negligible.

The next (K.296, in C major) was written in Mannheim for the daughter of his landlady (the "house-nymph") who showed considerable talent as pianist. The figurated tonic chord (conventionally, to establish the key) opens the first movement and adds a little imitative pattern to complete the S.I. There is a gay little march-tune in C (22) that seems to anticipate Figaro's *Non più andrai*; then a longish transition that brings the S.II (42) — as delightfully insouciant as a tune can be. The short development is all on subordinate themes, and the recapitulation, omitting the Figaro episode, is somewhat shortened. Both the *Andante* and the Rondo have little to say, but they say it charmingly, and the problem of polythematic design (the use of the S.II and other sub-themes) is solved — in part by the invention of easy transitions — quite adequately.

Six more violin sonatas were written in Mannheim (K.301–306). The fourth was completed in Paris, and all six were published there in 1778. Mozart still speaks of them as "clavier sonatas," the violin part being secondary in weight although essential to the texture. All but one (K.306, in D) have only two movements — the first always a sonata form, the second either an expanded Minuet (K.301, 303, 304), a Rondo (K.302), or a set of variations (K.305). The first movement of K.303, in C major, has an *Adagio* introduction which returns in the middle of the *Allegro molto*, with less of dramatic effect but to the same general purpose as Haydn's and Beethoven's use of the same device in the *Paukenwirbel* (Drum-roll) symphony and the *Sonate Pathétique*. K.306, in D major,

---

* Homer Ulrich, in his *Chamber Music* (Columbia University Press, 1948), excludes the duet-sonata from the category of chamber music. This exclusion is historically justified, since the duet did grow out of the solo piano sonata by the addition of an "accompanying" instrument. But it also grew into a true duet; and since it is with the sonata in this later stage that we shall have to deal, and since many examples will possess that kind of interest which seems most characteristic of chamber music, we shall include that form.

is the most pretentious of the group. Its main theme, sonorous but not very significant, is in the piano. It has a pattern in the bass which the violin doubles, and both go on thereafter with scintillant figures that make transition to the dominant. The S.II begins in that key, in the violin, but swerves into B minor for a time before settling in its proper key. The transition is again brilliant, with the Cl.S. expanded. The development is on bars 12–15 of the exposition (the more definite portion of S.I), so that this theme is omitted in the recapitulation. The first section of the *Andante cantabile* has a main theme in three-bar phrases, interestingly manipulated, and another in the dominant; after repetition of this section there is a new, very sturdy theme, rather eloquently spun out, that serves as development; then an abbreviated recapitulation, so that the whole movement closely resembles the sonata form. The Finale, on the other hand, is quite free in pattern. There is first an amiable little *Allegretto*; then, suddenly, a lively *Allegro* in 6-8, gigue-like and jocose, with two distinct but not highly contrasted themes; then the *Allegretto*, unaltered; then the gigue, with several novel additions and a turbulent climax; then a Cadenza for both instruments, *Allegro assai*, that subsides into the little *Allegretto*, with a dozen bars of the gigue for close. It is not very coherent, but it is great fun.

Five sonatas (K.376–380) appear to have been composed in 1781 in Vienna. They were published there in November along with the one in C (K.296) already mentioned as written for the Mannheim "house-nymph." They are thus among the first of Mozart's works to be produced during or after the break (June, 1781) with the Archbishop Hieronymus. That quarrel is of course not in any way reflected in the music. Neither is their greater maturity necessarily attributable to his natural desire to make the best impression possible upon those whose patronage he must now seek to live. But they are more mature, both in design and in substance, even though by comparison with such works as *Die Entführung aus dem Serail*, which Mozart hoped would establish him solidly in public favor, they are of little moment.

This maturity is of course visible in the structure. But unless structural skill is the only objective and the only attainment of an artist's effort, maturity implies also a ripening of human perception; and if this is so, it will be rational to explain structure in terms of that larger perception, rather than to account for perception in terms of structure. It was imperative, in Mozart's day, to establish the key unmistakably at the beginning of a movement. The S.I, in consequence, was often a figuration of the tonic chord—a design which hampered painfully any effort toward wider suggestion of experiential imagery. And in all these sonatas save perhaps the last (K.380), you will find melodic character emerging as the real core of the musical idea. This character is of variable vividness, but it is discernible not only in the main themes of most of the movements, but in the congruity of the several movements of a sonata with each other. This could be demonstrated, if there were space. We can only hint at it here; you will find further pursuit of it profitable.

K.376, in F major, announces that key in three chords only and then goes into its real topic — a spurt of elastic melody as actually alive as any "translation" of it into words would be chillingly dead. The violin does not repeat it, but finds another equally live strain, and the brief transition leads to the S.II — patently the perfect complement of the main theme. You will be hard put to it to find a name for the sort of experience that is imaged here. But if you play it in such fashion that the motion and the tension of the notes become "real"— become the portrayal of a spiritual activity in which you, as a person, are engaged — you will recognize that this music is a true counterpart of experience. And you will find the two later movements exquisitely in accord with the character of the first.

K.377, also in F, announces its key in a single chord and goes on, in its determined, down-hill treading, to suggest on the scale of the music room essentially that image of purpose which Wagner, in the *Ring*, on an immeasurably vaster scale and in the stentorian voices of the trombones, portrays as the consciousness of law to which Wotan himself must submit.* The theme of the *Andante*, to be varied, shows in its syncopated

---

*Commentators call this the Spear-motive; but the runes which Wotan must both enforce and obey are graven on its shaft. Wagner is spelling Determination with a capital D; Mozart no more than suggests it; but the core of the feeling is the same. Much more, however, than the mere fact of scale descent is involved, as may be seen by comparing this design with another of very different purport.

Gilda's aria, *Caro nome*, which expresses a wholly different state of mind, has a pattern highly similar to this. But not only are the scale-segments different (1 down to 2 and 7 down to 1 in Verdi; 3 down to 4 and 2 down to 3 in Mozart) — a distinction by no means without a difference. Mozart's violin, in *forte* triplet eighths, contributes much to the decisiveness of the piano, while Verdi's accompaniment only sharpens our awareness of the girlish vision of the Duke that now lives in Gilda's mind. For tension, in the Verdi, dwindles with the descent, while in the Mozart it increases.

Distinctions like these, by no means necessarily perceived in the verbal terms we clumsily use but conveyed through an intuition a thousand times swifter, are the real basis of performances which even dull ears recognize as meaningful or dull.

melody and its uncompromisingly solid bass a kinship with the first movement; and the *Tempo di Menuetto* gives a Finale far more in this general character than a bustling Rondo, in the convention of the happy ending, could have done.

K.378, in B flat, exploits at greater length than our impatient age will ordinarily welcome a kind of graceful amiability. Naturally, it is considerably ornamental in texture, and will delight the ear more than the mind. The three movements, however, maintain this primary character.

K.379, in G major, has a long and impressive *Adagio* as Introduction to a sonata-movement in G minor whose general level of tension will be found implied in the *Adagio*. The slow movement (again in variations) has a theme beneath whose naive surface an unsuspected wealth of experience is suggested; and this, a little hastened in the final variation, appropriately ends the sonata.

K.380, in E flat, is the most brilliant of the group — and the least distinctive in character. The *Andante con moto*, however, in G minor, springs from a deeper well, and the Rondo, whose subordinate themes keep pretty close to the implication of the main theme, is really exciting.

Three sonatas were composed in 1782 — K.402–404. All of them were left unfinished — for what reason, we do not know. K.402 is likely a product, first of Mozart's visit to Leipzig where he heard Bach's motets (sung by the St. Thomas choir) with such astonishment that he spread out the separate parts of one of them (no score being available) and put the piece together in his head; secondly of the influence of a new friend, Baron van Swieten, at whose house severe music only was cultivated, especially that of Handel; and thirdly of the enthusiasm of his wife, Constanze, for the fugal form. The sonata begins with a long *Andante, ma un poco Adagio*, in A major. Its slower speed makes singularly impressive the rhythm that was later to animate the Don Juan Minuet; but this is of course no dance. It serves, without in the least resembling a Bach Prelude, the same purpose as do those pieces in the *Well-tempered Clavier* — that of setting the mood for the fugue that is to follow.

The fugue was only half finished, and was completed by Abbé Stadler. The subject proves capable of many manipulations — of inversion, diminution, and an intricate stretto, all these being combined with impressive structural skill. But it is technically difficult and somewhat ineffective, the violin part somehow failing to mingle homogeneously with the three voices taken by the piano.

[51

The next sonata (K.454 in E flat) is the gem of the whole collection. Not only are the two instruments combined to the utmost tonal advantage of each, in a structure which is a perfect model of form. The quality of spiritual well-being seems to imbue every phrase, and each theme or episode as it follows another leads both players and listeners further into the region of sheer musical delight.

It was written for a young violinist, Regina Strinasacchi, with whom Mozart played the piece at her concert in Vienna. She first saw her part on the morning of the concert, and Mozart, who had not had time to write out his own, played from almost blank pages, as the Emperor Joseph found when he asked, after the concert, to see the sonata. It is the most familiar of the violin sonatas, and on that account we abstain from such enthusiastic comment as the music will evoke from any pair of sympathetic performers.

By comparison with this, the later violin sonatas — written for pupils or friends, and patently out of less compelling musical imagery — hardly demand discussion. K.570 was originally written for piano solo, and the addition of the violin part, although skillfully made, does not yield a perfect amalgamation. K.481 and K.526 have rather ephemeral musical substance, and K.547 was described by Mozart himself as written in an easy style for beginners. We shall therefore turn to the seven piano trios.*

The Trios

All the trios, apparently, were written for a small circle of musical friends, and it would appear from most of the pieces that the friends were not always very stimulating. The first (K.254) is in fact immature. It dates from 1776, and was perhaps written for Nannerl, who played it in Salzburg. The piano part far outweighs even the violin, and the 'cello, either doubling the bass of the piano or keeping silence, has hardly an individual note to play.

Neither is the next (K.496), written ten years later, formally a well-rounded sonata structure, for the 'cello is still subordinate, having nothing individual to say until the slow movement, and very little in the last except in the G-minor section. But the next (K.502), for clarinet, viola, and piano, is quite another matter. The viola is not deep enough to dou-

* There are really eight, but the one in D minor (K.442), like many of the violin sonatas, is negligible.

ble the bass, and is on the other hand so akin to the clarinet in tone, that both these instruments (genius here being stimulated by necessity) are fully equal in interest to the piano. Whether these instruments were chosen because of the delicate tonal problem they posed for the composer, or whether the delightful experience illuminated by the music demanded these instruments for its expression is a question the purist will answer in one way and the more naive listener in another. But the result is far more than the effortless solution of a structural problem.

The first movement (*Andante*, E flat, 6-8) approximates to the sonata form, but its S.II is patently an outgrowth of the S.I, so that the piece appears monothematic. The little turn-figure of the opening bar is so charmingly varied that its persistent recurrence is no more monotonous than the discovery of another wild rose on a clump of bushes. The Menuetto, which is grace itself, has an unusually long and interesting Trio, and is further amplified by an extended transition back to the Menuetto thereafter. The Finale (*Allegretto*) is on another facet of the one ruling mood. Its form is wayward, at first suggesting a loose sonata structure, then going on to a new theme in C minor and, after a brief return of the S.I, to another, very warm, in A flat, so that the S.I, when it returns, is almost a stranger. The trio was written for Franziska von Jacquin, one of his best piano pupils, who played the piano part with Mozart taking the viola. (It should be noted that the clarinet, according to the score, is indicated as an alternative for the violin; but the color of the piece is far more true to its character when the clarinet takes the part.)

The trio in B flat (K.502) opens with a little phrase in thirds whose romantic implication is abandoned (5) for a quite perfunctory continuation. This, together with the glittering figures in the piano which make the transitions, is all the thematic substance of the movement, for instead of S.II in the dominant we have only S.I, and the development, on a new tune, has only the weight of an episode. The *Larghetto* (E flat, 3-4) voices only long-approved sentiment, highly decorated — a thing made by rule. (You will have to admit that it is a good rule.) The Rondo, similarly, offers a full measure of conventional charm.

The next, however (K.542, in E major), is more vital. Its main theme is again in mellifluous thirds, but its flow is ample and always in character. The 'cello, hitherto no more significant than in Haydn, quite often emerges as leader of the discourse, and the episodes and transitions are always more than mere passages. The *Andante grazioso* borrows its graceful motion from the Gavotte and makes thereon an *objet d'art* that is about the last word in musical refinement. The Rondo (*Allegro*, 4-4 — but not 2-2 as virtuoso players are often tempted to make it) maintains throughout a glow of subdued gaiety that is difficult to "realize" in performance but, once seized, is irresistibly compelling.

The last two trios (K.548 and 564) are by comparison with this of little moment. K.564, like the violin sonata in B flat (K.570), was first written as a piano sonata. The other, in C, is again hardly more than a masterful but still dutiful exemplification of conventional sentiment. But Mozart's mastery is itself a thing to marvel at.

A trio for strings only is more difficult to compose than one with two strings and piano. But difficulties hardly existed for Mozart, so that his only example (K.563), which dates from 1788 when his technique was long since perfected, must be accounted for in some lack of public interest or in a perhaps natural preference for the more sonorous string quartet. The piece is cast in the six movements often found in the Divertimento — a fact perhaps indicative of the audience for which it was intended. There is first an *Allegro* sonata form in E flat, often ingeniously colored. The S.II, sung by violin with the 'cello a tenth below and the viola taking the actual bass, is a notable achievement in tone-color. The development shows how much meaning was hidden in the S.I. The following *Adagio* (A flat, 3-4) is so significant that it assumes very nearly the pattern of the sonata form, of course much condensed. The S.II seems to be only the S.I, in the dominant; but its continuation, on wide leaps above and below the close-packed chords in viola and 'cello, greatly expands the musical horizon, and the development, begun in E flat minor, briefly intensifies the sense of the main theme. The cheerful Menuetto offers a charming interlude, with little variety of character in the Trio, before the quaint *Andante* — variations on a theme so simple that it sounds like a nursery rhyme, but manipulated with such novel and yet always appropriate harmony that interest never lags. There is then another Menuetto, this time with two Trios, and a final Rondo, as gay as Schumann's Happy Farmer, whose tune the main theme faintly resembles. The whole trio is one of Mozart's most finished chamber works.

The Piano Quartets and Quintet

We have been long occupied with the chamber works involving the piano, and may thus go on to the three larger ones that remain — the two

54]

piano quartets and the quintet for piano and winds. The first of these is the piano quartet in G minor (K.478). This key seems to have been for Mozart what the key of C minor was for Beethoven — a tonal framework for stern and even rebellious thought. The imperious phrase which forms the core of the main theme, *unisono* in all the instruments, is complemented by a nervous upward leap and an incisive downward scale — no concession to pleasantness, but a more excited aspect of the same thought: for it has the same cadence, expanded. The continuation (9), less kinetic, is still focused on the same experience and culminates in another stern unison passage, made of the piano's answer to the string phrase. Then the opening phrase returns and is insistently pursued. Note that the repeated eighths (23) now recall the cadential rhythm of bar 4; the string figure in 28 suggests bar 9; and the piano's figure (also 28) is a fragment of bar 3. (The themes are shown in Ex. 7.)

EXAMPLE 7. MOZART PIANO QUARTET IN G MINOR, K.478

The transition (53) introduces the more mellifluous 3rds in which the S.II is to be cast. This theme (57) is identical in tonal contour with that which was later to form the A-flat episode in the Rondo of the Clarinet Trio (K.498), but its quite different rhythmic emphasis makes it convey a quite different implication. The tension is now lightened; a little figure in the piano (65) makes the Cl.S. (74); but the cadential phrases (88f) are still punctuated by the octave-leap in bar 2. The development is on an apparently new strain, but this is really S.I in a new guise, and the process of development continues after that theme has begun the recapitulation, and the S.II is now in G minor (instead of major) with many other alterations, so that this is really all a development section and is properly marked to be repeated. The Coda makes no concessions but sums up the discourse in stern unison.

[55

The gracious droop of the *Andante* (B flat, 3-8) does not reveal its underlying melancholy until the strings (9), in the lower octave, double the whole substance beneath and around that of the piano. Thereafter the note is unmistakable, both in the transition and in the S.II (35), with its *fp* ejaculations and its hushed pendant (39). The first transition serves for the return to S.I which, discreetly ornamented, begins the recapitulation.

The final Rondo (there is no Menuetto) is in G major (2-2). It is as gay as proper association with what has preceded could permit. The S.I hardly contains an expected note; yet it trips along as if quite unaware of its unusualness, and there are little hints of former thoughts (e.g., of the hushed phrase, from bar 39 of the Andante, appearing at bar 226) that maintain continuity with the earlier movements.

This piano quartet — really a new species of chamber music — was apparently intended as the first of three similar pieces. Another (K.493) was written some nine months later, but for another publisher; and the conclusion is ineluctable that the first project remained unfinished for lack of public interest. Seen in this perspective, the G minor quartet becomes another bitter chapter in that unconscious autobiography we are discovering in Mozart's music.

Structurally, the quartet in E flat (K.493) is modeled, in many features, after K.478. There are but three movements; the development in the first continues through the recapitulation; the slow movement (*Larghetto*, A flat) is again in 3-8 time and in a not dissimilar pattern; and the final Rondo (*Allegretto*, 2-2), gavotte-like in rhythm, has as delicate a tracery as the other. But while the consummate artist is evident, the man who was there so vividly portrayed is now a gracious bidder for public favor.

The Piano Quintet, for piano, oboe, clarinet, horn, and bassoon (K.452), is earlier than the two piano quartets, having been composed in 1784 for a concert of his own. He wrote his father after the concert that he considered it "the best thing I ever wrote in my life." Whether or not he revised that opinion during the seven remaining years of his life, the work is an indubitable masterpiece — one which (as Tovey has elaborately shown) Beethoven emulated but did not equal in his quintet for the same instruments, Op. 16. The difficulties Mozart had to surmount are all but imperceptible to the ear. How formidable they were should be at least suggested.

Since the "voice" of any wind instrument is more distinctive and less variable than that of a string instrument, the kind of phrase — and consequently the kind of theme — that will sound well on an oboe or a clarinet may be quite unfit for a horn or a bassoon. Moreover, the combination of these "voices," either with each other or with the piano, is tonally much more precarious than the combination of piano and strings. Thus the range of the composer's thematic invention and likewise his whole process of development are much restricted; for while he may easily invent brilliant or characteristic figures for each of the instruments, these figures may be quite unsuited for combination and wholly incompatible with the structural design of a movement or with its expressive character.

It will hardly occur to you that any of these problems arose. The range of intensity is indeed not great. Neither tragedy nor wild abandon is even suggested. The level is that of polite discourse on matters which, in the society here implied, concern the well-being of that society and reflect accepted views rather than disturbed convictions. That is, it is very "classic" music, and the actual depth of the good breeding that underlies classicism could hardly be better illuminated.

With a very few octave-transpositions, all the wind parts of this quintet can be played on the four instruments of the string quartet. Such a reading may serve to convey the contour of the piece, but — even more than with the violin substituted in the clarinet trio — it will dull the subtle color and falsify the musical character.

The String Quartets

We reach at last the most frequently heard of Mozart's chamber compositions — the string quartets. He left twenty-six of these, but sixteen of them are early works which, like Haydn's, we may ignore. Six of the remaining ten were dedicated to Haydn, from whom, he said, he "first learned the true way to compose string quartets." They outshine their model, but they also betray their origin. They were written from 1782 to 1785 — not as a "set" (only the last two have consecutive Köchel numbers), but as a carefully considered assemblage — the product, not of the enforced labor demanded by a commission, but of a labor of love.

From the pieces we have already studied, and still more from these quartets, it will be evident that Mozart was far more the conscious stylist than was Haydn. This need not imply that he was less compelled by expressive purpose. It only means that he was more offended by an inelegant turn of phrase. The happy turn, indeed, was highly valued by that audience which, in order to live, he must satisfy; and it is thus relatively seldom that we feel him writing out of the higher compulsion exerted by a true image of experience, transmuted by his imagination into musical substance and thus made communicable.

The first of the "Haydn" quartets, as we may call them, was written in 1782. It thus follows shortly after Haydn's "Russian" quartets — those in which the mere mechanics of fugal structure had been abandoned for a more subtle texture in which a distinctive rhythm or a melodic or harmonic twist had provided the basis for a psychological cohesion. Although he had written no quartets since 1773, he needed no second lesson. K.387, in G major, displays at once the "obbligato" voice-leading — the essential equality of all the component voices — that is the ideal of quartet texture (Ex. 8).

EXAMPLE 8. MOZART STRING QUARTET IN G, K.387

The opening theme, with its curious contrast of f and p within the two-bar phrases, is indeed somewhat "artificial" (in the eighteenth-century sense of "made by art"). It "says" but little; yet the graceful feminine cadence (4), enlivened by the four descending sixteenths of bar 3, is made to keep that smiling moment alive right up to the S.II (24). And what a delightful, chuckling humor that little tune has! The ensuing alternations of p and f (36), in its light, no longer seem artificial, and the long approach to the final cadence (begun with the four sixteenths of bar 2) stays in character throughout.

The development is longer than has been Mozart's wont. It is as adventurous as, in its context, it could well be. Several twinges of dissonance suggest how intense it might have become if the context had been forgotten, but Mozart never forgets the boundaries within which his imagination must be confined, and the movement closes on the note of graciousness with which it began.

The Menuetto, now featuring the *p–f* alternation in the mere chromatic scale, hints strongly at that transformation into the Scherzo which Beethoven was soon to effect. But the humor is here only an undercurrent. The chromatic scale is also assimilated to the grace that is still the predominant impression. The Trio, in G minor, strikes a somberer note but alleviates it ingeniously by interpolating an extra bar (9) and modulating, by way of colorful harmony, to B flat and then to D minor.

The *Andante cantabile* (C major, 3-4) develops for the most part the implications of its cadential figure (5) which extends the period to seven bars. Its rhythm also shapes the S.II (the solo D's in bar 30 could have been three eighth notes), so that this note of hesitant contemplation dominates the rather perfunctory beginning of S.I and imparts meaning to the many ornamental figures.

This quartet is of the period of the fugal violin sonata in A. The fugal beginning of the Finale is thus no surprise. But the assimilation of the fugal and the homophonic textures in a rounded sonata form is an anticipation of the *Jupiter* symphony and of the Finale of the *Eroica*. The main theme (G–B–E–C♯–D) resembles the G–A–C–B which Mozart often uses when a "learned" texture is begun. Quite humorously the fugal texture, when the exposition is complete, is broken off for the homophonic, which rules the transition; but the S.II (51) is again fugal, and it is soon combined with S.I (69), so that sonata and double fugue are ingeniously mingled.

Two quartets (K.421 and 428) were written in 1783. The first is in D minor (the only one of the six in a minor key), and it illustrates vividly the sensibility of the time to the contrast between major and minor. The main theme (first announced *sotto voce*) is for two bars a stern rhythming of D's. These generate an outcry, still subdued, and the whole phrase is embittered by the inexorable descent of the bass in half notes. The sudden *f* of the D's (5) is almost shocking; but even more significant is the abrupt *p* for the descent. The S.II (25) is gentle enough, but again the step-wise bass (now upward) intensifies it; the variation in triplet sixteenths becomes agitated rather than ornamental; and these sixteenths, now on reiterated notes, make even the F major of the cadence (the Cl.S.) forceful. The movement is appropriately succinct — only a hundred and seventeen bars.

The tinge of elegiac feeling hinted at in the subdominant (supertonic) harmony in bar 1 of the *Andante* is curiously intensified by the arpeggiations of the tonic chord and the ensuing subdominant phrase (4) which makes the period seem to group itself into 5 + 3 bars. The C minor stroke beginning the second section, with the following sudden *f* and the two dwindling cadences, hints more strongly at the note of tragedy, so that the unexpected drop into the main theme, by way of the one C-chord which comes in as IV in G, but turns out to be V in F (14), seems like an escape from catastrophe. The brief excursion into the warmth of A flat (35), after the stern chords preceding, is a grateful alleviation, but we feel, at the first return of the three reiterated A flats (43), that it is no more than that; and the elegiac note, when the main theme returns (52) after the stern chords, is now unmistakable to the end. Was ever a veiled misery so delicately probed?

The Menuetto, within its conventionally graceful motion, still keeps to the tenor of the thought that has governed all the quartet. The Trio, with its antic rhythm in the first violin and the pizzicato accompaniment, is thus extraordinarily grateful.

The Finale, like that of Haydn's Op. 33, No. 5, is a set of variations on a theme not unlike Haydn's. Mozart's, however, is vastly more allusive. The first violin's high A's against the continuation of the "tune" in the second violin strike a militant note quite outside the range of feeling suggested by the two opening bars, and this note gives a bitter taste to the whole musical substance. The turbulent syncopations of the second variation would hardly be rational without this background; the repeated notes reappear in a new guise in the third variation; and their almost complete absence from the fourth is as significant as any actual presentation of them could have been. In the last their original little hint of terror almost overcrows the theme itself.

What we glibly call tragedy appears, in this quartet, in very oblique perspective. All the same, it is tragedy.

The quartet in E flat (K.428) was composed during the latter half of 1783. Its main theme (*Allegro, ma non troppo*, 2-2) is more introspective than that of the D minor. It is far less stern, but in implication seems hardly less gloomy. Its concentration, however, proves far less sharp as the music proceeds. The harmonization of the theme (it first appears in unison) promises much inner illumination (12–15), but instead a transition begins whose chief feature is an interestingly manipulated but not very pregnant scale-descent. The S.II (40), beginning in G minor instead of the prepared B flat, also forsakes its first suggestion for rather perfunctory phraseology, and the warmth of the broad passage (56f) is almost negated by the scampering scales that close the exposition. The main theme, after one canonic imitation, disappears from the development in favor of the little figure that introduced S.II, along with some rather irrelevant arpeggiation. It is intensified in the recapitulation by a new counterpoint (113), but the rest is undeveloped.

The *Andante con moto* (A flat, 6-8) has a relevant fervency, much intensified by suspensions. The rocking accompaniment figure is hardly altered throughout the movement, so that the S.II offers little contrast; but the pull of the dissonances (e.g., at 15f.) is so novel that no more is to be desired. Here, without doubt, we have a harmonic imagination of the first order.

Vigor, hitherto not much in evidence, is so strongly presented in the first two bars of the Menuetto that only occasional repetition of this figure is needed to give vivacity to the whole piece. The Trio, in B flat, begins in C minor and reaches its real key only at the eighth bar. But it has reverted to the prevailing melancholy of the quartet, and its suavity is thus appropriate.

The Finale (*Allegro vivace*, 2-4) is indeed vivacious, departing wholly from the hitherto prevailing mood. Unexpected accents — e.g., the f on the two eighths instead of the tied E♭ in bar 62 — and the headlong speed of the brief passages of sixteenths, as well as the addition of a new melody above the last appearance of S.I (305), all serve to make acceptable this obvious intervention of a *deus ex machina*.

The fourth of these six quartets (K.458) was finished in November, 1784 — a year or so after K.428. Leopold Mozart spoke of the last three as being somewhat lighter than the first three. This is certainly true of the present work. The first impression, indeed, would suggest a stronger adverb than "somewhat"; but closer acquaintance will justify Leopold's phrase. For beneath the surface of this music, which may too easily be made to glitter coldly, there is a glow of spontaneous gaiety, hard for the performers to catch but, once caught, as infectious as laughter itself. It is really the spirit of comedy — more difficult for the creator to embody in his work than is the gloom of tragedy, and more difficult for the performer (whether actor or musician) to utter justly.

The quality most essential in performance is a kind of elasticity — a resilience first suggested in the little giggle of sixteenths that animates the theme in bar 5 and pops out at unexpected moments thereafter: in the vanishing scales (15–17); in the twitters that make transition to the S.II (42f); and in that theme itself, whose precise beginning and end it would be hard to pinpoint, but whose mood can hardly be mistaken. The development rightly avoids undue intensity by remaining in the dominant for sixteen bars, finding a new theme quietly in the ruling vein of thought. Then it turns to the S.II whose gay figure overrides the minor keys it is made to pass through. If the real mood is caught, the Coda will not seem overlong.

After so *riant* a movement a sober thought could hardly engage the attention. So the Menuetto (*Moderato*) comes next — a dance kept to the unexpanded dimension found in a Bach Suite, and showing all the grace with which the participants in the former gaiety would accede to the subsiding of that excitement. Thus the *Adagio* (E flat, 4-4) can begin with a thought that may be intensified to high seriousness. Instead, its mood is lightened (7) and the S.II (15) develops a romantic tension colored by a succession of "secondary" sevenths almost Wagnerian. There is no development, but only repetition with a gently sighing Coda and a mere hint of the S.I. The Finale (*Allegro assai*, 2-4), assuming an air of naivety that is really quite specious, finds a new note of gaiety and amplifies thus the underlying spirit of the whole quartet.

The fifth and sixth of the "Haydn" quartets (K.464 and 465) were finished on January 10 and 14, 1785. The fifth, in A major, is the most skilled of the six; the sixth, in C, the most imaginative. But since to realize an imaginative vision requires consummate skill, and to work out problems demanding skill requires imagination, that statement will likely be qualified by the performers into a momentary preference for whichever of the two is being studied.

The A major has as main theme for the first movement (*Allegro*, 3-4) a resilient four-bar phrase rhythmed like a minuet, and flowing with an ease that seems the antithesis of "learning." But at bar 18, where the viola begins to imitate the second violin, and 'cello and first violin continue, something of the high ingenuity of the whole structure is forecast. The transition (25–36), beginning in C, finds a colorful path to E, and the S.II (37), spurting into a triplet figure, is again fascinatingly imitated. Most of the close is made of S.I.; but four bars from the end of the exposition there is a tiny figure in the rhythm of the opening that, along with the S.I, forms the substance of a development almost incessantly polyphonic, yet as lucid and effortless as music can be.

The Menuetto itself cannot resist toying imitatively with its dancing phrases, but the Trio is content to ornament its sonorous texture with quick arpeggiations.

The *Andante* (D major, 2-4) is a set of variations on a rather curiously designed theme. Its first phrase is almost forgotten in favor of the second (4f), and the little syncopated figure (10) seems somewhat foreign to the thought. The variations are charming and well contrasted. The last is built over a drumming figure in the 'cello, and this, in the Coda, migrates successively to the higher voices.

The Finale (*Allegro non troppo*, 2-2) is a sonata-form movement with a single theme which does duty, in the dominant, as S.II, and there are a few free phrases of transition; but the one thought is put through an astonishing variety of contrapuntal paces. Beethoven thought so highly of this movement that he scored it.

The last of the "Haydn" quartets is the most frequently performed — doubtless because of the amazing *Adagio* that introduces it. It was probably this strange page which evoked from Haydn, when he was asked to explain it, the remark, "Well, if Mozart wrote it, he must have meant it." To the ear of today there is no perplexity, although the music strains the boundaries of tonality almost as far as Wagner was to do, seventy-five years later, in the Prelude to *Tristan*. Mozart's imagery, although his "subject" was far different from the passion Wagner was portraying, is just as penetrating. This Introduction and all the main themes of the following movements are shown in Example 9.

The tonality of the Introduction *is* C major, just as that of Wagner's Prelude is A minor; but it is so obscured by the A♭ chord (the lowered VI of C) and by the false relation of the ensuing A♮ that the simple V (on "two" in bar 3) has become uncertain. Thus its upward progression to D♭ seems perfectly logical, and the whole strain can repeat itself a tone lower. (Note that the three upper voices are in almost literal imitation.) Here, surely, is the "strangeness" of romanticism, all but at its peak before the actual romantic movement has begun.

The ensuing *Allegro* can be played as if it were quite unrelated to the

EXAMPLE 9. MOZART QUARTET IN C, K.465

Adagio. But though the tension is much reduced it has not dropped into insouciance. The G in bar 2 pulls against a subdominant harmony; its parallel, A (4), is more dissonant; and the descent from the peak of the curve (6f) is on a figure by no means perfunctory. This tension (slighter to our dissonance-drenched ears than to those of Mozart's day) colors the thought right up to the transition (25). A sub-theme (34) interjects a forceful note that makes the S.II (49) with its elastic triplets and its suave after-phrase all the more appealing. The triplets soon become swift sixteenths, recalling the sub-theme and generating a bold energy (66) whose widespread notes might have formed the Cl.S. had not the S.I needed reassertion as the topic of the development.

This section, in these quartets, is now becoming longer and more

64]

weighty than formerly. It is here wholly concerned with the S.I whose vigor is much intensified by the staccato figures (95), by the new counterpoint for S.I (100), and by the condensation of that small pattern into three arpeggiated (instead of step-wise) eighths before the two notes (also hastened) that make its breathless end. The recapitulation is somewhat shortened and the Coda is less positive than we, no longer ruled by the convention of the happy ending, might desire.

The *Andante cantabile* (F major, 3-4) has a rather elegiac main theme whose fervency is intensified by the *forte* ascent on the subdominant chord. A higher intensity is interjected (9–10); then, for the cadence, quietude is resumed and a transition begins. Its little figure (13), all huddled around a single note, imitated between violin and 'cello, and colored by gravely descending harmonies, maintains, in a more rarefied atmosphere, the mood of the theme itself. It is thus much more than a mere transition, for the S.II (26), still more hushed, is generated out of the repeated eighth notes, and is itself no more than a repeated note that becomes dissonant and resolves. It rises to the momentary high intensity already often developed (31); but its deepest implication is found in the next two bars where the darkening of the harmony (A to A♭) on the bare reiterated rhythm of the theme seems as pregnant as notes can well be. After a little the transition-figure (now with two notes added) leads back to the somewhat ornamented S.I and a somewhat extended recapitulation. Here, certainly, is pure music. But here also is pure poetry, seen in the half-light in which alone poetic visions are visible.

The Menuetto (*Allegretto*, C major) emerges graciously out of the lessening tension of the *Andante*, only the unexpected low F of the first phrase giving any hint of the energy of the *forte* phrase that follows. Neither is that vigor great enough to destroy the appropriateness of this movement as a sequel to the *Andante*. The Trio, in C minor, is again subtly right in striking a somber note. Observe the interpolated hint of the Menuetto (25–28).

The Finale (*Allegro molto*, C major, 2-4) has the mischievous gaiety so characteristic of Mozart. The main theme suggests that the form will be that of the Rondo, but the whole design turns out to be that of the sonata form. The second theme (53) is even lighter-footed than the first. It eventuates in a scamper of sixteenths that might have initiated the closing subject. Instead, its cross-accented culminant figure is slowed and there is a curiously romantic moment in E flat (88) before the dainty close of the exposition. The development is ingeniously contrived out of the main theme, in minor, abruptly contrasted with the second theme. The recapitulation (198) follows the plan of the exposition save that the romantic episode is now lengthened, and there is a quite extended Coda. The movement is clearly in the tradition of the happy ending, but this is by no means a heedless sort of gaiety.

The next quartet (K.499) was finished in August, 1786. It is an isolated effort — apparently, as Jahn thought, because "it met with no very general approval on its first appearance." It offers little of that immediate appeal characteristic of all the "Haydn" quartets, but seems nevertheless an important chapter in that unconscious autobiography we are tracing.

Its first movement (*Allegretto*, D major, 2-2) is so far dominated by its main theme that all the departures from that thought appear episodic. But this theme, perceptively read, suggests the contemplation of an experience by no means trivial. Its downward trend covers, *unisono*, a span of almost two octaves; the low A thus reached is repeated in five gentle footfalls; this rhythmic figure then recurs thrice, its tread falling on successive notes of the V7 chord, with a cadence figure (10–12) that for the first time shows conjunct melodic progression. Read as mere arpeggiation, this theme may appear quite dull. Read with insight, its implications appear increasingly deep.

EXAMPLE 10. MOZART QUARTET IN D, K.499

A sudden loud transition to B minor (23) brings a momentary sternness highly illuminative of the inner sense of the main theme, and a modulation to A then yields all the S.II that is to appear — a straining lyric figure on the subdominant (32). But this soon reverts to the five-note treading of S.I, and that theme, now in E major and with a singular warmth of color, comes back for a brief imitative expansion which, with an excursion to F sharp minor (58) and the introduction of a new rhythmic twitch, the sixteenth followed by the dotted eighth (65), will form the Cl.S. (83).

A little cadential figure in even eighths (97) becomes the background for the development, all founded on S.I and revealing still more of the significance of that theme. The recapitulation (141) follows the plan of the exposition but is often intensified by changes of register. Mozart marks this whole section for repeat and then adds a considerable Coda. The themes of this movement are shown in Example 10.

The following movements, like the first, demand imaginative reading. The subtle undertone of melancholy we have tried to suggest imbues them all, but it is so far hidden beneath the outwardly pleasant surface that performance in the conventionally bright and happy style will obscure it altogether. This seems to us particularly true of the *Adagio*, whose graceful theme and considerably florid texture are indeed in the highest sense ornamental; but it is true also of the dainty Finale which, if it grows too robust, will appear quite superficial.

Mozart's last three quartets (K.575, 589, and 590) were commissioned by King Frederick William of Prussia, to whom, as we have seen, Haydn's six quartets, Op. 50, were dedicated. The first (in D major) was composed in 1789; the last two (in B flat and F) in 1790. They offer to the royal virtuoso larger opportunity than do the quartets by Haydn, and in the skill with which the texture is woven they do not fall behind the previous works. Their spiritual substance, however, is far less significant. You will find in them many charming moments, but no such evocation of intimacy as the "Haydn" quartets offer.

To replace the quartet's first violin by a wind instrument was for Mozart an interesting experiment. Three such quartets exist: K.281 and 298, with the flute, and K.370 with the oboe. All three are rather slight in substance but charmingly worked out, especially the oboe quartet. Mozart disliked the flute, but no one would suspect it from this music. Its limitations, like those of the oboe, very considerably restrict the expressive range, but the pieces are so justly designed within the scope of the wind instrument that they have the charm of miniatures.

The Quintets

To add another string instrument (or a wind instrument) to the quartet was a more significant experiment. Mozart left, in all, nine quintets: K.46, 174, 406, 407, 515, 516, 581, 593, and 614. The first two we shall ignore. K.406, in C minor, is an arrangement for strings of the Serenade (K.388) for two oboes, two clarinets, two horns, and two bassoons. Its substance betrays the relatively restricted expressive range of the winds as compared with the strings; but the work, relatively easy to play, is still charming. It has a Minuet in canon, with a Trio *al Rovescio* — i.e., with the theme, begun in the second violin, answered in inversion by the first. K.407, for horn, violin, two violas, and bass, will allow a 'cello to substitute (of course with much loss of tonal color) for the horn. It was written for a friend, the hornist Leutgeb, for whom Mozart also wrote several horn concertos, and suggests the limitations of the player as well as of the instrument.

The two string quintets, K.515 and 516, were finished respectively in April and May, 1787. They offer, in the present writer's critical perspective, a most striking illustration of the antithesis between the classic and the romantic attitudes, and also — since they were written almost concurrently — of that congruity between those attitudes of which we spoke in the introductory chapter. The C major and the G minor symphonies, written, along with the E flat, in the summer of 1788, are analogous (even in key), and will seem to confirm our judgment. Each quintet is a consummate masterpiece.

The main theme of the C major quintet may appear, at first sight, unsuggestive. It is nothing but the arpeggio of the C major chord in the 'cello, completed (4) by a half-cadence high in the violin. But that arpeggio, imaginatively read, *looks toward* its completion in the violin; and once this expectancy is felt the theme becomes big with suspense. The whole pattern is repeated on the dominant, and again on the first inversion of the tonic. Then, after a pregnant bar of silence, violin and 'cello thrice reverse their role, the answer, deep in the 'cello, gaining pointedly in meaning. This breeds (rhythmically, out of the arpeggio) a figure of repeated F's (42) that soon forms the transition. The sudden interjection of the D flat chord (a sort of Neapolitan 6/4!) opens out a new and colorful harmonic region that is explored for some time. Then a more purposive rhythm on three quarter notes finally establishes the dominant key.

What then appears, however, is not the S.II but the S.I — the violin again leading; and it is only after a stretto on the answering phrase (76f) that the first violin, all alone, manages to find all the S.II that is to be offered: a quiet eighth-note figure with which the pattern of repeated notes is soon combined. This achieves a kind of luminous quietude, disturbed by a syncopated figure (115), but leading to spacious cadential phrases that form all the Cl.S. that is needed. The development is brief and appropriately hushed, dealing chiefly with the S.I and the quiet motion of the Cl.S. But through that very quietude it illuminates wonderfully the nameless spiritual region toward which the S.I aimed at the beginning.

We must curb an all but uncontrollable impulse to speak at similar length of the following movements. Descent from the high imaginative region so long occupied is appropriately accomplished by a rather grave Menuetto, again in C, but with a Trio in the darker subdominant. The ensuing *Andante*, in F, does not attempt to reach again the spiritual height of the first movement, but establishes itself on a plain halfway up to that eminence. The atmosphere is here warmer, but is not humid; the sentiment reflects the tone of a commoner but still wholly aristocratic experience, graciously enacted and graciously portrayed. The Finale can thus achieve the conventional happy ending without derogating from the earlier tone.

In the C major quintet the impersonal vision of the classicist is raised to a level which may justly be called serenity. In the G minor quintet the spiritual torment of the romanticist—his most appellant mood—is set forth even more vividly.

The main theme (see the accompanying illustration, Ex. 11) strikes at once into the core of the thought that underlies the whole first movement and, in a lesser intensity, the whole quintet. The first two bars are identical in rhythm, but very different in implication. The first phrase, tonally, is the rising arpeggio of the tonic chord—expressively, quite indefinite. But the second, a chromatic descent, is subtly harmonized (the C major triad, 6/4, after the F minor 6-chord, is still heard in the perspective of G minor), and in its light the inert first phrase gains much meaning. The third bar is so bowed as to depart from this rhythmic pattern, but this is a disguise rather than a contradiction, and the broader half-cadence (4) affirms the note of despondency. The first bar is then inverted and given an urgent continuation with an end, not on the perfunctory G the ear expects, but on the low D. Then the theme, in a singularly meaningful color, is repeated in the three lower instruments with a still more urgent continuation which enlists the two violins; and these are at once aroused to a highly romantic gesture on the diminished 3rd (20) that, along with momentary reference to S.I, leads to the second theme (30).

[69

EXAMPLE 11. MOZART STRING QUINTET IN G MINOR, K.515

Relativity of this theme to the first is heightened in two ways. It is in the minor instead of the conventional major tonality, and it is in the tonic key instead of the conventional relative. Its first simple ejaculation is bitter enough, but when the upward leap becomes a minor 9th it is intensified to an outcry.

Except for the dotted figure (44) and the chromatic twist (76) which, turning into a triplet figure, provides an interlude of relaxation, the rest of the exposition is on already established thematic matter. The short development, introduced by an expectant series of rising intervals,* does not greatly intensify the substance of the exposition; but this was itself of an intensity hardly countenanced by existing convention. We need not describe it further.

The tone of the ensuing Menuetto, pointed up by the ejaculatory chords (4, 6, etc.), is patently in character. It appropriately relieves, as the *Adagio* could not have done, the mood of the first movement. The following *Adagio ma non troppo* at first projects a warmth (heightened

* The rising 5th and 6th (94) may be seen either as a condensation of the preceding figure of S.I or as the incomplete S.II.

70]

rather than dimmed by the muting of the instruments) that, had it ruled the whole movement, would have seemed a too complete alleviation of the former bitterness. This note, however, is overridden by the heavy B flat minor of the S.II (18), whose thrust is much intensified by the ejaculations of the second viola. (Did Schubert, in the *Adagio* of his C major quintet, borrow from this his highly similar device — the tragic triplet figures in the second 'cello? See p. 151.)

The somber descent of this theme begins also the Introduction to the Finale, which makes as well a single reference to the dotted figure of the first movement. But the tone thereafter lightens, preparatory to the easy grace of the Finale. This (*Allegro*, G major, 6-8) is indeed a happy ending; but its gaiety is one which emerges rationally after the experiences already undergone, and the subtlety with which this vein of feeling is caught and maintained is as truly a mark of great art as is the impeccable structure.

Two more string quintets (K.593 in D, and K.614 in E flat) were written in 1790 and 1791 "at the earnest solicitation of a musical friend" who is not named. The first movement of K.593 has an impressive Introduction (*Larghetto*, 3-4) which promises more than the ensuing *Allegro* offers. This has a composite main theme whose three members seem rather alien to each other,* and the whole movement, charming as it is in effect, is rather diffuse in focus. The *Larghetto* returns to form most of the Coda. The main theme of the *Adagio* (G major, 3-4) is warm, and the S.II (16) appropriately agitated, but the image of experience it evokes is reflected rather than immediate. The Menuetto and the Finale are similarly delightful.

In the E flat quintet the opening motive, a rhythmic antic on the first two notes of the scale, so far rules the whole movement that the S.II (39), a derivative, is hardly distinguishable, and the Cl.S. (72) is merely a cadential figure superimposed on the motive. This description suggests monotony. Instead there is interest every minute, although the interest is of ingenuity rather than of imagination. The *Andante* (B flat, 2-4) has a naive little theme, rather freely varied; the Menuetto is similarly unsophisticated, and the final Rondo as insouciant as the chatter at a cocktail

* Hans Keller, in *The Mozart Companion* (Oxford University Press, 1956), finds high relativity in the first of these members to the opening strain of the *Larghetto*. The resemblance is indubitable, but the relativity would be more credible as a basic principle of structure if this thematic fragment had played a larger part in the movement.

[71

party. All these things, however, are drawn for us with the skill of a genius.*

To add a wind instrument to the string quartet was as intriguing an experiment as to substitute it for one of the violins in the quartet. Mozart composed two such quintets, one with added horn (K.407) and one with clarinet. The limitation we spoke of in discussing the quartets with flute and oboe confines also the scope of these more sonorous pieces. It is most noticeable in the horn quintet, since Mozart had to write for the "natural" horn which could play as "open" notes only those of the harmonic series. It thus had melodic freedom only in the top of its register, and the themes had to be designed with this limitation always in mind. The result is as natural as if there had been no obstacle; but comparison with the freer pieces for strings only will reveal the narrower range within which the composer had to work. This piece has three movements only, all rather short.

The clarinet, with a compass about equal to that of the viola, with a clearness in rapid passages exceeding that of the string instrument, and with a considerable variety of tone in its different registers, was a far less confining instrument to write for. It has, however, its distinctive tone-color; it cannot but be conspicuous against the string ensemble; and the thematic substance of this quintet had also to be invented with these facts constantly in mind.

The product, when one considers these necessities, is all but miraculous. The clarinet never "sticks out" like a solo instrument against a *tutti*, and never vaunts its agility at the expense of the violins. It leads, to be sure, in the lovely *Larghetto* which, like the slow movement in the *kleine Nachtmusik*, could have been entitled *Romanze*. But its lead is never ostentatious. Having been prominent for a time, as in the gay Menuetto, it keeps silent in the first Trio, naturally emerging in Trio II. And the Finale, a set of variations on a characteristically carefree mood, is managed with an instrumental *savoir-faire* that is the last perfection of aristocratic taste.

To double the 'cello with a bass viol was another (and much older) fashion of making a string quintet. The Serenade, *Eine kleine Nacht-*

---

*These two works quite possibly reflect — as do the quartets written for the Prussian king — Mozart's attitude toward his unnamed patron. Patrons were becoming harder to find; to please them was a pressing necessity; and the quintets thus form a not wholly happy chapter in his musical autobiography.

musik (K.525), has a rather diminutive sonata form for its first movement (it may well be taken as the March which opened the conventional Serenade); a gentle *Romanze* in gavotte rhythm for slow movement; a tiny Menuetto (the sections are all eight bars long except the last part of the Trio, which has twelve); and a tripping Rondo for Finale.* Since the 'cello and bass parts are identical, the piece can be played as a quartet with little loss, in a music room, of its character.

A delightful chapter in Mozart's musical autobiography — perhaps inappropriate at the end of a discussion of his serious works but too characteristic to be omitted — is found in the Horn sextet (K.522) for two horns, two violins, viola, and bass which Mozart called *Ein musikalischer Spass* (A musical joke). Hogarth could not have caricatured more effectively the pretensiousness of the would-be composer and performer, who may be taken as one person. His melodic wings will carry him no more than four bars at a time, and he comes to earth with a cadential thud at the end of every phrase. He has learned the outline of the sonata form, however, and his first movement contains all the essential features, even though they show no relativity to each other. In the lumbering Menuetto *Maestoso*(!) the two horns (*dolce*) have a chromatic passage of thirds for which the strings cannot find the proper harmony, and in the Trio the violinist-composer begins to show off, first in two octaves of the B flat scale and then in 10ths. In the *Adagio cantabile*, in C, whether from nervousness or out of a desire to be original, the first phrase of melody has an incongruous F sharp, while the accompanying harmony moves in consecutive 5ths. There are several eruptions of rapid scales (quite irrelevant) and at the end a cadenza that ascends to the end of the fingerboard. But the player's fingers are too big for the half step at this height, so that this composer wins the distinction of producing the first whole-tone scale in musical literature. The Finale (*Presto*) begins with a sort of rondo theme that falls into the relative minor and has to straighten itself out with two added bars in the tonic. The second section goes farther astray and is similarly rectified. Then, unable to continue this idea, the composer (not unlike some twentieth-century writers) begins a fugue on a ridiculous little theme whose knees cave in at the end of subject and answer alike so that it is quite unable to con-

* Donald Mitchell, in *The Mozart Companion*, notes the *Times* for May 6, 1955, as reporting the discovery of the MS. A first Menuetto appears to have been torn out. It would have preceded the *Romanze*.

tinue beyond the exposition. The smaller details are beyond description. The end is on three "chords" that anticipate polytonality.

One can hardly hear this piece without forming an image of some pretentious amateur, bidding for favor both as composer and performer. He is nearly unconscious of his misadventures, unless for his slips in performance; but he takes his composition *au grand serieux*, and here his constant ineptitudes yield a subtle musical humor that is about the funniest thing in the literature.

It is perhaps better not to read into it the bitter irony which afterthought, along the perspective of Mozart's declining fortune, may evoke.

Ludwig van Beethoven

1770–1827

WE FOUND the man Mozart, although we left him, rather incongruously, in a mood of ironic laughter, portrayed in his music as a man aware of the world and of its inexplicable contradictions. That "self-portrait" was doubtless refined and idealized (as were most of the painters' representations of him) by conventions of thought and utterance more concerned with surfaces than with underlying realities; but the man — *l'homme même* of Buffon's famous definition — was *there*.

The man Beethoven will be more evident. His childhood background — all but squalid — bred in him no such instinctive and in some degree squeamish sensitivity to what is hastily called beauty as that which Mozart absorbed by contact with aristocracy at its most ostentatious level. Neither, although his talent was commanding, had Beethoven the quick apprehension and the quicker facility of utterance of the prodigy. His talent, indeed, was too big — too comprehensive — for such immediate revelation. (So, of course, was Mozart's; like Beethoven's it had to be developed by experience; but experience, in its harsher, more fertilizing aspect, impinged upon him only later, and was accordingly more disturbing and harder to assimilate.)

Also, the portentous rumblings of the coming Revolution hardly reached Mozart's ear. In Bonn, a thousand miles to the west, they were more audible and Beethoven's underprivileged ear was more sensible of their vibration. His thirst for spiritual nourishment was, however, slaked by such contacts with the amenities of life as were offered by the von Breunings; his ambition was fired, not indeed to acquire but to excel; but his definition of excellence was formulated out of a wider and coarser background than was Mozart's youthful vision.

His music is thus seldom as exquisitely skilled as Mozart's. It shows more of the effort toward mastery. But, that mastery once acquired, it reflects a wider vision of the world and of the real objective of the artist.

The growth of that vision would be more clearly shown if we were to study his chamber works chronologically. But to show historic continuity is not our main purpose. We shall thus follow our established plan of taking up first the chamber music with piano, and shall begin with the sonatas for piano and violin which are more numerous and more representative of his genius than those for piano and 'cello.

The Violin Sonatas

Three of these, Op. 12, were apparently written in 1798 — the year of the *Pathétique* sonata for piano. None of them arises out of any such profound disturbance as generated that piece. The first, in D, seems rather an essay in construction than an utterance compelled by an imaginative vision. But the main theme of the *Allegro con brio*, while still on the arpeggio of the tonic chord, is rhythmed with a purposive vigor, and the continuation, still arpeggiating primary chords, gives lyric contour to the same impulse. The S.II (43) soon proves capable of ingenious cross-rhythm; its continuation (58) has welcome warmth; but the whole substance, in development, becomes somewhat redundant. A hint of the resourceful variationist that Beethoven will become is given in the slow movement. The sudden *ff*'s in Var. III are highly characteristic, and the murmuring of the theme within the syncopated harmony of Var. IV anticipates many a similar, profounder moment in later works. The theme of the Rondo-finale is more plebeian than Mozart's, but there are many charming lighter touches.

The second sonata, in A, begins with an *Allegro vivace* very slight in substance, but very ingratiating if the performers catch the requisite delicacy. The *Andante, più tosto Allegretto* (A minor, 2-4) is as substantial as, in its context, it could well be. The Finale (*Allegro piacevole*, 3-4), derives something of its character from the Minuet and, without ever departing from that graceful tone, manages to find both an S.II (54) and an S.III (120) that keep the hearer's attention alert.

The third sonata is the most pretentious of the three and (as is not always true of brilliant technical pieces) the most significant. An abundant rhythmic energy, highly characteristic of Beethoven, underlies the whole substance of the first movement. Note the sturdy bass (13), the properly non-lyrical quality of the S.II (37), and both the approach to the Cl.S. (50f) and that theme itself (58). The broad phrase in C flat at the end of the development (96), initiated by a darkening of the preceding staccato (from the Cl.S.), is thematically new; but it throws a new light on the excitement of the whole movement and also forecasts the coming *Adagio*.

This, a little surprisingly, is in a major key (C); but its sober melodic line, tensed by punctuating chords rather than relaxed by a suave figurated accompaniment and later activated by the double-dotted eighths, attains a stern eloquence. And when at length (23) the middle section sinks into the darkness of F minor the violin finds a song whose final phrase, over always unresolving dissonances, reaches such a height of suspense as music, hitherto, had hardly known how to portray.

The Rondo (*Allegro molto*, 2-4) has a more contrapuntal vigor than had the first movement. It thus forms a wholly appropriate Finale to the sonata, far more cogent than the happy ending so often demanded by earlier convention.

The next two sonatas, Op. 23 in A minor and Op. 24 in F, both dedicated to Count Moritz von Fries, were intended to form one opus. Their highly contrasted character suggests that purpose; some publisher's error defeated it. The first of the two is the least highly regarded by performers and listeners alike of all the violin sonatas. Yet the opening motive of the *Presto*, succinct and decisive, is real Beethoven; the S.II (30), in E minor instead of the more suave C major, gains thereby in appropriateness; the domination of that key right up to the end of the exposition is very purposive; but whether from the thinness of the three-voiced texture or for some obscurer reason, the tonal substance fails to body forth the weight of the idea. The *Andante scherzoso, più Allegretto* appropriately departs from the conventional loftiness of slow movements, voicing a sort of gentle banter which Beethoven will later learn how to make very attractive. Here it compels him to a sonata form, too long for the mood that he is expressing. The main theme of the Rondo (*Allegro molto*, 2-2) recurs twice without alteration in the first 112 bars, but so little thereafter that the form seems skewed. But, if you look for it, you will find in the music a very distinctive personality.

The F major sonata, Op. 24, is known as the "Spring" sonata, and the title (not Beethoven's) has never been protested.* The music in no way

---

* It was added, in a later edition, by the publisher A. Cranz.

directly represents the sights or sounds that delight us in that season, but it does portray our inarticulate response to the ever-new greening of the world. Form and character in the first two movements are both wholly lucid. It is the first of the violin sonatas to contain a Scherzo. This is an impish little piece. It makes the violin lose a beat in doubling the piano's theme, so that uninitiated listeners always think the player has made a mistake. Its value is not all in its humor, however. It freshens the atmosphere (a little clouded by the *Adagio molto espressivo*) so that the wonderfully gracious Rondo-finale can exert its wholly persuasive charm.

The three sonatas of Op. 30 are dedicated to the Emperor Alexander I of Russia. The first and third of these may perhaps be recognizable as commissioned pieces. (The composer was rewarded with a valuable ring.) The second is one of Beethoven's most significant works.

The first, in A major, is far less Beethovenish than is Op. 23. The sixteenth-note motive in the first bar contributes nothing to the character of the amiable main theme, nor has it enough in itself to yield any developmental weight. The *molto espressivo* prescribed for the *Adagio* (D major, 2-4) is native to the theme in the violin, but is over-intensified by the persistent dotted figure which also accompanies the S.II (17). The triplets (51) which at last relieve the figure do mollify the somewhat artificial sternness, but the theme itself (64) loses rather than gains by the substitution. It appears certain that Beethoven at first intended the tarantelle that ends the Kreutzer sonata to form the close of this piece. One can easily understand why he changed his mind, but not so easily how he could originally have related that breathless thing to the earlier movements of this work. In the actual Finale, *Allegretto con Variazioni* (A major, 2-2), the theme keeps its simple outline for four variations; the fifth, in minor, comes back by way of an excursion into B flat for the final, much expanded variation.

The second of the group, in C minor, is really the weightiest of all the violin sonatas. The main theme (*Allegro con brio* — with vigor) is grim and tight-lipped, reducing to its starkest terms the tension of tragedy. The implication of the long initial G, revealed in the sudden nervous sixteenths and the abrupt stop on the tonic,* is heightened by repetition

* Make the G grow by holding it a tiny fraction too long, precipitating the descent by making the sixteenths proportionately short. After the portentous *cresc.*, take the shortest of "catch-breaths." Then the *p* G will have the aplomb it must

78]

of the phrase on the subdominant. Then the broader eighths and the crescendo quarters, suddenly stilled on the ominously harmonized dominant (I and V *can* be ominous!) set the stage for an instrumental drama more concentrated than could ever be shaped were the composer hampered by words and actors.

Like the main theme, the action that follows has the import of tragedy. (The catastrophe, however, occurs at the end of the sonata.) The S.II (28) is reached after a brief, highly relevant transition. It is brittle and nervous — perhaps ironic in implication. It sinks into E flat minor for a moment and then, in huge two-octave strides, makes swift approach to the Cl.S. (52) whose vigor, no longer ironic, reveals an unsuspected facet of its nature in a momentary lyrical outcry (60).

There is no time, in so purposive an action, for the conventional repeat of the exposition. Against the main theme, deep in the bass, the violin invents a new, straining lyricism; the irony of the S.II becomes bitter; turbulent figures in the piano accompany the two-octave strides; and there is a terrifying return to the main theme (125), now overwhelming in its stark energy.

After the recapitulation there is a reminiscence of the somber development of the main theme; then a Coda that sums up the inexorable logic of the action. Beethoven's achievement of the *Eroica*, written less than two years after the Second symphony, and seen only in the light of that work, looks inexplicable. In the light of this piece it becomes more credible.

The *Adagio cantabile* (A flat, 4-4) looks both backward toward classicism and forward toward romanticism, and blends the two images into one of such loftiness as the twentieth century, defining loftiness as the exploration of outer space, seems to contemplate with impatience. The main theme might be called hopefully elegiac; the second (33), in A flat minor, with its thin staccato accompaniment for the broad cantilena in the violin,* has a breathless stillness wonderfully relieved by the legato return to the main theme. The two sudden eruptions of force (87, 96) are shocking but not out of context, for, like the fanfare after the *Adagio*

show. Murmur the first three beats against the violin, but articulate the sixteenths with it. You can simulate in this way the infinitesimal rubato you took with the theme.

* The repetition of this cantilena in the piano (41) is very hard to play lyrically, but it can be made so if the little finger imitates the dynamic curve just set forth in the violin.

[79

of the Ninth symphony, they recall implications in the first movement
that must still be contemplated.

The impudent Scherzo and its canonic Trio with a gruff bass imitating
the violin would doubtless have offended an eighteenth-century audience. It is superficially as incongruous — and intrinsically as right — as
are Shakespeare's clowns against the background of a tragic action. And
this becomes clearer when, with a portentous figure on the augmented
6th chord, we are plunged into the final act of the drama. The pattern
is a fusion of sonata and rondo forms,* but its logic is as inexorable as
that of the first movement. Even the abrupt cadence-chords of the main
theme (4–8) acquire a singular pathos (267f) as they approach the ineluctable catastrophe of the final *Presto*.

The third sonata of Op. 30, in G major, is more successful than the
first in its offering of what may be called royal entertainment. An over-
all grace of motion pervades the first movement — a grace that imbues
both S.II and episode; the slow movement — in a fresh key-color (E flat)
and in the mood and the expanded pattern of the Minuet — is wholly
accordant; and nothing could be more exquisitely conceived than the
Finale — almost a *moto perpetuo* — on a gently rocking figure of sixteenths beneath a gay little snatch of dance-tune. The pattern, as Riemann noted, is that of a *Rondo à la Musette* — a single, recurrent theme
over a pedal (drone) bass, tonic or dominant, with no more than brief
episodic excursions between. The departures from tonic and dominant
or relative are wonderfully timed for contrast, thus contriving a quiet
crescendo of gentle gaiety to the end.

The next, the great "Kreutzer" sonata, is so called from its dedication
to Rudolf Kreutzer, a notable violinist, in the service of that General
Bernadotte who was one day to become King of Sweden but who was
in 1803 ambassador to the Imperial Court in Vienna. It was at first dedicated to George Bridgetower, a London-born mulatto, a highly tem-
peramental violinist with whom Beethoven gave the first performance
of the work. His virtuosity prompted Beethoven to write it "in a very
concertante style, like a concerto." It was also, in a sense, composed
backwards, the last movement, as we have seen, having been originally
intended as the Finale of Op. 30, No. 1.

* A = S.I; B = S.II, rel. maj., 39; A = S.I, tonic, 92; C = S.III, tonic maj., 107 —
long developed; A = S.I, tonic (as recap.), 165; B = S.II, tonic *minor*, 201; A = S.I,
tonic, expanded, 256; Coda, 282.

In a way, then, this sonata oversteps the boundary between chamber and concert music.* Amazement must certainly color, but will not wholly comprise, any listener's immediate response to an adequate performance, for he will at the same time share in a progressive tumult of excitement — halted, mercifully, for the pregnant quietude of the S.II (91), but resumed thereafter at an even higher voltage to culminate in one of the most elemental outbursts of spiritual energy ever portrayed in tone (144).†

The theme of the *Andante con Variazioni* invites to intimacy as does hardly any earlier utterance of Beethoven. The variations, however brilliant, do not disguise this appeal. Indeed, the third, in F minor, intensifies it. And it is only because the larger apparatus of the orchestra gives weight to its substance that the Finale of the Seventh symphony surpasses this final movement in sheer abandon. (Supreme mastery of both instruments is needed to attain a sonority appropriate to the idea of this movement.)

Nine crowded years intervene between the Kreutzer and the last violin sonata, Op. 96, in G major. At first contact, you would think it the music of another man — as indeed it is. For this composer is Beethoven in his "third period" — a man whose unquenchable optimism is no longer militant but is tempered by a wisdom that sees art and life in what is probably the truest perspective ever attained by a musician.

The sonata speaks only of little things; but they are seen in the same perspective as the greater issues confronted in the last quartets. The tentativeness of the tiny phrase with which the *Allegro moderato* begins rules both its first expansion (3) and the derived arpeggiations that follow; their cadence-figure yields the transition; and the S.II (41) has a lighter gaiety, bred by this approach. Its deceptive cadence (59) releases an exuberance that takes definite shape in the Cl.S. (84) and carries over into the development.

The violin does not restate the simple theme in the piano with which

* This transgression is made more evident by the virtuoso violinists' current fashion of playing their part by heart, while the pianist — doubtless equally capable of memorization — plays from score as if his part were a mere accompaniment. Beethoven described the sonata as written *per il pianoforte ed un Violino obbligato*: i.e., the piano has the principal part; and this relation was long held to exist with all chamber music in which the piano shared.

† Hugo Riemann, editing the second edition of the German translation of Thayer's *Life of Beethoven*, quotes Czerny (Vol. II, p. 395) as saying that this theme was borrowed from an earlier piece of Kreutzer's (whence the dedication).

the *Adagio espressivo* (E flat, 2-4) begins. Instead, it comments on it — at first, *sotto voce*, but soon with the assurance of an improvisator whose imagination has taken fire; and when it at last plays the opening theme you will see why Beethoven first gave it to the piano only.

The Scherzo (G minor, 3-4) is impish and saucy; its Trio, in E flat, smiles more genially; and the Coda, in G major, ends with a whole-hearted laugh.

The Finale (*Poco allegretto*, 2-4) is really a set of variations on a tune that sounds as disarmingly naive as one of Haydn's rondo themes. The variations, however, are not after Haydn's manner, but disguise the theme by new figurations of its essential harmony. The fifth variation is a broad *Adagio espressivo*, as remote (but only as remote) from the theme as is its slow tempo. The sixth (*Allegro*) sounds as if it were to be the last, but it yields to a sort of fugue in G minor; then to the theme itself (lest you may have forgotten it); then, lest you missed its implication, to the last half of the theme, *Poco adagio*; then a moment of *Presto* for the end.

The 'Cello Sonatas

Like the ten violin sonatas, the five 'cello sonatas date from the three periods of Beethoven's creative activity. Two are from the first period; one from the second, and two from the third.

The first two, Op. 5, were written in Berlin, and are dedicated to King Frederick William II of Prussia — the patron, as we have seen, of Haydn and Mozart. But they were performed there by Pierre Duport, a brother of that Jean Louis Duport whose study of fingering and bowing on his instrument remains a standard text even today. These were the first 'cello sonatas to be written with an obbligato piano part. (Duport's were for 'cello and *continuo*.)

These are exceptional in that they have no slow middle movement. Each, indeed, has an *Adagio* introduction of considerable dimensions; but these are thematically unrelated to the following *Allegro*. The expositions in each sonata-*Allegro* are structurally very diffuse, but there is abundant melodic invention as well as constant care for keeping the 'cello free of entanglement with the accompanying figurations in the piano. The last movements are rondos, each in a distinctive vein of gaiety that is maintained without lapse throughout a movement which at first sight looks alarmingly long.

The next sonata, Op. 69, in A, dates from 1808 — that *annus mirabilis* which saw the birth of the Fifth and Sixth symphonies, the two piano trios, Op. 70, and the *Choral Fantasie* for piano, chorus, and orchestra which notably anticipates the Ninth symphony. The sonata speaks throughout in the distinctively male voice of the violoncello, avoiding the more feminine lyricism appropriate to the violin.

The first movement, *Allegro, ma non tanto*, 4-4, begins, with quiet assurance, in the 'cello alone. This theme is completed by the piano; then their roles are reversed. The transition, beginning in A minor, smacks of the S.I; the S.II (38) — a sweeping upward scale against simple imitations on the E major triad — is wholly appropriate, and it also makes transition to the Cl.S. (65) out of itself. The development, after sober reference to the broad opening notes of S.I, is largely an intensification of bar 3 of that theme. In the recapitulation, the S.I has a triplet accompaniment, and is wholly in the 'cello. The Coda (233), beginning with the S.I in D, again develops that theme, by diminution, up to a forceful statement of the whole theme in A, in bare octaves, ending with a few reminiscences of it.

The Scherzo that follows is one of Beethoven's most original creations. Its syncopated theme bumps over a cobblestone road, but our ride is exhilarating. The Trio (110), much smoother, gratefully appears twice.

There is no real slow movement. A short *Adagio cantabile*, in a vein as reserved as was the opening of the first movement, precedes the *Allegro vivace* (2-2) *— a movement in which, for the first time except, of course, for the Scherzo, the reserve is broken down. You cannot be sure how deep its geniality is until you hear the S.II (29), which has an indubitable gleam of passion in its eye. The man you glimpse behind this sonata does not, indeed, invite to intimacy. But he does command respect.

The two sonatas of Op. 102 were written in the summer of 1815. They are dedicated to the Countess Marie Erdödy, a pianist of some distinction and a long-time friend and patron of the composer. They do not fully exhibit the characteristics of Beethoven's third period, but they definitely depart from the second. They are only half as long as the earlier works, but their specific gravity is higher.

No. 1, which is really in one composite movement, begins *Andante*, 6-8, C major, with a phrase high in the solo 'cello that is then answered

* This time signature, since many passages are accompanied in sixteenths which must be articulate, seems to me an error.

by the piano and dwelt on in an imaginative way that suggests a rare moment of communion between two intimate friends. Then an *Allegro vivace* (A minor, 2-2) compacts its cogent exposition into forty-eight bars and the whole movement into a hundred and twenty-six. Its S.I marches broadly up the A minor scale and comes more precipitately down. But its line, unharmonized, is as sharp as a knife. The S.II (13), to which the only transition is a silence, is in a vein of protest whose insistence is heightened by the tortuous bass with its recurrent diminished 3rds. The implied event, if you imagine one, will not be happy. Another expectant silence makes transition to a brief *Adagio* in C, very slow and fully "third-period" in character, whose one troubled theme suddenly clears (*teneramente*) and yields to a reminiscence of the opening *Andante*. This, in turn, brings the final *Allegro vivace* (C major, 2-4) — a mingling of sonata and rondo with a development section in place of the S.III. The technical difficulties are not great, but the demands on the interpretative imagination are severe.

No. 2, in D, is externally more regular; but there is at the outset the same terseness as in No. 1, and, for the performers, a similar need to fill the compactness with meaning. For the tension of the rather obvious-looking S.I is high; the lyric contrast to its impatience, begun in the transition (21), is sharpened in the brief phrases of the S.II; but the decisive Cl.S. is wholly in character (43). The new color of the staccato eighths at the beginning of the development establishes the lyric continuation (63f) and makes more striking the "filling in" of the long D of S.I when the recapitulation begins (88).

The *Adagio con molto sentimento d'affetto* (F major, 2-4) is as deeply imbued with warmth as is the *Andante con Variazioni* of the "Archduke" trio; but it is more introverted, and breeds in consequence disturbed and rhapsodic musing rather than the steadier and loftier contemplation of the variations. The dark color is wonderfully established at the beginning,* and intensified in the stern rhythm of the continuation, so that the soaring in the D major section becomes really ethereal.

The *Allegro fugato* finale, as its title suggests, is not strictly fugal. Beethoven's counterpoint has seldom the assured ease of Bach's, nor does he scruple to indulge in such almost homophonic passages as that (102)

* Note particularly the trebling of the octave melodic line (15) and similar doublings (22, 51, 57); and remember that he who imagined this music could no longer hear it.

where the inversion of the theme is played in 10ths throughout. At 142
a new theme appears, making this into what may be called a double
fugue; but this theme plays a subordinate role in the piece.

The Piano Trios

Like his violin sonatas, Beethoven's mature trios date from all three
periods. Having a weightier tonal substance, they may be felt to illustrate those periods somewhat more vividly, but the characteristics are
similar.

We must first mention, however, several less important works. There
are two trios without opus number: one in B flat, in one sonata-form
movement, written in 1812 "for his little friend, Maximiliane Brentano,
to encourage her in piano-playing"; and one in E flat, in three movements (*Allegro moderato*, Scherzo, Rondo) which may be as early as
1785. There are also two sets of variations: Op. 44, in E flat, on a theme
so inane that one can hardly believe it to be by Beethoven (it was written
long before its publication in 1804); and Op. 121a (1816), ten variations
on a popular air from Wenzel Müller's opera, *Die Schwestern von Prag*
—*Ich bin der Schneider Kakadu*. This has a rather irrelevantly solemn
Introduction, ten variations on the song, and a Coda, *Allegretto*, that
makes a brilliant end.

Beethoven made his debut as composer with the three piano trios, Op.
1, published in 1795. They were dedicated to Prince Lichnowsky, himself enough of a pianist so that he advised Beethoven, whose writing for
the piano had been criticized for its difficulty, not to alter a note.*

The first of the three begins (*Allegro*, E flat, 4-4) with a conventional
but sturdy arpeggiation of the principal chords of the key. A note of
tension in the violin (10) warms the continuing phrases so that the S.II
(33) is appropriately sober. This, likewise, has an intenser pendant (51).
The transition (72) is brief, but the Cl.S. (80f) with its final syncopated
figure seems redundant. The development is rather thin, and the long

* The trios must have been given their final form during Haydn's second visit
to London in 1794–95. He heard them on his return, and advised Beethoven not to
publish the third, in C minor, which Beethoven doubtless thought the best of the
set. Some have supposed this advice to have originated in jealousy, but it is incredible
that a composer of Haydn's reputation, and of his frank admiration for such a youthful composer as Mozart, would have been moved by so petty an animus. Much more
likely, he feared that the sternness of the piece would alienate the interest of the
public. Indeed, in our present perspective, the first two trios seem almost over-
respectful of tradition.

Coda, although it assumes the dimension of a second development, adds little weight to the discourse.

The first two themes of the *Adagio cantabile* (A flat, 3-4) are unassuming in their pious conformity to the aesthetic creed of the day, but the S.III (55), in E flat minor, gains by contrast a bitter intensity. The Coda (not unnaturally in an early work) prolongs too much its leave-taking. The Scherzo is more daring, and the Finale (*Presto*, 2-4), beginning with the perky leap of a 10th and thus escaping the trammels of aristocratic reserve, is the most individual movement in the piece.

Op. 1, No. 2, in G, begins with a somewhat Haydnish *Adagio* that breaks into the *Allegro vivace* (G major, 2-4) on the 7th of the dominant and maintains that activity to the cadence. Activity, indeed, is the chief interest (by no means slight) of the whole movement, the S.II (72) dancing even more lightheartedly than the S.I. The development, always in character, returns to the S.I an octave higher than before and the recapitulation, thus begun, elaborates delightfully much of the whole substance of the exposition.

The *Largo con espressione* (E major, 6-8) has a placid surface, but an undertone of fervency appears (16) that becomes vivid with the S.II (26) and often (e.g., 40) colors the S.I itself. The Scherzo (G major, *Allegro*) begins a little gruffly but shakes off that mood almost at once for a lighter gaiety; and the Finale (*Presto*, 2-4), with its snare-drumming repeated G's, with the repetition of the theme in the piano on the dominant instead of the expected tonic, and with its jaunty S.II (74) subdued only for a moment by the more tranquil Cl.S. (105), provides far more than the conventional happy ending.

The third trio is by common consent the most significant of the three. (Beethoven's C minor mood is always portentous.) The pregnant S.I (*Allegro con brio*, C minor, 3-4), unharmonized until its cadence, is no mere assertion of the tonic key. Its impact is heightened by the *fermate*, so that it needs no immediate repetition. The continuing phrases have patent relativity and the whole progression to the S.II never relaxes until the flowing 6-chords (57) open the door for that gracious theme. But even this is soon darkened (80) so that the close, made of already established matter, intensifies the dominant mood. Clearly, this is music with more than a purely musical purpose.

The *Andante con Variazione* (E flat, 2-4) has a theme somewhat lighter than one might anticipate after the first movement. The variations, however, are no mere ornaments of the theme, but are imaginative transformations of it, whether of its actual line or of its harmonic substratum. They indicate a fact which will become more apparent, and will be vividly illustrated in the last trio — that Beethoven is the most imaginative variationist of all the great composers.

The Menuetto (C minor) does not exceed the conventional dimension of that dance. Neither is it at all in the character of a Scherzo. But it does effectively re-establish the C minor mood; and the downward scale that delicately begins the Trio becomes (69) a significant recall of that same design which was so vividly interjected at the close of the first movement.

The Finale (*Prestissimo*, C minor, 2-2), in sonata form, emphatically opposes the convention of the happy ending. It first presents an incisive arpeggio figure that sternly establishes the key, and then finds a rhythmically obsessed continuation that is wholly in character. As in the first movement, the S.II (69) is made to enter almost unannounced, and the S.I yields, most pertinently, the substance of the Cl.S. The development, which is mostly on S.II, thus gains a heightened significance. The *pp* ending, in the perspective of the whole trio, is an imaginative stroke of the highest order.

The Clarinet trio, Op. 11, was published in 1798. It was dedicated to the Countess Thun, the mother of Prince Lichnowsky to whom Op. 1 was dedicated. It was apparently written for performance by a clarinetist, Joseph Beer, who suggested the choice of the theme (from Weigl's opera, *The Corsair*) which, varied, forms the last movement. (Czerny says that Beethoven regretted this conclusion.) The clarinet, in this work, is not the essential tonal ingredient that it was in Mozart's Clarinet trio (see p. 52f). Only once does it descend below the compass of the violin into its colorful *chalumeau* register, and only in two bars does its part differ (except where the violin has double stops) from the alternative violin part. It does effectively color the main theme of the first movement, but the piano provides most of the atmosphere of the *Adagio* (E flat, 3-4), and the clarinet remains undistinctive in the rather undistinguished variations.

Ten years elapse between the Clarinet trio and the two which form Op. 70. We have already noted Beethoven's incredible productivity in this year, 1808, where his middle period reaches its peak. The trios are dedicated to the Countess Marie Erdödy, in whose house Beethoven at this time had quarters, and to whom the last 'cello sonatas were also dedicated.

The first, in D (*Allegro vivace e con brio*, 3-4), begins with an extraordinarily active theme which visual analysis can easily break down into five leaping repetitions of a four-note diatonic descent. But this breakdown will ignore the triple-time lilt of the theme which makes each lowest note of the four a springboard for the ensuing leap, but which gives the whole antic an elasticity hardly attainable by physical limbs. Neither is this activity the main purport of the theme. For it stops on a long F♮ which, since it is straining toward F♯, feels like an E♯. But the piano (6) first confirms its "F-ness" by giving it a B♭ bass, and then contradicts it by moving downward to A against the attained F♯ in the 'cello. And this begins a two-bar phrase of song, as urgent as was the leaping figure, that at once becomes the essential note of the discourse. A mere hint of the opening figure (35) starts the transition to the quite subordinate S.II (44), which, broadened, becomes also the Cl.S.

The development is very resourceful. It is as long as the whole exposition, and finds endless new implications in every phrase of the S.I, which dominates the whole section. The recapitulation (157), up to the return of the S.II, is almost another development, so that (rather unusually at this advanced stage of sonata structure) the development and recapitulation are marked to be repeated.

The *Largo assai ed espressivo* is of a slowness designedly oppressive.* It intensifies that impression by keeping to the same tonic as that of the first movement, only in the minor mode. But the minor tonality is only implied, not established, by the portentous D–A of the strings, so that the throbbing triad in the piano, under its answering motive — a sort of whispered commentary on the string phrase — is needed to confirm our sense of dread. The ensuing dialogue maintains this impression until the 'cello (9) begins a bitter song which the violin raises to an outcry (11). Two bars of resignation follow which the piano (14) protests violently, descending thereafter in a long tremor to a restatement of the opening, the dialogue being now between 'cello and violin, with the piano murmuring, tremolando, the underlying harmony.

---

* The notation in 2-4 time at first looks needlessly complex. But if you rewrite a few bars in 2-2 (or, still worse, in 4-2) time, you will find the whole substance taking on, for the eye, a sort of dead weight quite unrepresentative of the breathless suspense which must be, for the ear, the ruling character of the movement.

Our words probably imply melodrama. So does the title, "Ghost-trio," often applied to the whole piece. Performance, similarly, may all too easily overextend itself. But if the true note of the music is caught (*not* by mere timid suppression) you will find few pieces that evoke, as this does, the spiritual cramp of tragedy.

There is naturally no Scherzo. But the Finale (*Presto*, 2-2) is a wonderful portrayal of that state of mind, purged of baser emotion, which Aristotle deemed the proper spiritual effect of the contemplation of tragedy. For the ordinary note of gaiety is really quite absent. Instead, there is a warmer sense of well-being — a kind of spiritual clarity, rare and difficult to portray, that far outglows ephemeral jubilation. Hence, although the movement assumes sonata form, the subject-antithesis appears only as the variable surface of a single fluctuant mood.

The second trio, in contrast to the first, is all amiability. It appears to have interested Beethoven deeply, and to have been much slower in attaining its final form. There is structural novelty in the remaking of the theme of the *Poco sostenuto* Introduction into the S.II of the main movement (*Allegro ma non troppo*, E flat, 6-8). (A part of the Introduction also reappears in the Coda.) Something, however, makes for monotony in the total impression. A part of this seems attributable to the persistence of the feminine ending (2) of the main theme, in its near equivalent (4), and in the continuation of the S.II (46), which phrases of course reappear often.

The *Allegretto* (C major, 2-4) assumes the perennial rhythmic grace of the gavotte and puts that dance-measure through a fascinating variety of steps; the next movement (*Allegretto ma non troppo*, A flat, 3-4) is a similar idealization of the minuet; and the Finale (*Allegro*, E flat, 2-4), after flexing its muscles in a figure that will prove to be more than merely introductory, finds a theme more nearly jaunty than any so far heard in the trio, but still amiable. The S.II (59) is in G instead of B flat, and the Cl.S. (83), after a brief cadential strain, reverts to the opening figure for transition to the development. This is almost wholly animated by that figure, the S.II being only suggested against it (161). The recapitulation (187) is more altered in detail than in design, but there is an extended Coda that renovates all the substance of the movement.

The seventh trio, known as the "Archduke" because of its dedication to Rudolph, Archduke of Austria and a pupil of Beethoven, is not only the finest of the seven but is one of the noblest works in musical literature. It was finished on March 26, 1811, and was first performed on April 11, 1814, with Beethoven taking the piano part. (This was his last public appearance as pianist.)

We found Op. 70, No. 2 aiming, not wholly successfully, at amiability. This work aims at a much loftier portrayal, and succeeds. You cannot account for its success in terms of structural ingenuity. The "language" is indeed flawless, but its constant objective is portrayal, not rhetoric, and there is hardly a rhetorical device that is exhibited for its own sake. The tensions are mild and the motor impulses calm (these, in our view, are the elemental facts for expression); there is indeed a tonal richness unusual for Beethoven; but while these things contribute palpably to the conveyed image, they do not add up to the incalculable spiritual sum the music offers.

The main theme of the first movement (*Allegro moderato*, B flat, 3-4) is as simple as the golden rule. It is similarly uncompelling to a mind avid for excitement, but to one more broadly oriented it has a kindred meaning. Both theme and transition (from 29) have a leisurely design, and the immediate approach to the S.II (43-51) is a perfect preparation for that thought which a keen imagination placed in the submediant (G) instead of the conventional dominant. The continuation (6of) "says" nothing new, but it maintains admirably the achieved imaginative level, merging into the Cl.S. (68) which, on its repetition, retards a little regretfully its Neapolitan 6th cadence, floating thereafter on a cloud of undulant triplets that bring the wonderful exposition to a close.

The development, taking eleven expectant bars to establish the key of E flat, meditates long and fruitfully on the first phrase of S.I; goes on (133) to interpret similarly the following phrases; then quietly flies far above-ground over the strings that pluck bar 1 of S.II (inverted) to make a long and delicate approach to the recapitulation (191) and its appropriately assured Coda.

A Scherzo follows — down to earth, if you like, but not earthy, nor, indeed, really humorous. It begins its Trio on a creeping chromatic theme in B flat minor, set forth fugally; but this suddenly bursts into a thumping (160) which even the dullest ear will recognize as giving a momentary glimpse of Beethoven's very self, "in his habit as he liv'd."

This descent to earth was needful to give a measure of the elevation of the ensuing *Andante cantabile, ma però con moto* (D major, 3-4) — a set of variations that enact spiritual adventure of the highest order. You will not doubt for an instant the "reality" of this adventure; but neither the theme nor its variations will endure verbal "translation" or even description. The warmth and the color of the musical substance are alike unparalleled — certainly up to the time of this creation, and perhaps — if our long since color-drenched ears can form a true judgment of color values — even in our own day. Beethoven might justly have given this movement the superscription he gave the Solemn Mass in D — *Vom Herzen; möge es zu Herzen gehen.*

It leads without pause to a Rondo-finale, lighter in vein than anything preceding, and unfortunately capable of a kind of triviality in performance which, unless it is avoided (but it can be), tarnishes the impression so deeply imprinted by what has gone before.

The Piano Quartet

The only remaining work for piano and strings is the piano quartet, Op. 16. This is really an arrangement (but made by Beethoven himself) of a quintet for piano, oboe, clarinet, horn, and bassoon — the same combination as in Mozart's quintet discussed on page 56f. It was first performed, with the wind instruments, and with Beethoven at the piano, in 1797. Both versions were published in 1801.

It was doubtless written in emulation of Mozart's work. Like that piece, it has only three movements, the first introduced by an *Adagio*, the last a Rondo. Tovey has convincingly shown the superiority of Mozart's work, but that does not derogate from the worth of this piece. It was designed to give immediate pleasure rather than to arouse deeper contemplation, and succeeds admirably. In its arranged form it is exceptionally easy to play, even though three instruments are doing the work of four.

The String Trios

Although Haydn and Mozart had already shown the string quartet to be an ideal ensemble, Beethoven chose to begin his writing for strings alone with the slighter medium of the string trio. But this is no return to the antiquated "sonata" for two violins and bass of which Haydn wrote so many examples. It is from the first a true trio, with violin, viola, and 'cello contributing equally to the total interest, and the general pattern of the sonata form an established structural norm.

Yet these first string pieces do look backward. Op. 3, in E flat, while it has its first movement in regular sonata form, and follows that with a slender-limbed *Andante* (B flat, 3-8) and a Menuetto in E flat, has also a pensive *Adagio* (A flat, 2-4) and another Menuetto before the final Rondo. It smacks, that is, of the Divertimento. Traces of the personality of the composer are discoverable in all the movements, but he is most clearly revealed in the Rondo.

Opus 8, a *Serenade*, also looks backward. It begins with a March (the approach of the performers to the dwelling of an expected patron); makes its first appeal to the heart in a warm, if somewhat conventional *Adagio*; enlivens the scene with a dainty Menuetto; twice alternates a brief *Adagio* in D minor with an impish, still shorter Scherzo; dances delightfully to an *Allegretto alla Polacca* (F major, 3-4); makes five variations on an ingratiating little *Andante quasi Allegretto*; ruminates for a moment on the theme in B flat, and then goes out of sight down the street with a return to the opening March. The piece has indescribable charm. It is a pity that it is so seldom played, but it is by no means easy.

The three trios, Op. 9, are dedicated to Count von Browne, a *brigadier au service de S[a] M[ajesté] I[mpériale] de toutes les Russies*, whom Beethoven lauds as "the first Maecenas of his muse," * and to whose Countess the three piano sonatas of Op. 10 were dedicated. Beethoven describes the trios as the best of his works (up to this time, 1798), and the estimate is just.

The first, in G, opens with a broad *Adagio*, of whose continuing figure the last three sixteenths (3f), legato, initiate the S.I of the *Allegro con brio*. That whole figure, at the end of the development (123) ingeniously prepares the recapitulation. The S.II, beginning in D minor but really in F, is hushed and strangely tentative in contrast to the preceding vigor. The *Adagio, ma non tanto, e cantabile* (E major, 3-4 = 9-8) flows placidly throughout, but at a considerable elevation; the Scherzo, appropriate to that mood, has more of grace than of humor; but the final *Presto*, out of a mischievous beginning, develops a sturdy marching rhythm (23) which presently (38) leaves the ground altogether for a long soaring flight in B flat. The key relations between the subjects are often unconventional, but you have only to rearrange them in the "proper" keys to see how much of color is gained by this irregularity.

---

* He gave the composer a fine riding horse which Beethoven proudly bestrode a few times and then forgot that he owned it. After several months he was disagreeably surprised by a large bill for its maintenance.

The second trio, in D, is the least Beethovenish of the three. It is "drawn" from an unusual model, more Latin in feature than teutonic, but a very interesting figure nevertheless. The suave S.I of the opening *Allegretto* (D major, 2-4) is enlivened at bar 23 by a rhythmic nudge of thirty-seconds. The S.II (57) is anticipated by the persistent E's (39f) and by the rhythm of the 6ths in the viola, so that there is clear con-tinuity, and in the development the S.I acquires a triplet accompaniment very appropriate to its suavity. The gentle *Andante quasi Allegretto* (D minor, 6-8) has a similar character; the Menuetto, more teutonic, main-tains its flavor also in the light-footed Trio. The 'cello announces the S.I of the fleet Rondo (*Allegro*, 2-2), and is pretty conspicuous throughout. The S.II (70) is quite subordinate, and there is really no S.III. Instead, there is considerable development after the second appearance of S.I (106); and after its third entry (204) and the ensuing recapitulation, there is a colorful version of it in E flat (302) that initiates a long Coda.

The third trio is in C minor — a key which we have already found associated with a characteristic Beethovenian sternness. It will be found here, and in good measure. (The principal themes of all the movements are shown in Ex. 12.) The bald unison of the first phrase of S.I (*Allegro con spirito*, 6-8), with its augmented 2nd and its swelling crescendo, strikes a note of alarm that is clarified in the upward sweep to G and the impatient twitch of the sixteenths (4). These breathless notes wholly mitigate the weakness of the feminine ending, and are so managed in the continuation as to culminate in thumping chords (17, 19), and, in the enharmonic surprise (D♭ = C♯), to prepare an instantaneous transition to the S.II. The same rhythmic thump continues, the S.II beginning preg-nantly in A flat instead of E flat and reaching that key by way of another augmented 2nd (G♭ in bar 25 = F♯). A similarly high concentration of thought is pursued right up to the Cl.S. which forms a good deal of the development. Here, already, is the Beethoven of the second period.

The *Adagio con espressione* is in C major, 4-4. Maintenance of the same tonic gives a more pointed relativity to the first movement than could have been attained with any other key. The hesitant rise of the main theme and its momentary vanishing on the expectant A (1) suggest an undercurrent of depression beneath the apparent calm, and the in-tensity of that current is revealed in the more urgent melody of bars 3 and 5. The thirty-seconds of the transition (11f) are purposeful rather than merely ornamental, as the two stressed eighth notes at the end of each bar prove, and the S.II (14) — imitative between violin and viola — is shown by its straining continuation (16f) to have the same undercurrent as the S.I. The resumption of S.I in E flat (22) qualifies richly the sense of that theme, and in all the rest of the wonderful movement there is not an irrelevant note.

EXAMPLE 12. BEETHOVEN STRING TRIO, OP. 9, NO. 3

The clarity of C major in the Trio of the Scherzo points up, as did the same device in the *Adagio*, the peculiar intensity (here ironic) of the preceding C minor for the Scherzo itself. And the snarling triplets that begin the abrupt opening phrases of the Finale (*Presto*, C minor, 2–2) illuminate the sense of the continuation (5–8) whose simplicity, without this preliminary, would appear pointless. The S.II (29), appropriately, is in E flat minor; but it has a new, impassioned continuation (41) in the major that somehow imparts a more optimistic tone to the music — a tone felt clear to the end.

The String Quartets

In spite of his extraordinary achievement with this last string trio, Beethoven wrote no more in this form. He turned to the string quartet — a texture really less difficult to weave (because the fabric need never become thin), and one whose larger tonal resource gives both skill and imagination larger scope.

His first quartets, Op. 18, form a group of six, completed from 1797 to 1800 and thus representing nearly the culmination of what we call his first period. In structural skill they often show a mastery equal to Mozart's, but seldom his incomparable grace. In the weight of their substance they are mostly heavier, although aesthetics is as yet without an exact or even an approximate measure of that weight. His absorption in the effort is evidenced by innumerable sketches and by a letter to Karl Amenda (1801) which confesses that "I only now know how to write quartets properly." * How much the composition of the C minor trio contributed to that knowledge can only be guessed; but it must have been a great deal, for in sheer concentration the trio is the peer of any of the quartets. We shall single out for more minute examination only the three which seem to us the weightiest.

EXAMPLE 13. BEETHOVEN QUARTET IN F, OP. 18, NO. 1

No. 1, in F, is always cited as an example of Beethoven's skill in devising and handling a musical motive. The variety shown by this little opening phrase is indeed striking; but the real interest seems to us to lie, not in the first bar, which is merely the figuration of a single note, but rather in the resultant of the motivic energy acquired during the figuration — i.e., in the direction and the import revealed by the ensuing final note of the motive (Ex. 13). Observed as pattern merely, the figure soon becomes tedious. Observed as a source of energy, the figure becomes endlessly fertile. It animates the transition, whether as "turn" in the melody or as bass (30f) or as continuous sixteenth-note drive (105f) in the Cl.S., and keeps the expressive purpose continually in focus.

* Since the sketches go back to 1792, it is impossible to determine the precise order of completion of the quartets. The available evidence seems to show that the one in F, published as No. 1, was the second; No. 2, in G, was third; No. 3, in D, was first; No. 4, in C minor, was fifth; No. 5, in A, was fourth; No. 6, in B flat, was last; but the C minor may have been last, with the B flat the fifth.

Expressively, the *Adagio affettuoso ed appassionato* (D minor, 9-8) is a far higher achievement. Depth is manifest in the first bar; the spiritual burden transferred from it to the melody is heavy; but the bearers of it (chiefly first violin and 'cello) never complain that it is intolerable, even when the theme, tensed by the middle voices (48) and lashed by the thirty-seconds of the violin, is suddenly halted (59) and looks out over empty spiritual space with no more than a single footfall of support on the first beat of each of four otherwise blank bars. He who contrived this vision was a born dramatist.

The drive of the Scherzo is in keeping. The abruptness of bars 7–10 and the three-bar rhythm beginning the second section are but two of many characteristic features, and the relaxed running up and down the D flat scale after the bouncing C's that begin the Trio is a welcome relief.

The final *Allegro* cannot but remind the hearer of the Finale of the C minor string trio. Not to the advantage of the quartet; for what was there curt incisiveness now becomes, even by slight expansion (and by its major key), a kind of amiable capering. The simple sixteenth-note motion (19) thus acquires a laggard feeling which the unison stamping of bars 27–33 cannot enliven. But the S.III (136) is charming, and the new counterpoint which the S.I acquired (117) from the stamping scale, makes an interesting fugato, so that you will not too much regret the convention of the happy ending.

Quartet No. 2 in G need not detain us long. The first movement (*Allegro*, G major, 2-4) is quite conventional both in structure and sentiment — very well-bred, and a little too patently charming. The interest of the *Adagio* (C major, 3-4) is soon exhausted (the incessant feminine endings become almost obsequious) so that it has to resort to an Intermezzo (*Allegro*, F major), made on the diminution of the cadential figures of the *Adagio*. That brief discourse, elaborately ornamented, then returns. The Scherzo is more genuine. Its perky rhythm is delightful, and the Trio, which seems to have been suggested by a rising passage in the Scherzo (30) is ingeniously brightened by combination with a triplet figure. The Rondo-finale (*Allegro molto quasi presto*, G major, 2-4) has a tone of rather artificial gaiety which is hardly disguised by such pleasing devices as the unexpected over-the-fence leap into E flat (140) or the off-beat imitations on S.I (187). It seems hardly credible that this was the third and not the first of the quartets to be written.

That priority, however, is attributed by the scholars to the third quartet, in D. The two whole notes with which the S.I begins (*Allegro*, 2-2), and their interval, the rising 7th, considerably permeate its texture. (That interval, often narrowed, will still be suggested by the broad, two-note rhythm.) This broad rhythm is abandoned during the hop-skip transition (36f) but reappears, essentially, in what appears to be the S.II (51), and is perceptible in its pendant (68) which, by syncopating a single harmony in each of its first two bars, still recalls the whole-note rhythmic stroke.

The *Andante con moto* (B flat, 2-4) aims at no soul-shaking tragedy, but its whole substance preserves and amplifies the sense imparted by the first phrases of the main theme, sung by the second violin on its G string. The S.II (23), very slender, suddenly develops a high tension with its augmentation (30) of the three-note phrase with which it began. The restatement is considerably developed, with an appropriate epilogue.

The next movement (*Allegro*, D major, 3-4) is half-way between Minuet and Scherzo, with a short Trio in D minor. The first section of the *da Capo* is effectively repeated in the higher octave. The Finale (*Presto*, D major, 6-8) is a swift and impish sonata form. Higher and lower strings, paired, make a charming choreography for a main theme; the S.II (56) bounces as elastically as a rubber ball, and the whole substance, kept off the ground with consummate skill, makes a really happy ending.

The fourth quartet is in C minor. It lives up fully to the anticipation felt by every Beethoven-lover at sight of a work of his in that key. It is probably the most familiar of the quartets, and may thus be dismissed with a briefer analysis than its substance really demands. The principal themes, however, are quoted in Example 14. The main theme (*Allegro ma non tanto*, C minor, 3-4), with its pedal C and the stern *sf* on normally "weak" measures, is less urgently perturbed than was the string trio in the same key, but its range of contemplation is much wider. The S.II, whose embryo is patently bar 5 of S.I, considerably lightens the atmosphere, and this effect is intensified in the development (112) when the 'cello, in high register, takes over that theme. But since both themes are more lyrical than dynamic, forbidding the cumulative intensification possible with short, tortuously harmonized phrases, the development hardly reaches the tragic height implied at the opening of the movement. (Imitation and foreshortening of S.I at 94 and 102 yield less force than

EXAMPLE 14. BEETHOVEN QUARTET IN C MINOR, OP. 18, NO. 4

does the F minor version of S.II at 120, after the 'cello's F major singing of it at 112.)

Yet enough of the tragic mood has been portrayed so that a soulful *Adagio*, in the vein of the first quartet, would have failed to strike home. Consequently (but that it *is* consequent may not at first be apparent), what follows is a movement labeled *Andante scherzoso quasi Allegretto* (C major, 3-8), stepping daintily to a rhythm, danced fugally for a time but often becoming homophonic, that ultimately generates a sonata form. The S.II (43) and the Cl.S. (67) both feature the three reiterated eighth notes and the running sixteenths of S.I, so that there is no marked contrast;* but you will find the sober animation of this piece wholly appropriate.

The Menuetto (*Allegretto*, C minor), with its frequent *sforzandi* on "three," recalls the mood of the first movement, and the hastened speed prescribed when the Menuetto returns after the Trio intensifies that mood, which the Trio, in A flat, perhaps relaxes too much. Neither does the final Rondo, cast in the form so often used by Haydn, really bring the quartet to the conclusion implied in the first movement. The S.I has, indeed, a nervous energy akin to that of the opening movement; but the continuation (9) is only a perfunctory sequence which robs the ensuing opening phrase of half its force. The next section is still more amiable, and it may be because of this that the S.I is so often read (as it indeed may be) in a tone of light and even artificial gaiety. The final *Prestissimo* could hardly be taken as flimsy; but all its fire is hardly sufficient to give the movement weight appropriate to the character first announced.

* Cf. the last movement of the piano sonata, Op. 31, No. 2 — almost a "perpetual motion," but a fully rounded sonata form nevertheless.

The fifth quartet begins (A major, *Allegro*, 6-8) with a vivacity that smacks of the eighteenth century. The S.II, however, which appears in E minor (25) and halts for a moment of delight when it has found its "proper" major (37f), yields more than momentary tonal pleasure. There are many scintillant effects, harmonic and rhythmic, but also many perfunctory passages (e.g., 99f) which cause the music to lose its grip on the hearer. The total consistency which Beethoven will later impart to a movement in light character is not yet realized.

A Menuetto follows with its Trio, quite unusually, in the same key. Its melody, in octaves in the middle strings, has again the *sforzandi* on "three" we noted in the C minor quartet — with quite another expressive import. (Riemann's suggestion that the lower voice should predominate over the upper yields interesting results.)

The ensuing Variations (*Andante cantabile*, D major, 2-4) forecast the extraordinary interest that Beethoven will ultimately impart to this structural process.* They are no mere figurations of the theme, but new aspects of its intrinsic sense. Rather unusually, there is no variation in minor, but Var. IV, reharmonizing the theme chromatically, has all the tension of the minor key and provides thus for the wonderful glow of Var. V and the fascinating excursion into B flat with which the Coda begins.

The Finale, a sonata-*Allegro* (marked 4-4, but really 2-2) opens with a figure in the rhythm that will one day rule the C minor symphony. It maintains this activity right up to the S.II (36) which has the pattern, but not the harmony, of the second theme in the Rondo of the *Sonata pathétique*. The close, after the considerable display of vigor, seems singularly gentle.

The sixth quartet, in B flat (*Allegro con brio*, 2-2), begins with a theme of wholly Beethovenish vigor, a little suggestive of the later and far more vital *Emperor* piano concerto. The naturally energetic transition (33) will be effectively fugued in the development. The S.II (45) is quieter but

* Variation, which is really development, is a process which can be carried to greater heights of interest in music than in any other art. Painters and architects can vary motives, but not basic themes; but the musician, giving a new rhythmic contour or a new harmonic intensity to a familiarized pattern — itself also suggestive of emotional experience — can make of each new variant an almost new experience. The theme may of course be successively dressed in a variety of tonally bedizened costumes. It may also, since variation must be a constructive effort, provoke successive displays of mere structural ingenuity, indifferent to expressive character whether in the theme or in themselves. But that will not be Beethoven's method.

not intrinsically weaker, and the exposition, at the close, reverts to the second phrase of S.I. Exhilaration could hardly be more clearly expressed or more consistently pursued than it is in this movement.

The ensuing *Adagio, ma non troppo* (E flat, 2-4) figurates with such extraordinary delicacy the light-footed opening theme that the sudden drop of the S.II (17) into E flat minor, at first unharmonized, seems alarming; but a suave counterpoint, high above, soon alleviates that pang. Performed with absolute precision (and with no hint that this is difficult to do) the movement has something of the charm that will one day imbue the *Allegretto* of the Eighth symphony.

The ingenious syncopation that rules throughout the Scherzo (B flat, 3-4) can all too easily falsify the rhythm, turning it into a spineless, ambling 6-8. (Viola and 'cello must sufficiently mark their "threes" and "ones" so that the *sforzandi* in the violins will appear in the true perspective of 3-4 time.) The dainty capering of the Trio (a short violin solo) is patently akin in feeling to the delicacy of the *Andante*.

The last movement has an *Adagio* introduction (B flat, 2-4) entitled *La Malinconia* and directed by the composer to be played "with the greatest delicacy." (*Delicatezza* means also softness and refinement.) The "melancholy," although singularly intense, is kept within the bounds of B flat harmony up to the D minor 6/4 chord (8), which softens into the dominant; then the same strain is quietly harmonized in C minor, with its penultimate chord becoming a German 6th and resolving into B minor. From then on, harmony and rhythm seem more in accord with present-day expectations when melancholy is the theme; but the restraint of the opening is not less in character. And if the *Allegretto* of the ensuing Finale is not hustled into a bustling *Allegro*, that movement, whose quiet cheer has quite another undertone, will appear wholly relevant to the preceding (and presently recurring) *Adagio*. The undertone will be banished with the *Prestissimo*, but not forgotten.

The Razumovsky Quartets

Six years elapse before Beethoven again attacks the problem of the string quartet. The enormous forward stride marked by the composition of the *Eroica* symphony (1804) was no blind leap into an artistic no man's land, but the footfall of one who, although alone in this unexplored space, knew where he was and why he had come. To judge from many works following the *Eroica* — the *Waldstein* sonata; the B flat symphony;

the violin concerto; the G major piano concerto, and these quartets — it was for Beethoven a kind of Eden: a place of such spiritual serenity as he was never to find again. It is childish to look to contemporary event for an explanation of such a state of mind or of the works that portray or imply it. The inner assurance of power, established by the achievement of such a structural masterpiece as the *Eroica*, must have contributed to that state. But the *Eroica* was more than a structural masterpiece. It was the affirmation of a philosophy that had attained to more, even, than a lofty vision of heroism; and the serenity of these years must have been the product of innumerable contributions — awarenesses drawn from experience, surely (for his are not the visions of a dreamer), but unnameable, and tangible only to keen intuition.

Like every great composer, Beethoven came only gradually to see how far music could go in conveying these intimations. His expanding vision is more clearly perceptible through a study of all his works in chronological order; but the chamber works alone show it in true perspective, and the three Razumovsky quartets, Op. 59, clearly illustrate his growing imaginative power.

The first of these, in F, was begun on May 26, 1808. The other two were completed in the same year. They were commissioned by Count (later, Prince) Razumovsky (we adopt Nicolas Slonimsky's spelling) — Russian ambassador to the Imperial Court in Vienna, a warm friend of Beethoven, and a passionate music lover. He was to assume, two years later, the maintenance of the already established Schuppanzigh string quartet — accomplished performers all, who gave most meticulous study to Beethoven's chamber compositions. (Razumovsky himself, quite competently, often played second violin.) Such a group, in contrast to the contemporary orchestra, of whose ragged performances Beethoven often bitterly complains, must have offered a heartening stimulus to quartet-composition.

This first quartet is, to this commentator, the most subtly imaginative of the three. That quality is not immediately suggested by the S.I — a straightforward-looking tune in the 'cello against a persistent throbbing of tonic harmony. But if you sense the growing activity as the theme proceeds, it acquires a vitality that forbids perfunctory reading even of its first four bars. In those the tonic is touched but twice, not as phrase-end but incidentally; the same curve, but on the submediant and with the supertonic as its goal, takes a deeper breath; those same notes, now

[101

EXAMPLE 15. BEETHOVEN QUARTET IN F, OP. 59, NO. 1

in the sudden clarity of the first violin, follow on the thickening dominant 7th harmony and again rise above the G on which that phrase
paused; and the four rising quarters of bar 1 then become four swelling
whole notes — nineteen bars, in all, of the outward simplicity but the
far-ranging inner awareness of elemental well-being. After a few bars
of more colorful harmonic exploration (20–29) the tonic is quietly re-
established and bars 3 and 4 of the theme yield an amplification of the
mood as simple and as impeccably right as was the theme itself.

The S.II (60) is hardly distinguishable as a new theme. But a high
contrast would have ruined the impression thus far so subtly built up.
So, after an augmentation (now in half notes, 71–72) of the opening
notes in viola and 'cello, there is a passage of triplet figurations that "say"
nothing but still keep the mood from vanishing. A succession of obscure,
detached chords (85) recalls the relaxed attention; then the S.I generates
(92) a quiet, wholly appropriate Cl.S. (These themes appear in Ex. 15.)

The development follows without repetition of the exposition — an
exceptional procedure which Beethoven noted as such. It begins, also
exceptionally, in the tonic; it is long (103–243) and quite adventurous
harmonically, and it enlarges the sense of the themes rather than puts
them through ostentatious developmental paces. The recapitulation,
omitting the harmonic excursion at 20–28 (it closed the development),
soon assumes the color of D flat and so enriches the continuation that
when the S.I again appears as Cl.S. (338) it is sounded in an exuberant
ff that is even reinforced by *sforzandi* on "two" and "four" of its first
bar. But the Coda is not a noisy celebration.

Any imaginable *Adagio*, no matter how lofty, would have been
dwarfed in apparent altitude if it followed the high serenity of this *Allegro*. No one but Beethoven seems to have sensed this problem, and his
solution of it was at first quite misunderstood, even by Schuppanzigh.
The *Allegretto vivace e sempre scherzando* (B flat, 3-8) seemed a tasteless

102]

joke. It is not, indeed, immediately relevant. Its tone is one of amiable banter which can all too easily be sharpened into irony; but if this not too evident pitfall is avoided, the gaiety will be found appropriate to what has gone before.

A curious undertone of fear underlies the drumming of the 'cello at the beginning. It is dispelled at once by the antic tune in the second violin, but it comes again with the viola's unexpected A flats; and just when the first violin, on the same little tune, has adjusted our tonal perspective to that key, there is a similar leap over tonal fences into C flat, with the drumming now *cresc.* and harmonized. This is almost alarming; but the key of B flat was after all only around the corner, and it comes back with a new tune of smiling reassurance.

All this happens in 28 swift bars. The movement is 474 bars long; and quite obviously no conventional form existed in which this tactic of continual surprise could be effectively pursued. The core of the form lies in the drumming; the core of the banter is in the surprises, whether of unexpected key, sudden dynamic contrast, or new melodic phrase; and the total design is a marvel of ingenuity.*

You have only to play the *Adagio molto e mesto* (A flat, 2-4) immediately after the first movement to see that it could not have been placed there. Viewed in the present, somewhat skewed perspective of nineteenth-century romanticism, the desolate melody of the opening may indeed seem to "protest too much." But if the prescribed *sotto voce* is imaginatively respected, that accusation will not hold. The burden, too, is lightened by the S.II (24), whose temperature is lower. Its delicate ornamental background, also continued against the developing S.I (57f) guards against the danger of excess. It ends with a long flourish which runs without pause into the Finale, of which the S.I (*Allegro*, F major, 2-4), taken from a collection of Russian melodies by Ivan Pratsch, is in that source marked *Molto andante*. It is shown in Example 17. Beetho-

---

* There are at least eight of these phrases, with even more contrasts of key. Six of the phrases, with interspersed drumming, appear one after the other; the first two recur only at 155–176; a seventh (which never returns, and is really a "melodization" of the drumming) then appears (176–191) and the drumming itself is harmonically colored, only to subside suddenly into the fifth phrase (212), in a delicate staccato. After a sudden *cresc.* there is an astonished silence (236); then an eighth phrase alternates with the first (and the drumming), and this really starts a sort of recapitulation in which the first six phrases appear, *seriatim*. At bar 418 the eighth phrase recurs, alternating with the first two to form a Coda. (The drumming, marked A, and the eight melodic phrases are shown in Ex. 16.)

EXAMPLE 16. BEETHOVEN QUARTET IN F, OP. 59, NO. 1, SCHERZO

EXAMPLE 17. BEETHOVEN QUARTET IN F, OP. 59, NO. 1, THÈME RUSSE

ven's tempo falsifies its character, but makes of it a musical reality in its own right. The active vigor he reads into the theme is maintained by a hundred ingenious paraphrases of its motives, and, with the invention of a suave S.II (45), he shapes the movement into a wholly lucid sonata form. The imaginative level is much more mundane than that of the first movement, but the underlying joyousness is still akin to that wonderful utterance.

We must speak at less length of the two following quartets. Op. 59, No. 2, in E minor, is a not less original imaginative flight than was No. 1, but its aim is less high. The S.I, a two-bar phrase in E minor (6-8) is at first given a three-bar rhythm by the two silent bars which prepare and follow its repetition in F major. An undulant elasticity, and the waywardness in the matter of key suggested in that repetition, are its most conspicuous features. They are maintained throughout the transition (24), the S.II (39 — wonderfully appropriate to the S.I), and all the rest of exposition and development.

Nothing in this movement forbids the *Molto Adagio* (E major, 2-2) to follow. Beethoven warns that it is to be played *con molto di sentimento* (which does *not* imply sentimentality), and the core of the sentiment is set forth in the broad notes and the sober harmonies of the S.I, whose real implication, all but hidden, seems to be revealed in the lapse of the major dominant triad into minor (4). The first violin makes quiet and at moments poignant comment above the lower strings as they repeat the theme; then it sets going a soft march-rhythm (16). Against this the lower strings, in imitation, have a more urgent strain. The 'cello, against a significant pedal in the viola (octave F♯'s), finds a tense scale-descent (35) whose triplet motion is to rule most of the movement, and which will presently yield the S.II. How these things, sanely developed, complement the sense of the first movement the hearer will grasp (but not at a single hearing) for himself.

The *Allegretto* (E minor, 3-4) has a quirky, syncopated rhythm and pursues a similarly twisted harmonic course. Its Trio, in E major, is on another Russian tune from the same source, where its tempo is marked *Andante*. Beethoven gives it quite another than the character it originally possessed.* It is here given a fugal exposition against a countersubject in triplets, and is further manipulated (e.g., in canon between the violins at 111) with much gaiety.

EXAMPLE 18, BEETHOVEN QUARTET IN C MAJOR, OP. 59, NO. 3

The Finale (*Presto*, E minor, 2-2) begins with an exuberant march-tune, so solidly in C that the first discovery of the true key of the piece (7) seems like a mistake, and it is only after several "rectifications" that E minor is at all firmly established (42f). The S.II, gratefully relaxed, is in B minor (70). The S.III (this is a Rondo) is a masculine song, begun (146) in viola and 'cello in C against a figure from S.I. It veers gradually toward the flat keys of the circle, and the S.I presently appears in B flat, with its last bar yielding considerable development. The S.II (216) is extended as before, but the S.I returns (276) and rules to the end, hastened to *più presto* and at last resting on a pedal E to give it its true key-perspective.

The last quartet of Op. 59, in C major, although it begins, like Mozart's quartet in the same key, with a slow Introduction, vague and prophetic

---

* It is a patriotic hymn, entitled *Slava* (Glory), which plays a large role in the Coronation Scene from *Boris Godounov* (Ex. 18).

in suggestion, turns out to be the least allusive of the three. For that prophecy is not fulfilled. Frank energy will be expected from the iambic ictus that begins the *Allegro vivace*, but neither is that suggestion fully realized. The first violin, solo, invents for the apparent S.I a dancing figuration of the dominant 7th; follows with its counterpart in F and D minor; and when at last the real key has been found and acclaimed, *forte*, what turns out to be the real S.I (at least, in the exposition) is a kind of paraphrase of the violin's solo, physically rather than spiritually energetic. Neither does the S.II (a paraphrase of the transition-figure begun at 30) broaden the imaginative horizon. The development, perplexingly, chooses to discuss the solo version of the S.I; plays for a while with the S.II, and then (121) begins a sonorous syncopation of the iambic motive, presently made more exciting by rhythmic diminution. But in all the bustle of the first movement there is hardly the feel of a strong purpose.

The *Andante con moto, quasi Allegretto* (A minor, 6-8) is quite another matter. Its gentle melancholy, although never obsessive, is unrelieved, and even when the quiet eighth-note motion of its melodic curve undergoes a painful depression of its intervals (e.g., at 60) the twinge is brief. Within its limited horizon, suggestive of folk-song, the impression is that of a kind of smiling misery such as Schubert often voices. It recalls Matthew Arnold's phrase about "the almost intolerable pathos of Burns's verse"— intolerable because it is so nearly unconscious. A more difficult movement to interpret justly would be hard to find.

The Menuetto, in C, is marked *Grazioso*, and fulfills exquisitely that prescription. It offers, too, precisely the needed alleviation after the *Andante*. The gentle excursion of the Coda into flat-key atmosphere will seem a strange preparation for the unbounded vitality of the ensuing Finale, but you will agree that nothing could have pointed up that vigor more strikingly.

The Finale (*Allegro molto*, 2-2) is a huge fugue, on a theme ten bars long that crackles like a dangerous live wire. The polyphony is hardly orthodox. When the first violin enters as fourth voice the second violin doubles its theme, and the viola and 'cello are also in octaves, so that there are only two parts instead of four; but the purpose here was not to make a model fugue but to express superhuman vitality, and fugal structure was obviously secondary to that triumphantly achieved purpose.

In the six quartets of Op. 18 a man of no mean stature was portrayed. The figure limned in Op. 59 has grown, in six years, almost incredibly.

A new, assured technique gives external evidence of that growth. But it would be a critical error to suppose the growth to be exogenous. There is a new, propulsive vision within — a new awareness of meaning in music. To symbolize that meaning far outruns the capacity of language; but its ultimate reference, as our comments have often dared to insist, is still human experience. Beethoven never doubted that reference. But Op. 59 is only the beginning of his discoveries.

The "Harp" Quartet

In comparison with Op. 59, the novelty of the next quartet, Op. 74, in E flat, is not striking, but it does reveal a considerable fermentation of the romantic brew. It was written in 1809, a year after the Fifth and Sixth symphonies, and is dedicated to Prince Lobkowitz, to whom (along with Count Razumovsky) those symphonies were inscribed.

It has an Introduction (*Poco Adagio*, E flat, 4-4) whose tone is patently meditative. On what sort of experience it meditates, you may judge for yourself if you will allow the yielding curve of the opening motive, its gently dissonant texture, and its "open" phrase-ends to hint at matters more than purely musical. For these things characterize the whole Introduction and anticipate the tonal speech of romantics as yet unborn.

The main theme of the *Allegro* first asserts the E flat key, somewhat obscured in the Introduction; then it borrows its most distinctive curve from the opening motive of the *Adagio*. A single repetition, in the viola, establishes its thematic significance, so that the pizzicato "harping," which has given a nickname to the quartet, suffices to maintain the atmosphere, along with the recall of the forceful chord of the first bar and the characteristic tensions of the *Adagio*. A brief running transition leads to the S.II — itself begun suggestively out of key (33), and complementing the sense of the S.I rather than offering distinctive contrast. The Cl.S., another complement, is appropriately only a cadential figure. The development begins with colorful *stretti* on S.I; then the 'cello invents an extension that soon rises to white heat. This is slowly dissipated, and the harping makes expectant approach to the recapitulation. This differs little from the exposition, but a Coda follows (180) that is really a second development.

The *Adagio ma non troppo* (A flat, 3-8) is no conventional excursion into long-charted lofty sentiment. It portrays a mind less tensed than when the quartet began; but it is that same mind in action. The S.II (22), depressed into A flat minor, strives to right itself into C flat major, but the effort is singularly painful, and the ultimate escape into the original key is similarly moving. The S.I returns (61), much enriched, and you will expect no more than the floridation of the whole discourse. But the S.II is replaced by a new and much more hopeful theme in D flat (84), sung by the first violin and then by the 'cello. The darkness of A flat minor cannot be wholly dispelled thereafter, but it is largely banished (112) by the S.I, now low in the first violin, with an accompaniment of delicate staccato in the second, and with harping in the viola. Beethoven's *espressivo*, marked against the cadential tonic-dominant chords near the close (161), if justly interpreted will verify our reading of the sense resident in the whole movement.

The Scherzo (labeled only *Presto*) is in C minor, and is almost as obsessed with the famous "C minor rhythm" as was the symphony in that key, written the year before. In its context it sounds a little ungentle, but you will soon find its frank vigor grateful. The Trio (*Più presto, quasi prestissimo*), still in 3-4, "is to be imagined as if in 6/8." Its main figure goes up and down the scale with a considerable clatter of heels. It is distributed, fugue-fashion, among the four voices, acquiring as countersubject a sort of *canto fermo*. On its last appearance, after a double repetition, the Scherzo is kept *piano* throughout, acquiring a long Coda that leads without pause to the Finale.

This is an *Allegretto con Variazioni* (E flat, 2-4). You will find its theme — of disarming simplicity — precisely what was anticipated by the approach. (Try to imagine a strenuous conclusion. It is unthinkable.) Its basis throughout, except at the cadences, is a tiny three-note dotted rhythm ("two-a| one") with the melodic stress on "two." The variations, hardly more sophisticated than the theme, pursue its essential harmonic contour, but each one finds a new melodic figure in a new rhythmic pattern. The sixth variation, *un poco più vivace*, is much expanded and makes an end, *Allegro*, on the melodic figure of Variation III.

The Last Quartets

Although the next quartet, Op. 95, was written in 1810, and is not properly to be reckoned among the "last" works, it anticipates so many of the characteristics of that final period that it must at least be regarded as marking the transition to it. At any rate, the halcyon days of Op. 59 and Op. 74 are over. Known external events, although they must have contributed to the serenity of those days, do not explain it. They are equally inadequate to account for the change. Precarious health, growing deafness with consequent isolation from the active musical world, financial troubles (momentarily lifted in 1810), concern as to the character of his brother Karl's wife and the fate of their little son, and the frustration of his own cherished plan for marriage — these and other worries occasioned by his own erratic behavior, impose no burdens which his own indomitable spirit had not already proved itself able to endure. The last works, more clearly than recorded external facts, prove that a new philosophy is forming — a philosophy that embraces more than had been dreamed of in that forthright interpretation of the world that is so confidently put forward in the works of the second period. That confidence generated a style that may be called imperative; the style of the third period, in contrast, is subjunctive.

Evidence of this change is discernible in Op. 95 — in the more tentative character and the unconventional design of themes; in an evident impatience with the accepted canons of formal structure; in a much more frequent use of harmonic obliquity; and in the abrupt conjunction of ideas that would formerly — if conjoined at all — have been linked by explanatory transition. The main themes of the quartet are quoted in Example 19.

The quartet is in F minor. It has the shortest first movement of all the quartets — only 152 bars. The essentials of the form are all condensed within this space; yet the movement (*Allegro*, 4-4) does not seem lean. The S.I begins with an exasperated ejaculation, enforced by a silence; then a whip-sawing of C's, up and down, against similarly rhythmed tonic and dominant chords. But the ejaculation, repeated on G♭, fades at once to *piano* (7) and becomes ruminative; and even though it returns, fragmented (16) and then complete (19), the gentler tone has to supervene for only 3 bars to reach the S.II — a gesture so warm that it quite o'ercrows the momentary rage.* This theme (25), in D flat (not the orthodox A flat), maintains that key right through an extraordinary excursion on the A major scale (39) which is really an intensified passing-note — a long A between the A♭'s of bar 38 and the B♭'s of 41–43. (There are three analogous passages, 50, 108, 119.) The ejaculation, subdued to a murmur, underlies the rumination to form the end of the exposition.

* It is perhaps not irrelevant to recall the innumerable recorded outbursts of Beethoven's temper and his later abject apologies.

EXAMPLE 19. BEETHOVEN QUARTET IN F MINOR, OP. 95

The development (61) begins, startlingly, with the ejaculation in F major, and spends its brief 23 bars on that theme and its first continuation. The recapitulation (83) accordingly omits the first 18 bars of the exposition. The S.II now begins in D flat as before, but goes almost at once into F major (94). The Coda (130) begins with the S.I in D flat and makes turbulent arpeggiated comment on it until the end, where it fades into uneasy silence.

The ensuing *Allegretto ma non troppo* is in the unexpected key of D major. The *mezza voce* prescribed for the 'cello's hesitant descent of the scale and for the ensuing melody is essential if the subjunctive character that governs the whole piece is to be realized. The melody hovers on the border of G minor — so far that the brightness of the unequivocally major moments yields a subtle sense of strain, and the viola's D's (26–27), similarly, have a strangeness almost foreign to their primary tonic sense. The S.II (33) is in G minor, fugally set forth, and its well-constructed polyphony yields many significant harmonic twinges. After a tense climax the fuguing subsides into the hush of the opening, with the 'cello theme now obscurely harmonized; then, against a new and very delicate countersubject, the fuguing begins again, this time leading to a return

110]

of the S.I, so altered in register and so extended as to form an extraordinarily suggestive epilogue to the movement.

Without pause the equivalent of the Scherzo follows — an *Allegro assai vivace, ma serioso*. This strange qualification seems to refer to the Trio, to which the elastic figure of the Scherzo soon yields; for this has a sort of chorale in the three lower strings, above which the first violin has a single persistent figure.

A brief *Larghetto espressivo* (F minor, 2-4) warns that the tone of the coming *Allegretto agitato* (F minor, 6-8) will not be very optimistic. This begins on the animated figure of the last notes of the *Larghetto*, striking a note of unrest by no means desperate, but persistent and never alleviated. The S.II (32) is merely a tense rhythmic interlude before the return of S.I (51), now fragmented and polyphonically intensified. The interlude returns (82); the ensuing S.I all but vanishes; a new rhythmic figure (110) that promises invigoration is negated by the creeping chromatic viola beneath a sort of surrender in the first violin; then, *molto leggieramente*, comes a lively figure in F major for Coda, pleasant indeed, but not wholly consistent with the implications of what has gone before.

Quartet in E flat, Op. 127

The next quartet, Op. 127, in E flat, came to being fourteen years after Op. 95, in 1824. It was commissioned, along with two others, by another Russian nobleman, Prince Galitzin, who, like Razumovsky, was a string player (a 'cellist) able to take his part along with professional players. The commission came at a moment of deepening personal trouble, and was couched in language so appreciative of Beethoven's genius that he was much heartened. This may have been the trigger that released the image of happiness that glows throughout the work; but this music is far more than an elated response to unexpected good fortune. It portrays the mind of an optimist assured, in the face of all contrary evidence, that his optimism is sound. We found Op. 59, No. 1 to be in a kindred vein. In that work, however, although it is quite without rhetorical emphasis, something of the grand manner is discoverable. Here there is nothing of the sort. The imaginative level, effortlessly attained, is even loftier; but there is no conscious pride in that attainment. He is only trying to make the goodness of that imaginative region as self-evident to you as it is to him.

The main themes of the whole quartet are illustrated in Example 20.

[111

EXAMPLE 20. BEETHOVEN QUARTET IN E FLAT MAJOR, OP. 127

There is at first a firm sonority (*Maestoso*, E flat major, 2-4) only six bars long. It will show, when it recurs, more relativity to the main movement than appears at first sight. Its last note is an under-trilled C, and the main theme of the unhurried *Allegro* (3-4) begins on that active note. Its curve is beautifully rounded, moving with a quiet zest that is without the least trace of anxiety, yet with an assurance implied rather than affirmed. Something of that implication is revealed in the quite homophonic continuing strain, *forte* (23), out of which a brief contrapuntal transition is derived that leads to the S.II in G minor (41). But this, only a little more tense, reverts after repetition in the second violin to the S.I ('cello, 57), now in G minor, and there is presently an extended, hesitant cadence on the dominant of that key.

The development begins with the *Maestoso*, now more sonorous, the S.I following, in the same G major key. An extraordinary sense of elevation is conveyed by a sequential rise on the second bar of S.I. That theme presently reverts to the flat-key color (117); undergoes a high diminished-7th intensification; expands its characteristic interval of the 4th; and then, by way of the augmented 6th, the *Maestoso* emerges once

112]

more, *ff*, and in the full glare of C major (135). But this is not the end
of the development. Bars 2 and 3 of S.I find new counterpoints — first
a dainty staccato scale; then a little three-note figure; the rhythm of S.I
is invigorated ("one," staccato; "two," *sf*; and "three," slurred); and at
last S.I returns in E flat (167), beginning a recognizable recapitulation.
The homophonic pendant (23 = 183) is now high in the 'cello, with the
S.II (215) in E major, and there is much enrichment of the texture, although it leads downward to the expanded cadence that ended the exposition. The *Maestoso* does not return to begin the Coda, which no longer
strives for intensity, for the quiet assurance of the S.I is now doubly
assured.

The Adagio, *ma non troppo e molto cantabile* (A flat, 12-8) is a rein-
terpretation, by a master now all but clairvoyant, of that sense of loftiness
which had been often portrayed by lesser composers, to the evident satisfaction of listeners with imaginative wings no stronger than theirs. Beethoven had always known the high altitude of this region, and had more
recently explored it in the slow movement of the piano sonata, Op. 106,
and in the *Adagio* of the Ninth symphony. In both those works, the
region is shown at two levels (i.e., with two themes), and in the symphony the process is that of variation, as it will be here. But since there
is here but one theme, the concentration is higher, and its tension harder
for the listener to maintain.

The theme is very simple — perfectly symmetrical, wholly diatonic,
and quite unimpassioned. Propelled by no more than a leisurely-assem-
bled dominant 7th chord and by three up-beat notes, the first violin
draws, for four bars, an effortless curve; the 'cello repeats it; once more
the violin leads and the 'cello follows; then, with two bars of undulant
cadence the music alights on the level of the variations. The 'cello now
makes a kind of appoggiatura-approach to notes that, in the theme, were
wholly consonant, and the texture, richly polyphonic, enhances the
gentle pull of these dissonances. For the next variation the measure
changes to 4-4, *Andante con moto*. An even greater elasticity is attained
through a most delicate scheme of syncopation in the violins against incessant staccato sixteenths in the lower strings. The third variation, approached by a unison D♭ that turns into C♯, is in E major, *Adagio, molto
espressivo*, 2-2. The motion is slowed for contemplation and almost halts
at the eighth bar, on a very "modern" augmented 6th chord whose reso-
lution-tone, B, is played by the 'cello along with the dissonant C♮ against

A♯'s in the violins. The final E's drop to E♭ for return to the original key. In the fouth variation, again in 12-8, the 'cello and violin again dialogue a more remote version of the theme. Then comes another excursion to E and an episode on the three up-beat notes that introduced the theme; the first violin floridates in running sixteenths the first four bars of the theme; the three lower voices similarly figurate the next four; there is an expectant pause; then the whole tonal fabric softly returns to earth.

To find a sequel for such a scene as this must have been an imaginative problem of the first order. Beethoven's solution is brilliant — not in tonal glitter but in psychological appropriateness. It is marked *Scherzando vivace* (E flat, 3-4). Spurred by four pizzicato chords, the 'cello begins a lightsome hopping which, along with a smoother phrase, yields a brief and quite regular Scherzo form. But there follows, instead of a Trio, a quaint five-bar phrase in 2-4 time that provokes a development of the Scherzo as long as the Scherzo itself. Then a real Trio appears (*Presto*, E flat minor) — a wayward streak of *pp* melody that suddenly grows loud and boisterous to form its second section. There are endless ingenuities of rhythm and texture, yielding a structure more varied than in the scherzi of the Seventh and Ninth symphonies.

The Finale (E flat, 2-2) has no tempo mark, but the impetuosity of its "kick-off" leaves no doubt as to its speed. The most propulsive motive (5) is an outgrowth of the kick-off,* and the music thereafter hardly departs from this character. There is of course a lessening of energy (21), and a distinguishable S.II presently appears (55); but there is no real contrast of mood. The form is thus a sort of Rondo. A stamping climax (237) seems to presage the end. Instead, the energy dwindles, the pace slows, and the key changes to C major. Then, *Allegro con moto (comodo)*, comes a trilling in 6-8 time and a scamper of triplet sixteenths that emerges into a new version of the propulsive motive of the opening of this movement — and, if our derivation is correct, of the opening motive of the quartet.

The Quartet in B flat, Op. 130

The quartet in B flat, Op. 130, was really the third of the quartets written for Prince Galitzin. It was begun, along with the A minor, in March, 1825, but was published earlier than that work, which was ac-

* It may have been generated out of the opening of the first movement. Substitute B♭ for the C with which that theme begins; make the first four notes eighths and the fifth a half note, and you have this motive exactly.

cordingly numbered Op. 132. The Finale of Op. 130, as first written, was the *Grosse Fuge*. Artaria begged Beethoven to write a shorter and more suitable Finale, and Beethoven, for once, acquiesced without protest. But the present Finale could not be completed until 1826. Artaria published the quartet as it now stands in May, 1827.

The brightness of its surface makes this the most appealing to the ear of all the last quartets; but longer acquaintance will prove that its glow really comes from within. The first movement, like that of Op. 127, begins with an Introduction (*Adagio ma non troppo*, B flat, 3-4). (The themes are shown in Ex. 21.) This, however, is more integral to the *Allegro*. It appears more often and has a little figure (7) that will help to form the transition to the S.II of the *Allegro*. The Introduction is warmly romantic, contributing more of that character to the *Allegro* than it would have shown if its running S.I and its trumpeting countertheme had been self-dependent. For the S.II (53), in G flat, would never have been the offspring of that parent. The whole movement, with its

EXAMPLE 21. BEETHOVEN QUARTET IN B FLAT, OP. 130

many available structural elements, is not wholly in the classical sonata-form perspective, but that outline is perceptible as the ground plan of the structure, and the details need no description.

Its brightness will have whetted rather than exhausted our appetite for pleasure. What follows, accordingly, is an excursion into another corner of that field — a sly little Scherzo (*Presto*, B flat minor, 2-2) whose inner gaiety the minor key at first masks. But it cannot suppress a smile, in major, and the beginning of its second section (9), and the Trio (B flat major, 6-4), all on one hopping figure, is all but boisterous. The return to the Scherzo (50) is comically made on an enormous augmentation of the upward scale that ended the Trio, followed by three quaint chromatic slithers in the first violin, solo.

The *Andante con moto, ma non troppo* (D flat major, 4-4), after the Scherzo, is wholly welcome. The additional direction, *poco scherzoso*, seems a little strange as a qualification of the romantic tone struck at once in the harmonically unstable anticipations of the theme; but it should serve, rightly interpreted, to guard against overemphasis of sentimental implications in the theme itself, begun by the viola (3) against a staccato figuration of the harmony in the 'cello and then taken over by the violin. The song is brief. It evaporates (10) into a dainty staccato figuration that makes as if to cadence in F (19), but the first violin, all alone, takes an expectant D♭ and drops from that note onto the main theme in the unexpected and delightful key of C major. This, still more daintily accompanied, makes transition to the S.II (26) in A flat, *Cantabile* — a wing-borne little tune whose flight is made the more aerial through its design as a three-bar period. Its continuation suddenly becomes a paraphrase of the introductory bars (36–37), and the S.I then returns. The music now pursues its former course, harmonically altered so that the expectant long note (now G♭, 54) brings a brief development, by imitation, of the S.I. The S.II is now in D flat (61); there is another transition to the paraphrased opening; then a slowly fading Coda, taking its leave on the S.II. For sheer charm this movement has hardly an equal. Perhaps that, after all, was what *poco scherzoso* was to imply.

But the usual sense of that word is more nearly exemplified in the next movement, *Alla danza tedesca* (*Allegro assai*, G major, 3-8), whose teutonic grace, if not exactly courtly, is captivating. It first shapes a tiny Minuet-form — two sections complete in twenty-four bars; then a waltz-like Trio whose first section, still in G, is led by the first violin. But its second section, led by the 'cello, has the same tune in C; and instead of the formal *da Capo* there is a sort of playful development. The S.I comes back (81) with sixteenth-note figures in its accompaniment, and these the first violin makes into a delightful paraphrase of the main theme. The little tune, broken into one-bar pieces, is roguishly distributed among the instruments to make the end.

Next comes the famous "Cavatina" (*Adagio molto espressivo*, E flat, 3-4) which Beethoven said he could never think of without a tear. Its simple melody, entering against a flowing figure that often recurs in the accompaniment, has a tranquil surface; yet it is really drawn from a deeper well whose quality the first violin reveals (40) in tense (*beklemmt*) fragmentary phrases in the established 3-4 measure against the throbbing C flat harmonies, essentially in 9-8, below. The brevity of this outburst, contemplated, is tragic; and in its light the melody, returning, is no longer so simple.

The present Finale was written at Gneixendorf in 1826, during that visit to his brother Johann from which Beethoven returned to Vienna with the fever that was to prove fatal. This is his last completed composition.

The music is perhaps less allusive than the former movements — to catch again the creative mood after a year would hardly be possible; yet it is surely more appropriate than the great fugue, and, of course, less fatiguing to the listener. The main theme is a gay little tune that he might have invented twenty years before — except that he would hardly have begun it in the "wrong" key of C minor. It rights itself after four bars, but this disorientation is a trick that will often be turned. The S.II (39) has trouble in escaping the attraction of B flat as tonic, but it does finally establish F as its key, and its signature rules, even beyond the end of the exposition of what is as much a Rondo as a sonata form. The development, after a few antics on the S.I, has a wholly new theme in A flat (if you like, the S.III of the Rondo). It is very suave in contour, moving almost incessantly in even eighths and yielding a grateful contrast. You will almost have forgotten the S.I when hopping octaves in the viola (158) announce its return. But it now appears in F, and is put through many developmental paces before its return in its proper key (237). From then on, the pattern of the exposition is discernibly followed, and there is a sort of Coda which rediscovers the theme we called S.III; but the piece seems really designed — by no means heedlessly — as a sort of comedy of errors, and half the fun is your own uncertainty as to just where you are.

Quartet in C sharp minor, Op. 131

The next quartet, Op. 131, in C sharp minor, is by common consent the greatest of these last works. Its seven movements, once described by Beethoven as *zusammengestohlen* (really out of experience), do not clearly follow either the design or the movement sequence of conventional sonata form, nor can any other considerations of pure musical propriety account for their sequence. Yet, for the percipient ear, the quartet offers the most revealing chapter of any in that musical autobiography which we have often noted as implicit in these works.

This is a narrative, piecemeal yet coherent, not of event but of the impact of event, upon a mind perhaps as capable of interpreting the final meaning of event as any that ever lived. Music cannot, indeed, portray event. But it can portray our feeling-response to event. For this response — in considerable measure an emotional state — language, which can portray event, has but a feeble and ineffective vocabulary. We use language here, of necessity; but our words do not and cannot define the music they describe, except in its structural aspect. Rather, the music defines — and vastly re-defines — the words.

The seven movements of Op. 131 (really five, since two of them are short introductions) are all played without pause. (The themes are shown in Ex. 22.) The first movement (*Adagio ma non troppo e molto espressivo*, C sharp minor, 2-2) begins with the fugal exposition of a somber theme, deeply burdened but neither desperate nor rebellious — the contemplative attitude of a mind both acquainted with grief and strong enough to endure it.* The fugal texture is free, the theme being frequently altered as to interval and the second phrase being far more in evidence than the first. Its staid motion is hardly varied until the key changes to G sharp minor (54) and the second phrase is "diminished" (the quarter notes become eighths). There are *stretti* (the theme taken against itself), e.g., at 93–94, and at 99–100 where the theme in the 'cello is augmented against its original form in the violin; but these devices are

* The tonal tension is toward the subdominant with the *sf* on A, the tonic being touched but once and on the weak half of the bar; the three half notes, followed by gravely moving quarters, give an accordant impression of motor energy. The theme is analogous to that of the fugue in the same key in Bach's *Well-tempered Clavier*, Bk. I.

118]

EXAMPLE 22. BEETHOVEN QUARTET IN C SHARP MINOR, OP. 131

not displayed for their own sake. The grip of the music is strong; the implied experience stern.

The second movement (*Allegro molto vivace*, D major, 6-8) brings a welcome relief from strain. The main theme, in the first violin, flows quietly in a sort of circle, returning upon itself (6) and slowing its pace for a moment before it is transferred to the viola.* The first violin completes the viola's theme and then finds a long gracious curve of descent which may be seen as transition. Then (24) it begins, solo, a somewhat more exuberant phrase which may be taken as S.II, for this design will embody the essentials of sonata form. Although this theme begins in D it soon modulates to A and comes to an indefinite close on the dominant of F sharp minor (48). Then it unconcernedly begins the S.I in E, again repeating its tiny *rit.*, and goes on to a kind of development involving new harmonic colors in such profusion that one might almost think the later Wagner was here at work. The culminating *unisono* swoop of all

* Conceived as implying two beats in the bar, Beethoven's *molto vivace* makes his *un poco rit.* (7) impossible to execute naturally. Implying six in the bar, it dictates a tempo in accord with the character of the theme and makes the *rit.* manageable, although one is tempted to begin the *in tempo* with the viola's theme on the second half of bar 8.

[119

the instruments on the S.II (172) will be felt as the logical outcome of this singularly vivid portrayal, pursuing undeviatingly the 6-8 motion of both its themes, of a mind somehow freed of all the trammels of artificiality.

What Beethoven designates as No. 3 is an eleven-bar Introduction (*Allegro moderato*, F sharp minor, 4-4), made of a few incisive solo phrases, recitational and insistent, that effectively presage the portrayal of another sort of experience. That experience, richer than the foregoing two, is too full of implications to be set forth in the guise of either fugue or sonata form.

No. 4, accordingly, is a theme and variations. The theme (*Andante ma non troppo e molto cantabile*, A major, 2-4) is hesitantly syncopated, its phrases being uttered alternately, bar by bar, by the two violins. The viola contributes essential harmonic sonority while the 'cello, pizzicato, enhances the hush which the theme's antiphony imposes. (Imagine the theme played, as it could be, by a single violin. It will lose all its hesitancy — which is half its character.) Var. I has the theme, no longer syncopated but condensed and in low register, in the second violin. The first, in the pauses, interjects warm, almost recitational phrases; then violin and 'cello exchange roles. The second half, as in the theme, grows richer and rhythmically more active. Var. II, *più mosso*, against a march-rhythm begun in the middle strings, resumes the antiphony, first violin and 'cello alternating phrases that suggest rather than directly vary the theme. These become more extended, surrounding the march-rhythm in richer sonority, and the end is on a vivid figure, *unisono*. Var. III (*Andante moderato e lusinghiero*, i.e., coaxingly, A major, 4-4) reshapes the theme into little phrases, at first dialogued between 'cello and viola, then between the two violins, and at last with the two parts doubled. Var. IV (*Adagio*, 6-8) figurates the theme itself almost unrecognizably in a texture unbelievably light-footed. Var. V (*Allegretto*, 2-4) quietly syncopates the essence of the thematic line, making an interlude of calm before the deeper disturbance to come. Var. VI (*Adagio ma non troppo e semplice*, 9-4), adopting the rest on "one" that gave the theme its hesitancy, wraps the theme in an elastic succession of chords, *sotto voce*, that at length allow a melodic line to emerge. The repetition of the first eight bars, an octave higher, is pointedly punctuated by a little figure of sixteenths deep in the 'cello that plays a larger part in the second half of the variation. A little epilogue of quiet runs is added. Var. VII (*Alle-*

gretto) begins in C major, making light of the theme for eight bars; then it returns to A major and adorns it in shimmering trills; then it begins the C major version in F, but hurries it out of the way; returns to A and makes an end on little cadential figures.

Without more than a breath-pause the 'cello gives out in a single bar the basic motive of four notes that will rule the ensuing *Presto* (E major, 2-2). The theme, mischievously gay, almost runs off the track into C sharp minor; rights its balance an octave higher; runs off again, this time to B major; then teeters with one foot on B until (*Molto poco adagio*) it has got the other up to G♯ — surely third and fifth of the E triad? — and then goes off merrily into G♯ minor on the basic motive (37). This is wrong, too, as it soon finds (44); and at last, having settled in E it prances delightfully to a cadence. At once (69) it finds a new theme (*piacevole*) under whose spell it remains until the 'cello, with its loud introductory bar (167) brings back the S.I. The rest is in the same vein. The last appearance of the S.I (470) is for a time quaintly whistled *sul ponticello*; then a swift crescendo, bowed regularly, brings the end.

Three incisive G♯'s, however, announce No. 6 (*Adagio quasi un poco andante*, G sharp minor, 3-4) — a moment of meditation on a pensive little four-bar theme in the viola which the first violin repeats with a curiously disheartened, Neapolitan-6th A♮ (9) in its cadence. There are only twenty-eight bars, but if you ponder them you will find here a significant comment, both on No. 5 and on the more vital energy that follows.

No. 7 (*Allegro*, C sharp minor, 2-2) begins with two swift, angry phrases, detached; then launches into a vital march whose tune, rhythmed by all the lower strings in steps identical with its own, has a threatening energy. Smoother phrases follow (21f), but the tension of the augmented second allows little relief. The S.I returns for a moment, modulating to E for the S.II (56) — a swift downward scale-figure with a huge leap after its lowest note to high, rhythmed B's (*poco riten.*) that both initiate similar figures in the other instruments and generate a broad counterpoint against them. An impressive, broadened cadence brings the development, begun with the S.I in F sharp minor (78). Against this the first violin makes a terrible counterpoint in whole notes rising scale-wise, and when this is taken up by the 'cello (110) for all seven notes of the scale and eventuates in the *unisono* ejaculation of the detached opening phrases, the import of the music is pretty clearly revealed. The development ends with an obscure murmuring in three-bar rhythm over a sort of imprisoned bass (147) that resolves into C sharp minor and the recapitulation. There is a new bass motive (170) that colors the main theme; an impressive dwelling on the leaping figure of S.II that starts (262) a frightening turmoil on the angry ejaculations of the opening and the tension of the augmented second, and this leads to a long *unisono* approach to, and reiteration of, the ejaculations. The scale-counterpoint in whole notes (now descending) accompanies the main theme (314); an interpolated D major scale (329), analogous to that at bar 39 of the first movement of the F minor quartet, Op. 95, gives a moment of Neapolitan-6th tension; the renewed excitement of the main rhythm is broken off with the unfinished opening ejaculation (347); and a Coda follows, on that phrase (strangely tamed), on the dragging descending scale, and on the main theme itself, slowed after a little to *Poco Adagio*. But six bars in the original *Allegro* and in the brilliance of C sharp major make the end.

The Quartet in A minor, Op. 132

The quartet in A minor, Op. 132 (Ex. 23), is the second of those written for Prince Galitzin. Sketches show that it was first conceived in 1824, and that the first and last movements were far advanced before the illness (in April, 1825) which is so eloquently commented on in the Song of Thankfulness. Four movements only were apparently first intended. That song is thus an afterthought.

The first movement begins (*Assai sostenuto*, A minor, 2-2) with a burdened motive, all in half notes, built up from the bottom in free imitation and uttered in a *pp* that much enhances the implications of its dissonance. (The main themes of all the movements are shown in Ex. 23.) After eight bars of this unrest the first violin, still on the characteristic diminished 7th, interjects a streak of sixteenths (*Allegro*, 4-4) below whose final E the 'cello, in treble register, sounds the main motive of the movement — a phrase on the first three notes and the leading-tone of the A minor scale. The first violin repeats this against the *Adagio* motive. Its continuation involves more pungent dissonance (the diminished 3rd) and eventuates in a portentous downward dotted rhythm on the B flat triad (the Neapolitan 6th), a cadential stamping (four quarters), and a single bar (*Adagio*) in the first violin, all on the mere A minor triad but severely meaningful. The same general procedure, somewhat intensified, is then pursued. It makes unexpected escape (33) into the orbit of F; a

EXAMPLE 23. BEETHOVEN QUARTET IN A MINOR, OP. 132

new rhythm is rapidly generated (38–40f), accumulating a force that seems to portend catastrophe; and suddenly the S.II emerges (48) — a warm, lyric phrase in the second violin over a triplet-eighth accompaniment that is carefully marked *non ligato* to keep the theme from dissolving in its own warmth. The first violin, taking this theme at a higher level, contracts its minor 3rd into a diminished; but it avoids further insistence on this bitter interval and the music settles quietly on its tonic, F (57, *dolce*), in passages that are frankly joyous. Thereafter, however, the S.II has a little two-bar epilogue (71), warmer than ever, and in a moment the exposition is ended — but with a 7th added to its final chord.

The development is almost all on the main theme and the *Adagio* motive, and it illuminates them fruitfully. You cannot tell where it ends, but suddenly the rhythms of bars 38–40 reappear (149), bringing the

[123

S.II and the rest of the exposition with some expansions. The Coda (195) is really a new development, subtly heightening the sense of both themes. The final bars, out of a dissonant murmur on the diminished 3rd, rise to high tension.

The next movement is a sort of Scherzo (*Allegro ma non tanto*, A major, 3-4). Its pattern, on a rather large scale, is quite conventional; but its humor is so pensive that if Beethoven had used that title it would have seemed misapplied. The S.I is really composite. A figure of three rising quarter notes (half-step + third) in four bars first defines and then obscures the key. Then it becomes the counterpoint to a clinging phrase, set forth in an endless variety of tensions which the first note of the accompanying figure (as rising appoggiatura) creates. There is no contrasting theme.

The Trio is equally intriguing. The first violin, with its open A sounding continuously as drone, plays, high above, a placid but by no means inanimate tune. This the second violin accompanies with a figure of even eighths (half of them also A's) that make a gracious countermelody. (The analogy with the Musette, a frequent bagpipe interlude in Gavottes and other dances, is obvious.) There is this time a contrasting section (142) — a fluid melodic strain that migrates from instrument to instrument while the others gently tap the triple rhythm. Not a *forte* is marked in the whole Trio until near the end, where a gruff objurgation in viola and 'cello culminates in four minatory-sounding bars of duple time. The *da Capo*, however, is not made until a mollifying reminiscence of the beginning of the Trio has been heard.

The next movement (*Molto adagio*, 4-4) is indubitably related to Beethoven's personal experience — his recovery from the illness of April, 1825. He entitles the piece "Sacred song of thanksgiving of a convalescent to the Deity, [written] in the Lydian Mode." * We ourselves, and probably Beethoven also, since the music is not strictly modal, will hear the music as rather precariously in the key of F.

The first division of the piece is altogether hymn-like. Like a brief organ-prelude, a phrase of eight even quarter notes precedes each of the five iambic "lines" (eight half-note "syllables" long) of the hymn — the "organ" always *piano*; the hymn-phrases swelling. The fifth "line" is like the fourth, except that its last three notes bring the dominant of D major,

---

* The Lydian Mode is an old ecclesiastical scale, having B♮ instead of B♭, but whose "Final" (an ending-tone far less positive than our tonic) was F.

in which key the second division of the movement is cast. This is entitled *Neue Kraft fühlend* (feeling strength anew). It will vastly amplify
our image of the gratitude expressed in the hymn. It is marked *Andante*
(D major, 3-8), and moves with an elastic rhythm and a vitality full of
the hopefulness of convalescence rather than with the energy of fully
regained strength. Its first sixteen bars, almost throughout, are alternately
f and *p*. The rest is more delicately figurated, with a wonderfully tentative approach (52–53 and 62–63) to its climactic peaks.

Each of these divisions is then varied. The hymn, in the first violin,
unaltered, is harmonized in syncopated figures in the lower strings, gaining greatly in fervency with this texture. Then the *Andante*, still keeping
its alternation of *f* and *p*, is perhaps rather re-scored than varied, although
the figurations are more florid. Then the *Adagio*, now marked *con inti-
missimo sentimento*, sets a warm florid version of the organ-strains against
the lofty chanting of phrase after phrase of the hymn itself — all this in
such unexpected distribution of the parts that many more than four
voices seem to be singing. A more genuinely worshipful utterance would
be hard to find.

Next comes a little interlude (*Alla marcia, assai vivace*, A major, 4-4),
really invigorated, that becomes faster and faster and leads to the Finale
(*Allegro appassionato*, A minor, 3-4).* A surging figure of accompaniment in the three lower strings sets the tone of the movement even before
the urgent theme, feverishly energized, begins.

The surge of the theme is more impetuous than that of the accompaniment; the insistent E's (5–6) rise to a G that could have remained
in A minor but leads to an uncertain cadence in C; and the same cadence
(18) for the repetition (doubled by the viola) finds its outlet in D minor.
This continuing strain (it is no mere transition) is intensified by a driving
two-note figure (34) that makes the dissonant high F that follows all the

---

* This theme, in D minor and as yet far less distinctive in expression, appears
among sketches for Schiller's *Ode to Joy* and was first intended as a possible main
theme for the Ninth symphony.

The word *appassionato* is a very rare qualification among Beethoven's directions
for performance. After the *Largo appassionato* of Op. 2, No. 2, it does not appear
until Op. 106, where it is secondary to *Adagio sostenuto*, and only once more, in
the *Allegro con brio ed appassionato* of Op. 111. It does not appear in the symphonies, and we have not met it thus far in the chamber music. (It was not Beethoven's
title for the piano sonata, Op. 57, and though the world has welcomed that title, it
was applied only to a later edition, and by the publisher.) Beethoven's music again
defines the word, rather than the word the music. But never before has he spoken
with the personal, immediate urgency of undisguised romanticism.

more bitter, and the same note in the 'cello, below the figure (43), has the immediacy of Schumann. The S.II (52) begins in G but is half the time in E minor, and its culmination (64), on an insistent 'cello figure whose bass, in the viola, descends to give each repetition new harmonic force, generates an outcry (68 and 76) whose descending curve subsides on a yielding note of regret into the returning S.I (92), again in A minor.

But the three eighth notes of its continuing strain (113) soon undergo a restless development; then, since these notes are rhythmically identical with those of bar 1 of the S.I, that theme returns — for the moment in D minor (169) but soon in the original key, and there is a somewhat condensed recapitulation. The undulant curve that ended the exposition on a note of regret now takes on an ominous note of excitement; it grows faster and louder; it borrows the main theme; and the result is a long Coda, *Presto*, soon emerging into A major, that is no longer addressed directly to the Deity but still displays its *neue Kraft* with full recognition of its source.

The Grosse Fuge, Op. 133

The Grand Fugue which was intended to form the Finale of the B flat quartet, Op. 130, was published as Op. 133, in 1827. Whether Beethoven erred, either in substituting the finale which Artaria requested, or in substituting the choral movement of the Ninth symphony for whatever orchestral form he might have given to the finale of the A minor quartet, is a question probably best answered by the decision rendered by his rather superior mind. The Fugue, at any rate, is quite big enough to stand alone.

In the form-perspective of Beethoven's day, when homophonic idiom had largely supplanted polyphonic, this piece might well be seen as his *Kunst der Fuge*. It is far less explicit than Bach's great work in exploring every nook and cranny of fugal technique, but it is a masterly demonstration of compositional skill. And it is more than that. It demonstrates Beethoven's determination not to open that grim mouth of his without saying something of human import.

A detailed analysis would be tedious and only half intelligible. We show, therefore the two main themes as Beethoven presented them in his *Overtura* (Ex. 24), and attempt to describe only the principal features of the complex structure which follows. (Our bar-numbers begin with the first Fugue.)

EXAMPLE 24. BEETHOVEN GROSSE FUGE, OP. 133

Theme A, tortuous and introspective, is the real main theme of the work. (Theme C, shown above A in the bass in quarter notes, is only a subordinate, yet fertile, countersubject.) Theme B, violently active, is structurally co-ordinate with A, so that we have to deal with a "double" fugue. But this is constructed in what we shall describe as five sections, highly contrasted in tempo and character accordingly as A or B is given the leading role.

Theme A, *pp* in the first violin, introduces B as main theme of Section I and will form its counter-subject as shown in our illustration. The four voices enter with B in downward order to form a quite regular fugal exposition. The following manipulations contain no other matter until a new counter-subject in triplet eighths appears (33) along with B in the second violin and A in the viola. This combination persists until the jerky rhythm of the opening is resumed (69) in an episode on fragments of B and A. Theme B then returns complete (85) in the 'cello, but with the triplet counter-subject now shaped into an eighth and two sixteenths. But the triplets return (113), for a time banishing B altogether; but it comes back (128) and broadens its leaps to make a decisive end for the section. Since the fugue began, not one *p* has been marked.

Section II, *Meno mosso e moderato* (G flat, 2-4), begins with the first four notes of A, in sixteenths, and toys with them, accompanied by C, until 142 where both themes combine as we have shown them. Theme A, now in its natural contemplative character, presently appears in canon between 'cello and violin (168); the texture of sixteenths thickens and swells to the only *f* in the section (197), then subsides to a faint murmur in B flat minor.

Section III (*Allegro molto e con brio*, B flat major, 6-8) at once establishes A, in the active rhythm shown, as principal theme. It is tossed about, like Paolo and Francesca blown by the winds of Hell, until a cadence is made in A flat (247). Now the 'cello emerges with A in augmentation (a note to a bar), while the second violin, out of three-note fragments of the theme, inverted and in swift motion, makes a new fugue-subject that is regularly "exposed" in all four voices. The 'cello's augmentation later reduces, for one bar of the theme (e.g., 254), its dotted half note to two dotted quarters, *ben marcato*); and this added impetus, repeated, sharpens the focus of the motion until the first violin (326) begins a new counter-subject against the augmentation of a half of theme A. Its foreshortened two dotted quarters become very incisive. This carries on until a halt is made in E flat (389), when fragments of theme B, *p* for two bars only, return reshaped into 6-8 meter and in a frantic *ff*. These lead at last (452) to a combination of A, augmented and inverted in first violin, B in second violin, A (original) in viola, and the rhythm of A in the detached slurred eighths shown in our illustration in the 'cello. It comes to a cadence in A flat.

Section IV briefly returns to the *Meno mosso* of Section II, but with A in the violin against its inversion in the viola. It abandons this (485) for a transition, *accelerando*, to the *Allegro molto e con brio* (6-8), at first on A and in a portentous *p*; then, retaining hardly more than the rising half-step of A's first two notes, there is a long build-up of half-subdued excitement, filled with hints of the two main themes but less polyphonic in texture. It ends with little snatches of themes B and A as we showed them.

Section V, the Coda, then begins with loud, broadly syncopated statements of theme A (*Allegro molto e con brio*, 6-8). The theme reverts for a moment (656) to its swift form; broadens again as it dwindles to *pp*; there is a kind of hesitant groping (677) for a foothold; and finally themes A and B combine in an unrelieved crescendo to the decisive end. As with the fugue in the A flat piano sonata, Op. 110, fugal structure is quite abandoned for a more cogent purpose which, indeed, was apparent from the beginning.

The Quartet in F, Op. 135

Beethoven's last quartet, that in F, Op. 135, was finished in the autumn of 1826 at Gneixendorf where, as we have seen, the new Finale of Op. 130

was written. It is about half as long as the other "last" quartets, and is in a lighthearted vein far removed from the tone of those works. But its charm is as compelling as is their depth, and its facture is as delightful as its humor. Its chief themes are shown in Example 25.

EXAMPLE 25. BEETHOVEN QUARTET IN F, OP. 135

The first movement (*Allegretto*, F major, 3-4) begins with a little phrase in the viola whose low pitch and minor harmony would appear quite somber were it not for the flippant little quirk in the violin that follows it. The rest of the theme, on a smiling figure echoed upward above a pizzicato bass, is probably more naive in design than in implication. The succeeding phrase (10f) seems really sober, but it ends with a gay little upward scale and the diminution of the opening motive. This motive then modulates errantly, apparently aiming toward C major; but it goes right past that key into F (24), and the first violin, against a Haydnish accompaniment, finds there the S.II — a strain whose even sixteenths, merely by avoiding the hop of the previous dotted rhythm, become fluid and gracious. The hop can't be long resisted, however, and after a few recurrences its infectious lilt generates a new figure in triplet sixteenths (38) which makes transition to the cadence that ends the exposition.

But that cadence is deceptive. The development that follows is compact, yet comprehensive. It returns (101) to the opening phrases, now *f* and in imitation, making a somewhat abbreviated recapitulation. This ends with another deceptive cadence (159), after which there is a remarkably fresh-sounding Coda.

The Scherzo (*Vivace*, F major, 3-4), with its syncopated rhythm, faintly suggests the Scherzo of the A major 'cello sonata, but its humor is much more genial. The scale-wise theme of the Trio, nudged by an eighth-note motive, turns out to be endlessly productive of interest so that it quite outdoes the Scherzo itself.

The *Lento assai, cantante e tranquillo* (D flat, 6-8) appears to have been an afterthought. There is evidence in the sketchbooks that Beethoven at first intended the quartet to have but three movements. But this, in its tiny dimension (it has a theme only eight bars long, with four variations) is in keeping with the rest of the quartet. In sentiment, it seems to some commentators to sink too far into sorrowful contemplation, and to others to soar too high into regions of mysticism, to be compatible with the rest. To us, it seems to do neither. The note of playfulness is indeed abandoned, but its seriousness is only a manifestation of the warmth which lay, largely hidden, under the surface of the first movement.

Each variation adds, to its reshaping of the theme, an extension of the cadence — a useful as well as an expressive device, since the theme itself has not that extension, and the first variation is so similar in tone that one might well suppose it to be a part of the theme. The second variation, in C sharp minor — somber-colored and in a strangely hesitant rhythm — is indeed tense; but the next variation gives immediate relief, and the fourth, a most delicate figuration of the theme, has only the undertone of pain that all warmth, even that of passion (of which there is here no trace), must possess if it is to appear genuine.

The origin of the last movement, which Beethoven titled *Der schwergefasste Entschluss* (the hard-won decision), has been much — and fruitlessly — debated. The piece is narrow enough in implication to relate (as no deeply felt composition ever does) to a single event; but any one of a dozen events might have been its source.*

* The three notes for *Es muss sein!* are the first notes of a canon that Beethoven wrote, more than half in fun, demanding that Schuppanzigh be paid for his per-

Two motives, one set to *Muss es sein?* (Must it be?) and one to *Es muss sein!* (It must be!), precede the music and form its thematic bases. That for *Muss es sein?* begins the piece (*Grave, ma non troppo tratto,* i.e., dragged, F minor, 3-2) in a vein which might be taken as serious if it were not for the roguish fashion in which *Es muss sein!* is made to reply. The design is that of a compact sonata form, in which the S.II (45) is nothing but the legato phrase (17) which follows the "It must be!" that begins the *Allegro* (F major, 2-2). After the development the *Grave* returns (171) with its weight amplified a couple of G's by the furious tremolo of the violins — perhaps the first appearance of this theatrical device. There is a free recapitulation, ending with slow and distorted ejaculations of *Es muss sein!*; then a Coda, begun pizzicato and kept *pp*, even when bowed, until the last four bars which insist, *ff*, that It must be!

The String Quintet in C and Some Lesser Works

Artaria published in 1797, as Beethoven's Op. 4, a string quintet which was really the Octet for wind instruments, later published as Op. 103, not merely arranged but recomposed. The Octet was probably written in Bonn; rearrangement yielded a more significant work; but its interest is chiefly for the close student of Beethoven's style, and we shall pass it by.

The only quintet originally for strings is Op. 29, written in 1801, and therefore after the completion of the first quartets, Op. 18. The writing for the instruments is very effective, but the concentration on the musical idea is perplexingly diffuse in comparison to that shown in the quartets. The first movement (*Allegro*, C major, 4-4) begins with a promising, deeply introspective theme, set forth with admirable simplicity. Yet the transition to the S.II (often so logical in the quartets) is made on a mere babble of triplet scale-figures, and the S.II itself (41) has little interest beyond its pleasant design, except that it is in the submediant (A major) instead of in the dominant. Because of this irrelevance the S.I, although kept largely in the foreground in the development, fails to realize the implications it first suggested.

The *Adagio molto espressivo* (F major, 3-4) begins its main theme

formance of the B flat quartet if Dembscher, who wished to have the quartet played at his own home, were to receive that favor. Dembscher asked, *Muss es sein?* and the canon was the answer. The only other words of the canon-text besides *ja, ja, ja,* are *Heraus mit den (sic) Beutel!* (Out with your purse!). For the whole story see Hugo Riemann's revision of Thayer's *Life of Beethoven*, Vol. V, p. 200f.

with a significant upward surge; but it descends at once into the insignificant complacency of a long ornamental cadence.* The S.II also (24), although approached by rather remote harmonies, with the suggestive tension of its four-note figure enhanced by the drive of accompanying reiterated sixteenths, comes to a lame conclusion. The intermediate theme (43) is quite factitious, although it makes the *fausse reprise* of the main theme (58) appear as a moment of real insight. The ensuing repetition, although much enriched in texture, adds nothing to the thought.

The Scherzo has a sort of lumbering energy, but little of Beethoven's characteristic humor; and the Trio, although in a smooth legato, keeps the same pattern of three notes to a bar (there is not a divided beat in either Scherzo or Trio), with a certain monotony the inevitable result. The Finale (*Presto*, C major, 6-8) has a swift and flickering rhythm for its S.I, but the S.II (55) is a harmonic formula only, and is approached by such a long succession of even eighths that its entrance is without freshness. The development ends with a curious innovation – a quite new section, *Andante con moto e scherzoso*, A major, 3-4 – and the recapitulation begins thereafter, refreshingly, in F. The *Andante* returns, in C, and there is a brisk Coda, all on the main theme.

There are several works for small groups of wind-players – a duet in G for two flutes (1792, but published only in 1901); three duets for clarinet and bassoon (also 1792?), in C, F, and B flat – the third being a sonata-form movement plus a set of variations; and two trios for two oboes and English horn. The earlier of these is known as Op. 87, although it was probably composed in 1795. It is of extraordinary interest, not only as a tour de force in texture (there are never more than three notes sounded simultaneously, yet the harmony never sounds thin) but as a musical composition in itself. There are four movements – a compact but well-rounded sonata form; a slow movement that makes the English horn into a remarkably satisfactory equivalent for the 'cello in a string trio; a Minuet, also called Scherzo; and a jolly rondo for finale.† The other work for this combination is a set of variations on *Là ci darem la*

* Compare the not dissimilar first bar of the theme of the *Adagio* in Op. 127. The upward drive is there much more tranquil, but its implication of character is maintained throughout the theme, while it is here quite negated by the perfunctory cadence-formula (2) and the graceful ornament of the next two bars.

† Some find this piece more enjoyable when performed by two violins and viola, or by a less homogeneous combination of wind instruments, but I remember at least two performances by players in Henry Wood's Queen's Hall Orchestra which roused the high approval of packed houses at Promenade concerts.

mano, written in 1797. It is hardly less skillful, but its substance is nowadays less interesting.

The sonata for horn and piano, Op. 17, was written in 1800, just after the string quartets, Op. 18. Written, of course, for the "natural" (valveless) horn, it posed severe problems in melodic invention. They were solved with skill, but the combination of two rather incompatible tone colors, added to the difficulties in design, makes the piece more a curiosity than a delight.

The Septet, Op. 20, for violin, viola, 'cello, bass, clarinet, bassoon, and horn was not intended as a "pot-boiler." It turned out, however, to be just that, being reminiscent enough of Mozart and the Divertimento to be immediately charming, and at the same time so patently the product of sound musical intuition that familiarity did not weaken its appeal. It was perhaps an essay toward Beethoven's first independent orchestral piece, the Symphony in C, Op. 21.

There is first a sonata-form movement with a brief but arresting introductory *Adagio*; then a quietly pensive *Adagio cantabile* (A flat, 9-8), voicing that familiar vision of loftiness in which the still-existing aristocratic regime appeared as the best of all possible worlds; then a *Tempo di Menuetto*, another version of which forms the last movement of the little piano sonata, Op. 49, No. 2; then a theme with five variations, as delicate as an ormolu clock and ticking quite as audibly; then a Scherzo (*Allegro molto e vivace*) with a refreshingly plebeian undertone; and finally an almost impish *Presto*, introduced by a short *Andante con moto alla Marcia* that is darkened into E flat minor to make more vivid the major key that follows.

Franz Peter Schubert

1797–1828

No OTHER music is as unselfconscious as Schubert's. Even after he has turned from song to instrumental music, having found things to utter which are beyond the range of melody as singers know it, the stream still flows — as clear and as unaware of its source as any hillside spring, and just as perennial.

He was shy and uncomfortable in the world of men, and even in the more manifest regions of the world of art — in those that are haunted by men from the world of affairs. Those men are indeed earnest seekers after that strange insight into human impulse which the arts, at their best, have always offered, and, however meager their understanding, they repay the artists generously for their offerings. But inevitably the conventions that rule in the world of affairs have their influence on the world and on the effort of the artists. Sophistications generated in the world of affairs breed their counterparts in the world of art; falsities, unavoidable in each, are reflected by or absorbed into the other; and so subtle is their interaction that only long critical experience can distinguish — and even then can distinguish but precariously — the false from the true.

For the enduring appeal of the arts is to the imagination — a faculty in some measure existent in all of us (else, as we have argued, art would have no public), but one all too easily obfuscated by the irrelevancies of erudition. The hallmark of creative imagination is spontaneity; that of erudition is caution; the two, even more than politics, make strange bedfellows; yet art is the union of what is essential to each.

Creative imagination, at any rate, Schubert possessed, possibly in greater measure than any other musician in recorded history. The learning which must guide such an imagination if it is to create works intelligible to men of lesser intuition, he had to gain almost wholly by his own effort; and that effort was naturally fumbling. His first mastery was in the field of the song, for his melodic invention was inexhaustible, and the stimulus to that invention, offered by the lyric impulse in the guise of words, was not only a spur but a corrective against uncontrolled invention; for the poem kept in focus the experience which it was the business of his music to vivify.

But the range of purely lyric impulse is narrow. That impulse is not, indeed, wholly destroyed when the complexities of contemplated experience submerge it and turn the exploring mind toward philosophy; for philosophy itself strives toward that simple summation of experience which lyric utterance attains. And what Schubert came to see was a vision similar to that set forth in the works of Beethoven's last period — a vision far beyond the range of lyric speech, but not beyond the range of music.*

He turned, therefore, increasingly to instrumental music as the vehicle for utterance of this broader vision. In the field of orchestral music, two incredibly lyrical symphonies were the outcome (the Unfinished, dismissed nowadays by erudition as hardly worth attention, being lyrically the most remarkable). But his achievement was equally high in his last chamber works. He was primarily a pianist, but he had learned the violin at school so that he could take the viola part in the quartet ensemble ready-made in the family: his two brothers, Ferdinand and Ignaz, taking the violin parts and the father the 'cello. He wrote many quartets for this group — unpretentious efforts, but good schooling for the future. We shall ignore these, interesting as many of them are for the student of style, and shall describe only those which display a determined, rather than an incidental achievement. The number of these, however, seems astonishingly large when we remember Schubert died when he was only a year older than the Beethoven of the Op. 18 quartets.

The Violin Sonatas

The duet for piano and violin — a little strangely, since the violin is the nearest instrumental equivalent of the voice — was hardly a favorite

* Bach, likewise, saw the essentiality of the lyric impulse and preserved it astoundingly in his greatest works, whether vocal or instrumental. It is most unfortunate that erudition, in our day, has become so purblind in its occupation with structure that it has all but lost sight of this impulse as the guiding principle of his work.

combination with Schubert. There are three easy sonatas (usually called sonatinas) Op. 137; a sonata in A (often called *Duo*) Op. 162; a sonata for Arpeggione; * a set of variations (Op. 160) on the theme of the song, *Trockne Blumen*, from the song-cycle, *Die Schöne Müllerin*; and a *Fantaisie* in C, Op. 159.

The three sonatinas are short, easy, and apparently elementary, but their melody is so haunting and their structure so lucid that they have not lost their appeal, even today, unless to the very sophisticated. They were written in 1816. The first movement of the second is already a significant venture into what may be called instrumental (in contrast to vocal) melody — a venture whose success depends on harmonic progression, permitting melodic intervals quite unsuited to the voice. The harmonic image is compelling.

The sonata in A (1817) is on a larger scale. Its S.I (*Allegro moderato*, 4-4) begins deep in the piano on a quiet dotted rhythm that might turn out to be either sad or gay; but the violin enters against it (5) with so smiling a counterpoint that the note of pain is banished. The Scherzo (*Presto*, E major) follows appropriately after the temperate first movement. It has a sprightly shift from three-bar to two-bar rhythm at the beginning, and many impish contrasts of *p* and *f*. The suavity of the Trio is a perfect counterfoil. The following *Andantino* (C major, 3-8) is perhaps a little too delicious; but the Finale (*Allegro vivace*, A major, 3-4), borrowing from the main motive of the Scherzo for its S.I, is of a freshness wholly delightful.

Neither the *Rondeau brilliant* nor the *Fantaisie* — both of them virtuoso pieces whose technique was soon quite outshone by Paganini's amazing tricks — properly belongs in the category of chamber music. The Variations were primarily for flute and piano, and lose somewhat when the violin is substituted for the flute, since there is little of the sonority of the G string available. The song which yielded the theme comes at a rather late stage of the young Miller's fatal love affair. The Introduction (E minor, *Andante*, 4-4) appropriately foreshadows the mood of the song, but the variations, progressively more ornamental, quite depart from its character.

---

* This was a six-stringed instrument, fretted like a guitar but bowed like a 'cello, whose lowest note was the E above the 'cello's C. Schubert wrote its part an octave higher than it sounds. It can thus be played on the viola, except that six-note chords have to be condensed into four notes.

The Trios, Opp. 99 and 100

Although Schubert played the piano, especially when he accompanied Vogl in his songs, in a fashion which evoked the highest praise from many hearers, it was not, for him, the intimate vehicle which Beethoven found it to be. In chamber-music combinations, likewise, he seems seldom to strive for that difficult blend of color which one finds, for example, in the variations in Beethoven's *Archduke* trio. To avoid the overweighting of the bass when the low register of 'cello and piano are united, he often uses only the higher register of the piano, doubling in the octave the single real part he is giving it. The effect is eminently clear and brilliant, but the whole tonal resource is not employed. This fault — if it is right to call it so — becomes less conspicuous as his experience grows; and while his treatment of the piano is seldom as satisfying as that of later chamber composers, this weakness is hardly noticeable in his last chamber works with piano, the two trios.

There are but two trios for piano and strings: Op. 99, in B flat, and Op. 100, in E flat. Of these the first is the more interesting. Both were written in 1827, when full command of structure and expression had been gained, and when the gloomy song-cycle, *Die Winterreise* (The Winter Journey) was also in process, of conception if not of execution.*

Op. 99 begins (*Allegro moderato*, B flat, 4-4) with a theme as resilient as any that was ever conceived. Its foundation is firm — the tonic chord, unchanged for three bars, in incessant eighth notes; a propulsive figure in the pianist's left hand vitalizes it; and the theme itself, revealing its energy in the triplets into which its first long notes burst, ends its phrase on a swoop of sixteenths that covers all but four octaves. The repetition, a tone higher, feigns an excursion toward D flat but instead of the swoop makes an illuminating diminuendo and comes gracefully back into its key, *piano*. Now, for fourteen bars, there is only the mood, maintained

* Commentators are often perplexed when works of such different character are produced by composers at the same time. If it were true that music is and must be the immediate emanation of a composer's mood, this perplexity would be well founded. But, although his work stems from experience as truly as that of any other artist, it does not reflect the musician's *immediate* experience or his momentary mood. It reflects experience as it has been long known and pondered; and there is no reason why the creative act cannot be performed, whether by composer, poet, or painter, in defiance of a temporary mood opposed to that of his immediate project. What he needs for that effort is not a mind overcome with the emotions he is portraying. It is a mind illuminated by the imaginative understanding of the experience which, in its emotional aspect, is his real "subject." Only against that background of understanding can he judge whether his music is true.

by the triplet figures and the propulsive bass; but the theme comes back (26) very softly in the piano, and this time the continuation leads to the S.II (59).

This, in the 'cello, is the perfect complement to the S.I. It reveals, indeed, the inner awareness out of which the main theme sprang; and that Schubert conceived it thus seems proved by the persistence of it, or of an octave-figure derived from it, right up to the development. The S.I, hinted at against the octave-figure as the exposition ended, rules the development for a time in a panorama of modulatory colors. Then the S.II, accompanied by the triplets from S.I, takes over (139), its rhythm being soon excitingly diminished (167). Two *fausses reprises*, each revealing its uncertainty in a slight retard (191 and 202), precede the real recapitulation (211) which begins suggestively *pianissimo* and with the S.I in the piano. This is somewhat shortened and, with its *forte* areas considerably reduced, appropriately contemplative.

The theme of the *Andante un poco mosso* (E flat, 6-8) has an elegiac tinge, almost submerged in flowing harmonies of a color new to the ears of Schubert's day, but so often dwelt on by later romanticists that their appeal to present-day ears is much weakened. The middle section, relieving by syncopation the over-gentle swaying of the 6-8 measure preceding, is considerably more intense, and the sudden quietude of C major (67) has the feel of a gentle hand laid upon an overwrought shoulder.

The Scherzo (*Allegro*, B flat) is such a mingling of impishness and grace that one cannot tell which predominates; but that does not lessen one's delight. The Trio, in E flat, has the simple texture and the four-bar contour of a Ländler, and at slower speed would be no more than that; but it does serve to make grateful the *da Capo*.

The Rondo (*Allegro vivace*, B flat, 2-4) begins with a theme that at first sight looks quite trivial. But within its first eight bars there are six different motives that will be made to change their melodic intervals or to combine with each other in countless different ways, so that the theme, which if literally repeated would soon pall intolerably, maintains and heightens its spontaneity quite miraculously to the end. The most striking feature is a long episode in 3-2 time which makes the rhythm of the first three bars into what Beethoven would have designated as a *ritmo di tre battute*. But there is also a sterner transition-motive (52) that combines, first with a new tune made on the dotted rhythm of bar 5 of the S.I and then with itself (78) in canon; and there is even a suggestion (262 and

596) of the *hemiola* — a fifteenth-century device which shifted what we call 3-2 time into 6-4, combining, as here, both rhythms. This Finale extends to 653 bars, but it is not too long.

That fault, however, is all too evident in the E flat trio, Op. 100. Its first movement is 634 bars long and its last 748. The S.I of the first *Allegro* (E flat, 3-4) is firm without distinctive strength, so that the 'cello's more suave continuation (16) yields only a perfunctory contrast. The S.II (116) is rather an invented counterpoint to its accompaniment (still on the suave curve, in triplet figuration), than a thematic contribution to the discourse. The highest contrast is offered by the transition-episode (48) on a delicate staccato rhythm.

The slow movement (*Andante con moto*, C minor, 2-4) is appropriate to the apparent but unrealized intention of the first movement. It begins with a quiet march-rhythm that supports a heavily burdened but by no means weak-kneed theme in the 'cello whose implication is wonderfully summed up in the dropping octave G's (15) of its second strain and the ensuing upward leap of a tenth to a moment of undisguised pain. The rhythm of the bar with the leaping tenth generates (41f) a quieter strain in E flat that soon tramps heavily on the pattern of the dropping octaves. The S.I returns, building a high climax in F sharp minor (110f); the rest, with the S.I *più lento* for Coda, is a reworking of these things.

The Scherzo, in E flat, is all in canon — a device obviously borrowed from Mozart or Haydn which evidently cost Schubert some labor, for it lacks his usual spontaneity. But the unlearned Trio is exuberant.

The Finale (*Allegro moderato*, E flat, 6-8), like that of Op. 99, begins with a trivial-looking theme. It is far less varied in motive, so that variety is gained by rather artificial contrasts of subject — what may be called S.II, in C minor, 2-2 (73); its continuation in 6-8, rhythmically in the pattern of S.I and accompanied by streaking runs in the piano; and, quite unexpectedly, the main theme of the *Andante con moto* (279 and 697), against the tramping rhythm characteristic of both S.I and S.II in the violin, and an agitated chord-figure (marked *appassionato* but also *pp*) in the piano. Total coherence, whether of substance or design, is hard to discover.

The "Trout" Quintet, Op. 114

The last chamber work with piano we shall study will be the quintet in A, called the "Trout" quintet because of the variations on Schubert's song, *Die Forelle* which (probably as requested) form an interpolated movement, the fourth, in what is thus a five-movement scheme. It was written in the summer of 1819, at Steyr, whither Schubert had gone on a walking tour with his friend, Johann Michael Vogl, the sympathetic interpreter of his songs. He found there a wealthy amateur 'cellist, Paumgartner, who commissioned the work. The strings are violin, viola, 'cello, and bass — that being a combination ready at hand, but also similarly used by Hummel. It is Schubert's first mature chamber work. How far he went beyond it we shall see when we study the string quartet in G; but we shall never understand how such a distance could be covered in eight years by one who was physically hardly more than a boy when he died.

A little spurt of arpeggio in the piano begins the *Allegro vivace* (A major, 4-4) — a figure that will gain in significance as the music proceeds. The real S.I follows — a placid thought in the strings, in two eight-bar strains punctuated by the arpeggio. The piano then quietly plays the theme in octaves, high above the strings which provide the harmony. (The notes are different, but the sense is the same.) Its tone is limpid and clear against that background. Now the middle strings (25) begin a motion in eighth notes, the piano returns to its arpeggio, then finds still another variant of S.I; and the former design is repeated, the eighths becoming triplets against the theme in the piano. Rhythms and figures then unite for transition toward E major, secretly generating, on the way, a warm duet between violin and 'cello which might be called the S.II (68). That role, however, seems to us best filled by the contented little tune which the piano begins, solo, at bar 84. Another little duet emerges, between violin and piano (100), before the swift sixteenths that foretell the close of the exposition.

The development begins on a broadened, dotted-quarter rhythm (the diminution, if you like, of the dotted-eighth figure in our S.II), which gently underlies the S.I. Its evolutions will be easily followed. The recapitulation (210) begins in D, the subdominant — a lazy-looking device of Schubert's, since it brings the S.II back, when it comes, in its proper key, the tonic, without the trouble of readjusting the modulations.* You will find a good many omissions of originally exposed matter that gratefully shorten the section.

The *Andante* (F major, 3-4) begins with a gentle curve in the piano,

---

* Since S.I, S.II, and Cl.S. are conventionally all in the tonic key in the recapitulation, this trick has its justifications.

but after its first phrase it remembers the dotted rhythm of the S.II of the first movement, and enlivens with it the gracious theme. Then it wanders into F sharp minor, finding a strain suggestive of an interlude in Schubert's familiar *Serenade*, and comes out of its lingering warmth into the S.II — as lithe a rhythm as imagination ever enacted. At the end of this, G magically becomes the leading-tone of A flat, the S.I comes back in that key, the *Serenade* returns in A minor, and the lilting close is in F.

The Scherzo (*Presto*, A major), is as gay as the *Andante* was pensive, a little quirk in its harmony (5–6) generating much of the fun. The Trio, in D, is much quieter, smooth string phrases being answered by tinkles high in the piano.

The fourth is the interpolated variation-movement. In the song, the trout-fisherman finds the water muddied (really, by passion). Here it remains clear. The variations are decorative and transparently pursuant of the theme. Only in the last does Schubert use the little flicker in the piano which so vividly contributed to his "picture" in the song.

Like the Rondo of the B flat piano sonata, the Finale (*Allegro giusto*, A major, 2-4) begins with a loud, naked note (here, an E). Out of it comes a whimsical little theme, dialogued between strings and piano for a long time. The S.II (84) is in D — whether with the leading thought in the piano or the violin is hard to say, but the piano wins out with its leap to the *fz* B; and it continues (112) with another strain in its high octaves that suddenly remembers S.I. The strings remember it better than the piano, for they take it over (135), and the piano makes a lyric flight in triplets around it. All these things run together, pell-mell, in a mischievous *pp*, dwindling almost to nothing on quiet cadential phrases in the piano. Then come detached ejaculations of upward arpeggio (the opening of the quintet?); more quiet; then a roar on the D chord for the close.

With a loud B the development section starts. But it is no development. It is only a recapitulation of all that has gone before, beginning in E and ending in A, just as the exposition began in A and ended in D. But the adventure, in the new keys, looks quite different.

The String Quartets

We turn now to Schubert's string quartets — to the four, that is, which show his highest mastery. From 1812 to 1817 he wrote, besides some fragmentary attempts, ten complete quartets, only two of which have more than the interest which attracts the student of style.* Even these two we shall ignore, in favor of the greater works. The first we shall study is itself only a single movement, the *Quartettsatz* in C minor, D. 703, written in 1820. (An *Andante*, in A flat, was projected.)

The main theme has, for Schubert, a new sort of intensity and a wholly unwonted conciseness — two bars only, *Allegro assai*, 6-8, C–b♮–c, B♭–a♮–B♭ | A♭–g–a♭, G–c–e♭ | where capitals indicate the strong beats of the measure. Each note is repeated — i.e., in sixteenths. The dynamic is *pp*. The instruments enter with the subject consecutively, as in a fugue; but the rules of fugal answer are defied, for the first three all begin on middle C and the 'cello an octave lower. The counter-subject is nearly the inversion of the subject, also in sixteenths. With the viola's entrance a savage *cresc.* begins, up to the D flat chord (9), on the arpeggio of which the violin, solo, descends, in hard, staccato eighths, *ff* for one bar, *fp* for the next. Can this be Schubert, the lyrist?

It is; but he has found a new lyricism. The D♭ falls to B♮, then rises to E♭ (not happily), and begins the theme anew, in eighth notes, more nearly legato. This is only an approach to what might appear as the S.II (27) — a melody quite in the earlier vein. But the 'cello (19) has already begun to support the legato S.I with a rumble in its own rhythm (along with the viola's tremolo of sixteenths on a pedal C); and this rhythm underlies the new melody,† imparting to it an unrest which the melodic line itself does not even hint at. The outcome (61f) is a turbulence patently related to the S.I and supported by its motive, but now visible as inherent also in the transition melody.

The real S.II begins, rhythmically, with bar 93 (the accent on D in the next bar is agogic). Again the S.I underlies it, and is incorporated in its continuation (105) in a gentler curve, G–F♯–F♮–E. The mere cadence-formula of the Cl.S. (125) is supported by a mere undulant figure from

---

* The ten are as follows, numbered according to the thematic catalogue of Otto Erich Deutsch: D.18, beginning in C, ending in B flat; D.32, C major; D.36, B flat (these written in 1812). To 1813, three: D.46, C major; D.74, D major; D.87, E flat (pub. as Op. 125, No. 1). To 1814, two: D.94, D major; D.112, B flat major (pub. as Op. 168). To 1815, one: D.173, G minor. To 1816, one: D.353, E major (pub. as Op. 125, No. 2).

† To devise a characteristic rhythm for accompaniment is of course nothing new. *Gretchen am Spinnrade* and *Erlkönig* had long since shown that device at its most vivid pitch. But to borrow a primary motive as contributory to a thought of highly contrasted character is quite another matter.

S.I; but the sudden roar that begins the development, although stilled at once, is portentous. Indeed, the whole development is vague. Its melody faintly resembles the curve of the Cl.S., but that reference seems pointless. It is what it seems — quite new, and quite tentative, for its brief flights end in frustrations. Neither do these lead to a reassertion of the S.I. Orientation comes with the transitional theme (195), now in B flat; and what follows is recapitulation of the whole earlier substance from that theme on. The cadential figure is as quiet as before, and the music seems to have evaporated. But now, like Samiel in *Der Freischütz*, comes the sinister S.I, just as it was at the beginning, to "explain" whatever can be explained of this subtle drama. It is hardly strange that he left it without the conventional complement of *Adagio*, Scherzo, and Finale. Convention could no more supply the sequel to this piece than to the Unfinished symphony. But he had learned "the true way to write string quartets."

Schubert's next quartet was that in A minor (D.804), published as Op. 29. It was written in 1824. Its spiritual theme is no mystery like that of the *Quartettsatz*. It is only the musing of a lonely mind — a theme familiar to every artist (and probably to yourself), but never before so simply and so personally expressed.

It begins (*Allegro ma non troppo*, A minor, 4-4) with a quiet figure of accompaniment in the second violin, underlain by a rhythm that after a dotted half gives a little throb of sixteenths at the last beat of the bar. The theme confines itself for twelve bars, quite without protest, to the first five notes of the scale. It does not even know that it is resigned, and when after a long extension the theme comes back in major (23) its escape from the 5th-range that first confined it is wonderfully bright. There is, to be sure, a pretty strong hint of the other side of the picture, given in the sudden A minor cadence (32) and the following passages; but the S.II (69) is as calm as the S.I, and has implications just as deep. The development is spurred to something like self-realization, and there is a kind of ruefulness in the quietude with which first its rhythm and then the theme itself is resumed after the crisis (140f). But the recapitulation (168) needs only to repeat the tale to make it more vivid than before.

The *Andante* (C major, 4-4) begins, like the piano *Impromptu* in B flat, with a reminiscence of one of the many incidental numbers Schubert wrote for *Rosamunde*, a fantastic play by Wilhelmine von Chézy, librettist of Weber's *Euryanthe*. The theme is so naive that you may think it hardly worth attending to; but if you lend it a little more than your ears you will find that it voices a strange sadness — a kind you will be grateful to experience. And the manner in which this thought is maintained, with never an excess of emphasis and yet always with enough tension to keep the subtle experience in focus, is a manifestation of far more than artistic skill.

The Menuetto (*Allegretto*, A minor) is again indescribably right, of course in texture, but also in character. It is indeed a dance, but it is for spiritual limbs, not physical, to enact, and the image of experience it evokes could find its equivalent only in similarly insubstantial words.

The Finale (*Allegro moderato*, A major, 2-4) makes a more credible pretense of gaiety, but — perhaps because of the context now so fully established — it is never untrammeled, never wholly frank. It never exults. The main theme, with its accents on "two," has a sort of peasant-dance suggestion at which you may smile for a moment; but the weight is a little too heavy to bear, and that fact is not concealed. The S.II (72) is in C sharp minor, and in a rhythm by no means sprightly — the skitter of triplets above it (114) is a very thin disguise — and there is not a moment of insouciance in the whole movement. But what music ever spoke more truly?

Quartet, "Death and the Maiden," Op. posth.

Neither the sun nor death, La Rochefoucauld says, can be contemplated fixedly. Yet there is nothing more compulsive to the imagination than the source of life, or the mystery of its end; and whether we are aware of it or not, an almost constant intimation of each is in the back of our minds. Face to face with death, we veil it in its conventional apparatus, and in that guise it does bear fixed contemplation. The poet Claudius brought this familiar surface of it rather sharply into focus in a song, *Der Tod und das Mädchen*, which Schubert set to music in 1817. His music, competently uttered, pierces considerably beneath that surface. At any rate, its contemplation, fascinated, is considerably less oblique.

The impact of the song is sharp. To expand the discussion could not but weaken its impact. Yet the quartet, although it diffuses our focus, widens our horizon on the experience and brings it home, perhaps with more permanence than does the sharper blow dealt by the song.

The first movement begins (*Allegro*, D minor, 4-4) with two arresting trumpet-calls whose up-beat triplets then march toward a broad introductory strain. What will appear as the S.I proper (15) also marches determinedly, impelled by the triplets, at first in two five-bar strains. Thereafter its harmonic purpose becomes a little bewildered, and only circuitously can it reach firm assertion on the opening fanfare (41f). The continuation grows less anxious, coming to rest in F major (61) and beginning the gentle S.II, all harmonized in 3rds and 6ths. (Its periods, like those of S.I, add a fifth bar for translation to the higher octave.) But in the higher register the theme becomes harmonically perplexed; the triplet figures of accompaniment are hastened to sixteenths, and the agitation culminates in a violent *unisono* passage (112). But this S.II has become an obsession, and the close of the exposition is on it.

The development, likewise, although the tramp of the march with its propulsive triplets strives for the foreground, is still ruled by the S.II right up to its climax (186). Thereafter the S.II is reduced to a figure in the viola, while the march-rhythm, with its up-beat triplets but not in its original design, approaches the opening fanfare (41 = 200). The rest is recapitulation up to bar 297 (= 139), where a long low D begins a very tense Coda in which the first form of S.I has its only repetition (*più mosso*). Then, over a more despondent marching in the middle strings, the first violin plays a brief threnody. In this movement, surely, the technique of the *durchkomponiertes Lied* is exemplified without words.

The *Andante con moto* (G minor, 2-2) is from the song. But it begins with the inexorable march of Death toward the Maiden, who has shrunk from him crying, "Don't touch me!" He answers, "Give me your hand, you fair and gentle form: a friend am I, not an avenger. Be of good cheer, I am no fiend; you'll sleep within my arms quite softly."

In the variations that follow, the almost static (but on that account most impressive) theme is mostly kept in low register, the violins having persistent rhythmic figures which color pointedly the somber harmonies. At the end of the last variation, these figures, agitated sixteenths, dwindle to triplets for the Coda; again to eighths on a pedal B♭ for a *ppp* repetition of the theme; then they vanish altogether as the theme rises to a higher octave and appears in the singularly poignant major key for the fall of the curtain.

In the now established context, the drive of the Scherzo (*Allegro molto*, D minor) is all but terrifying. Its impact is the more forceful in that its brevity is almost curt. The Trio, in D major, offers alleviation; but it cannot but hesitate (80, 96) as the dotted rhythm from the Scherzo comes to the surface, nor escape the minor key as it repeats its second strain (101).

The Finale (*Presto*, D minor, 6-8) is a frantic tarantelle. Its S.I has a surface of fevered gaiety, but the core of it is all but brutal. It rules for sixty bars, when another pattern (rhythmically, bars 7 and 8 of S.I) begins transition to S.II, halting for breath before it begins that theme (88). The merely musical adventures of these two themes are absorbing — so much so that one may too easily forget their origin in that partial and oblique contemplation of death which is all we humans can endure.

The Quartet in G major, Op. 161

This, Schubert's last quartet, was written in 1826. The first movement appears to have been performed at the only concert he ever gave of his own works, on March 26, 1828 — the first anniversary of Beethoven's death. The concert was a great success, yielding more money than Schubert had ever had at one time in his life; but it received little notice in the musical journals — probably because Paganini had just come to Vienna, and within a week was to rouse such a furore as no other virtuoso had ever provoked. The quartet (if it was the G major) was an appropriate choice for that anniversary. It is indeed too long, for Schubert was never to learn how not to fatigue the attention of his hearers. But it explores, in its own way, a region of the mind which no one but Beetho-

EXAMPLE 26. SCHUBERT QUARTET IN G MAJOR, OP. 161

ven had hitherto entered, and that great figure, had he seen the music, would have been further confirmed in his opinion that "this Schubert was a genius."

The first movement (*Allegro molto moderato*, G major, 3-4) forecasts in its first four bars the tensions that are to rule not merely this movement but the whole quartet (see Ex. 26). The bare G triad grows louder for two bars. At the last instant of that swell the B♮ becomes B♭, and on the down-beat the G minor chord is ripped with full force out of all the instruments. The twitching figure that follows is in the same tense character. All this is repeated a 5th higher, and two depressed phrases follow (E♭–D, E♭–D), the last D with a "hold." This, however, is really introductory. A more continuous thematic line (S.Ib) follows. It compacts into single phrases the twitch (3) and the drag (E♭–D); the 'cello, under tremolando harmonies, takes the thematic figure downward from G through F and E flat back to G; then, suddenly *ff*, the G triad of the opening returns, leaping up an octave (33); the twitch grows fiercer and the leaping octaves, hastened and syncopated, build an accumulation of force that Beethoven might well have envied. It halts on the dominant of B minor (63) and the S.II appears.

Without its troubled rhythm, this theme would be the old appealing melody of Schubert the songster.* With it, the appropriateness to the developing scene is complete. The theme is repeated with shimmering figures high above, suggestive of orchestral color, but these mingle with the texture when imitations on the theme follow (90f) against an increasingly tremolando background. Then the 'cello has a more legato version of S.II (110); the imitations — perhaps redundantly, although they are in different voices — reappear, as does the S.II with the shimmer and a pizzicato accompaniment; and *unisono* scales at last announce the end of the exposition.

The waver into which the exposition sank begins also, confusedly, the development, but the S.Ib soon appears, followed by S.Ia in its leaping-octave form and its former syncopated turbulence. This sinks into a quiet G minor chord (278) which begins the recapitulation — the minor harmony now being jerked into major; but the force is now mild and the twitch subdued, with its sixteenths tamed into eighths. Against an un-

---

* Tie the two syncopated notes that begin each measure into a dotted quarter, play the theme legato, and you will have it. Then note the pathos the syncopation contributes.

expected triplet accompaniment S.II is now transformed into a quiet figuration (292); the 'cello, as before, takes it downward; after an outburst of the octave-leaping S.I, it finds a new, warm counter-theme to play against the S.II (343); and even the cadential octave-scales seem less intense. The contradiction, major-minor, although it is brought to an end quite positively on the major, still seems unresolved.

The *Andante un poco moto* (E minor, 4-4) is no warmed-over dish of conventional loftiness. It probes, as did the first movement, into that region of the mind which the last quartets of Beethoven explored, and of which Schubert, unaided, found fuller understanding than any later composer until Brahms.

Out of loud B's, patently the dominant of E minor, the 'cello emerges with a tentative, discouraged sort of strain, allowed only at the end (10) — and then obliquely — to come to rest on the tonic. It continues above a long pedal C in the viola, and would be in that key were it not for the F♯'s that disturb its rest. The subtlety of this persistent avoidance of adjacent obviousness is wonderful. After a return of the initial loud B's, an F♮ in the 'cello's first strain seems to establish the theme in C; but the cadence, quietly but inexorably, steers it back to E minor.

E's, treading softly on each beat of the measure, descend to D's in G minor; there is a sudden loud outburst of that chord, arpeggiated in dotted rhythm, and of the diminished 7th; there are alarming ejaculations and a sort of choked outcry (the G–B♭ of the end of the fourth line of Ex. 26); then the most "modern" harmonic distortion ever invented up to this time.*

Prepared as before, this whole extraordinary passage recurs a tone lower; then, with singular pathos, the S.I returns (81) in the violin; then in the 'cello with a fluid counterpoint above; and with loud F♯'s (108) the recapitulation begins. It follows the course already laid out and ends, as often with Schubert, in the tenuous sweetness of the major key.

* The G of the diminished triad (C♯–E–G) at "four" of bar 53 really becomes F double-sharp; the triad then, quite correctly, *expands*, resolving to C♯ minor on the way to its real goal, G♯–B♯–D♯, as 6/4 chord (with bass G♯). This would have been quite comprehensible, even if startling, as modulation. But the "outcry," G–B♭, follows as if there had been no modulation. It belongs to the following diminished triad (B♭–D♭–E — the E = F♭) which expands, similarly, to B♭ minor; for the G of the outcry, added to this triad, merely makes it a diminished 7th chord. The ultimate goal of the whole passage is the G minor of bar 58; and the strange excursions are thus similar to the interpolated scale of A minor at bar 39 of the first movement of Beethoven's F minor quartet, Op. 95.

The two following movements, for whatever reason, fail altogether to carry out the implications of the first two. The rhythm of the Scherzo (*Allegro vivace*, D major) forecasts, with but little of its buoyancy, that of the Scherzo in the Great C major symphony; and with this its only thematic substance the interest lags, even though the movement is short. The Trio (*Allegretto*, G major) is a sort of Ländler over a D pedal, again without contrasting idea.

The Finale reverts, but now only humorously, to the contrast between minor and major. The form is that of the Rondo, but between the S.I and its first recurrence (257) there are at least four distinguishable tunes: one out of *opéra bouffe* (60); another in D (93), a sort of march driven by the persistent tarantelle-rhythm; another in B minor (171) on swaying 6ths; and finally, as a grateful pause for breath, another in B minor whose first three notes each fill a whole bar. The movement is brilliant and, in another context, would be delightful. But it does not belong here.

The String Quintet in C major, Op. 163 (posth.)

No such lapse as that which we have just had to note is even suggested in this, the last and the greatest of Schubert's chamber works. As one experiences it, whether as performer or listener, it seems the most intimately compelling utterance in the whole literature. Never did the outwardly shy soul of this infinitely gifted artist reveal more fully its inward wealth, and never has the tide of inspiration been more effortlessly held at its flood. Of the vanity of musical learning, or of the lesser trickeries that rouse ephemeral admiration, there is not a trace. There is indeed a consummate skill. But it is a skill too subtle for learning to atomize, and analysis will have no place in your conscious response. You seem just to drink in music, in draughts too big for your gullet.

Yet, when you are filled, you will know that this was more than just music. It was somehow a great draught of experience. There was no portrayal of event. No imaginable occurrence could have been so rich in spiritual vitamins. This is the summation and the essence of a thousand experiences — a metaphor, not for event but for a pretty large fragment of life itself.

There is at first — as if a Moses had tapped the rock in Horeb — a welling out of tone. (Analytically, it is nothing but the C major chord, con-

fined within an octave but bulging in volume for two whole bars.) *
Then something within the octave bursts (into a mere diminished 7th),
and as the pressure subsides the upper C emerges as melody — rising to
Eb, falling gently to G, and still more gently rebounding. So far, the
melody has floated on the stream of tone. Now it leaves it, spurting
lightly up to G, and descends, with two light and two more clinging
steps, to a half-cadence prolonged by a tiny high G chord. (See accompanying Ex. 27.) Then the whole strain, the first 'cello now leading,
begins again on the second of the scale but a 7th lower in pitch. An
augmented triad (21), singularly portentous, initiates a transition that
grows rapidly to a stern climax on naked B's and then, more slowly,
climbs the scale to a huge entrance of the main theme, now in both 'celli.
Arpeggios, vigorously active, figurate in all the upper strings the harmonies that at first were only sustained chords, and a new continuation is
contrived that leads to the orthodox dominant key for the S.II. But a
surprise is in store for us!

For the two 'celli pull apart from this note and bring in the new theme
(60) in the warmer tonality of E flat major. No mere scrap of tune, this,
but a full-throated melody indescribably appropriate to the S.I. (The
violins, above, have an elastic figure which, in a somewhat altered design,
will accompany the pensive theme of the *Adagio*.) Soon (79) the lyric
flame ignites the violins; first violin and viola begin a canon (they don't
keep it up, but who cares?) against more active figures until unmistakable cadential feeling (117) presages the close of the exposition. But in
the midst of this (138) there comes a little somber march-rhythm that
will form the topic of most of the development.

This section, 113 bars long, is consistent not only in itself but with the
whole idea of the movement. For while its topic is indeed the subordinate
march-rhythm, that phrase is itself clearly relatable in contour to the
first three bars of S.II; and this soberer aspect of that thought, now explored, is a vital contribution to that draught of experience which we
have spoken of as the "subject" of the quintet. Its staccato becomes legato; it curves upward as well as downward; it is agitated by a syncopated accompaniment; but it is still a relative of S.II. The recapitulation

* Compare the opening of the G major quartet and ponder the significance com-
pressed into this elementally simple device. Two whole regions of experience are
implied — one by the drop of B to Bb; the other by the splitting of G into the third,
F#–A and the drop of E to Eb. But these implications do not reside permanently in
these notes. They are *put there* — and not by skill but by imagination.

EXAMPLE 27. SCHUBERT QUINTET IN C MAJOR, OP. 163

(267), in part because of this development, is so altered as to be also developmental in purport.

The *Adagio* (E major, 12-8) begins with a theme in thirds, like the S.II of the first movement, whose warmth has a heavy undertone of weariness. Its pensive note is extraordinarily intensified by the persistent commentary of the first violin, in a figure like that which accompanied the S.II in the first movement, but now much expanded in meaning. The sustained but rather mild tension subsides toward the end of the section; but the tang of the subdominant is pretty strong (C♮, its minor 3rd, is frequent), giving mild warning of what is to come.

For pensiveness now turns black. Trilled E's rise to F♮; a loud syncopated rhythm in F minor begins (29), and the second 'cello's minatory triplets * strike that dark note even before violin and first 'cello declaim,

* Compare the figure given to the second viola in the *Adagio ma non troppo* of Mozart's G minor quintet (18f).

[151

in no uncertain tones, the acuteness of its pain. The hush of the transition back to the S.I is awesome, but when the tone of pensiveness is resumed (64) new figures in both violin and second 'cello surround it — musical graces, to be sure; but also the graces which, whether real or imaginal, make dark thought endurable.

The Scherzo (C major, *Presto*) strikes with intentional rudeness a plebeian note all but shocking at first contact. But once we have adjusted to its frank vigor it becomes not only exhilarating but patently akin to that broadening image of experience we have been envisaging. Its relativity will at least be affirmed by the extraordinary Trio — *Andante sostenuto*, in F minor, and in 4-4 time — whose declamatory recitation seems like a *memento mori*. (Wagner's inexorable trombones, portraying Fate in the *Ring*, may well have been suggested by bars 3 and 4 of the Trio.)

Quite appropriately the Finale (*Allegretto*, 2-2) begins in C minor, coloring thus the theme to make it somewhat akin, in character if not in design, to the Scherzo. Only after eighteen bars, with excursion into several keys, does it appear in its intended C major key. This shifting of tonalities is a persistent feature throughout the piece. The first phrase of the S.II (46) is almost Brahmsian, but its second lightly throws off that weight, and when the violins take it into higher register it becomes more buoyant still. The first phrase, adding the turn as ornament (110), quite loses weight and begins, like S.I, to shift its keys; but it has a warmly sonorous afterthought (127), *molto espressivo*, in the two 'celli. Then the viola, in octaves, outlines a gradual harmonic rise that brings the return of S.I (169). This is put through many developmental paces, presently jigging in a dotted rhythm so lively that it soon cannot choose but retard its pace for a moment. There is then a declension to a halt, and a recapitulation begins with S.II in C (268). The Coda is made of S.I, *più allegro*, then *più presto*, coming to a resounding cadence that expands the penultimate dominant 7th into a tense augmented 6th chord.

In the A minor and the D minor quartets, Schubert contrived concluding movements consonant with their preceding substance. In the G major, whose experiential reference is more obscure, he failed to do this, and the conclusion of the quintet, scrutinized from this angle, is itself not wholly successful, however great our delight as we listen. But the reference of its first three movements is to an even more indefinable (if more pleasurable) region of the mind. Schubert died at thirty-one. Have we any right to ask of him more than he gave?

Octet, Op. 166

This engaging piece, for clarinet, horn, bassoon, string quartet, and double bass, was written in 1824 at Steyr, on commission from Count Ferdinand Troyer, a competent clarinettist who was chief steward to Archduke Rudolph. It was written in February, finished on March 1st, and had a private performance later in the spring. Its first public performance was under the direction of Schuppanzigh, on April 16, 1827. Having six movements, the work suggests the eighteenth-century Divertimento; but there is no reversion to the superficial, merely entertaining purpose mostly aimed at in that form.

The first movement is a fully rounded sonata form. It begins with a quiet *Adagio* (F major, 4-4) whose dotted rhythm will rule in most of the *Allegro* to come. But the S.II of that movement is also anticipated, so that the *Adagio* is only the *Allegro* half-awakened. But a blither strain than the S.I would be hard to find. It is only the arpeggio of the F chord, but with a half-step thrust from below, always as propulsive up-beat, toward every note but the last, which is taken by a joyous leap.* The S.II (49), in the clarinet, begins in D minor. Its oft-repeated leaping 6th gives quite another lilt to the dotted rhythm, but maintains a high relativity in character. In the horn (60), for which the theme must have been first designed, since it is on "natural" notes, it acquires a most appropriate mellowness. But the 6ths, in the violins become 8ves (71) and then are narrowed to minor 2nds (77) without impairing the sense of the theme. But these minor 2nds are also the intervals of the thrusts in S.I, so that more than rhythmic continuity is suggested. Finality (the function of the Cl.S.) is suggested by the cadential figure in the violin (95) and the leaping G's (they sound as C's) in the horns in the next bar; but the actual close of the exposition is still pleasurably distant. The development, largely ruled by the dotted rhythm, suddenly remembers

* Compare the third theme in the first movement of the Kreutzer sonata (144), a considerably similar figuration of the E minor triad. The thrust-notes are all off-beat eighths; the propulsion, a hundred-fold more energetic, comes from the first three E's and their booming bass, and the character is so different that the comparison may seem strained. But it will strongly support our contention that the meaning of music lies in its portrayals of tension and motion, rather than in its structural patterns as such.

the introductory *Adagio* (183), a part of which, in augmented notation, makes approach to the recapitulation (203). The Coda (310) is in an eagerly hastened tempo, but it slows for the horn to bring a pleasant remembrance of S.II.

The second movement always seems to recall the *Ave Maria* which Schubert set to Ellen's prayer from Scott's *Lady of the Lake*. (The song was written in 1825. Whether this music suggested it is a question probably unanswerable.) The gentle theme is much enriched by added 3rds and by beautifully consonant counter-melody which, incidentally, cannot escape the infection of the dotted rhythm. The middle section is quite improvisatory, although it never wholly loses sight of the main idea. When the theme returns thereafter in the violin (78), the first sixteenth of the accompanying figure becomes two thirty-seconds — a tiny structural alteration, but suggestive out of all proportion to its size.

The Scherzo (*Allegro vivace*, F major, 3-4), if the analogy with the Divertimento is pursued, will seem a modernization of the Minuet. Its rhythm is rough and peasant-like, and it persists under the even flow of the new tune in the clarinet (51). The Trio, in C, is undotted throughout, but its placidity is enlivened by the 'cello's unbroken staccato.

The fourth movement (*Andante*, C major, 2-4) is a set of variations on a tune from a play with music by Mayrhofer which Schubert had composed in 1815. The variations are not abstruse. If such had been intended, another context and another theme would have been essential. The fifth variation is in C minor, but the persistent figure of thirty-seconds in second violin and viola excites (and is intended to excite) only a mild agitation. The sixth is a delicately woven tonal web in A flat, the key being a highly appropriate departure from convention. It gets back to C by adding an F♯ to the A flat triad and resolving it to G. The last variation (*un poco più mosso*) is brisk, disguising the theme in a shimmer of thirty-seconds in the first violin. These, in the Coda, become hardly more than a murmur beneath snippets from the theme ingeniously distributed among the winds and the first violin.

The fifth movement is a real Menuetto (F major, *Allegretto*), but it smacks more of the nineteenth century than of the eighteenth. The Trio, in B flat, makes much out of a triplet figure that was only an incident in the second half of the Menuetto.

The sixth movement begins in F minor (*Andante molto*, 4-4) with mock-heroic ejaculations in the rhythm (here double-dotted) of the first movement, ending with Schubert's favorite augmented 6th approach to the dominant of F. The ensuing *Allegro* (F major, 2-2) begins in the strings alone with what feels like a march, although our imaginary steps are confused when the first phrase turns out to have only three bars. The next has five, however, so that we go on happily to the four half note C's that compel the jubilant stomping end of the tune. The S.II (93) is on a two-bar phrase that hums quietly in 6ths or 3rds and then takes its first bar through more vigorous evolutions. But this first bar is rhythmically and melodically similar to the second bar of S.I, so that we really don't know which of the two themes we are hearing — or, indeed, whether the S.II isn't just another version of S.I. At any rate, we march right into a brief recall of the Introduction, made more flamboyant than ever by bravura passages in the violin, and so to the Coda, *Allegro molto* and *accelerando*, shouting at the top of its lungs at the mere joy of being alive.

Felix Mendelssohn-Bartholdy

1809-1847

MENDELSSOHN's chamber music, like all the rest of his output, is what might have been expected from a man of extraordinary talent, educated almost wholly by contact with the best things, the best people, and the best ideas to be found in his privileged world. He and his sister Fanny were not sent to school, but were taught at home by private tutors — the most competent available. Their teachers were strict, their lessons thoroughly learned, and their progress such that comparison with Mozart and his sister was inevitable.

Felix's taste, thus stimulated from above, was highly exclusive, for stimulation from below was neither offered nor, in all probability, countenanced. The excellence toward which he aimed, and which he pursued all his life with indefatigable zeal, was thus so clearly defined that he was repelled by anything incompatible with the principles he had all but unconsciously learned to accept. He championed his ideals valiantly within the growing circle of admirers which his talent and his urbanity attracted; but from opposition arising outside that circle (i.e., from below) he retreated after the first shot.

His music reflects this disposition. It is a model of design and of discrimination in color; but its objective is pleasure, and it shuns the deeper reaches of pain. He never suffered the obsession that drove Beethoven and Schubert to their most exalted discoveries, and Heine showed keen penetration when, after paying tribute to Mendelssohn's undoubted abilities, he spoke of his most salient characteristic as a "passionate indifference." *

* Wir bewundern bei diesem Meister zumeist sein grosses Talent für Form, für Stilistik, sein Begabnis, sich das Ausserordentlichste anzueignen, seine reizend schöne

Being a brilliant pianist, Mendelssohn wrote his most effective (but not on that account his best) chamber music for combinations involving that instrument. There are three piano quartets (Opp. 1, 2, and 3); a sextet (1824, published later as Op. 110) for piano, violin, two violas, 'cello, and bass; two sonatas for piano and 'cello, Opp. 45 and 58; and two trios, Op. 49, in D minor and Op. 66, in C Minor. Only the trios have any current favor, and we shall begin with those, ignoring the others.

The D minor trio opens with a broad theme in the 'cello (*Molto allegro ed agitato*, 3-4) which is expanded in the violin and completed in the piano doubled by the strings. The piano then finds a more excited rhythm (40f) which, without forgetting the S.I, makes a brilliant interlude before the S.II (118) — a well-sounding, rather placid theme, announced by the 'cello and amplified by the other instruments. An agitated triplet-figure in the piano signals the coming close of the exposition, which is not repeated. The development begins (186) with the S.I in A minor and dutifully manipulates this and the other themes without adding much to their significance. The recapitulation (368) is much shortened and there is a brief Coda, *assai animato*. The piano part is very scintillant, and is difficult to manage without outshining the strings.

The *Andante con moto tranquillo* (B flat, 4-4) is exquisitely modeled in every detail. Its main theme seems haunted by that of the *Adagio* of Beethoven's violin sonata in C minor. The S.II, in B flat minor (32), heightens the tension somewhat but it hardly disturbs the ruling tranquillity. More than any other of Mendelssohn's slow movements, it sums up for this commentator the undercurrent of his genteel philosophy. The Scherzo (D major, *Leggiero e vivace*) is so far dominated by the chipper little tune that is its main theme that nothing else stands out in contrast. If you hunt for it, however, you can discover an S.II (28); the S.I returns, in rondo fashion (47), but is developed extensively with no sign of an S.III; and there is a recapitulation (118) with a Cl.S. (hinted at in the development at 105f, but really cadential from 157) so that this is an approximation to sonata form. There is no Trio.

Faktur, sein feines Eidechsenohr, seine zarten Fühlhörner und seine ernsthafte, ich möchte fast sagen passionierte Indifferenz. (We admire in this master chiefly his great talent for form, for style, his ability to master the most exceptional difficulties, his charmingly beautiful structure, his fine "lizard-ear," his delicate tentacles, and his earnest, I might almost say passionate indifference.) (*Musikalische Berichte aus Paris*, Paris, April 25, 1844.)

The Finale (*Allegro assai appassionato*, D minor, 4-4) is less impassioned than the superscription implies. The S.I has a somewhat sinister undertone; the S.II (53) offers only a slight contrast, retaining somewhat the dactylic rhythm of the S.I. The S.III (142) is a broad theme in the 'cello, gratefully liquefied by a triplet figure of accompaniment. The sonata-rondo form is wholly lucid and the brilliance, not only of this movement but of the whole trio, makes it one of the most effective pieces in the repertoire. The sense of intimacy, however, is hardly awakened.

That sense is more apparent in the second trio, Op. 66, in C minor. It is tinged with the character that seems for so many composers to inhere in that key. The S.I (*Allegro energico e con fuoco*, C minor, 4-4) is at first only a restless figure of arpeggio, but it acquires a sober melodic complement (22) with accompanying sixteenths derived freely from the opening figure. The S.II (62), more lyrical, has a patently kindred tension. Its rhythm also generates the brief and properly inconspicuous Cl.S. (87). The development begins with canonic imitation on the opening figure; the melodic complement is then dwelt upon, as is the S.II, perhaps too expansively for the incisiveness which the actual thought seems to demand. Canon on the opening figure again marks the recapitulation (221), and there is much — perhaps too much — comment thereafter.

The mellifluous *Andante espressivo* (E flat, 9-8) is hardly accordant with the implications of the first movement. The somewhat more burdened S.II begins in E flat minor (39) but it cadences in G flat, and the swifter sixteenths in the accompaniment do not much mitigate the monotony of the too-undulant rhythm. The Scherzo (*Molto allegro, quasi presto*, G minor, 2-4) is a nervous *moto perpetuo* whose excitement fluctuates interestingly above and below the norm of tension set at the beginning. There is a short trio in G major, all well below that norm. The Finale (*Allegro appassionato*, C minor, 6-8) begins with an upward-leaping minor 9th in the 'cello whose implication of passion is at once overridden by the lilting scale-descent that completes the phrase. The S.II (50) is buoyant but not impassioned. The S.III (128) has a curious resemblance to the chorale-like phrase scintillantly ornamented in Chopin's C sharp minor Scherzo. This, in C, begins the brilliant Coda.

The String Quartets

The temptation to brilliancy, into which Mendelssohn's fleet fingers inevitably led him when the piano was involved, was absent or was effectively resisted in his writing for strings. He left six quartets, two quintets, and an octet. Two of the quartets are early (Op. 12, 1829; Op. 13, in A minor, 1827); three are "middle-period" works (Op. 44, No. 1, 1838; No. 2, in E minor, 1837; No. 3, in E flat, 1838); one is "late" (Op. 80, in F minor, 1847). As often with Mendelssohn, the later works show an increasing mastery of some details of structure, but reveal little widening of his musical horizon. (For example, the *Midsummer Night's Dream* overture was written in 1826. The remaining numbers are seventeen years later; but, with the exception of the *Notturno*, they show no real imaginative advance.*) Indeed, if we were right in thinking intimacy to be a primary value of chamber music, the earlier works have more of the virtue than the later. We shall choose but two for comment.

The substance of the E flat quartet, Op. 12, is indeed not weighty, but it is wholly genuine and unpretentious. The first movement, after a brief Introduction (*Adagio non troppo*, E flat, 4-4), presents its two quiet, not highly contrasted themes (*Allegro non tardante*) in a manner wholly in accord, both with tradition and with their gracious, well-bred, and really sentient character. The texture is not polyphonic, but neither is it pianistic; the development is not very exciting, but it would be false to the thematic substance if it were; and the whole impression is that of a simple experience which turns out to be memorable far beyond its promise.

Instead of a Scherzo, a *Canzonetta* follows — a dainty little tune in G minor (*Allegretto*, 2-4), whose charm is displayed without any bedizenment of virtuosity. The equivalent of a Trio follows (*più mosso*, G major) — a sort of oblique variant of the *Canzonetta*, to which a simple *unisono* bridge makes return. The *Andante espressivo* (B flat, 3-4) is quite Victorian in its gentility, and it enhances that character by giving a feminine ending to almost every phrase. An unexpected vehemence of recitation arises out of its *largo* continuing strain, provoking a somewhat agitated comment on the main theme, whose original quietude is never restored. The Finale (*Molto allegro e vivace*, E flat, 12-8) begins in C minor with a scamper in the general character of the tarantelle; this is sobered into a quiet strain (*dolce tranquillo*, 130); the scamper begins again and becomes a violent *unisono* as the exposition ends. A new theme, which may be seen as S.III in a sonata-rondo form, begins the development, which brings back the S.I in E flat but also develops it somewhat.

* Compare the original and the "Paris" versions of the *Tannhäuser* overture. (The interval is two years shorter.)

The new theme also returns, and its 4-4 time rules to the end, recalling, in contrast to the bustle of the tarantelle, the quietude of the first movement.

The quartet in D, Op. 44, No. 1, is more accordant with our usual image of Mendelssohn. It begins (*Allegro vivace*, 4-4) with an excited, firmly rhythmed swoop on the arpeggio of the tonic chord. The phrase-end is unfortunately only a Mozartian, trumpet-and-drumming cliché (4) — a perfunctory completion of the really buoyant energy of the first two bars. (Mendelssohn may have sensed this, for the drumming plays little part in the development.) A swerving figure follows (13) which, after a return of the S.I, will introduce and form a part of the S.II (59) — a thought considerably tinged with the vitality of the main theme. The S.II is the chief topic of the development until the S.I reappears (166) revealing itself in many new aspects. The recapitulation (230) adds little to the discourse.

A suave Menuetto follows, also in D, singularly lacking in rhythmic impulse. Its Trio is mainly given over to a flow of eighth notes in the first violin, which figure also yields the Coda. The slow movement (*Andante espressivo ma con moto*, B minor, 2-4) has a really poignant theme, very simple and appropriately accompanied by a counterpoint in the second violin with pizzicato chords below. The S.II (37), in D major, is only slightly contrasted. The lapse into D minor at its second bar is an impressive stroke. Seldom does Mendelssohn speak as intimately as he does here. The Finale (*Presto con brio*, D major, 12-8) is rather orchestral in texture, the brief motives of its S.I being set off by intervening *unisono* fanfares, and its whole impression of lively bustle rather annoying after the truer contemplation of the *Andante*. Its S.II (60), like the continuation of S.I, is a pleasant descending line. Altogether, little is accomplished beyond a conventional happy ending.

The String Quintets

There are two string quintets — Op. 18, in A (1826) and Op. 87, in B flat (1845). The first is singularly amiable. Written in the same year as the *Midsummer Night's Dream* overture, it is similarly well-proportioned and well-textured; and, like the string quartet in E flat and other early works, it offers a genuine invitation to intimacy. The engaging S.I of the first movement (*Allegro con moto*, A major, 3-4), minuet-like in rhythm, is followed by a more animated figure of transition (35) which proves so fruitful in interest that the S.II's entrance (80) is long delayed. That theme, however, is of little consequence, and the Cl.S. (102) is only an offshoot of it. The development is thus naturally mostly concerned with the S.I, which it really amplifies. The movement is perhaps overlong, but if you allow its serene mood to rule your attention you will not become impatient.

An Intermezzo follows (*Andante sostenuto*, F major, 3-4). Its main theme, quite undisturbed at the outset, makes toward intensity (17) but subsides for the C major S.II (26). When the S.I returns, however (42), it really speaks out, evoking rather significant development. The rest is repetition, more highly ornamented. The Scherzo (*Allegro di molto*, D minor, 2-4) has a mock-serious theme, exposed fugally and maintained as a *moto perpetuo*, except for a few grateful breath-pauses, without either S.II or Trio. The Finale (*Allegro vivace*, A major, 2-4) has a glittering surface but a more perfunctory gaiety.

The second quintet, written nineteen years later, abandons the appeal to intimacy, but is otherwise hardly more mature. Its S.I (*Allegro vivace*, B flat, 4-4) spurred by tremolando harmonies, has little inner strength. Neither is the S.II (53) more convincing. The *Andante scherzando* (G minor, 6-8) was perhaps intended to be less naive than it seems. But the following *Adagio e lento* (D minor, 2-4) strikes a genuine note of somberness, at first subdued but becoming stern with the S.II (17), whose compelling rhythm supports a strain as nearly tortured as any Mendelssohn ever penned. A gentle episode in A (30) offers a welcome alleviation, leading to the return of S.I; but that theme is now nearly shorn of its character by the graceful triplet figurations that adorn it. The shuddering tremolando harmony beneath its last return (79) smacks of the melodramatic, and the D major Coda thus seems rather like the apparition of a *deus ex machina*. The Finale (B flat, 4-4, *Allegro molto vivace*) enters bravely in the trappings and the suits of joy, but the real stimulus to festivity is not apparent.

The String Octet

The Octet, Op. 20 (1825) is the earliest of Mendelssohn's mature chamber works, and is perhaps the best of all. It is for four violins, two violas, and two 'celli — in substance, a doubled string quartet, but it is not so grouped. The first movement (*Allegro moderato ma con fuoco*, E flat, 4-4) begins with an exuberant theme, all on the notes of the tonic triad until the very end, but its eyes shine with genuine exhilaration that is maintained (somewhat abated in the episode, 21f) right up to the entrance of the S.II (68).* Even that theme, although naturally more sedate, is kept within the established expressive range by frequent interjections from S.I. The development begins on elongated strides of the S.I in the lower strings, and the vigor of the whole thought is enhanced by an apparently new motive (137). This, however, gets its second bar from the first episode (21), and those three quarter notes make transition to the development of the S.II (164). A stimulating *unisono* passage announces the recapitulation (216) which greatly shortens the exposition and adds a fiery Coda.

The *Andante* (C minor, 6-8) presents its thought in sharp focus by building its S.I out of a single motive. Triplet figures presently color the texture, with an exquisite sub-theme (29) emerging into the quiet streams of descending scale that form the S.II (41). Out of these things a beautifully rounded movement, always consistent with their implications, is built up.

The Scherzo, however, is the gem of the octet. It is in G minor (*Allegro leggierissimo*, 2-4), to be played *sempre pp e staccato*. Its slightly impudent eighth-note theme, with the mischievous sixteenths that accompany it and also form its pendant, is dismissed with soft woodpecker taps in thirty-seconds which, one cannot but regret, are never heard again. But there are other delightful things — the little march-tune that follows the taps; the sly four-note figure (65) that closes the section; and the trilled antic (113) made of the cadence of a sixteenth-note figure from the S.I (95). These are put together to form a sequence of breathless interest. Virtuosity is not demanded of the individual players, but the piece is nevertheless extremely difficult to put together.

The Finale (*Presto*, E flat, 2-2) begins with a four-bar fugue theme in the second 'cello that enters in rising succession in each of the other instruments. Its slightly clownish humor is heightened by the shortening of the entrance-interval when the theme reaches the violins. A stamping on half notes follows (33); the fugue theme comes back (51) accompanied by the stamping, now hastened to repeated eighths; another half-note phrase (73) begins to thump against it; a four-note scale-rise makes a new accompaniment for the stamping; fragments of these things are

* When it descends to the 'celli (9), the theme suggests that of the opening of Strauss's *Heldenleben*.

tossed about; the half-note phrase from bar 73 returns (133) and becomes conspicuous; a huge climax is built up, out of which the first violin emerges to make a solo transition; and at last the fugue theme returns (189), accompanied by a new, broad phrase which, if it persisted, might make this a double fugue. Instead, the fugue theme becomes (as it has before), a subordinate figuration; there are more combinations; and all at once the theme of the Scherzo turns up (273) to add to the jamboree.

Obviously, as has often been noted, there is a similarity between this piece and the Finale of Mozart's *Jupiter* symphony. You will hardly expect a sixteen-year-old boy to rival a thirty-two-year-old Mozart; but you will have to admit that the boy is a genius.

Robert Schumann

1810–1856

SCHUMANN's musical sensitivity, which in some lights will appear even keener than Mendelssohn's, was very differently nurtured. Not even Kuntzsch, his only music teacher in the little town of Zwickau where he grew up, had any true measure of its depth; and while it was fed by many cultural contacts (his father was a publisher), it underwent no formal discipline until he went to Leipzig (1831) to study law. He had shown, as a child, an exceptional knack for improvisation, and had begun to shape some of these fleeting musical images into little piano pieces and songs; but whereas, at seventeen, Mendelssohn had already acquired the skill that produced the *Midsummer Night's Dream* overture, Schumann had not even begun the study of harmony or counterpoint or the principles of musical form. His father's death in 1826 deprived him of the surest support he had so far enjoyed for his musical education.

His mother, overindulgent of his many weaknesses but determined that he should *not* pursue the disgraceful career of professional musician, was finally convinced of her error by Friedrich Wieck, the teacher with whom he began serious study in Leipzig. But Robert soon ruined his prospects as pianist by the use of a mechanism he designed for equalizing the strength of his fingers, and composition became in consequence his primary interest. This study, directed by Heinrich Dorn, was desultory, but he was awakened to the significance of structure. He presently turned to Bach who proved, in the long run, to be his most informative teacher. No other romanticist — not Mendelssohn himself — discovered so clearly that strange addition to the vitality of even a conventional chord which comes from the melodic leading of component voices into and away from that chord.

Both his improvisatory genius and his novel use of polyphony — not only in the Bachian patterns of canon, fugue, etc., but in the contriving of enriched, more modern harmony — contributed greatly to the interest of his chamber music. He began with this genre only in 1842, after having established a distinctive style of writing for the piano (1830–1840), a considerable competence (by no means as assured as Mendelssohn's) in orchestral writing (1840), and a most percipient manner, akin to that of chamber music, of wedding vocal melody to an accompaniment which, as much as the melody itself, portrayed the inner sense of the verbal text (1841).

The Violin Sonatas

Following our established plan, we must notice briefly the two sonatas with violin. They were both written in 1851, in a period of what is generally recognized as declining power. The first, in A minor, Op. 105, is for piano and violin; the second, in D minor, Op. 121, is for violin and piano. This often unnoticed distinction is not without a difference. Hitherto, in the duet sonata, the piano had been recognized as the principal part; in the D minor sonata the violin assumes that role; but as yet the virtuoso manner is avoided.

The surging main theme of the A minor sonata is very characteristic of Schumann, and the whole first movement maintains its level without lapse. The slow movement is brief and very suggestive — a song without words so vivid that if the violin part were within a singer's range the poets of the day would surely have tried to contrive a text for it, as they did for the wonderful *Abendlied*, originally written for piano duet. The last movement is chiefly on a lively figure, often imitatively treated, and quite captivating; but the violin part — to the eye quite unassuming — poses such awkward problems for the left hand that the sonata is seldom played.

The D minor sonata is much longer and more imposing in idea, but the thought is diffuse and the structure (perhaps on that account) so repetitive that the mind, if not the ear, is wearied.

The Trios

There are three piano trios. Two were written in 1847, the third in 1851. Although Schumann's severe illness beginning in August, 1848, is regarded as the first step in the mental derangement that finally overwhelmed him, the first of these trios, Op. 63, in D minor, has all the elasticity of his youthful works, but shows also the mastery yielded by his arduous self-instruction.

It begins (*Mit Energie und Leidenschaft*, D minor, 4-4) with a compelling theme in the violin — two three-bar phrases, nearly identical but so connected and so harmonized that the repetition is all but imperceptible. The musical substance is buoyantly active, the tension of the diminished 3rd giving it urgency and the rolling arpeggios of the accompaniment, with their firm but never stolid bass, completing the musical image of unleashed passion implied in the superscription. There is a short, derived interlude, then a repetition of the theme with an abrupt cadence, making way for the transition — no mere bridge, but a sharper definition of the already abundant energy. The S.II (25) in the piano, less tense than the S.I but no less eager, is repeated in the violin against its canonic imitation in 'cello and piano, and eventuates in a mingling of the two themes to close the exposition. All this is accomplished in fifty-four bars.

The development varies these things interestingly, subsiding, on the march-rhythm of the bridge, to an expectant pause (82). Our expectation is met by a quite new theme, high in the piano in tripletted chords, soft-pedaled. To this both violin and 'cello, whistling *sul ponticello*, play an almost eerie bass.* The development, making much of this interpolation, is extended. The recapitulation (162) thereafter is a welcome rehearsal of the exposition. The Coda (211) pointedly brings back the chorale theme just before the end.

A Scherzo follows, in F major, 3-4, labeled only *Lebhaft, doch nicht zu rasch* (Lively, but not too fast). Like the first movement, it is buoyant and energetic, but there is no tragic undertone. The Trio flows and flows, on the smoothest of undulant scale-waves, and makes an almost unforeseen return to the Scherzo.

The slow movement, *Langsam, mit inniger Empfindung* (Slow, with intimate feeling), is in A minor, 4-4. It begins with a ruminant theme to which the 'cello (10) makes eloquent answer. The harmonies are somber and tense, with the diminished 3rd again in evidence. The middle section,

---

* This new theme, chorale-like, resembles more than faintly that of Schubert's song, *Der Kreuzzug*. A monk watches from his barred window the embarcation of a regiment of Crusaders. His heart's desire is to go with them, but his vows forbid. He half consoles himself with the reflection that life is itself a crusade into the promised land; but all that his voice can utter, beneath the chorale in the accompaniment, is a stiff and imprisoned bass.

in F major, somewhat faster and animated by a triplet rhythm, sings with more abandon. The first section then returns, somewhat shortened, and leads without pause to the Finale (*Mit Feuer*, D major, 2-2).

If you had fears, during the slow movement, that the composer's powers were waning, you will be at once reassured. The S.I is full-throated and joyous with a steady, exuberant tonal flow in the piano supporting the theme whose drive, not spurred by dotted rhythms, is big with latent energy. An alternative strain (17) with a more released vigor, leads to a repetition of the theme in the unexpected key of F, but the continuation returns it to D. Without transition the S.II appears (59) — very quiet, moving almost scale-wise and in even quarter notes, but still exuberant. A hint of S.I (67) appears for a moment against it, but the culmination is on the vigorous alternative to S.I. A more active figure (121) is interestingly combined with both main themes; a sort of horn-call is added (171); out of the turmoil the S.I returns, but in G. It is quite excitingly fragmented, patently as an approach to its original form and key for the recapitulation (257). The Coda, continually hastened, gives quick glimpses of all the themes.

The other two trios, although shaped by the same skilled hand, are less significant. The second, Op. 80, in F, is from the same year as the first. Its opening motive (*Sehr lebhaft*, 6-8), with its determined convergence on the tonic and its energy enhanced by dissonant harmonies over a propulsive rising bass, promises a highly stimulating musical adventure. That promise is not kept. Already at the end of the theme (8) its vigor has waned; repetition of the more pregnant opening, in B flat, cannot effectively revive it; the apparent S.II (52) has little individuality; the songful Cl.S. (106) is pleasant to hear but, like King Charles II, is "an unconscionable time a-dying." The development (135) soon abandons the virile beginning for a rather factitious excitement, generated out of the continuation of that theme, staccato, together with a new theme in long notes (155) imitatively treated, and it ends with a long discussion of the Cl.S. The recapitulation (274) mercifully omits that theme until the end of the accelerated Coda, but the promise is still not kept.

The slow movement, *Mit innigem Ausdruck* (with intimate expression), D flat, 4-4, is romantically songful but with more intensity than depth. The third movement, *In mässiger Bewegung* (moderate speed), B flat minor, 3-8, is an interesting anticipation of the sort of Intermezzo that Brahms will often substitute for a Scherzo. The Finale, *Nicht zu rasch* (not too fast), F major, 2-2, has a vague and indecisive S.I — the musical embodiment, no doubt, of an image suggestive but not clearly focused; and the rest of the movement, interesting enough in its contrapuntal ingenuities, still fails to achieve purposeful coherence.

The third trio, Op. 110, is dedicated to Niels Gade. It seems, to this commentator, possibly a sort of musical characterization, such as Schumann used to improvise as a child, of that amiable composer. The graceful sweep of the S.I (*Bewegt, doch nicht zu rasch*, G minor, 6-8) is accompanied by a similar figuration, and this sort of motion, supporting also the less active S.II, rules the whole movement. The second movement, *Ziemlich langsam* (rather slow), E flat, 12-8, is in a related mood but is quite short, so that the mild contrast of the middle section in 9-8 suffices to maintain the attention. The next (*Rasch*, C minor, 2-4) is the most individual movement in the trio. It is again Intermezzo-like, with a sort of conscious naivety that is quite charming. The last is marked *Kräftig* (vigorous), *mit Humor* (G major, 4-4). *Humor* does not imply comicality, but rather capricious mood. To our vision, this is no better realized than is the uncertain character of the Finale of the second trio.

Two larger works with piano remain to be studied — the piano quartet, Op. 47, and the piano quintet, Op. 41. These and the string quartets were all composed in 1842. Never had the flame of Schumann's genius burned brighter than in this year. It was fed, no doubt, by the consciousness of acquired mastery, gained by the composition of more than a hundred songs in 1840, and of two whole symphonies and the *Overture, Scherzo and Finale* in 1841. But by the end of the year (the piano quartet dates from December, 1842) the flame had begun to burn itself out, and signs of the mental illness that was to overwhelm him were evident not long after.

The Piano Quartet, Op. 47

The quartet begins with a brief Introduction (*Sostenuto assai*, E flat, 4-4) in which the main motives of the principal theme of the following *Allegro ma non troppo* (2-2) are broadly set forth. They there take on a new brightness, but still retain their romantic warmth. Schumann's warning, *sempre con molto sentimento*, is observed in the piano's short solo passages between the motives, but it is more fully felt when the 'cello (36) begins a lyric expansion of the first motive. Thereafter the

S.I returns, and with no other transition the S.II appears (64) — a sharply rhythmed scale-figure, begun in the piano and imitated in the strings. But the imitations are soon given wholly to the piano, the first of the motives from S.I appearing against them incidentally in the violin. These things form the only topic thereafter, and the exposition closes with a return of the *Sostenuto*. The development begins with the S.I in D minor; its four-note figure then makes a sonorous dialogue between piano and strings into which fragments of the piano's solo passages are interjected, and these figures, *unisono* in the strings, at length make exciting return to the recapitulation. This, somewhat condensed, ends with a brief reference to the Introduction. The Coda, *più agitato*, sums up lyrically the chief sense of the movement.

The Scherzo (*molto vivace*, G minor, 3-4) is crisp and brittle, on a theme that begins *unisono* in piano and 'cello and later appears in canon. It sounds a little gruff at first, but it sparkles pleasantly when it rises to higher register. There are two Trios, the first on a smooth legato theme still in G minor and also imitative. The first section of the second is all on antiphonal chords, syncopated by tying "three" to "one, two," with never a down-beat to identify the "one." Yet a careful performance (of course in absolutely strict time) will make it float in the air, as the notation suggests.

The *Andante cantabile* (B flat, 3-4) begins with a passionate song in the 'cello that is the very essence of the romanticism of Schumann's day. After a repetition in the violin, the piano comes to the fore with a blurred, syncopated variant of the melody — the only imaginable version of it that the piano could utter in competition with the strings. Then there is an interlude in G flat (4-4), more soberly contemplative, but with much inner warmth. Thereafter the song returns in the viola beneath arabesques in the violin; violin and viola make a canonic duet on it; it returns to the 'cello against low, soft harmony, murmured in sixteenths in the piano and sustained in the strings; and there is a Coda whose B flat pedal bass is sounded in the octave by the 'cello, its C string having been tuned down a whole step.

The Finale (*Vivace*, E flat, 3-4), although it is well made, often exciting, and sometimes moving, adds little to the impression made by the foregoing movements. An opening fanfare yields to a warm 'cello theme (22); a kindred phrase is added (38); the S.II (93) is in contrast all staccato, working up to lively imitations on the fanfare. A third theme in

A flat, smooth and flowing, is welcome to the ear but seems hardly pertinent to the discourse. It does not recur. The rest is essentially recapitulation, varied and ingenious, but hardly more.

The Piano Quintet, Op. 41

The piano quintet, composed in September and October, is the most popular of all the piano quintets in existence. Music more abundantly joyous could hardly be imagined; but this springs from a deeper well than does the merely joyous. The beginning (*Allegro brilliante*, E flat, 2-2) is on incisive, half-note strokes whose exuberance captures the ear from the first note. The piano, in gentler interludes, expands the sense of the theme and paves the way to the S.II (57) — a tender dialogue between 'cello and viola which the violins presently enrich with appropriate harmonic color. The main theme returns to close the exposition. The development, begun in obscurity, is soon cleared. The third and fourth bars of the S.I, made into one bar by diminution, yields a figure in the piano which modulates far afield, growing to a resumption of the main theme to begin the recapitulation. The only variant from the exposition is a short but vivid Coda.

In the second movement (*In modo d'una Marcia. Un poco largamente*, C minor, 2-2) the funereal suggestion is ineluctable; yet the quality of sadness is somehow not burdensome. As in the great March in the *Eroica*, its second strain is in C major, and its warmth is enhanced by a blurring of the rhythm of the accompaniment (triplets of quarter notes in the piano against even eighths in second violin and viola). The March returns, followed by a Trio (*agitato*) in F minor, at first violent, in triplet figures that become imitatively tangled but are later subdued to a murmur, against which the viola hoarsely recalls the March. The former continuing strain follows, now differently colored, and in F. Then the March comes back, impressively, in the first violin, the lower strings sounding the harmony in a dull pizzicato. (Schumann did not mark staccato the piano's doubling of these chords, but he surely must have intended it.)

The Scherzo (E flat, *molto vivace*, 6-8) shows what an elemental joy there is in a purposeful scale. There is really nothing else here than the scale and the thud of it as it reaches its goal, but the interest never lags. There are two trios — the first, quiet, with undulant arpeggioed triads for accompaniment; the second, in A minor (2-4), a fidgety *moto per-*

petuo with an occasional hint of the Scherzo's scales against its incessant sixteenths. The Scherzo naturally returns thereafter.

In contrast to the Finale of the piano quartet, this one is an incredible addition to the already rich offering of the preceding movements. It begins in C minor (which we are perhaps to take as the submediant of E flat) with an incisive theme, akin to the opening of the first movement but more active still, forcefully struck out of the piano against thick harmony in the strings. Its more sonorous pendant (21) is a perfect complement. The S.II (44), in G major, is a derivative (by rhythmic diminution) of the pendant. Against it the viola (52) finds another phrase that presently takes over altogether and prepares for a brief but vivid recall of the S.I in E minor. A broad rhythm of half notes with one half bar in triplet quarters (95f) follows the recall.

There is now a low murmur in the piano against which the viola (98) begins to remember the transition to S.II. When it has got hold of the whole phrase (115), the first violin finds a new melody in the half-note rhythm of 95f to play against it. The transition-phrase, however, predominates and marches straight to a recall of the S.I in C sharp minor (136). This is really a recapitulation, but it evokes another joyous tune (224) beautifully blurred by Schumann's favorite trick of syncopation, that would appear as Cl.S. to the sonata form it completes if it had also ended the exposition. It will have that function, by and by. But there is first a Coda to this sonata form. The S.I in the piano becomes the theme of a fugato to which the second violin supplies a counter-subject; then the transition-figure from 52, in the strings, is again combined with the broad theme from 115, now in the piano; and a tremendous climax arises which appears about to end the piece.

But it ends on an expectant dissonance, and the real Coda of the whole movement follows. The pianist's right hand whacks out the S.I *of the first movement*; his left hand and the second violin play against it the S.I of the Finale; the other instruments make of the same stuff a resounding fugue that reaches its peak (378) on a ritard; then, *piano*, comes the syncopated Cl.S., growing also to a tumultuous conclusion on the main theme. For sheer joyousness, this piece has hardly its counterpart.

The String Quartets

Schumann's three string quartets, his only essays in this form, were all written in the first half of 1842. He had made intensive studies of

Haydn and Mozart in preparation for the effort, but there is no imitation of his models. Coming from so original a mind they are naturally unorthodox in form. His musical images were from the first (as may be seen from his early piano pieces) pretty directly generated out of experience; the development of a musical idea was for him the pursuit of that image (to be sure, in its musical rather than its programmatic guise); and the accommodation of such imagery to the more abstract design of the sonata form was always an awkward structural problem.

The first of the quartets to be written (Op. 41, No. 2) is a vivid illustration of his manner of dealing with the problem. Its main theme *Allegro vivace*, F major, 3-4) has all the élan of the early Schumann; he develops it fascinatingly, and is so absorbed with it that he can find neither the substance nor the place for a second theme; the Cl.S. (68f) begins the development, but soon has to yield to the main theme and its derivatives, so that the recapitulation is without its proper emphasis as summation, and there is only a long series of chords, artificially alternating *f* and *p*, for Coda.

The gentle song that is the theme of the *Andante, quasi Variazioni* (A flat, 12-8) is too long to be varied systematically (hence the *quasi*). The Scherzo (*Presto*, E flat, 6-8) rephrases interestingly its basic pattern of six eighth notes and, like the variations, finds many colorful modulations. Its Trio (C major, 2-4) is a welcome relief from the persistent triplet feeling of the *Andante* and the Scherzo. The Finale (*Allegro molto vivace*, F major, 2-4) begins with a light-footed patter of sixteenths that recalls the Finale of the B flat symphony. Its S.II is again the Cl.S., and forms the basis of much of the development, which, by comparison with the exposition, is disproportionately long. This seems to us to explain why this quartet, in spite of its many interesting moments, is seldom performed.

The second quartet to be written is that published as No. 3. It is much more orthodox in form than the F major — which may account for its popularity. It begins with a short Introduction (*Andante espressivo*, A major, 4-4) in which the main theme of the following *Allegro molto moderato* (3-4) is hinted at — the hint being the descending 5th with which that theme begins. This is an ingratiating curve, maintaining its added-6th dissonance for three bars before its resolution on the tonic. The continuing strain is an even simpler two-bar phrase, yielding appealing tensions as it is imitated, bar after bar, in downward succession. The

S.I, returning, also proves imitable, but this device is not pursued. The S.II, in the 'cello (46), complements rather than contrasts with the S.I. A passage of higher tension, *ritenuto*, and a brief recall of S.I end the exposition. The development, short and rather perfunctory, is all on the S.I, so that the recapitulation begins (154) with the S.II. A tiny Coda (206) recalls the main theme once, builds up its characteristic descending 5th, and subsides. You may not have received the pleasure that a strongly designed sonata form offers, but you will feel that you have participated in a significant experience.

The second movement (*Assai agitato*, F sharp minor, 3-8) is the most original in idea of the four. Its timid, hurried theme, all in detached, syncopated phrases, becomes the basis of a set of variations, each one an unexpected response to the troubled experience whose import you can gather from the theme. The first variation, curt and driving, gives the lead to the 'cello, then to the viola, with brief continuing phrases in the violins. The second, in 2-4, makes a fugue-subject out of the theme and exposes it with almost furious energy. The third (*Un poco Adagio*, 3-8), turning the theme into a continuous instead of a broken line, imitated between first violin and viola, makes its intrinsic shyness more visible. The last (*Tempo risoluto*, 3-4) angrily brushes away the tear that almost spilled over and then adds a quiet epilogue, mostly in F sharp major.

These quartets were dedicated to Mendelssohn. The beginning of the *Adagio molto* (D major, 4-4), with its quiet reserve and its persistent feminine phrase-ends, sounds like a conscious adoption of that master's manner. The alternative strain in the viola (8), however, is quite another matter. It evokes an altered version of the main theme, expanding its cadence into a long sequential descent. A dotted rhythm begins, with portentous phrases above and below it; the main theme's first phrase, in A minor, and the viola's alternative become big with tension; the tramping of the dotted rhythm grows funereal; and all at once the main theme, against a fluid triplet figuration, emerges in all its original quietude. The dotted rhythm begins again, and all this is repeated in higher register. The Coda is a fading of the scene against the dotted rhythm, all on a pedal D.

The Finale begins (*Allegro molto e vivace*, A major, 2-2) with what seems to this commentator another Mendelssohnian phrase — a gay jingle, quite superficial, and out of accord with all the foregoing impressions.

[173

It halts abruptly (14) for a more Schumannesque strain which may be taken as the S.II in a free rondo form. The jingle returns and a third theme, in F sharp minor, appears (49) with the jingle again its outcome. Then follows another section marked *Quasi Trio*, in F major and in a graceful gavotte rhythm. All these things recur thereafter, the jingle yielding an extended Coda.

The quartet in A minor, Op. 41, No. 1, was the last of the three to be composed. It begins with a rather extended Introduction (*Andante*, 2-4) whose musing theme has a gentle melancholy very characteristic of Schumann. The *Allegro* following is in F major (6-8) — a departure from orthodoxy, but quite forgivable, for it imparts a warmth to the S.I, which might otherwise seem a little dull. But there is real, if quiet, urgency in the elastic lift of its first two bars and in the "squeeze" of the ensuing syncopations with their unmarked down-beat; and this little fact of feeling, amplified by higher tension and varied harmonization as the theme is repeated, turns out to be the topic of the whole movement. For the upward 4th, replacing the upward 3rd in the cadence of the theme (72), immediately becomes the S.II; and there is no other matter save the little interlude (50), rather extendedly developed, in the whole piece.

After so quiet a first movement, the Scherzo naturally follows. It begins (*Presto*, A minor, 6-8) with a couple of drum-taps that introduce and piquantly accompany the theme — a four-bar figure in which gaiety is somewhat less subdued than in the first movement. Again there is no contrasting theme. An Intermezzo (C major, 2-2) serves as Trio. The *Adagio* (D minor, 4-4) begins with an arpeggio figure in the 'cello, recitational in tone, which both announces the mood of the movement and supports its upward-looking melody — a theme whose resemblance to that of the Adagio in Beethoven's Ninth symphony is clear. There follows an intenser interlude and a return to the theme. The theme of the Finale (*Presto*, A minor, 2-2) has a gavotte-like up-beat measure, and that rhythm, highly activated, governs the whole exhilarating piece. Even the *Moderato* interlude before the Coda broadens the same rhythm, first into quarters and eighths, then, still perceptibly, into whole notes.

These quartets, as first essays in a very exacting species of composition, are certainly a remarkable effort. One cannot but regret that he did not pursue it further.

Johannes Brahms

1833–1897

BRAHMS's musical education, like Mendelssohn's, was directed from above. Unlike Mendelssohn's, it was mingled with many strong influences from below. Brahms's father was a hack performer on horn, viola, and double bass who had — until his son enabled him to glimpse it — no notion of the possible range and depth of musical art. But he was bluntly honest; and his rather diffident son, adopting that attitude as the best policy even in matters of art, pursued it doggedly, sometimes to his great material disadvantage.

He was a docile student, executing the disciplinary tasks which Cossel and Marxsen, his masters in piano and composition, set him, with fewer mental reservations as to their value than are common in some talented youth. He felt in consequence little kinship with the "futurists" (Liszt and Wagner); but he found in Schumann, in 1853, a kindred spirit. For beneath that surface which Marxsen had so carefully polished lay a musical nature as ineradicably romantic as Schumann's. Quite romantically, Schumann attempted (in the famous article, "New Paths") to launch him in the musical world as a kind of Messiah who should redeem musical art from the sinful state into which the futurists were leading it.

That article was really a grievous error of judgment. It elevated the young man to a position which he knew he was as yet unable to fill. Yet the ideal implied in it was precisely his own, and he could not but try to live up to the prospectus. Much aid came from the great violinist, Joseph Joachim, two years his senior, who had already proved his own ability as composer. The two undertook a course of musical self-education, sending each other, weekly, counterpoint problems for correction. Joachim soon recognized Brahms's superiority, even though his skill was as yet inferior to his own; but his support continued and was of the utmost practical as well as critical value.

Brahms continued his studies alone, gaining ultimately such a command of compositional technique — but within an area far more restricted than that of the futurists — as only the greatest masters, Bach, Mozart, and Beethoven, had possessed. How far these studies impeded his native imagination is a question to which no certain answer can be given. That there was an impediment can hardly be doubted. It is most visible in the works of the late 'fifties and early 'sixties, when such themes as that which yielded the Handel Variations are tussled with.* But it is less evident in the chamber works than elsewhere, and even this brief sketch of Brahms's preparation will suggest, as his career amply proved, that chamber music was the type of utterance most congenial to his nature.

The Duet Sonatas

There are seven duet sonatas, all for piano: three with violin, two with 'cello, and two with clarinet. All except the first 'cello sonata are late works.

The first of the violin sonatas, that in G, Op. 78, is not his first essay in that form. Schumann, in 1853, had recommended one (unknown thereafter) for publication by Breitkopf & Haertel; two others, whose composition Gustav Jenner certifies, also fell a victim to that relentless self-criticism which was Brahms's inveterate habit. The sonata in G was written in 1878, after the first two symphonies had at least tentatively proved the validity of Schumann's prophecy. His early struggles for fame and bread were now over; he was able to enjoy a delightful summer residence at Pörtschach; and the resultant spiritual calm is reflected not only in this sonata but in the concerto for violin and the second piano concerto. (Compare the similar period, around 1806, which yielded Beethoven's Fourth symphony, the G major piano concerto, and the violin concerto.)

This work might be regarded as Brahms's "Spring sonata"; but it is far more akin to Beethoven's Op. 96 than to his Op. 24. It is often called

* No one can dispute the interest of the variations, and the fugue, which aroused Wagner's ungrudging approval, is an almost incredible preservation of true Bachian fire. Yet, in the *Variations on a Theme of Schumann*, Op. 9, which are hardly less skillful, the true imaginative germ (evident in Schumann's little theme as it is not in Handel's) is made to grow into such a revelation of musical personality as I cannot find in the Handel variations — even the much-lauded twentieth.

the *Regenlied* sonata, since Brahms, after Schubert's example, based a good deal of the music on his song of that title (Op. 59, No. 3). The first movement opens (*Vivace ma non troppo*, G major, 6-4) with the main theme in the violin over a deceptively simple accompaniment of two chords to a bar; but the elastic reiteration of these supports a melodic line of wonderful ease and fluidity. (The rhythm is directly borrowed from the song.) The high serenity of the theme is presently amplified by wide-ranging arpeggio figures in the piano, accompanying first the continuation of the theme and then the repetition of it. The S.II (36) offers so little contrast that it seems like another continuation, and ends with a reminiscence of S.I. A leisurely episode that serves as Cl.S. ends the exposition. The development (82) begins with the S.I in the piano, accompanied by the two-chord rhythm, now pizzicato in the violin; but it soon grows to a high sonority (*più sostenuto*) on the running passages, and contrives an intricate inter-rhythming of the episodic figure from S.I. The recapitulation somewhat enriches the exposition, but only enough to heighten the charm of the experience whose portrayal is the real objective of the music.

The *Adagio* (E flat, 2-4) begins with a contemplative theme to which the violin refers only after it has made excursion into a darker episode. For what follows is dark indeed—a funereal rhythm (*più andante*— i.e., somewhat faster) in the piano, again on the motive from the *Regenlied*, answered by a tense melodic strain in the violin. These things, of a significance for which language has no symbols, make up the middle section and lead back to a much enriched repetition of S.I. The Coda recalls both March and S.I.

The Finale (a gay Scherzo would be unthinkable) borrows directly from the *Regenlied*—starts a quiet *moto perpetuo* in the piano against which the violin turns the song into the main theme; finds a somewhat gayer S.II (29) that has a lighter second strain; then reverts, rondo-fashion, to the S.I. But the S.III of the rondo form is a reminiscence of the main theme of the *Adagio*—not, however, slowed to that tempo, but fragmented so that it may also bear reference (*tranquillo*) to the march rhythm of that movement. The S.I comes back and the Coda (*più moderato*), again reminiscent, ends almost nostalgically on an augmentation of S.I.

The next violin sonata, Op. 100, is apparently—but only apparently— slighter in substance. Its character is indicated, as far as one word could do it, in the superscription of the first movement: *Allegro amabile.* The piano sets forth the main theme (A major, 3-4), apparently casting it in simple four-bar periods; but the violin, echoing the fourth bar, turns them into five-bar groups— an addition whose value you can test by playing the theme without these fifth bars. (It makes sense; but how square it becomes!) Piano and violin reverse their roles for two periods; then, after a short, vigorous transition, the S.II, still more songful than the S.I, is set forth, the piano again leading. After a more energetic continuation the violin repeats the theme, suavely accompanied; but the continuation now becomes the Cl.S. (79). The development is at first only contemplative, but it is activated when some quite intricate imitations appear on the three-note motive of the first bar of the sonata.* The Cl.S. is then imitated canonically at the 9th below and at the distance of a single beat, and then, charmingly expanded, forms the end of the development. The recapitulation of the S.I is shortened, but that of the S.II is complete. It subsides into a passage of highly percipient contemplation (219) before the Coda.

The next movement begins (*Andante tranquillo*, F major, 2-4) with a fervent song in the violin; but this is broken off after only fifteen bars for a *scherzando* theme, piquant and gently mischievous, which is much more extended. The *Andante* comes back, remaining a little longer; then the gay theme returns, *vivace di più* (a little faster) and very hard to play as delicately as is essential if its fine humor is to be projected. Then the *Andante, sempre più dolce*, with a final hint of the Scherzo, makes the end. Pause a moment to consider the imaginative resource of one confronted with the task of continuing the intimations of the first movement, and who can find so perfect a solution.

The Finale is a *Rondo varié* — really on one theme, for the interludes between its recurrences are hardly more than episodes. That theme is another song, first sung by the alto voice of the violin's G string. The first episode begins on the questing diminished seventh, but at bars 45–46 the violin cadences on the descending phrase from bars 19–20 of the second Andante; then the piano finds a tranquil figure in its high register to which the violin plays the bass; and this same line, taken by the violin

---

* The resemblance of this phrase to the first bar of Walther's Prize Song in *Die Meistersinger* was of course noticed by the tune-detectors. One of them, mentioning the fact to Brahms, was dismissed with the characteristic remark, "Das sieht jeder Narr" (Every fool sees that).

when the piano descends to a lower level, forms a new counterpoint to the returning theme (63). The continuation is a development of phrases of the theme (particularly its first phrase), but there is no really new matter until a new variant of the theme appears (112), now in the piano, with its phrases detached and syncopated and a *leggiero* staccato bass, delicate beyond description (and again very difficult to play). The diminished-7th interlude follows, shortened, and the theme, in obviously cadential fragments, makes the close.

The third violin sonata, Op. 108, in D minor, was begun at Thun in Switzerland in 1886, along with Op. 100, but was finished later. It is in a very different vein — hardly tragic, perhaps pessimistic, but with much warmth beneath its austere surface. The main theme (*Allegro*, 2-2) is very lean in texture, the violin carrying it far above the piano which, in syncopated octaves, has only the one contrapuntal "voice." The impression is grim but compelling, and the sudden release of energy (24) comes as no surprise. The S.II (48), in F, is not an antidote. It might be so, were it not for the three *sforzandi* on the second eighth of "two" and the inability of the theme to withstand the gravitational pull of D minor. The close (174) is on a two-note phrase dialogued between piano and violin over flickering arpeggios that can barely sustain its lessening weight.

The long development, all *sotto voce* over the throbbing of a persistent pedal A, is on the main theme whose second and third bars emerge at intervals out of a figure derived from the syncopated accompaniment of that theme at the beginning. The tension of this stillness, although the harmony is never sharply dissonant, is high, so that the approach to the recapitulation (117f), shimmering in a new and exquisite color, is extraordinarily grateful. That color is continued against the returning S.I in the violin (131), mitigating the original grimness; but the ensuing release of energy (as at 24) is more startling than before. The S.II appears in D, but the dialoguing, instead of dwindling, grows forceful, so that the Coda (219) begins on the S.I with its harmony now filled out and the theme itself becomes an outcry not to be suppressed. It does subside, but onto the long pedal (now D) of the development. There is another shimmer that fades as the violin sinks in preparation for a last utterance of the theme, *sostenuto*, and with a bitter *sf* at its peak.

The *Adagio* (D major, 3-8) is a marvel. In fewer notes than you would expect to find in Mozart it sets forth a gravity of thought that seems to embrace all that is really essential in the widening philosophy of the intervening hundred years. For the essential of a philosophy is not in the mechanics of its reasoning but in the attitude of mind that its conclusions generate — in the feeling that grows out of understanding; and to embody that understanding in any medium of communication is a service which even great artists are seldom able to render. The first sentence is long (seventeen bars), and even then its cadence is not final. Behind the hesitant two-note motive from the accompaniment (1–2), now on the diminished 7th, the violin rises to an interlude in 3rds, on the minor subdominant of A, whose warmth illuminates the sense latent in the whole movement. The two-note motive then becomes melody in the piano; the violin reiterates it; then the piano in a descending sequence on tinier intervals makes a wonderful approach to the returning main theme. This, shortened, but with a triplet figure for accompaniment, reaches the same illuminating phrase in 3rds as before, repeats it and extends the repetition, descending to a final reminiscence of the opening bars of the theme.

The following Intermezzo, entitled only *Un poco presto e con sentimento* (F sharp minor, 2-4), seems in its context the most engaging of all the pieces in this vein which so often substitute for the Scherzo in Brahms's sonata structures. It has but one theme whose varied repetitions, set off by episodic excursions, grow always more fascinating. But if you ponder it you will see that this gentle humor is appropriate to what has gone before.

The Finale (*Presto agitato*, D minor, 6-8) is the kinetic counterpart of the first movement — externally, a tarentelle-rondo; internally, an ironic comment on the human comedy. Like the Kreutzer sonata, it strains the tonal power of the violin beyond its capacity; but that very strain is essential to the irony.

The 'Cello Sonatas

The 'cello sonata in E minor, Op. 38, was begun in 1862 and finished in 1865 — the period of the F minor piano quintet, with which its sober first movement shows considerable kinship. It had at first four movements, an *Adagio* intervening between the first movement and the *Allegretto*.* In contrast to earlier chamber duos which gave the piano the leading role, this is a sonata for violoncello and piano. It is ruled through-

* Dr. Josef Gansbächer, to whom the sonata is dedicated, begged Brahms to let him see the rejected movement, but his entreaty was wholly unavailing.

out by the 'cello's male voice, never attempting that competition with the violin which the huge compass of the instrument makes possible, but which too often suggests a human falsetto. Yet the musical substance is so vital and its presentation so lucid that there is never a moment of monotony.

The main theme (*Allegro non troppo*, E minor, 4-4), begun in the lowest register of the 'cello, surges upward for a moment, completing its first strain in two stentorian drops of octave and 9th. Then it continues in its middle register, the contrast highly appealing. Repetition of the theme in the piano, high above the 'cello, offers no contradiction of its sense but rather a new aspect of its character. Neither does the gentle episode (42) that makes transition to the S.II weaken the impression already given. The firmness of the S.II (58) would have had no impact without it, and it helps to point up the clarification offered by the quiet serenity of the Cl.S. (79) in B major. The development parades no intellectual subtleties. It only magnifies the most evident feature of the themes — their strength, which is by no means all physical. It would be hard to find a movement which, with so little evidence of compression, keeps the essence of a type of spiritual experience so constantly in focus.

The 'cello theme in the *Allegretto quasi Menuetto* (A minor, 3-4) is so charming that you will perhaps not notice the melodic interest of the piano's associated theme. A similar interchange appears in the S.II (38) which is more waltz-like. The Trio, in F sharp minor, derived from the minuet theme, dances under a diaphanous veil of color thrown by the ingenious figuration of the piano — so alluringly that you will almost resent the return of the *Allegretto*.

The Finale (*Allegro*, E minor, 4-4) is an ingenious amalgamation of fugue and sonata forms. It begins with a powerful fugue-subject — two stern, leaping-octave E's followed by an incisive triplet figure — announced by the piano. The answer, in the 'cello, is given a sturdy countersubject in even eighths, and the third voice — the right hand in the piano, taking the S. — is accompanied by that CS. in the 'cello and by another in the left hand of the piano. Both these countersubjects are later made so conspicuous that the texture approaches that of a triple fugue. But the S. softens its energy, even in *ff*, by adding the 3rd to its former melodic line (26); the texture gradually becomes harmonic rather than polyphonic; and the first countersubject (53), now *p*, legato, and imitated by inversion in the right hand, becomes essentially the S.II of a sonata form to which the 'cello supplies arpeggiated harmony. A colorful development follows in which harmonic and polyphonic textures are mingled. The recapitulation begins (132), not with the fugal subject alone but with the answer in the piano and its first countersubject in the 'cello, and much of the former exposition is then gone over. A breathless *più presto* Coda proves that Brahms, if he cared to, *could* exult.

The second 'cello sonata was composed in Thun, Switzerland, in 1886, along with the two violin sonatas in A and D minor and the C minor trio. It is much more brilliant than the first, freely exploiting the highest register of the instrument above an accompaniment far more colorful than was there offered. Indeed, the opening (*Allegro vivace*, F major, 3-4), with its ejaculatory 'cello theme over a *tremolando* accompaniment, verges on the melodramatic. It subsides, however, making on its last phrase the transition to the S.II. This, in the piano (34), stands in a large open space and is architecturally imposing, but its relation to the S.I seems to this commentator one of position rather than of cognate sense. The development heightens the dramatic aspect of the S.I by plunging suddenly into F sharp minor, with its *tremolando* accompaniment higher, louder, and more threatening than before. A tonally subdued but expressively tumultuous discussion ensues, after which the 'cello takes over the *tremolando* while the piano softly reiterates the motive on the upward 4th with which the S.I begins, augmented, begun on the beat (instead of the sixteenth up-beat), and modulating downward over a chromatically descending bass. It arrives thus at a huge augmentation of the S.I (every note a whole bar long) which begins the recapitulation. The Coda (176) summarizes both main themes.

Kalbeck thinks it possible that the *Adagio affettuoso* (F sharp major, 2-4) is the suppressed slow movement of the E minor sonata. It would indeed have been out of place there, but its structure seems to belong to the 'sixties rather than to the 'eighties. The S.I, in the piano against a pizzicato bass, is slow and tense; the S.II, in the 'cello in F minor, is more relaxed, and the piano, before taking it up, makes a colorful paraphrase of it in 6ths and 3rds. The S.I returns (44); its accompaniment when taken over by the 'cello is more figurated, and it rules to the end.

The Scherzo, marked *Allegro passionato* (F minor, 6-8), seems to borrow its thematic line from the Finale of the Third symphony. Its humor is grim and, in its *mezza voce* utterance, faintly terrifying. It is clarified, when the 'cello emerges from its low register (11), into a sort of angry impatience — the "passion," apparently, implied in the superscription. An obscure excursion into E minor and a violent outburst in F minor intensify the general impression. The Trio, in F major, is mostly emollient but has its moments of tension.

The Finale (*Allegro molto*, F major, 2-2) is a Rondo, quite happy and often excited, but in ways far removed from the implications of the first movement and the Scherzo. A vigorous S.II in A minor (23) is followed by a more suave version of the S.I, and that by the S.III in B flat minor.* The rest is a somewhat elaborated rounding out of the form. The whole sonata is more attractive to the ear than the E minor; but the total impression is less compelling.

The Clarinet Sonatas

The two clarinet sonatas, Op. 120, were written in 1894, after the clarinet trio and the clarinet quintet had aroused wide interest. Richard Mühlfeld's playing on the instrument which Brahms called "the nightingale of the orchestra" had inspired those two pieces, and the sonatas were an aftermath.†

The first of the two is in F minor. It begins (*Allegro appassionato*, 3-4) with a dark theme in the piano, unharmonized. The clarinet adds another strain, rather obliquely harmonized, whose long upward leaps hint more directly at the passion indicated in the superscription. Both strains are then dwelt on. The S.II (53) is more agitated than the first theme, and its full energy is released in the piano's augmentation (61) against sweeping arpeggio figures in the clarinet. The development begins (90) with the S.I ruminantly elongated in the piano, and continues to bring that theme to the fore, but the S.II forms the peak of the section. Only the S.II is at all literally recapitulated. The Coda (*sostenuto ed espressivo*) begins on a phrase in triplets over a C pedal that goes on until detached phrases from the S.I make the rather dejected end.

The *Andante un poco Adagio* (F minor, 2-4) begins with a suspenseful theme in the clarinet over harmony remarkably oblique for Brahms and a rhythm that plods rather than marches. The piano does not take up

* The tune-detectors seem not to have noticed here a strong hint of *Vesti la giubba* — of course, as the novelists say, "purely coincidental."

† "It would be nice if you brought along your B flat clarinet," Brahms wrote on the eve of Mühlfeld's visit to Ischl where Brahms was summering. The trio and quintet having been written for the clarinet in A, this was a sufficient hint that something new had been created.

this theme but offers (23) a quiet reassurance in D flat. There is no other substance, but the impression is strong. Brahms felt that the clarinet blended better with the piano than any other instrument, and this music strongly supports that opinion.

The *Allegretto grazioso* (A flat, 3-4) would become a Viennese waltz if it were danced in a gayer tempo and by a more lighthearted person than the one you can glimpse throughout the sonata. It is shaped like a Minuet with a perceptible but only slightly contrasted Trio in the middle. The Finale (*Vivace*, F major, 2-2) throws off the somber mood, marching buoyantly (but not in goose-step) to the stimulating one-two, *one* rhythm that can be felt throughout the movement.

The second clarinet sonata, in E flat, is in high contrast to the first. It begins (*Allegro amabile*, 4-4) with a fluid theme of wide range and many long skips, wholly suited to the clarinet. The S.II (22) is less "amiable" than the S.I. It is at first in close canon at the 5th between the clarinet and the bass of the piano, but its sternness is at once lightened in a sort of paraphrase in the clarinet. The development exhausts the resources of both subjects. The second movement, *Appassionato, ma non troppo Allegro* (E flat minor, 3-4), smacks somewhat of the waltz but is too intense for that character. Its Trio (*Sostenuto*, B major) is very warm and essentially gentle in contrast to the main portion. The Finale is a set of variations on another amiable theme. They are both ornamental in effect and ingenious in design, the theme, especially in the fourth variation, being quite deeply buried under persistently syncopated harmony. The fifth (*Allegro non troppo*, 2-4) suggests that it will be expanded to form the end of the movement, but that function is fulfilled by still another very free and ornamental variant in E flat major.

The Trios

The trio in B major, Op. 8, was Brahms's first mature chamber work. It was written in 1854, and was first publicly performed at Breslau on December 18, 1855. About a week later it was played in Boston, Massachusetts, by William Mason and Theodore Thomas, later the founder of the Chicago orchestra.

This, however, was not the version of the trio which is known today. Brahms made over the whole work in 1889, but insisted that it be labeled only as a revised version and retain its opus number. The Scherzo is the only movement to remain virtually unaltered. Comparison of the two versions is impossible in our space, but is also needless since only the later one is nowadays performed.

The main theme of the first movement also remains. It reveals the twenty-one-year-old composer, as do his other youthful works, as a remarkably old young man. Nowhere, indeed, will you find in his music the bloom of youth that colors so engagingly the early works of Schumann and the other romantics. But only the bloom is missing, for the actual sense of aspiration, the hallmark of romanticism, is still there. The current of his thought, measured in volts, may seem low, but measured in amperes it is high. The theme is first doubled at the third above by the 'cello; then the violin is added, reshaping the three half notes into three quarters; but these three notes form the culmination of the rather long exposition of the theme. They are diminished to three eighths (52); they yield a triplet figure of accompaniment for a new, dotted-rhythmed phrase; and the S.II (74) is thus reached. It is a thin line in the piano, completed by a dotted rhythm, and this, like the S.I, is considerably developed, so that there is only a brief cadential triplet figuration for Cl.S. There is hardly a note in the development that cannot be traced to these things. The recapitulation (197) is much shortened.

The Scherzo (*Allegro molto*, B minor, 3-4) has a blunt, rather stolid theme which rules the whole movement, even accompanying an anticipation (augmented) of the Trio (101). This, in B major and *meno allegro*, is at first warm and a little nostalgic, but it swells to a high affirmation at the end. The Scherzo of course returns, and there is a brief, obviously cadential Coda.

The opening phrase of the *Adagio* (B major, 4-4) may plausibly be derived (as may also the main theme of the Scherzo) from the opening theme of the trio. Not so, however, its high fervency which, to our mind, is but faintly illuminated by such a derivation.* The two strings quietly

* I do not dispute the possibility of this derivation. A creating musical mind will of course be obsessed with a tonal pattern that is proving fertile. That pattern, fermenting subconsciously, *may* generate — as here — others of quite astonishingly diverse character. But that they are so generated is no guarantee that they will be usable in the context of an already consciously formed and critically pondered creation. Brahms could have turned these notes, consciously or subconsciously, into forty other patterns, all of which he might have rejected as incompatible with the imagery of experience that was really guiding his effort. (Did he not remake the trio because that imagery had been insufficiently rendered in the earlier version?) To erect this half-conscious, purely tonal operation into a governing principle of musical creation is to assume that tonal cohesion is the first creative law. It is a law; but it is the last, not the first. And I suspect that a good deal of logic-chopping music in the twentieth century has been made out of this reversal of principle.

assent; different but equally cordial comment is offered to the piano's twice-repeated proposition; the two musical forces join, and the 'cello emerges (33) with a tenser strain in G sharp minor which the violin at length takes up. When the main theme returns, as before, the piano accompanies the comment of the strings in a delicate triplet figuration high above.

The Finale (*Allegro*, B minor, 3-4) strikes at once a note of subdued but pointed agitation with a 'cello theme that begins on the submediant, clings precariously to the dominant (F sharp), cannot find a tonic resting-place in all its seventeen bars, and for cadence pauses, *ritardando*, on the supertonic. Then the violin takes the theme over a more disturbed harmony, twice cadencing *ritardando* as before, and then beginning a restless transition to the S.II (64) which is frankly in D, with a welcome brightness and an accordant vigor. The S.I returns (111), first in the piano and then in the strings, proceeding toward G sharp minor and what may appear as the S.III, although it is all made of the S.I and its cadence, and is a sonata development rather than a rondo-theme. It rises to a full-throated climax (183) and goes on to the S.II (205), developing it and the S.I to a conclusion very affirmative in force but still perturbed by the indecision that underlay that theme.

The Horn Trio

The next trio, Op. 40, is for piano, violin, and horn; but since it was published with parts for viola or 'cello as alternative to the horn, and is more accessible in that combination, we shall depart from our plan and discuss it here. It had to be made, of course, with the peculiarities of the horn constantly in mind, and the regular sonata form was thus precluded; but you will hardly notice the irregularity if the essential current of the thought is kept (as it will be) in the foreground of your attention.*

* Brahms wrote for, and demanded in performance, the "natural" (valveless) horn. It can produce, as "open" or natural notes, only the tones of the "harmonic series"— those produced by the division of the air-column into fractions — half, third, quarter, fourth, etc., up to the 16th which is the practical limit. For the horn in Eb, these notes are: Eb below the bass staff (No. 2 in the series; No. 1, an octave below, is unmanageable), Bb, Eb, G, Bb, Db,* Eb, F, G, Ab, Bb, B♮,* C, Db, D♮, Eb. (The notes marked with an asterisk are out of tune with our scale, but can be rectified by the performer.) Intervening, "stopped" notes can be produced by inserting the hand in the bell of the horn. Blown loudly, their quality is very different from the open notes; blown softly, the difference can be made all but imperceptible.

EXAMPLE 28. BRAHMS HORN TRIO, OP. 40

The trio was composed in May, 1865. Brahms's mother had died on February 1st. The music is no threnody, composed for that event; the Scherzo and the Finale are quite untainted with grief; but there is such gentle retrospection in the first movement, and such an agony of tenderness in the *Adagio*, that the association is ineluctable.

The first movement is a quiet *Andante* (E flat, 2-4) whose main theme, mellow like the tone of the horn which dialogues it with the violin, is complemented by, rather than contrasted with, another in the piano (29) which the horn and the violin take over and amplify. (See the themes of the trio in Ex. 28.) There is another (*poco più animato*, B flat, 9-8) that offers a contrast in motion and mood, but not an antithesis. The first theme, slightly varied, and the third recur, and the epilogue is on the first. There are no structural tricks, but the image of experience is kept in focus.

A Scherzo follows (*Allegro*, E flat major, 3-4), its theme again designed to be playable on the horn; but its first statement, *unisono* in the piano, disguises that need. Its last four bars are a decisive phrase in 2-4 that will yield later development. The horn helps to harmonize this and the ensuing repetition of S.I, and adds a subordinate strain (61) to the structure before it takes up the opening theme. This is quaintly augmented (121) and otherwise elaborated before the Trio (*Molto meno Allegro*, A flat minor), with its sober theme in mellow 3rds topped by the horn, appears. The Scherzo returns thereafter.

The *Adagio mesto* (E flat minor, 6-8) begins in the piano *una corda* with a theme — perhaps rather a figure — of four bars, sorrowful indeed, but still more gentle. Violin and horn then sound the real main theme, in the same vein but more tense; the horn, solo (19), has a new strain, really the S.II, which violin and piano take up and develop. At length it is combined with the piano's opening figure (43); the main theme comes back, presently attaining a kind of brightness in G flat major, and after the piano makes a little epilogue the horn, above the violin, turns the S.II into a phrase in E flat that is ineffably illuminating. It comes once more, in F, with the violin above; the piano makes the S.II into an oblique strain in the same key; the music hastens a little, and the S.I, *forte* and *passionata*, begins a peroration that, although it fades on the piano's opening figure, is no longer forlorn. Sensitively read, this seems to us the most imaginative slow movement in all Brahms's chamber music.

The Finale (*Allegro con brio*, E flat major, 6-8) smacks strongly of the hunt. The violin and piano have the bouncing theme which ends with a jolly *Ho-la* — really, a horn-motive that appears often thereafter. A second subject group — an exuberant shout (45) and an eager upward swerve (67) — together with a cadential descent in what feels like 3-4 time complete the exposition. The development, not of course learned, is wholly joyous.*

The Trio in C major

The trio in C, Op. 87, was begun in 1880, along with that in C minor, Op. 101. That in C was finished in 1882; the C minor, not until 1886. The C major, although its structure is unassailable, seems the least popular of the trios — perhaps because its four movements, although compatible enough in character, are linked by no compelling association. Each movement is of high interest in itself, but — for this commentator at least — they do not fuse into an indivisible whole.

* Dr. Josef Gansbächer, calling on Brahms on the morning after he had received the news of his mother's death, found him playing Bach's *Goldberg Variations* while the tears streamed down his face. Brahms told the news, still playing. Is it fanciful to find, in these last two movements especially, a kind of musical analogue of his native behavior under emotional stress?

The first four bars of the main theme (*Allegro*, 3-4), *unisono* in the strings, project a sturdy and purposeful energy that is heightened by the ensuing chromatic ascents and the more active motion of the almost unpunctuated continuation up to its peak (11). A similar drive animates the continuation, yielding another thematic phrase (21) whose crowded imitations reach a high intensity and make doubly convincing the S.I which returns in full force. The S.II (57) is gratefully warm (its first three chromatic notes recall bars 5 and 7 of S.I), and like the S.I it has an intensifying continuation (80). The Cl.S. (102) maintains its *grazioso* dotted rhythm to the end of the exposition. The development, beginning at a low level on S.II (117) has a turbulent undertone of triplet motion that prepares a very affirmative return of S.I and a development of it whose culmination is in the broad augmentation of that theme (165) in D flat. The recapitulation (209) is no mere rehearsal of past events, but is rather an amplification of their sense. The Coda, *Animato*, is mostly on the augmented S.I, but the last bars return it to its original form.

The following *Andante con moto* (A minor, 2-4) is a set of variations on a deceptively simple-looking theme, evidently invented out of a ferment of Hungarian folk-song. It begins with two identical four-bar periods; the third period is rhythmically similar until its fourth bar, apparently excited by the upward leap of a 5th (D–A) it took in its second bar, takes that leap again after an eighth and goes up to C; repeats the ascent, and then, disguising its rhythmic symmetry, drives itself into a brief lyrical frenzy on the same impetus. There is a quaintly regretful four-bar conclusion. The variations, on a theme of such a character, are naturally more ingenious than expressive, but they do amplify interestingly the rather odd character of the theme.

The Scherzo (C minor, 6-8) is fleet and distant. The piano flickers eerily in the background, leaving the thematic substance largely to the strings. The Trio (*poco meno presto*, C major) has in contrast a childishly simple theme, elaborated in the second section sufficiently to mitigate the perhaps oversharp contrast.

The humor suggested in the superscription of the Finale (*Allegro giocoso*, C major, 4-4) perhaps lies chiefly in the five-bar pattern of the theme, which persists right up to the S.II (43). This hops cockily in the 'cello against tinkling triplets in the piano. The S.I, returning (53), keeps to the same texture for a time but turns into a development which makes great fun out of the figure of four eighth-note chords that accompanied the S.I at the beginning. The recapitulation (117) is shortened. The Coda begins (171) with an augmentation of the S.I, but soon hastens it even to diminution. Then, on its inversion above combined with its original form below, it stamps gaily to an end.

The Trio in C minor

Elizabeth von Herzogenberg, after receiving the trio in C minor, Op. 101, wrote to Brahms that she found the music "better than all his photographs as giving a true portrait of the master." Any portrait of Brahms in his maturity will suggest a strong character, but this music — at any rate in its first and last movements — illuminates that character as no physical portraiture could do. The themes, the chief lineaments of the portrait, are shown in Example 29.

EXAMPLE 29. BRAHMS TRIO, OP. 101

The main theme (*Allegro energico*, C minor, 3-4) limns the essence of spiritual strength with the utmost conciseness; its continuation (11), in firm dotted figures that contrast with the pervading triplets of the theme proper, seems wholly inevitable; a return to that theme (22) adds to its power, and the shortest of transitions, patently just as purposeful, brings the S.II (38). Here, if ever there was one, is a song of manliness, sung in octaves in the deep sonority of both violin and 'cello and accompanied by no more than firm arpeggios of its essential harmonies, likewise in octaves in the piano. All this comes out with full sonority, although there are only two real parts. A much thicker and more activated version of this theme, with the briefest of cadential figures for close, brings the development. (Brahms crossed out the repeat of the exposition.) This begins, *forte*, on the S.I, but after six bars it becomes suddenly (and illuminatingly for the portrait) *piano*. Only when it reaches toward the rhythm of bar 11 does it begin to grow in force. That alternative strain, indeed, substitutes for the S.I in the recapitulation, which we recognize as having started only when we hear the continuing passage (from bar 5f) that followed the theme when we first heard it. The S.II, in C, returns regularly (150); the dotted-rhythm figure is vigorously insisted on; but the S.I, in the bass of the piano and then quietly augmented in the strings as well, makes the end.

The next movement is a delicate and highly allusive Intermezzo (labeled only *Presto non assai*, C minor, 2-2). I call it allusive without being in the least able to tell in words what it alludes to. That it contributes greatly to the portrait I am sure you will agree, and perhaps that is a sufficient index of its meaning. Its texture is thin, almost to transparency, even when its first light steps begin to march more firmly (30) in F minor. As if this had been the Trio of a Scherzo, the first part returns (95) and ends on a quiet augmentation of its first phrases.

If, allowing our fancy a liberty of excursion beyond the literal suggestion of the music, we say that the *Presto* portrayed a glint in the eye of our "subject," the following *Andante grazioso* may be allowed to portray a smile relaxing his ordinarily firm lips. The theme (C major), alternated between strings and piano, follows a bar of 3-4 time with two of 2-4, pursuing this engaging device consistently, even in the middle section (a little more intense) where 9-8 is followed by 6-8. The intimation is so charming that you will be tempted to repeat the movement; but if you do that you will distort the total portrait.

The Finale (*Allegro molto*, C minor, 6-8) is a rondo-sonata form, as succinct as the first movement, less pregnant in actual idea, but almost as compelling in vigor and brightness. A considerable fund of humor underlies its externally rather stern aspect. This is visible near the end, when the main theme, returning in C major (191), turns its original staccato into a nonchalant legato in the *Meno allegro* tempo of the second subject.

[191

The Clarinet Trio

The Clarinet trio, Op. 114, is the first of Brahms's affairs with "Fräulein Klarinette," as he called the instrument to whose charm he was subjected through Richard Mühlfeld. The fading of that obsession is set forth in the two clarinet sonatas, already described; we shall see it at its peak in the Clarinet quintet, Op. 115, written in the same year (1891) as the trio; but the passion is even now pretty strong. With the string quintet, Op. 111, Brahms had made up his mind to compose no more; but that decision gave him such a sense of freedom that his old energy returned, and the affair with the clarinet was just the spur needed to give it direction.

The trio begins (*Allegro*, A minor, 2-2) with the main theme, unaccompanied, in the 'cello. The clarinet takes it over, amplifying it in both its range and its faintly regretful character. The piano (13) adds a more rhythmic afterthought; these things provide the transition; and the S.II (43) – again in 'cello answered by violin – only deepens the impression so far given. (The 'cello, against the answer, has the theme inverted.) The development (83) begins with the S.I, low in the 'cello in E minor, but is mostly concerned with a phrase from the transition (see 33f). The recapitulation begins (138) with the augmentation of S.I in the clarinet which breaks its line, by syncopation, into an extraordinary amplification of its sense. The Coda, *Poco meno Allegro*, is on swift, whispered scales that suggest a plagal cadence in A major.

The *Adagio* (D major, 4-4) begins with an elegiac theme in the clarinet which the 'cello repeats, finding thereafter a continuing strain in a rhythm suggestive of the gavotte. The piano (15) to the accompaniment of the strings (and afterwards accompanying them) counters with an answering strain in A – a thought whose brightness is a little darkened by the frequent lowering of the submediant to F♮. Miss Clarinet (22) then sings the S.II in D – a broad phrase, impassioned but restrained, which generates a more evident unrest. Hints of the S.I begin to appear and the 'cello returns to that theme. The rest is elaboration, exquisitely colored, of these things.

The third movement is neither Scherzo nor Intermezzo, but a rather flabby waltz (*Andantino grazioso*, A major). The Finale (*Allegro*, A minor) alternates and mingles 2-4 and 6-8 time, the 2-4 mitigating the somewhat overgraceful pirouetting of the 6-8. Neither movement lives up to the promise of the first two.

The Piano Quartets

There are three quartets for piano and strings, Opp. 25, 26, and 60. The first two of these were begun in 1856, but finished in 1862. The C minor was possibly begun even earlier. It was at first in C sharp minor, the change of key having been determined by some unknown condition. The first is the most popular of all — probably because of its Gypsy-rondo Finale.

Brahms had not yet learned the technique of condensation which is so characteristic of his later works. Yet, although he cannot resist the temptation to develop an idea as soon as it has been announced, his continuations are so logical that there is never a moment of indecision in the design. The wealth of his invention here appears almost Schubertian, and Schumann, had he lived to hear this work, might again have spoken of its "heavenly length." The principal themes are quoted in Example 30.

The S.I is so expanded that you will suppose the broad tune that

EXAMPLE 30. BRAHMS PIANO QUARTET IN G MINOR, OP. 25

[193

emerges in the 'cello (50) to be the S.II. Instead, it is an anticipation, in D minor, considerably resembling the real S.II which appears, in D major (79), soaring on eagle's wings. This has likewise a continuing strain (102); the S.I follows, developed rather fragmentarily (130) so that the development proper may be felt to begin here; but the tentativeness of the harmonic progression and the dwindling of energy seem to us to make this passage function as closing section. The real development, then, will begin (161) with the S.I in its original form. The manipulations thereafter — especially the canonic imitations on S.I (206f) — reach a terrifying intensity; this is alleviated by development of the first continuing strain (237, from 11); the S.I is again forcefully suggested (259), and the recapitulation, thereafter, approached by rising *unisono* repetitions of this one suggestive bar, begins with the *ff* establishment of G minor (265). This is much shorter than the exposition, rehearsing only essentials. The Coda (343) makes a stirring crescendo out of the ever-rising figure from bar 1.

The Intermezzo (so entitled) which takes the place of a Scherzo may appear to ears inured to twentieth-century dissonance to offer a surfeit of linked sweetness. The lilt of the S.II (34), however, is an ample compensation. The Trio (*Animato*, A flat) is still in 9-8 time and is not much faster than the *Allegro ma non troppo* of the first section; neither does it offer much contrast, its five-bar periods being so suavely constructed that this irregularity is hardly noticeable. Like the Intermezzo, the Trio has two sections; but the theme of the second is only complementary to the first.

The theme of the *Andante con moto* (E flat, 3-4) seems at first of a Victorian primness. Its second strain, however (17), is underlain by chromatic harmony that reveals much latent energy, and when the theme appears in the bass of the piano (40) it is clear that a heady brew is fermenting. The triplet rhythm of the accompaniment becomes (essentially) dotted; a surging imitative phrase emerges against it in the strings; and the middle section of the piece (*Animato*) turns into another *Marche des Davidsbündler contre les Philistins* like that which ended Schumann's *Carnaval*. (Like that march also, it is in triple time, but your spiritual muscles will tramp to it just as triumphantly.) The return of the first theme is at first in C major (the key of the march), but both this and its re-establishment in E flat are now newly colored so that there is no sense of anticlimax.

The vitality of the *Rondo alla Zingarese* (Gypsy Rondo) that follows is so exuberant that verbal description is desecration. Brahms's interest in Hungarian melody (which, like Liszt, he did not differentiate from Gypsy music: Bartók and Kódaly revealed that difference only after Brahms was dead) had been exemplified in his *Hungarian Dances* — the fruit of his tour with Reményi in 1853. It finds here its amplest outlet. The three-bar period of the opening rules the structure almost throughout. There are five themes. The first begins the rondo; the second (31) turns the F♯–G cadence of the first into a springboard from which its scale-figure shoots up; the third (80) is a pizzicato figure in the strings with a swift *leggiero* scamper in the piano for accompaniment; the fourth (155) *Meno presto*, is in G major; the fifth (173) is complementary to the fourth, forming with it (together with some reference to earlier themes) the middle section of the rondo. There is a long *quasi Cadenza* elaboration before the first theme returns (362), *Molto presto*, to end what is probably the most exciting piece of chamber music ever put together.

The quartet in A major, Op. 26, contrasts with the G minor as does the Second symphony with the First, or the A major violin sonata with the D minor — all being illustrations of Brahms's way of making two pieces, of the same genre but of different character, all but simultaneously. It is much brighter than the G minor, and at first sight may appear less significant; but on thorough acquaintance you will likely revise that opinion. The main theme (*Allegro non troppo*, 3-4) makes with its first four bars in the piano a rather indifferent impact on the ear, the tonal tension being slight and the rhythm no more stimulating. Moreover, it breaks off at the end of four bars for a continuation in the 'cello that is quite unrelated in contour, rhythm, or character; reversal of the original roles of strings and piano offers little more excitement; but the piano's continuation of what was the 'cello's phrase begins to be disturbing, and when the first phrase of the theme — *unisono* in the strings, apparently in F sharp minor, and suddenly *ff* — is contradicted by the same phrase in the piano, fully harmonized and in A major, it is evident that a considerable force is about to be unleashed. An energizing motive (39), its first three notes suggestive of the first triplet-notes in bar 1, but the whole design an anticipation of the coming S.II, yields the transition to that theme which appears, in E, at bar 53 in the piano. (Note the hint of S.I in the 'cello beneath.) This theme is warm and lyrical, but it is also generative of a more lilting continuation (57) which plays a large part in the close of the exposition. This lilt also begins the development, but the main emphasis is on the S.I. The recapitulation is essentially the exposition with the conventional key-changes. The Coda reveals an unexpected possibility of imitation in the S.I.

The *Poco Adagio* (E major, 4-4) begins on a note of quietude with a theme in the piano whose serene curve is wonderfully enhanced by the rocking bass and the slight blurring of its line by the figurations in the muted strings that surround it. The two five-bar periods in which the theme is cast contribute to its mild tension which is suddenly heightened by the A♯ (4). This note, indeed, extends the period to five bars, for another A♮ would have compelled a perfunctory cadence, and another analogous progression extends the second period. As the quietly reaffirmed cadence sinks to a murmur, a harp somewhere in the cellarage (it is really the piano) interrupts the murmur with an obscure swoosh on a diminished seventh. As it recurs the murmuring strings are roused to an outcry, first in G minor, then in F minor, but its purport is not revealed. The S.I returns, figurated as before, in the strings, but its outcome is now an impassioned melody in the piano (42), a part of whose burden is the four-note descent from bar 5; but the outcry is also interjected (51). The strings alone now begin a long transition (58) on what might have become a third subject if its purpose had not been merely a return to the S.I. This appears (85) in octaves in violin and 'cello, now unmuted, while the piano, *una corda*, has the former gently blurring string figures. The harping returns and continues as accompaniment to the S.II. The Coda is on the S.I, more richly colored than ever.

The Scherzo (*Poco Allegro*, A major, 3-4) has little gaiety and no humor — perhaps because both will abundantly appear in the Finale. Its suave S.I is followed by a more active transition-figure; the S.II (33), a little warmer, ends the first section; all three are extensively elaborated in the second. The Trio, in D minor, treats its vigorous main theme in canon, but follows it with a quiet strain that for some reason has the rhythm of the main theme of the Scherzo.

The Finale (*Allegro*, A major, 2-2) is gay and lively, but its blood does not boil as does the Gypsy Rondo's. Indeed, the persistent jingling of the main theme's syncopated motive, even though varied, begins to sound artificial before the S.II (84) is reached. This is broad and sonorous at first, acquiring animation through several added motives. Instead of returning to the S.I, the music runs on to the S.III (143) – broad and sonorous like the S.II – and the S.I reminds us that this is a Rondo by reappearing (206) in its original form. It is invigorated by a new counter-subject (243), and the substance is enlivened by various new combinations with subordinate motives. The Coda (*Animato*) jingles excitedly to what most hearers regard as a long-delayed close.

The quartet in C minor, Op. 60, is the least popular of the piano quartets. It was apparently the earliest to be conceived. Its first movement dates from 1855, the period of Schumann's last illness, when not only that sorrow but the long-concealed but indubitable passion of Johannes and Clara Schumann was posing for the young composer a psychological problem of no mean dimension. When the quartet was at last finished Brahms spoke of it as the portrait "of a young man in a blue frock coat and a yellow vest"— Goethe's "Young Werther," whose sorrows were in those days commisserated by many tearful readers.

The *Allegro non troppo* (C minor, 3-4) begins with two bars of sustained C's in the piano. Then the strings set forth the main theme – an exceptionally literal portrayal of grief for Brahms, who is usually more reticent. The continuation, begun a tone lower, intensifies the melancholy; then, with sudden force, comes a tense rhythmic variant of the theme (31) that is just as suddenly stilled for a long transition to the S.II. This, in the piano (70), seems remarkably complacent in this context, but the ensuing variants and additions, more sharply rhythmed, retrieve the mood. (The 'cello's pizzicato (86) is the first bar of S.II, disguised.) The exposition ends, as the development begins, on the two-note figures of the S.I. They are the basis of a high intensification which goes on to the variant of S.II first heard at bar 86. There are interesting canons on this theme over a long pedal G, so that the *unisono* triplet G's at bar 196 replace the introductory C's and begin the recapitulation, which is considerably developmental.

The Scherzo (*Allegro*, C minor, 6-8) is virile and impatient. Its main theme is rhythmed on the two-note motive set forth at the beginning (with an up-beat), but it grows more songful (17) at the end. The S.II (23) appears in the strings without any transition. It imports a nervous twitch into what still seems a continuation of the two-note rhythm, and eventuates in the same songful continuation as the S.I. A third theme (72) has a more fluid contour, although it retains the twitch. This, developed, serves as Trio to the Scherzo.

The *Andante* (E major, 4-4) begins with a long 'cello theme in which the note of pain struck by the flatted (Neapolitan) C in the first bar is often enough recalled so that it rules the total impression. An intenser variant in the violin also makes transition to the S.II (34) — a clinging, gently syncopated strain in B major whose appeal is not exhausted by its considerable length. On its last two bars the piano makes gentle comment to which the strings, in dialogue, reply (66f), the 'cello's first bar being the first of S.I. The return begins (78) with the main theme high in the piano, its clear tone being singularly expressive against the richer figurations in the accompanying strings.

The Finale (*Allegro comodo*, C minor, 2-2) seems a product of what churchmen sometimes describe as spiritual dryness. The main theme, in the violin for twenty-eight bars, is accompanied by a rather plodding *moto perpetuo* figure in the piano; the S.II (54), above the equivalent of 6-4 time which has already been established in the piano, largely retains the pattern of four quarter notes with which the S.I began; and the end of the exposition is a chorale in E flat in the strings with four lines of text obviously implied. The written-out *fermata* at the end of each line is accompanied by an arpeggio figure in the piano. After a development on the chorale and the first phrase of S.I there is a kind of *fausse reprise* in B minor (188). The real recapitulation (216f) has the S.I in the strings, *unisono*, against the *moto perpetuo*, also *unisono*, turned into a triplet figure; the S.II is in violin and 'cello instead of violin and viola as before; the chorale is in C instead of E flat and is sententiously extended in the piano for approach to the Coda (328) which really adds nothing to the sense of the movement. Where the real Brahms was while this piece was being composed is to us a mystery.

The Piano Quintet, Op. 34

This is rightly the most frequently performed of all Brahms's chamber works. It took its final form in 1864 after being cast as a string quintet (with two 'celli), rejected as too thick, and as a sonata for two pianos, which was too cold, the warmth of string tone being essential. (But the two-piano version was published.) The chief themes of the work are illustrated in Example 31.

The main theme (*Allegro non troppo*, F minor, 4-4) is a commanding line, set forth *unisono* by piano, first violin, and 'cello. Its continuation is actually in the strings (compare these notes with the last half of bar

EXAMPLE 31. BRAHMS PIANO QUINTET, OP. 34

17 in the piano), but this is accompanied by a diminution of the theme into sixteenths which inevitably attracts the attention. Thereafter it is extended in the strings, still *unisono* and with terrifying strength, and almost completed in the piano; but the first violin (23) takes up its obviously penultimate bar and begins a transition, still on a note of considerable anxiety, to the S.II, in C sharp minor (34). The hopping of its first motive seems intended to dispel that mood altogether, but the next bars continue it, and the ensuing strain (in the viola, accompanied by its inversion in the 'cello against a pedaled blur in the piano) carries the real burden of the theme, as may be seen in the continuation (57f). A warning thump in the piano (74) gives notice that the exposition is about to end. The dotted rhythm (76) that is the most conspicuous feature of the Cl.S. is smoothed to even eighths; the resultant three-note figure is augmented rhythmically, and the close then comes on the first three notes of S.I, augmented. They accompany as the development begins, an oblique version of the theme itself, remote and of uncertain aim, that becomes (122) an intricate canonic imitation on the first phrase of the S.I; the S.II is similarly imitated by inversion in the piano (137); the main theme, in fragments, returns (160); its diminution, as at bar 5, emerges,

[199

and the full force of the theme is again unleashed to begin the recapitulation. The Coda begins (*Poco sostenuto*) in quiet contemplation of the S.I to which a countersubject is added in the second violin; these yield to a still quieter harmonization, high in the strings, of the theme-fragment in the 'cello; then the piano begins (*accel.*) to surge toward the excited diminution of the main theme, and the end is a tumultuous outpouring of its strength.

The *Andante, un poco Adagio* (A flat, 3-4), whose main theme is all cast in mellifluous 3rds, has a sort of sweetness very appealing after the sternness just experienced.* The key changes (33) to E major; second violin and viola begin a triplet figure that evokes from the piano a more assertive melody (all in 6ths) which rises to considerable tension; then the main theme returns, with passing reference to the theme in 6ths, for the close.

The Scherzo (*Allegro*, C minor, 6-8) is not only wholly in character with the first movement but illuminates that experience vividly. Three thematic ideas, all presented in the first twenty-one bars, yield the essential substance. The first, a rising arpeggio of the submediant (A flat) triad over pizzicato C's in the 'cello, faintly suggests the Scherzo in Beethoven's A major 'cello sonata, and also the Scherzo of the C minor symphony; the second, in 2-4 time, is of a frank and alarming energy; the third, again in 6-8, is an outcry, affirmative but not yet triumphant, that was hinted at in the cadence of the second. (Its adoption of the "C minor rhythm" of Beethoven's symphony must have been conscious; but that rhythm was not solely Beethoven's property.) There is a Trio in C major, on a theme somewhat akin to the third theme of the Scherzo but quieter. Its second section begins with a prickly double counterpoint, staccato in 'cello and piano, then inverted in piano and first violin, but this yields to its first theme and so to a return of the Scherzo. The tramp of the basic rhythm never lets up either in Scherzo or Trio.

The Finale is introduced by a ruminative *Poco sostenuto* (F minor, 2-2) whose first phrase — a rising octave that ascends further by a semitone — suggests the theme and the mood of Wagner's *Faust Overture*. Its obscurity is lifted when a tense phrase appears in violin and 'cello (13), highly appropriate to the implications of both the *Allegro* and the

---

* To this commentator's mind, whose opinion had better be expressed in a footnote, the whole movement is out of accord either with the preceding or the following movements. This is of course not a denial of its charm, which is patent to any ear.

Scherzo. The *Allegro non troppo* (F minor, 2-4) begins with a quiet theme that plods doggedly in the 'cello against a more active but no more joyous accompaniment in the piano. After a legato complement and a momentary inversion of the 'cello theme (54), the piano takes the S.I and the strings its accompaniment. Then in a sudden *forte* the stuff this theme is made of is revealed, not only in a paraphrase of the theme but in a new theme, a little faster (95), whose dynamic is kept low but whose tension is high. It begins to be released (126) when a three-note phrase from the S.II, in eighths in the second violin and in quarters in the first, begins to be accompanied in triplets by the piano. As it subsides from its high climax a paraphrase of S.I appears that leads to the original form of that theme. What follows is recapitulation, with conventional key-changes. A quiet transition (322) leads to the final section (*Presto, non troppo*, C sharp minor, 6-8) which begins with a transformation of S.I and presents the chief thematic substances in the furiously active new rhythm. A sudden hush (440) allows the 6-8 transformation of the S.I to add a single eighth (in place of the former eighth rest) at the end of its second phrase; the S.II is thus accompanied, its descending 5th more and more subdued. Then on a throbbing syncopation a resounding conclusion is built up.

The String Quartets

Beethoven's incomparable achievement in the field of the string quartet was as obstructive a deterrent to Brahms's creative imagination as were that master's nine examples in the field of the symphony. Brahms never dreamed that he could outdo Beethoven in either field. He only hoped that his own works, in comparison, would not appear too unworthy of the ideal which, indeed, he knew himself to share with Beethoven. Even that attainment was so difficult that he wrote — and destroyed — twenty string quartets before he would publish his first examples, Op. 51, Nos. 1 and 2. These were finished in 1865. They differ as do the two first symphonies of ten years later — the first being strenuous and purposive, the second more relaxed. Both are structurally faultless — unless a too-exclusive attention to structure is a fault.

The opening theme of the C minor quartet (*Allegro*, 3-2) is almost heroic in its upward, dotted-rhythmed sweep, the breadth of the triple measure contributing not a little to that character. (See the accompanying illustration, Ex. 32.) Repetitions of its abbreviated motive end on

JOHANNES BRAHMS

EXAMPLE 32. BRAHMS QUARTET IN C MINOR, OP. 51, NO. 1

highly active notes (F♯, A♭, A♮), adding still more urgency, and the following phrases, no longer with a hiatus between, complete the masterly line. The ensuing sustained octaves in the viola, punctuated by cadential chords, and the drooping violin phrase (11) accompanied by the dotted rhythm, seem at first to contradict the initial impression of exuberance; but they rather serve to give it a wider frame of reference. The S.I returns (23) in viola and 'cello; the eighth-note pulsations on the pedal C at the beginning become leaping octaves high above; and after its cadence the droop from bar 11 makes, in two bars, the transition to the S.II. This begins (35) with a figure on the famous C minor rhythm, but it emerges into a spurt of melody in the first violin accompanied by a strong line in the 'cello and colored by modulation into G flat major. All these things combine and alternate until a two-note figure on the dotted rhythm, gradually descending, prepares for the Cl.S. (62) whose quiet line blossoms into a floridation in the first violin. The S.I, in E flat minor (75) in the 'cello, really begins the development although the double bar comes

202]

eight bars later. From this beginning you will expect the impetuous drive of the S.I to heighten its note of exultation. To our mind, this fails to happen. Both main themes are ingeniously and sometimes excitingly combined, and rise to a high climax, but the tension is too brief to be really affirmative. The recapitulation (133) begins with a contemplative augmentation of the S.I; the impetuosity is resumed thereafter, but the force is not enhanced. The Coda, in 2-2 time, begun on two notes of the droop (11), perforce turns the dotted rhythm of the S.I into a pattern of even eighths, gaining in speed but losing in spiritual force, for the figure seems reduced to a mere arpeggio. The quiet end of the movement in C major, on an augmented fragment of S.I, seems an inexplicable negation of the original sense of that theme.

The ensuing *Romanze* (*Poco Adagio*, A flat, 3-4) is structurally akin to the *Allegro*, for the dotted rhythm is almost incessant throughout the first section. The tone is mildly elegiac. What will appear as the S.I is in the first violin, although its accompanying substance yields the thought most amplified in the sequel. The structure is cast in three-bar periods. A triplet figure, quite tentative, begins the second section. Harmonic flux is the chief characteristic of the design, now in two-bar periods, but tense melodic phrases here and there emerge. The dotted rhythm of S.I, in E major but aimed toward A flat, signals the return of the opening, which is now accompanied by the triplet rhythm. The strain we called the S.I, however, is absent. It recurs only in the 'cello (55), accompanied by florid sixteenths in first violin. Before the close the middle section is briefly recalled.

The form of the Scherzo, but not its humor, appears in the *Allegretto molto moderato e comodo* (F minor, 4-8) that follows. Persistent motion on a motive of two conjunct sixteenths yields the S.I.* Even with its countersubject in the viola, its steps are almost weightless, nor is the S.II (15) more than half on the ground. The second section gives the viola's countersubject first to the 'cello and then to the first violin, presently lightening its slight weight by a variant in triplet sixteenths (38). The Trio (*un poco animato*) is in F major, 3-4 — an artlessly simple tune accompanied by a pedal A in the second violin that alternates the open A string with the same note on the stopped D (a favorite tonal effect with Brahms).

* Is it an echo of the *Allegro* figure that forms a part of the main theme of Beethoven's piano sonata, Op. 31, No. 2?

The Finale (*Allegro*, C minor, 2-2) asserts in its first two bars the dotted rhythm and the descending diminished 7th from the S.I of the first movement; then completes its S.I with a design which, against a sturdy descending bass, first follows an emphatic half note with a two-note motive in eighths and then precedes the eighths by the half note. The drive of the theme is clearly intended to recall the first movement, but it seems to us far less compelling. A sub-theme — a sonorous phrase in second violin and viola (33) — appears on the way to the S.II (50), which is gentler but also insistent. The S.I returns quietly in the first violin against its inversion in the viola (70), sinking to a half-cadence in E flat (81) from which low level the development begins. This deals *seriatim* with the more important subjects, but is no more intricate than the considerably involved exposition. It exhibits those themes in somewhat new lights, but with no visible climactic purpose, and ends with a hesitant approach to C minor and the recapitulation.

If the expectation aroused by the vivid swerve of the opening of the quartet is taken (not unnaturally) as a forecast of the purport of the whole quartet, that expectation will be disappointed by the conclusion. The structural interest in the all but cyclic unity offered by the persistent dotted rhythm is indubitable; but while structural unity is essential to the effective utterance of an expressive purpose, the two are not (as theory seems to suppose they are) identical.

Quartet in A minor, Op. 59, No. 2

The quartet in A minor is less ebullient than the C minor but is in our view more consistent in expressive purpose. Its main theme does contain a somewhat cryptic reference, but that, as it turns out, contributes to the general expressive sense. When Brahms and Joachim were, as one might say, fellow students, Joachim had adopted a sort of motto as characteristic of himself: *Frei Aber Einsam* (free but lonely), whose initial letters, F–A–E, were often turned into musical notes, in themes. Brahms chose for himself the motto *Frei Aber Fern* (free but distant); and the notes F–A–F, from the second of the *Ballades* for piano, Op. 10 to the Third symphony, Op. 90, very often appear in his themes — of course in varied guise. The four half notes, A–F–A–E, which begin this theme, comprise both mottoes: in A–F–A, the inversion of the intervals (3rd, 6th) of F–A–F; in the last three notes, Joachim's motto intact. (Both quartets were intended to be dedicated to Joachim; a misunderstanding caused a dedication to Dr. Billroth; but the original intention remains in the music.)

Observe in the theme (*Allegro non troppo*, 2-2) not only the mottoes but the tentative circling around, rather than the assertion of, the tonic; note also the appoggiatura suggestions in the viola (E–F, D♯–E, etc.) as well as its fluid triplet motion; watch how the suspense is sustained throughout the twenty bars of the theme, and you will probably conclude that something more than abstract design is here intended to be sensed. A little figure of eighth notes gently animates the continuation, yielding appropriate intensity on the way to the S.II (46) which, if your imagination has been aroused, will appear as exactly what you expected and hoped for. (Observe the triplet quarter notes that recur in the viola.) This is almost as long as the S.I, and is enriched by repetition with the viola above the second violin and a new *lusingando* counterpoint in the first. Quiet reference to the S.I ends the exposition. The development is neither intricate nor obscure. The recapitulation (183) figurates the S.I but is soon normal, and the Coda (*più animato sempre*) merely enlivens the already vivid impression.

The *Andante moderato* (A major, 4-4) seems like a more intimate version of the S.II of the first movement, for a similarly floating design, darkened by the Neapolitan-6th bass, is its evident burden. Ejaculations in F sharp minor (43), twice calmed by antithetical gentleness in C sharp major, evidently release something new in the undertone of the S.I, for that theme returns in the unexpected warmth of F major (77) before the 'cello, back in A major, takes it over.

The ensuing *Quasi Minuetto, moderato* (A minor) is very graceful, a little melancholy, and quite conventional in form. Its Trio (*Allegretto vivace*, 2-4) in major is a delightful surprise, as is the momentary return of the *Minuetto* in the middle of it. This vivacity probably engenders the figuration that somewhat adorns the minuet on its return.

The Finale (*Allegro non assai*, A minor, 3-4) is patently the complement of the foregoing movements. Its S.I is cast in three-bar rhythm throughout, ending (25f) in a free augmentation of the opening thematic line; the transition, in four-bar phrases, leads quietly to the S.II (43) — an all but waltz-like strain. At its end the F–A–F motive turns up (72), beginning the transition back to the S.I. This, however, is now in four-bar rhythm. The last two notes of the waltz-like sequel generate a new motive (161) that is turbulently imitated and culminates in a roaring *fortissimo.* The S.I returns, again in three-bar rhythm (198); the S.II follows, but now in the 'cello (238); the Coda (293) begins with the S.I in canon; fragments it into two-note phrases; augments it *pp*; then, *più vivace*, diminishes it in continuous eighths and ends on its figure, *unisono*. In the whole quartet there is far less of cyclic motive-recurrence than in the C minor quartet; but there is far more of expressive continuity and of imagery.

The Quartet in B flat, Op. 67

The quartet in B flat, Op. 67, is the last that Brahms wrote. It is lighter than the others in substance and perhaps more difficult to interpret adequately. It is at any rate the least often performed, and is as often condemned as praised. The S.I (*Vivace*, 6-8) suggests a hunting-horn, but the cross-rhythms of its continuation imply more sophisticated adventure. Lively scale-wide passages make transition to the S.II (34) and continue against it. It sways on the border of F major and is repeated in lower register, emerging in F minor. The Cl.S. (58) — a jerky little figure in 2-4 time, alternates and combines with the ruling 6-8 meter. The development begins with a quite new theme — a *sotto voce* wave of sound that alternates with the hunting theme (now legato) until the 2-4 figure takes over and is pushed to a climax. Then the new theme leads back to the recapitulation. In the Coda the 2-4 and 6-8 rhythms are somewhat intricately combined.

The *Andante* (F major, 4-4) has a songful, rather complacent main theme, sung by the first violin after two introductory bars. There is a quasi-tragic interlude (it is hardly an S.II) in D minor (29) whose tension suddenly lessens, turning at last into a floridation in the first violin and wending its way back to the main theme, now somewhat more richly accompanied.

The following *Agitato* (*Allegretto non troppo*, D minor, 3-4) gives its theme to the viola against a persistent figure in the other strings which are all muted. The theme pulls constantly against gentle dissonances, but the agitation is slighter than that ordinarily implied by the superscription. When the violin takes it over the viola supplies a new counterpoint. The S.II (25), again led by the viola, is in a similar rhythm but has a broader sweep. This ends with an augmentation of the S.I (51). A brief interlude ends with a fascinating pedal A in the viola in syncopated octaves (80) against which the first violin hints at the S.I, supplying, when that theme returns in the viola, a triplet figuration. The Trio, in A minor, is a sort of free variant of each of the main themes of the *Agitato*.*

The Finale is a *Poco Allegretto con Variazioni* (B flat, 2-4) on a naive little tune of the kind Brahms loved to sophisticate. To be sure, there is more than sophistication; yet that seems the main purpose. In the last variation the hunting theme from the first movement is combined with the tune, and the epilogue is made in the same fashion.

The String Quintets

The quintets for strings are late works, the first, Op. 88, having been finished in 1882 at Ischl in Switzerland. Brahms himself called it a product of Spring, and the music patently reflects the mood of that season. The addition to the string quartet is a second viola, after the example of Mozart and Beethoven.

The first movement (*Allegro non troppo ma con brio*, F major, 4-4) opens with a complacent theme, that at first gives small promise of future interest. The slightly altered repetition of its four-bar strain cadences on the dominant of D; wider intervals in the same general design reveal more of inner strength and evoke a livelier rhythmic pattern (22) whose continuation begins to glow with the warmth of the S.II toward which it is leading. This is in A, in the viola, at first essentially in 6-4 time, and has all the lilt of the first *Liebeslieder* waltzes. Its repetition in the violin closes the exposition. The development at first meditates rather remotely on the S.I; an intermediate phrase from the first transition (34f), now with an added triplet counterpoint, yields a growing animation; an apparent attempt to return to the S.I (111) is denied by the hopping rhythm of the first transition; but that theme summons all its strength (129) in canonic imitation and the recapitulation soon follows, the S.I now *f sempre*, with double-stopped triplet harmonies beneath.

The slow movement begins (*Grave ed appassionato*, C sharp minor, 3-4) with an intense, bitter strain in the 'cello, a third above the first violin. As in the *Andante* in the A major violin sonata, this theme is brief, and the equivalent of a Scherzo follows (*Allegretto vivace*, A major, 6-8). This dances lightly through a conventional Scherzo form, yielding to a much elaborated version of the *Grave*. What follows is likewise a livelier variant of the swifter movement (*Presto*, A major, 2-2). Although

* Kalbeck quotes Georg Henschel's diary as recording Brahms's assertion that this *Agitato* was the tenderest thing he had ever written.

the theme is much disguised, it is recognizable in the violin's refiguration, and the Scherzo form is again intact. The *Grave* returns for the close, with no reference to the Scherzo.

Slow movement and Scherzo having been combined, the Finale follows (*Allegro energico*, F major, 3-2). This takes the form of a free but contrapuntally elaborate fugue. Its subject, begun on two heavy chords, is an almost viciously energetic succession of driving eighths in the first viola. It is answered by second and first violins in order, then in octaves by second viola and 'cello, so that the texture is in four parts, not five, until a new dotted rhythm, resembling that of the 2-4 motive in the Scherzo of the F minor piano quartet, presages a transitional theme (29) and an indubitable S.II (35). Although this is presently combined with the fugue-subject, it is evident that a sonata form is being amalgamated with that of the fugue. Another motive in triplet quarter notes expands what we have called the S.II (37), which is in A, and the broad three-note phrase that underlay the dotted rhythm is conspicuous in the close of the sonata-exposition. The development, beginning at bar 55, is of course wholly polyphonic, and the recapitulation (110), which could not reasonably rehearse the fugal exposition at the beginning, is vastly altered. The Coda (*Presto*, 9-8) is held to *pp* until bar 169, when a swift crescendo up to five stamping C's introduces the fugue-theme in an augmentation so ingenious that the *Presto* tempo seems enhanced.

One cannot resist the notion that, loath as Brahms was to be compared with Beethoven, there was behind this piece a remembrance of the fugal Finale in the C major quartet, Op. 59, No. 3. All in all, Brahms does not come off so badly.

The string quintet in G, Op. 111, is Brahms's last work for strings alone. Kalbeck proudly tells how, on hearing the piece, he guessed (and Brahms acknowledged) its inspiration to have come from the Prater — a huge park, given to the people of Vienna by the Emperor Franz Josef. Unlike Schönbrunn with its formal gardens, its clipped trees, and its "Gloriette" (a sort of Grecian temple atop a distant hill), it is no princely residence, but a true playground, dotted here and there with merry-go-rounds and topsy-turvy swings and other challenges to the daring, but offering also alluring invitations to seclusion. But the quintet is far more than the record of a day spent in the park. The main themes are shown in Example 33.

It begins (*Allegro non troppo, ma con brio*, G major, 9-8) with a re-

EXAMPLE 33. BRAHMS STRING QUINTET IN G, OP. 111

sounding 'cello theme, booming against an accordant uproar of *tremolando* harmony — the very exuberance of youth, reawakened and revalued in a deeply experienced mind. The S.II (26) and a figure suggesting cadence (46) both emerge so naturally out of the whole current of musical event that the exposition (only fifty-eight bars long including its first ending) forms a single composite impression. The development, quite naturally, does not attempt to heighten the excitement. Rather, it gives it a new color by beginning on a murmur in B flat, around and out of which fragments of the S.I grow clearer; a new, lightly leaping motive is introduced (84) whose antic 6ths and tapping eighth notes (at first in a three-bar rhythm) assume new and exciting patterns up to bar 100, where the *tremolando* of the opening returns and at 105 the 'cello booms out (if it can — the theme is too big for the instrument) the up-beat of the S.I and the recapitulation begins. The first violin takes it over at once, with more brilliance but less force; the S.II is retained in full; and the Coda (162), at first *p*, finally releases all the exuberance of the main theme.

The main theme of the *Adagio* (D minor, 2-4) resembles, in its essential curve, the *Allegretto* of the Third symphony, retaining its nostalgic core but shunning its alleviating grace. The sudden C major that follows (3) is only apparently antithetical, for downward chromatic slippages to the *tremolando* cadence (8) darken the first viola's somber line. The violins' recitational interjection and the viola's paraphrase of the opening of the theme prepare a sort of variation of that thought (16), now in the timid violins. Recitation and more extended paraphrase bring another variant of the theme in G minor (33). Its ruminant, triplet-figured cadence is now expanded, *molto diminuendo*, but the triplets' sudden protest (48) generates a third variant of the theme in D major whose sequel, marked by a sort of syncopated tongue-and-grooving of the dotted-rhythmed arpeggio figures, becomes highly agitated. The simple theme, now in the violin, finds a singularly appropriate close in D major.

In place of a Scherzo there is what someone has called a *Valse triste*. (Its first three bars do indeed anticipate Sibelius's famous tune.) Its theme (*Un poco Allegretto*, G minor, 3-4) still smacks of the park (the Prater is no Coney Island), its gentle melancholy being relieved by a gayer Trio.

The Finale (*Vivace ma non troppo presto*, G major, 2-4) begins with a naughty little gesture in B minor in the viola. The first violin, taking it up *forte*, corrects the faulty key. It soon finds for transition a little beckoning three-note motive, triplet-accompanied, and a quaint, folk-like S.II (52) in that essentially 6-8 rhythm. The impish sixteenths of the opening soon warn that the S.I will return. It does (80), and there is what the theorists call development thereafter. The listener, more perceptive, will call it great fun.

The Clarinet Quintet, Op. 115

The Clarinet quintet, Op. 115, is a richer fruit of that same interest in the "orchestral nightingale" which yielded the Clarinet trio, Op. 114. Both pieces were finished in 1891, and both were written for Mühlfeld, whose performance in them, to judge from comments I have heard from actual hearers, has never been equaled.*

Two bars on a fluid figure in 3rds, indeterminately in D or B minor, descend to an anticipation of the main theme in the minor key.† The

---

* I *might* have heard him, with the Joachim quartet, in London. Some fool among my acquaintances said, "Don't go; Joachim plays dreadfully out of tune," and I, a still bigger fool, stayed away.

† This anticipatory phrase is identical in tonal contour with that of the alto voice beginning the *Agnus Dei* in Bach's B minor Mass, and is similarly repeated sequentially. There is of course no thought of borrowing, here; the faster tempo also veils the suggestion; yet I cannot banish the notion that something of Bach's understanding of the words, *qui tollis peccata mundi, miserere nobis*, was in the back of Brahms's mind.

clarinet then enters, improvising around the figure (in D) and so effectively blending clarinet with strings that no sense of discrepancy ever
arises thereafter. The clarinet's low register yields the bass for the theme
proper (14), first in the 'cello, above the viola, then high in the two violins. (See the illustration, Ex. 34.) A forceful staccato figure (25) snaps
the deep absorption and begins the transition to the S.II. This begins in
the clarinet (37) at high tension, subsides to a moment of hesitancy,
then, in the clarinet, leads to the Cl.S. (58) — at first in three-note phrases
that toss contrariwise in clarinet and 'cello and release tensions that have
been thus far unrevealed. The development recalls for a moment the
improvisation, seizes upon the sixteenth-note figure of the opening, and
rapidly piles up a turbulent climax; then (*Quasi sostenuto*) the rhythmic
figure from bar 25 begins to march with funereal tension while above
the tramping lower strings clarinet and first violin reshape, legato, the
staccato phrase from bar 26 and presently the S.II (112). The S.I reappears (*in tempo*, 127) in the clarinet answered by the 'cello; these two
make a figured chromatic descent, and at 136 the opening figure begins
the recapitulation. The close is on the hushed phrases that began the
movement.

The *Adagio* (B major, 3-4) is in a related but still more elegiac mood
and, although less complex than the first movement, is even more impressive. It gives almost constant prominence to the clarinet; yet, al-

EXAMPLE 34. BRAHMS CLARINET QUINTET, OP. 115

though the strings are muted, they do not seem subordinated. The broad theme, in the clarinet, is heavily weighted by the persistent pull of syncopation and the frequent Neapolitan lowering of the 6th of the scale in the harmony. Triplet motion in the lower strings somewhat softens its impact. Both violins share in its continuation, returning the lead to the clarinet (25) for a sequential approach to the theme and the theme itself. A lingering cadence brings a change to B minor (42). A clarinet cadenza then leads to the middle section (*Più lento*, 4-4). Here snatches of the main theme are floridly ornamented by the clarinet, but the strings have also their share and the amalgamation of ornament and basic substance is complete. There is a quiet, impressive conclusion.

An *Andantino* (D major, 4-4), palpably intended to avoid the shock of a too-abrupt plunge into more worldly concerns, begins the third movement. Its theme, although quite naive, is wholly welcome. The main part of the movement, however, is a swift variant of this thought (*Presto non assai, ma con sentimento*, 2-4). The ingenuity of the transformation is amazing, but analysis of it in any but the dullest of technical terms is a problem so baffling that we have had to forgo it.

Even after this lighter movement the shock of a brilliant or even a weighty Finale would be unendurable. What appears is therefore a set of variations on a theme hardly less naive in appearance than that of the Andantino. It begins (*Con moto*, B minor, 2-4) in the violins, the clarinet interjecting only incidental complementary phrases until the end, where it plays the last eight cadential bars continuously. The dimensions of the theme — two sixteen-bar sections, the last repeated — are duplicated in each variation; the contour of the theme, on the other hand, is reshaped with each, and is sometimes hard to recognize. In the second section of the third variation a figure of sixteenths appears which, although still in 2-4 time, clearly suggests the figure that opened the quartet. In the fourth (in B major) second violin and viola continue the suggestion; and in the fifth, which is again in B minor and in 3-8 time, the resemblance becomes unmistakable. In this way the Coda is able to return to the opening four bars of the quintet as its topic. Intellectually, the device may seem somewhat forced; expressively, it is wholly satisfying.

The String Sextets

Consistently with our plan, we return from Op. 115 to Op. 18, the sextet in B flat. The jolt is considerable, yet it is less than that we experienced in turning from Beethoven's Op. 135 to his quintet, Op. 29. For Brahms's early works, preceded by a most unusual intensity in self-critical study, show fewer signs of artistic experimentation than those of any other great composer. A discrepancy is of course evident — not wholly reassuring as to the value of that self-criticism. For there is in the first sextet an abandon — a melodic fluency all but Schubertian — that could not survive such critical pruning; and a wisdom greater than Solomon's would be needed to give ultimate decision as to which was the higher value.

The sextet was written in 1859–60. It had no other predecessor in the field of chamber music than the first form of the trio in B major, Op. 8. (The first piano quartets were as yet unfinished, and Brahms's effort with the orchestra had gone no farther than the two Serenades, Opp. 11 and 16.) Yet the handling of the instruments is always wholly competent, whether as to their individual technique or their combination. The principal themes are shown in Example 35.

EXAMPLE 35. BRAHMS SEXTET IN B FLAT, OP. 18

The main theme of the first movement (*Allegro ma non troppo*, B flat, 3-4) begins in the first 'cello's tenor register with viola and second 'cello below. It is quite unpretentious rhetorically, although its first period is imperceptibly lengthened to five bars by the repetition of bars 2–3, and its quiet flow — carefree but far from flippant — establishes at once the mood of the whole movement. The first violin, with a preparatory bar (it is not, integrally, a fifth bar of the second period) takes over the theme intact and expands it in a colorful modulation that finally uses the full sonority of the sextet (the second viola is silent for twenty-two bars) and reaches its peak (35) as effortlessly as it began. Even after the climax

[213

has subsided the original melodic impulse persists, evoking a warm triplet figure from the first violin — obviously in approach to the S.II. This, beginning in A (61), at first cadences somewhat unstably in its "proper" key (F major), but its repetition in the higher octave rises buoyantly to F sharp (in D); then, again in the lower octave, it finds that F, after all, is its true key. (This shift between major and minor, as we saw, is a favorite device with Schubert.) At once, as if the melodic spring would never cease flowing, the first 'cello finds a continuing strain (85); violin and viola repeat it; and there is still another (115) that ends the exposition. Aside from a combination (173) of the triplet figuration evoked by the S.I with a four-note motive that completed the 'cello's continuation of the S.II, the development is more indifferent to "learning" than is usual with Brahms.

The *Andante, ma Moderato* (F major, 2-4) is a set of variations on a theme that can be piously read as a sample of folk-song structure. But if the incessant, *forte*, "one, two" march of the accompanying chords makes the first viola and then the first violin, who have the theme, realize what they are saying, such a draught of melody comes out as will add more than a cubit to the stature of any hearer who holds out his cup to it.*

There is nothing else to do with such a tune than to make variations on it. Brahms had already proved himself the most imaginative variationist since Beethoven, and these reshapings of the primary implications of his theme largely confirm that status. They figurate the essential harmony — the first in sixteenths, the second in triplet sixteenths, and the third in thirty-seconds (with surging scales that recall the last of Beethoven's Thirty-two Variations in C minor); then the fourth, in D major, still *forte*, slows the motion to even eighths and "sings unto the Lord a new song," as tense as the theme but shorn of a part of its sternness. The fifth, over a bagpipe drone in the second viola and suddenly *piano*, has a quiet lilt which none of us would have had the wit to imagine as another implication in the theme, and the last returns to the theme in the first 'cello, with its sections now not repeated, and makes a Coda on its final cadence.

A gaiety more vigorous than light appropriately imbues the following Scherzo (*Allegro molto*, F major, 3-4). Having but one theme, it is short.

---

* We used to call it, in the little chamber group to which my wife and I belonged, "the Crusaders' tune."

Note the interesting rhythmic shift of the first note from "one" to the up-beat "three" at the imitative beginning of the second section. The Trio (*Animato*) cleverly extends its eight-bar period to ten bars, supporting its melody on the opening figure of the Scherzo. Its theme also yields the Coda.

Energy heightened beyond that of the two preceding movements, even if it could have been portrayed, would have failed in impact. The Finale, accordingly, is a Rondo on a main theme whose sedateness is in strong contrast. The regularity of its design is almost painfully orthodox, and its sentiment, to our ears, similarly demure. It rules, with a brief intermediate strain, for fifty-six bars. The S.II (72), approached by a transition in three-bar rhythm, has a continuing strain more interesting than itself. The S.I returns (138) with its former continuing motive which is vigorously developed (180f), forming thus the S.II of the Rondo. The S.I reappears (278) with its phrases divided between violin and 'cello to begin a recapitulation. Another version of the S.I follows (389), first violin and first 'cello now taking each a single bar, and on this theme and its first continuation the Coda (*Animato, poco a poco più*) is reached. Here the first viola, scampering over the essential harmonies of the S.I in sixteenth-note arpeggios, is accompanied pizzicato by the other strings in a diminution of the three-note motive from bar 33. But they soon take to their bows for the jolly end.

The Sextet in G, Op. 36

The Sextet in G, Op. 36 (Ex. 36), written at Lichtenthal in 1864, is more frankly autobiographical than any other of his chamber works. We know only by inference that the C minor piano quartet related to the suppressed passion of Brahms and Clara Schumann. This piece contains in its actual notes a reference to the all-but-announced engagement of Brahms to Agathe von Siebold, the talented daughter of a professor of medicine at the University of Göttingen. Although it was Agathe who explicitly refused a proposal that was probably never spoken, it was Brahms (made aware by his friend, J. O. Grimm, of the high tide of gossip their association had aroused) who wrote her that "he could not wear fetters." How deeply his rude phrase hurt her he perhaps never realized; but his own longing also remained, and the first movement of the sextet seems to us to tell, however guardedly, how deeply it rankled even after five years.

[215

EXAMPLE 36. BRAHMS SEXTET IN G, OP. 36

The first movement (*Allegro non troppo*, G major, 3-4) begins with a waver between the open G of the first viola and the adjoining F♯ — the G being a pedal that continues for thirty-two bars beneath the theme in the first violin. This is a deeply contemplative melodic line, rising without rhythmic propulsion through the two fifths, G–D and E♭–B♭ (a bar for each note), veering into E flat and back to G, and then, only a little more actively, retracing its quiet curve. (See the illustration, Ex. 36.) The continuation (33) has the new color of B major, but keeps a similar contour; the waver, no longer a pedal, accompanies the returning theme in the 'cello (53); and that thought does not release its hold until an intense scale descent in the 'cello (95), imitated in the upper voices, makes extended approach to the S.II, in D (135). This, still in the 'cello, although only slightly contrasted in rhythm, is lyrically warmer than the S.I, and when the first violin repeats it in F, doubled first by the 'cello and then by the viola, it begins to be perturbed. At the peak (162) there comes an outcry, thrice uttered, on the notes A–G–A–B♮–E, and against the B the second violin suspends a D. Now B♮, in German, is called H; and these notes thus spell AGADHE, which is as near AGATHE as it is possible to come in the restricted alphabet of music. The outcry, in lower voices and transposed to other tonal levels, remains conspicuous until the close of the exposition on the S.I. The development

216]

JOHANNES BRAHMS

begins with a canon in contrary motion on the S.I; the opening waver appears (249) and is expanded against many new manipulations of the subject; but all this is subordinated to the wider exploration of the character of the theme. The recapitulation (343) is quite regular, with the outcry of course transposed to D, where its note-names spell nothing, but still mean *Agathe!* The Coda (*Un poco sostenuto*) finds still more of character in the S.I.

This Scherzo (*Allegro non troppo*, G minor, 2-4) naturally follows the *Adagio* mood of the first movement. The main theme is angular in rhythm and a little blunt and wayward in design, but it soon smooths itself into a *tranquillo* triplet figuration. Against this the theme appears in inversion, syncopated and briefly fugued. The Trio (*Presto giocoso*, G major, 3-4) is a swift, plebeian little waltz whose frank gaiety is tamed (165) by a quiet reshaping of its melody, legato. The return is rounded off by a tiny Coda, *Animato*.

Hanslick, after his first hearing of the *Poco Adagio* (E minor, 4-4) described it as a set of variations "on no theme." His confusion was understandable, for the brief theme, although cast in three four-bar sections resembling the simple A–B–A design, does not return precisely upon itself. Moreover, it is composite. Two rising 4ths, obviously recalling the rising 5ths that open the first movement, are accompanied by a chromatic descent (in even eighths in the second violin, but figurated in triplets in the viola); and this descent proves to be of equal significance with the more conspicuous rising 4ths. It takes the lead, in first violin and viola, in the first variation, while the rising 4ths (in pizzicato eighth notes) appear as accompaniment in the first 'cello. The chromatic descent, figurated and moving contrariwise in upper strings and 'cello, begins the second variation. The next (*Più animato*) begins with a leaping octave in a marching rhythm that enters in quick succession on B's, E's, A's and a D — i.e., on the essential 4ths of the theme — each voice continuing on a triplet figure. In the next variation the octaves leap downward, and at the same time viola and second violin fill in, scale-wise, the 4ths B–E and F♯–B; but the general contour pretty effectively hides these minutiae. The next, at first still more obscure in its derivation, but begun in a delicate and graceful *piano*, eventuates in a direct statement of the rising 4ths, quarter notes in the first 'cello, and in half notes in the violin with the chromatic descent against it. Then, *Adagio*, and in E major, a quiet figuration of the 4ths, slowed from sixteenths to eighths and finally

[217

to quarters, makes the serene end. You may think that Hanslick, after all, was not wholly wrong.

The relation of the last movement to the sextet thus far is hard to see. There are two contrasted structural features — a glittering figure in sixteenths (*Poco Allegro*, G major, 9-8) that serves as S.I, and a quiet melodic flow, *tranquillo*, that follows (7) as the figure subsides. But the contour of the opening figure, in the same quiet motion, follows (15) in the first viola; the sixteenths reappear (29); and against them the first 'cello (34) has another pattern — a sequence of descending 5ths — that serves as Cl.S. in a remarkably short sonata-exposition (only fifty-two bars long). Development and recapitulation are similarly compacted. The Coda, *Animato*, maintains the sixteenths in *moto perpetuo*, but the flowing S.II emerges for a time against them. The remote spirituality of the earlier movements hardly survived in the *Adagio*. It is unimaginable that it could have been continued in a Finale, where convention expects something akin to the happy ending of the eighteenth century. But the disappointment of those who expect the impossible, however unjustifiably, is still a disappointment.

The "Brahmins" believed, and it may still be plausibly argued, that Brahms endowed us with the most highly civilized music we possess. Its technical finish is unassailable; its substance is free of impurities; on any of our precarious aesthetic scales it registers indubitable weight; its excitement is never merely inflated; and the image of experience it reflects is not only in accord with long-established ideals but is often considerably above them. But while his work was thus a rampart defending the high conventions of civilization, it was also a barrier against excursion into the "wastes" that lay outside the walls.

It was not so with Beethoven, who was more at home outside the walls of convention than within them; who fed his imagination on fresh rather than preserved fruits; and whose musical images of experience retain, in consequence, even for the twentieth century, an almost untarnished veracity. One could wish that Brahms had gone, earlier and more often, not only to the Prater but to still more uncultivated fields.

We turn now to a sketch of the musical effort in those fields. We shall find no figure of the musical stature of a Beethoven or a Brahms. But we shall find in these virgin soils many musical plants that can become acclimated to our own and cross-fertilize and fructify for the richer nourishment of the musical spirit.

Nationalistic Chamber Music

T H E structural perfection of Brahms's chamber music is probably as great as is humanly attainable. But that perfection, except in its smaller detail, is not wholly due to his effort. It is the culmination of that long line of endeavor which began with Haydn and which our study has in some measure illuminated. It was thus an inheritance wholly Germanic in character, even though the origins of chamber music were Italian.*

* Italy and France inherited the language of ancient Rome and transformed it into their vernacular (Romance) tongues. Something of ancient literary taste survived along with that inheritance, to emerge when the vernacular tongues, at the hands of Dante and the Provençal poets, became literary languages. That taste was greatly clarified and its principles were reinforced by the revival of the ancient learning, so that the (to us) considerably artificial literary classicism that was formulated — most authoritatively in the France of the 1660's — was accepted there and in Italy as it was never accepted in Germany or England.

Again, this acceptance of what was regarded as august literary authority was apparently related to the acceptance of Roman Catholicism as the authoritative universal religion. At any rate, those countries in which Catholicism was to dominate were those in which the classic literary ideals were pursued, while those in which Protestantism was to flourish were those in which the classic traditions were least followed. The association is difficult to establish factually, but the coincidence is too complete to be accidental; and since the rejection of the classic tradition (as in England and Germany) was evident even before the Protestant movement began, it is at least arguable that a national disposition or temperament, rooted in long traditions of outlook and behavior, was a significant factor in either attitude.

Music, in this writer's view, offers if not a fuller, at least a more immediate revelation of disposition and temperament than any other art. In that view it thus appears natural that Italy and France should follow the lure of opera, which, offering the closest counterpart of classic drama, was the musical form most accordant with their national instinct and their artistic tradition. It was similarly natural that Germany should develop such musical forms as the symphony and its more intimate relative, chamber music. The nationalistic movements now to be noted will appear as similarly natural.

Native musical imagination, the primary stimulus to any high creative effort, was no more prevalent in Germany than in other lands. In Italy and France, where it was developed against quite other cultural traditions, it yielded quite another product — the opera. Learned culture — somewhat prideful, as learning often is — ruled in opera, and ruled out all expression of national character as it was revealed in the music of the folk. In other nations — Russia, Bohemia, Hungary, Norway — that same native musical impulse, doubtless equally strong, lay fallow until it was fertilized by the effort of perceptive minds, encouraged to creation by foreign example rather than intimidated by it to mere imitation.

RUSSIAN

The consciousness of Russia as a musical nation was aroused by Michael Glinka (1804–1857) whose opera, *A Life for the Tsar* (1836) revealed the existence of a vast body of folk music hitherto ignored by the intelligentsia. It awoke the national consciousness to an extraordinary degree, starting the most vigorous nationalistic movement to arise in Europe. Glinka ventured also into chamber music, with a *Pathétique* trio, two string quartets, and a septet; but the opera, the symphonic poem, and the song were his principal interest. Dargomyzhsky, pursuing dramatic realism as well as national musical idiom, contributed to the new movement, and these two were followed by a group — Balakirev, Borodin, Cui, Mussorgsky, and Rimsky-Korsakov — announced to the world by Vladimir Stasov as "The Mighty Company," but generally known as "The Five," who pursued the nationalistic ideal with such fervor that Tchaikovsky (whose Russianism was non-militant) was not included among the company. Of these five, only Alexander Borodin (1833–1887) produced chamber music of note.

Alexander Borodin (1833–1887)

He, like all the Five except Balakirev, was not a professional musician. His chief effort was in chemistry and medicine, to which he made important contributions. Balakirev strongly urged him to cultivate his evident musical talent, and while his second symphony is still current in the orchestral repertoire, and his opera, *Prince Igor*, with its familiar *Polovtzian Dances*, and his symphonic sketch, *In the Steppes of Central Asia*, are perhaps more characteristically Russian than his chamber music, one of his few works in that genre is still very much in the repertoire.

This is his second string quartet in D, finished in the last year of his life. It will be evident from the tone of the opening movement (*Allegro moderato*, D major, 2-2) that the sonata form as an ideal structural pattern was of relatively slight interest to him. The main theme, a graciously undulant line in the 'cello, contains several motives which suggest possible development, but none of them is put to that purpose. The first violin takes over the theme (5) quite lyrically a 4th higher (but over the same pedal D), and finds a more lilting continuation with a couple of tripping sixteenths (10) that will soon prove infectious. The two versions are amiably dialogued against quietly active harmonies in the middle strings; a cadence on the dominant of A seems to announce a second theme; but what appears is a new variant of the sixteenth-note figure from bar 10, over pizzicato chords — the transition to the S.II. This (57), in both violin and 'cello, really begins in F sharp minor but finally lands in A. The transition-figure returns in the 'cello (77), driving toward what we take to be the Cl.S. of the exposition (*Animato*) — a chromatic descent in the viola — briefly expanded. The development (108) begins on the S.I in F major; yields to the S.II (127) and to the transition figure (145); and quietly returns to the recapitulation (180). Colorful excursion into flat keys now heightens the interest but the design is kept in focus.

The Scherzo (*Allegro*, F major, 3-4) is no more heedful of the conventional form than was the first movement, but is just as lucid and still more charming. Its main theme is a tripping figure of one bar in the first violin. Against this the viola has a counterpoint on the descending 5th which, inverted to the rising 4th and in 3rds in the two violins (29), becomes an infectious swaying waltz-tune, *Meno mosso*. The original figure returns (100), alternated between second violin and viola and building up to a jubilant new motive (128) that forms the climax of the piece. There is a brief recapitulation (192) and a Coda that seems to intend a brilliant close but thinks better of it and vanishes in pizzicato.

The third movement is the familiar *Notturno* (*Andante*, A major, 3-4) that has been heard in countless rearrangements. Its main theme, first heard in the 'cello, is nostalgic but is careful not to protest too much. The implication of its essentially descending line is heightened when the violin repeats and extends the theme. Vigor is then interjected (48) by an upward, sixteenth-note scale (*più mosso*) that culminates in a figure made from the first two bars of the main theme. It is ingeniously overlapped in the violins, revealing its origin in the 'cello (67) and reverting at last (111) to the S.I in the 'cello, hesitantly imitated in canon by the first violin. The two violins prolong the canon, and the scale-figure is twice interjected into the Coda.

The Finale begins (*Andante*, D major, 2-4) with the statement of two short patterns — one in higher strings, the other in lower — which are then combined in 'cello and viola to form the main theme of the movement (*Vivace*). The S.II (90) is blithe and elastic, somewhat in the vein of the waltz-tune in the Scherzo. After a return of the two opening phrases, only the second of which is now *Andante*, there is the hint of a third subject (241). These things are shaped into the sufficient likeness of a sonata-rondo form. A certain resemblance to the Finale of Beethoven's Op. 135 (*Muss es sein? — es muss sein!*) can easily be seen. Whether it really originated this movement is another question.

Peter Ilyitch Tchaikovsky (1840–1893)

Tchaikovsky, although black-balled by the critics for membership in the Mighty Company, still seems to us in America as a more vivid exponent of Russian national character than any other nineteenth-century Russian composer except Mussorgsky. His interest in chamber music was slight, so that he left but three string quartets, a sextet (*Souvenirs de Florence*), and a piano trio. None of these retains as fully as the Borodin quartet the appeal of that exceptional, non-professional piece. All of them, on the other hand, have more of what we think of as Russian character. Tchaikovsky is perhaps a little more observant of the canons of sonata form; but of that form as the greatest German masters saw it he has little awe.

The first of the quartets, Op. 11, in D, was written in 1871, before the Second symphony. His understanding of the individual instruments is already complete and his intuition for their combined sonority quite sure (his skill in orchestration was always unfailing); but his musical images are so largely melodic and lyrical that the structure remains largely that of accompanied tune, even though he is fertile in the invention of attendant, often scale-wise, melodic figures. He can hardly contrive, however, the kind of succinct, pregnant musical phrase whose implications must be revealed by development as the German masters conceived it.*

* How much of our faith in the German ideal of structure by development is due to our long indoctrination — essentially, brainwashing — in the tradition of German

The first quartet begins (*Moderato e semplice*, D major, 9-8) with a theme of such ruminant character that it can be intensified only by repetition and the addition of new accompanying voices; the second theme offers little real contrast, and the whole movement, although the conventional outline of the sonata form can be discerned, gives the impression of improvisation on a sudden suggestion of idea rather than a considered discourse. The *Andante cantabile* (B flat, 2-4) caught the popular ear and has been arranged for almost every thinkable combination of instruments. Its second theme, accompanied pizzicato by the 'cello, is even more songful than the first. Both movements seem to have (*mutatis mutandis*) the texture and the purport of drawing-room piano pieces. The Scherzo is more energetic, and the syncopations in the Trio sound — at any rate to our ears — thoroughly Russian. The Finale (*Allegro giusto*, 2-4) is patently of folk origin although the themes, so far as we know, are Tchaikovsky's own. Vivacity is skillfully maintained, but the total impression is frothy.

The second quartet, written in 1874, although less frequently performed, seems to this commentator more interesting both in substance and structure. It has an Introduction (*Adagio*, 6-8) without key-signature

superiority in structure is a question to which the brainwashed — we ourselves — are unlikely to find the true answer. The virtues of the system, even when that system is learnedly expounded by the theorists (who are the indoctrinators) are manifest and largely indubitable. But they may be attained — as a more skeptical glance at Brahms's achievement than we gave in our study may indicate — at the expense of a certain measure of spontaneity, which is also a virtue. Hugo Wolf's complaint of Brahms — *er kann nicht jubeln* (he cannot exult) — is not the protest of a child deprived of its bottle. It is a plea for the recognition of an element as essential in musical utterance as is structure — the element of experiential imagery. (You do not exult over nothing.)

Indoctrination has taught us that rhetorical perfection, as such, is a thing to be admired even when the purpose of utterance is submerged in the process of utterance. That process is also indubitably effective for the rectification of a faulty image of musical experience, such as exultation. But you will not rectify a faulty image of that sort by the mere perfecting of the rhetoric of your utterance as rhetoric. You will only distract the attention of your hearer from the essential (e.g., the imaged exultation) to the subordinate (your cleverness).

National characteristics in music are not mere rhetorical gestures. They stem from experience — inherited, communicated, shared, and cherished — as the portrayals of accepted national behavior-patterns. To apply to nationalistic music the critical yardstick of German sonata-structure is thus a dubious critical experiment. Neither Borodin nor Tchaikovsky shows any high realization of the value of the sonata form as an artistic abstraction. To complain, then, as we shall have seemed to do, of their indifference to this august structure-pattern is really to confess at least a measure of indifference to values of imagery in their music far more essential than that of abstract structure.

and in no definite key, which twice resolves an intriguing tangle of dissonance into a somewhat tortuous imitative substance and then continues in a cadenza figure for the first violin. You will expect the tiny imitated theme to be incorporated into the main movement, but it never reappears. Yet that movement (*Moderato assai*, F major, with signature, 4-4) seems to us a wholly appropriate sequel to the Introduction. The main theme, with a three-note chromatic figure for counterpoint, floats flexibly around the tonic. It is made to rise in intensity and pitch by rather obvious harmonic sequences (Tchaikovsky always relies on this device), but the impression of character is not lost. The transition to the S.II is on a more excited syncopated rhythm (42); that theme (56) has a marching strut and is accompanied by scampering staccato scale-figures; and the development (there is no Cl.S.) is approached by another brief cadenza in the first violin. The development is mostly on a fragment of the S.I, again manipulated sequentially, but the color-interest is high. The recapitulation (132) is much intensified, but the Coda (196), still on the S.I, is appropriately quiet.

The Scherzo (*Allegro giusto*, D flat) is on a lively dance-figure that follows two bars of 6-8 by three heavy stamps in 9-8. Both this theme and that of the Trio (*l'istesso tempo*, A major, 3-4) have a distinct Russian flavor. The *Andante ma non tanto* (F minor, 3-4) begins with two bitter-sweet phrases of protest on the augmented 6th followed by a three-bar hint of resignation. This note continues to be struck, somewhat polyphonically, throughout the first section. The second, in E major, is on a more agitated theme that rises syncopatedly over agreeable chromatic harmony. Elaborate figurations in all the accompanying instruments then yield a tense sonority. The return of the S.I is at first tainted with a similar agitation, but the somewhat overlong leave-taking is quiet. The Finale (*Allegro con moto*, F major, 3-4) is almost throughout in the rhythm of the Polonaise — a never-failing whip to languid nerves.

The third quartet, in E flat minor, was written in 1876. Its key, unusual because rather uncomfortable for the strings, is quite appropriate to the composer's prevailing moods of melancholy; but the piece as a whole lacks the interest of the other quartets.

Neither does it seem needful to study in detail the last of Tchaikovsky's chamber works — the piano trio in A minor. It was written in 1882, "to the memory of a great artist"— Nicholas Rubinstein, a friend, but often a severe critic of Tchaikovsky's work. The first movement, entitled

Pezzo elegiaco, begins in a mildly elegiac vein but soon forsakes it for a mingling of brilliancy and passion, interesting in itself but incongruous with the opening note which is quite lost in the long dissertation. The last two movements are really one, since they are all variations on the simple theme, announced by the piano — ten two-bar phrases, grouped 3 + 3 + 4, and all identical in rhythm except for the third, sixth, and last which end on the down-beat while the others end on "two." In the first section there are eleven variations, among them a waltz, a mazurka, and a fugue (which may be omitted), often colorful and displaying the piano to advantage. The second section (*Variazioni Finale e Coda*) turns the theme into a sort of *Marche des Davidsbündler* à la Schumann. Fifteen pages are marked for a merciful *ad libitum* omission.

Aside from an amiable piano trio by Anton Arensky (1861–1906) and the 'cello sonata of Rachmaninoff (1873–1943), in which the composer's pianistic skill seems to us too much in evidence, there is no other nineteenth-century Russian chamber music which demands mention in our rather restricted survey.

BOHEMIAN

Surrounded by nations more powerful than itself, Bohemia, although its people formed a distinctive ethnic group which from the close of the Thirty Years' War maintained its native customs, became in the eighteenth century so far an appanage of the Austrian Empire that even its native language was all but suppressed, and its external cultural influence nil. Nationalistic sentiment, however, remained strong, and it was perhaps only natural that it should be expressed most fully in music — which is not the language of diplomacy.

No such musical awakening as that effected by Glinka in Russia is chronicled, nor did Bohemia produce any "Mighty Company." But it did produce two important nineteenth-century composers, one of whom still remains an outstanding figure.

Bedrich Smetana (1824–1894)

A similar faith to that of Glinka drove Smetana to celebrate in music the glories of his native land. His effort mostly took the forms of opera and the symphonic poem (*The Bartered Bride*, and "The Moldau," the second of six orchestral pieces collectively entitled *Ma Vlast* — My Country — are known to every concert-goer); but for more intimate revelations he turned to chamber music. Two string quartets and a piano trio in memory of the death of his little daughter are his only output, but the quartet in E minor — *Aus meinem Leben* (From My Life) — is still a favorite.

This is frankly but in no way offensively programmatic. It first portrays the enthusiasms and the desperations of youth; a Polka (a Bohemian dance, originating around 1830 and long the rage in all Europe) then suggests another aspect of gaiety; the slow movement tells of his love for Katharina Kolář, his first wife and helpmeet (she was a fine pianist); then a lively folk-dance illustrates the composer's delight in folk music. But it comes to a sudden halt and a high E — a persistent ringing in his ear that heralded his approaching deafness — begins to sound in the first violin, and the sorrowful end is soon reached.

The main theme of the first movement is a recitative-like ejaculation in the viola (*Allegro vivo appassionato*, E minor, 4-4) — almost verbally explicit; the S.II (71) is similarly unmistakable as a feminine influence. There is no other essential subject-matter. The development (121f), almost all on the S.I, becomes polyphonic by accompanying that theme with a triplet figure first generated out of its exposition. The recapitulation, omitting the S.I, brings back the S.II in E major, and the Coda is a tamed version of the S.I. The *Allegro moderato à la Polka* bounces right off the floor at its first bar and maintains its agility until the second violin (47) introduces the S.II — a sort of trumpet-tune. The Trio, beginning in D flat, has little else than its new, more elastic rhythm, but the first violin (122) at last finds graceful melody above it. In the *Largo sostenuto* (A flat, 6-8) the hero (impersonated by the 'cello) comes on stage in a solo recitative. Then the violin begins to sing in warm and movingly harmonized strains of an experience which the dullest ear would recognize as amatory. After the brief S.II (46) the 'cello takes the S.I against gentle floridations in the violin, and the heroine answers with the S.II. The Finale has been sufficiently described above.

Smetana's second quartet, in D minor, portrays "the whirlwind of music in the head of one who has lost his hearing." It is somewhat more elaborate in texture, since it presents transformations of its themes in illustration of the much less concrete "events" involved in its program. His model was evidently the Lisztian symphonic poem, which tells its story by giving new shapes, and consequently new character, to its basic themes. But the quartet hardly requires analysis.

Antonín Dvořák (1841–1904)

In almost any work of Dvořák's, although he never speaks the musical language obscurely, a foreign accent is detectible. It suggests a background of experience somewhat strange to our own but never alien — a background we know at second hand, from our grandfathers. He has more than a fair measure of learning, but he never parades it; and the intimidation we often feel when confronted by learning is never aroused when he speaks. The Dance, almost unknown to America as a communal expression, was for him what it was to his people — an utterance of inherited national sentiment and an evidence of solidarity.

His first teacher was the fiddling village schoolmaster at Nelahozeves (Mühlhausen) where his father was innkeeper and butcher. An organist at Zlonitz where he was sent to school at twelve taught him the rudiments of organ, piano, and theory, enough so that when he went to Prague at sixteen his violin earned him a precarious livelihood. When Smetana became conductor of the National Theatre Dvořák gained from him not only much new insight into orchestral music and performance but a deeper understanding of the folk music he had grown up with. He composed almost constantly (a string quintet, two symphonies, and even an opera were later destroyed), acquiring a skill which won for his first Slavonic Dances equal recognition with the Hungarian Dances of Brahms. The sonata form remained for him a vehicle for attaining musical coherence rather than the high abstraction which it sometimes seems to have become for Brahms, and there are perhaps no perfect models of that form among his works. His texture is seldom really polyphonic, although he is never at a loss for well-manipulated figures of accompaniment. His rhythms are often literally adopted from the music of his people, but he knows how to adapt them to larger purposes. His harmony is colored by the free modulation common to all his contemporaries, but it has a highly personal tang. His melody, even in those works written in America (1892–1895), was never (he asserts) directly borrowed, but was written only in the spirit of Negro song as he heard it. Only a deep imaginative insight could have yielded the spontaneity either of those works or of his more frankly nationalistic pieces. But that same faculty is the chamber-musician's richest resource, and we shall find Dvořák using his wealth to good purposes.

The Chamber Music with Piano. No more than passing mention need be made of his two duets for piano and violin — the Sonata in F, Op. 57, and the Sonatina in A, Op. 100. The sonata has never been popular. Dvořák, only a fair pianist, seems not to have been aware of the depths and subtleties of piano tone which Liszt and Chopin had so sensitively explored, and the two instruments somehow refuse to blend toward a tonal purpose which, to the eye, looks attractive. The sonatina does not suffer from this defect. It is much slighter in substance but is very engaging, and provides for many a student a good initiation into the experience of chamber music.

The piano trios, according to our plan, are next in order. The first of these, Op. 21, in B flat, has much melodic appeal, but is so repetitious that the mind, rather than the ear, becomes wearied. Its main theme (*Allegro molto*, 2-2), a spacious lyric phrase, is heard thrice at different levels before its diminution (19) begins to provide rhythmic energy; a complementary strain (31) has a similar sequel; the S.II (72), a dance rhythm, keeps going with more repetition than development to the end of the exposition (157); the long development presents rather obvious expansions of the S.I, and the recapitulation, although it adds considerably to the sonority of the S.II, adds little to its real interest. The sonata form is for Dvořák as yet a pattern obediently filled out, rather than a vehicle suited to purposeful communication. The *Adagio molto e maesto* (*mesto?*), in G minor, 2-4, has its soberly contemplative theme in the piano. Its end (8) is so remote as to seem inconsequent, and repetition in the 'cello makes its purport no clearer, although it has the annoying interest of obscurity. The S.II (36) in A major is not highly contrasted, nor does the staid augmentation of S.I at the end appear really impressive. Both the *Allegretto scherzando* (C minor, 2-4) and the Finale (*Allegro vivace*, 6-8), although their intent is visible, fail to realize it — partly through unskillful drawing and partly through excessive length.

The second trio, Op. 26, in G minor, was written shortly after the death of the composer's daughter. It is more somber in tone than the B flat, but similarly diffuse. We go on, therefore, to the trio in F minor, Op. 65, written seven years later, which is quite another matter.

Its main theme, *pp* in unison strings (*Allegro ma non troppo*, F minor, 4-4) is a sober thought, compacting many implications into its brief three bars. The piano makes an excited flourish out of its last dotted motive, suggesting a fuller repetition of the theme. Instead there comes quite another motive (9) — three loud chords with a tense outcry following — cognate in character with the first and amplifying its sense. Repetition of the main theme in the piano (17) restores its perspective. Still another subordinate thought (29), with the motive from bar 9 attached, makes transition to the real S.II (66) in the 'cello in D flat, very songful and definitely akin to the character thus far exposed. A more rhythmic syncopated motive gives this theme expansion similar to that of the S.I and makes a rather too-extended transition to the development. This begins with an oblique version of the S.I in the piano (117). After its leaping 6th has made modulation to B major, the strings put the theme through several sequential paces; at 136 its rhythm is much activated; at 164 the motive from bar 9, augmented, becomes highly intense, preparing for the thunderous return of the S.I and the considerably enriched recapitulation.

After the fashion of Brahms, the next movement is no Scherzo but an *Allegretto grazioso* (C sharp minor, 2-4) that might well have been entitled Intermezzo. It has a quaint, square theme — as true a portrait of Dvořák as Elizabeth von Herzogenberg found the C minor trio to be of Brahms. Its angular phrases — externally almost awkward, internally extraordinarily tender — are put through modulations rather than developed, but the smiles and frowns on the knobbly face never lose interest. There is a Trio (*Meno mosso*, D flat) on a long, flowing curve whose second strain reaches impressive heights — or depths —of human warmth.

The *Poco Adagio* begins with a 'cello theme that should confirm Dvořák's assertion that he did not, in America, directly borrow Negro melody but only wrote in the spirit of it. A latent desolation, neither black nor white, is here as patent as in the *Adagio* of the "Negro" quartet. The minor subdominant harmony of the opening bar becomes more heavily flatted as the theme continues, and the second strain (11) cannot evade that influence. The S.II in G sharp minor, stern and incisive against a figurated tremolando, is imitated between violin and 'cello. Its second strain, in B major, warm and lyrical, at last finds the way back to A flat and to the S.I, now in the violin (74). There is a thoughtful epilogue.

The Finale (*Allegro con brio*, F minor, 3-4) is, in pattern, almost a Scherzo; in character, a Slavonic dance. The Trio, in E, borrows some of its rhythm from the S.I, thus offering more similarity than contrast. The movement is bright and attractive, but to our mind it has little relativity to what has gone before. Indeed, the recall of the main theme of the first movement, in triple time and *grandioso*, before the *Meno mosso* Coda, seems quite irrelevant. But this is not the first instance in which we have found a composer at a loss when reaching his Finale.

Dvořák's last trio, Op. 90, called the *Dumky* Trio, abandons the classical sonata form and offers a succession of six *Dumky* —"laments" or "elegies" are perhaps our nearest equivalents of the Little Russian word. The *Dumka* has ordinarily a sequel, called *Furiant*; it is fast and excited, but the "fury" we naturally read into the word is not essentially implied. It is also tempting, but possibly wholly fanciful, to see in this sequence the survival of an established custom which we noted in the dance music of the middle ages — the dance-pair. A slow dance-measure was immediately followed by a fast one, the melody of the second being a transformation of the first, and a second pair might still be made of the one theme.

An analogy, if not a real historic sequence, is evident here. The first *Dumka* (*Lento maestoso*, E minor, 2-4) is followed by an *Allegro quasi doppio movimento* in E major whose dainty figure in the piano is a new version of the descending 6ths that accompanied the 'cello's tense melody in the *Dumka*. Both are then reworked, piano and strings reversing their former roles as melody or accompaniment, with the fast section (*Allegro*) prancing even more gaily than before. You will go far to find such delightful insouciance as is here expressed by a mere figurated descent of the scale. The second *Dumka* (*Poco Adagio*, C sharp minor, 4-8) follows without pause. It is very somber — really a *Marcia funèbre* — with an elemental, wide-spaced one–two, one–two for rhythm and a few choked notes in the 'cello for melody. The piano, for a little, takes the theme into the clarity of C sharp major; with the 'cello it recedes into the minor but finds another release in E; then the piano, harping a modulatory descent, surrounds the 'cello's slow extinction. The delicacy of the following *Vivace non troppo* is a model of appropriateness. The piece reaches its *furioso* peak only gradually. March and *Furiant* are then reworked, piano and strings exchanging roles. In the third *Dumka* (*Andante*, A major, 3-4), similarly designed, the piano, after setting the rhythm, has to play the melody "with one finger"— i.e., without a note of accompaniment — as severe a test of touch as could be devised. The following *Vivace non troppo* (A minor, 2-4) is on the figure of the two culminant bars of the *Andante* melody — a sparkling transformation. The reworking is freer.

The fourth *Dumka* (*Andante moderato, quasi tempo di Marcia*, D minor, 2-4) is detached from the preceding unbroken succession. Its alternative *Allegretto scherzando*, in A minor, is a reshaping of the 'cello's quiet melody in the March, and there are more alternations and variants than in the preceding *Dumky*. Before the fifth a long pause is prescribed. This is not a characteristic *Dumka* at all, but is rather an exciting Scherzo (*Allegro*, E flat, 6-8) with some fluctuations of speed but no high contrasts of character. The sixth, however (*Lento maestoso*, C minor, 4-8), reverts to the former pattern with a sudden *Doppio movimento, Vivace*. The whole trio, an exhilarating excursion into what is for us a foreign scene, is a similarly grateful departure from the sacrosanct sonata form.

There are two piano quartets, Op. 23 in D and Op. 87 in E flat. The quartet in D is one of Dvořák's earliest mature compositions — very personal but diffuse in structure. It has but three movements: a rather loose sonata *Allegro*, a very Slavic Theme and Variations for slow movement, and a combination of Scherzo and Rondo-finale that seems to this commentator to fall between the two stools of form on which it tries to sit.

The main theme of the other (*Allegro con fuoco*, E flat, 4-4) is a *unisono* phrase in the strings, more determined than purposeful. This impression is heightened by the continuation — an incisive figure in the piano that turns its nervous dotted rhythm into declamatory triplets, only to end on a subdued reference to the theme, now in a quiet legato (8). Dialogue on these things, with the S.I progressively diminished to eighths and sixteenths, brings a sonorous version of that theme (26); then the dotted rhythm sets out in search of an S.II which the viola finds, in G (43), and which dominates the rest of the exposition. The S.I, in E flat, begins the development and — sometimes diminished, sometimes augmented — rules that whole section. An apparently false reprise of the S.I (146) turns out to be the true beginning of the recapitulation. The S.II soon follows, momentarily in B major; but it reverts to E flat and yields to the S.I which, now frankly diatonic and very muscular, begins the Coda (196). There is a passage of interesting harmonic obliquity (*Poco sostenuto e tranquillo*) on the two factors of the S.I before the emphatic close.

A suave 'cello theme begins the following *Lento* (G flat major, 4-4). The piano twice paraphrases its two-bar strains; the violin (12) in a kind of free augmentation, makes comment on it; the piano has a more insistent figure that modulates to C sharp minor, and the S.II, tense and declamatory, follows in that key. The rest is little more than the same substance with the parts for strings and piano exchanged. The third movement (*Allegro moderato, grazioso*, E flat, 3-4) — a sort of *Ländler* — suggests

Brahms's substitution of Intermezzo for Scherzo. No more than the earlier movements does this smack of the Bohemian scene or the composer's individuality, but it is a charming movement all the same. The Trio (*Un pochettino più mosso*, B major) dances alternately on tiptoe and thudding heel, anticipating at the end the *da Capo*. The Finale (*Allegro ma non troppo*, 2-2) begins in E flat minor on a marching theme that sounds as if it were the fulfillment of a commission to celebrate an occasion in which the composer had only a halfhearted interest. The S.II of the sonata form (66) is a soaring tune in the viola; the development is mostly on the S.I, whose four initial rising eighths, in augmentation, are for some time interestingly combined with that figure in its original form. There is little else to report.

The piano quintet, Op. 81, in A, vies with the "American" string quartet as the most popular of Dvořák's chamber pieces. It begins (*Allegro, ma non tanto*, 2-2) with a curiously Verdian main theme in the 'cello over an undulant piano accompaniment. The violins continue it in a squarer, more energetic rhythm; it returns in the piano (53) with a new sequel in triplets, making transition to the S.II (92) in C sharp minor which also serves as Cl.S. Both themes are interestingly developed, with sonorous imitations on the S.I and a considerable rhythmic drive generated by the S.II. The recapitulation (294) is much condensed, and the sonorous Coda (406) will reveal a perhaps unobserved kinship between the two main themes.

The slow movement (*Andante con moto*, F sharp minor, 2-4), entitled *Dumka*, begins with a short refrain in the piano that prepares for the main theme in the viola. To this dejected, narrow-horizoned strain the piano, high above, adds a simple, limpid counterpoint, and interjects its refrain between the viola's phrases. The violin (*Un pochettino più mosso*) offers an alleviating contrast in D which the piano continues in the minor mode. Interesting recombinations of main theme, its counterpoint, and the refrain conclude the section. What would ordinarily be taken as *Furiant* follows — a transformation of the refrain into 2-8 time. Thereafter the *Dumka* is reworked.

The Scherzo, subtitled *Furiant* (*Molto vivace*, A major, 3-4), is really a swift, lithe waltz, quite unrelated to the *Dumka*. The Finale is a gay rondo (*Allegro*, A major, 2-4) whose main theme is introduced by varied repetitions of its cadence formula. It first enters (12) on the up-beat, but when the piano takes it over (17) it begins on the down-beat with a curious alteration of its rhythmic energy. The cadence-formula of the introduction is further developed, its augmentation (47) suggesting a new theme in the offing; but this does not arrive until bar 83. It is at first a little stolid, but it develops a rhythmic tic (104) that enlivens it. Its continuing strain (120) ends with the opening cadence-figure, and the S.I is thereafter considerably developed, the augmentation of its sixteenth-note pattern serving as a third subject for the rondo. The S.I returns (266) to begin a considerably altered recapitulation.

The String Quartets. Three of Dvořák's six mature string quartets must suffice to give an idea of his handling of this difficult form. The quartet in A minor, Op. 16, is the first chamber work to which he gave an opus number. It has the same virtues and the same faults as the B flat trio, Op. 21. The quartet in D minor, Op. 34, like Smetana's trio, is a reflection of his sorrow over the death of a child. Also after Smetana's example, this quartet has a Polka. The quartet in E flat, Op. 51, is the first to show both full command of the structure and also his musical personality.

It begins, not with a succinctly stated subject but with a quiet arpeggiation of the E flat chord (*Allegro ma non troppo*, 4-4) out of which the first violin, with a little sixteenth-note hop on the supertonic (4) shapes the essence of the S.I. The hopping spreads over the instruments like an infectious smile; it generates a few spurting scale passages; it finally hops whole octaves upward, and all at once the S.II (37) emerges — a mere swerve above and below its central tone, F, but the perfect realization of what has all along been promised. Endless repetitions of this little two-bar figure follow, so ingeniously harmonized and figurated that they never grow stale. The figurations, in fact, are nothing but the little hop from the S.I. That theme, in E minor, begins the development. It appears in augmentation at bar 92, along with a recognizable variant of the S.II in the 'cello; it is also diminished (103) and otherwise manipulated, so that there is no precise beginning of the recapitulation. Indeed, the S.II emerges unexpectedly (124) just as it did before, in its "proper" tonic key, to let you know just where you are. The Coda reverts for a moment to the original form of the S.I (178) and goes on to make an improvisatory end on the same thought.

The following *Dumka* (G minor, 2-4) is appropriately subtitled *Elegie*. Its simple theme, to which the 'cello strums accompanying chords, makes no parade of grief, but cannot keep a tell-tale abruptness out of its cadence, which comes in the third bar as the viola begins its repetition of the little theme. The retarded cadence of the more fluid strain that follows (9) has a similar import, for the ensuing escape into B flat is indeterminate and restless. Neither does the middle section (39) — approached by that same cadence — free itself from the unobtrusive influence of the opening. Its beginning, in B flat, is also its end (67), on the tensest upward climb in the whole piece. The *Vivace* (G major, 3-8) that follows is a transformation of the *Dumka* theme. Its gaiety does not seem forced until it appears in the perspective of the *Dumka* itself as it does when it makes the brief Coda. (Most readers will probably reject this quite personal impression.)

The next movement is a *Romanze* (*Andante con moto*, B flat, 6-8). Only one of the two protagonists essential to such an episode is portrayed; indeed, one suspects that the physical presence — to say nothing of physical contact — of the other, at this budding stage, would reduce both characters to blushing incoherence. The event, quite patently, is wholly imaginal; but if you take it as "purely musical" you will blindfold your imagination.

The Finale (*Allegro assai*, E flat, 2-4) releases the tensions of *Dumka* and *Romanze* effectively through the bodily muscles. The dance is called *skočna* in the Czech language; the nearest English equivalent is *reel*; but the name matters little. Neither does the form, which is that of the rondo: the S.II (40), at first still in E flat and in five-bar rhythm (3 + 2), then in B flat (58), three-bar; S.I (84); S.III, *Poco meno mosso*, second violin, developed fugally; S.I, developed (191f); recapitulation of S.I (248), and of S.III (294). What we called S.II does not recur until the very end. If you call it a mere sub-theme the whole pattern will become a sonata form. What really matters is the gaiety, irresistibly infectious.

Partly for lack of space, but also for their lesser interest, we omit discussion of two quartets, Op. 61, in C, and Op. 80, in E, and go on to the "American" quartet, Op. 96, which, along with the string quintet in E flat, Op. 97, and the "New World" symphony, was written during the composer's brief residence in this country, 1892–1895. (He summered at Spillville, Iowa, a Bohemian community where the homesickness he contracted in New York was much alleviated.) It is the shortest and the simplest of all the quartets, and perhaps on that account the most popular; but its quality — unless structural intricacy is to be accounted a primary virtue — is high.

The main theme of the first movement (*Allegro ma non troppo*, F major, 4-4) is played by the viola against *tremolando* F major harmony in the violins. It arouses a strong impulse to a shuffling of the feet, and is purely pentatonic in design; but those features do not necessarily stamp it as of Negro origin. The S.II (44), likewise pentatonic, is more songful and, to this ear, more Negroid. The S.I serves as Cl.S. to end the exposition, and is the chief topic in the development. At its recapitulation (112) that theme finds a new bass and greatly expands its final sixteenth-note figure. The S.II (156) is at first even quieter than before, but the 'cello seizes it for an intensification before the whipping-up of the S.I that makes the end.

The following *Lento* (D minor, 6-8) cannot but recall the *Largo* of the New World symphony. Both themes are pentatonic and each contemplates a horizon too distant to be reached, yet more to be desired than any attainable region. The texture is exquisitely woven and is so appropriate to the thought that you may not even notice it — which is probably what Dvořák desired.

The Scherzo (merely superscribed *Molto vivace*, F major, 3-4) is doubtless as Bohemian as it is American, for the dance-impulse is unaware of nationalism. The first phrase (still pentatonic) is very cocky; the second (5) a mere "hesitation"; the first, in F minor and augmented (49) makes the alternative sections which, if you like, you may call the Trio.

The Finale (*Vivace ma non troppo*, F major, 2-4) first sets going a marching rhythm, and then makes on it a tune that will be taken as S.I; but another one turns up (33) that begins on the up-beat and has the same character. A sudden shift to A flat (69) brings the S.II — a smoother strain, but still based on the march rhythm. After considerable preparation the second version of the S.I returns, rondo-wise (123). It grows very excited, then subsides into a broad chorale-like strain (155) that serves as S.III. The structure of the rest does not need to be described. Its gaiety cannot be.

Confronted with the choice between Dvořák's last two quartets, Op. 105, in A flat, and Op. 106, in G, we choose the latter as giving a fuller view of his mastery. Or, of his fuller mastery; for this music, although unmistakably Dvořák's, is no longer unmistakably Bohemian. There is also a clearer vision of the sonata form *as* a form — a vision doubtless sharpened by his study of Brahms, although there is no aping of Brahmsian idiom or of Brahmsian device. Rather, there is ascent from the individual to the general: from the folk to the world: or, if you like, from the attitude of the romantic artist to that of the classicist. But there is no ivory-tower aloofness. There is only a keener awareness of the essences of the musical experience as distinguished from its more ephemeral and often more appealing qualities. The music sounds more stern than any earlier work. Really, it is only more deeply earnest — and actually warmer. The themes are illustrated in Example 37.

EXAMPLE 37. DVOŘÁK QUARTET IN G, OP. 106

The main theme of the first movement (*Allegro moderato*, G major, 2-4) is almost wholly rhythmic in interest: three incisive upward leaps with the last prolonged on a nervous shake; then the mere triplet-figurated descent of the tonic chord to a mere tonic-dominant halt. (But observe that this takes five bars, not four, of musical time.) The same design recurs, but on the VI (the E minor) triad; then, foreshortened to two bars, on the IV (C major), the II (A minor), and the V7 (D); but this resolves to the dominant of E minor, and only now does the appeal of melody begin to be felt, in the two-note figure that descends from the high A (17) on the scale of that key. Two new motives now emerge: the dotted rhythm (20) in second violin and the little phrase (25) of three detached, two-note groups — both on the essential "one-two, one" of the opening bar. These hints now fuse into a single composite impression that comes into sharp focus with the outcry of the 'cello (59), thrice aimed toward the yawing augmented triad. A moment later the first violin finds a little figure of triplet eighths that will prove to be the essential substance of the S.II (80) in B flat (a key-color far more indicative of its sense than the orthodox D major would have been). Being only a figure it can be moved upward or downward or change its intervals as the over-all melodic purpose may dictate; and that purpose has a considerable latitude. The suggested S.I (140) serves as Cl.S. leading rapidly to the development (154), resolutely begun on the two-note figure from bar 25. All these things are there not merely combined but coordinated toward a purposeful climax. The recapitulation (262) remakes the exposition toward that same purpose, even the two final chords being an augmentation of the opening leaps. No mean musical intelligence contrived this piece.

The *Adagio ma non troppo* (E flat, 3-8) does not adopt the easy formula of *Dumky–Furiant* but explores to its last cranny of implication the one theme on which it is built. The method is not that of formal variation. It is rather, if the word is not taken too literally, a kind of narrative method, expanding individual phrases according to their weight rather than their dimension. The intensifications, involving gradual hastenings of the tempo, become a little oratorical, but the urgency is never feigned.

The Scherzo (*Molto vivace*, B minor, 3-4) has a bitter tang, somewhat in the vein of irony. That impression is softened by what are essentially two Trios — the first in A flat (95), the second in D (231). The Finale begins with a short Introduction that sets forth (*Andante sostenuto*, G major, 4-4) the four descending scale-notes of the S.I of the *Allegro con fuoco* following. This little 2-4 theme sounds like the beginning of a heedless Rondo. But its four-bar strain, ending with a thump on the downward 5th, stops for two more thumps in the rhythm of the leaps that opened the quartet, and these form the main substance of the continuing phrase. The S.I returns briefly (36) with its four-note descent extended in a long series of thumps; the descent is then made on a triplet figure (50); it is smoothed to four legato quarters (88) and vanishes, leaving only the thumps, pizzicato, behind. Then (114) a second theme appears, in E flat; the S.I returns in its first form, subsiding on the four legato quarters which repeat the *Andante sostenuto* (now notated in 2-4) and extend it to a close on the dominant of E minor. But what emerges is the fluid S.II of the first movement; its S.I follows (269); and from now on these themes either combine or alternate with those of the last movement, enlarging its horizon and establishing the structural unity of the whole quartet.

It is rational to see this unity as the attained objective of a structural purpose more comprehensive than any we have observed in the earlier quartets. It is also rational to see both structure and unity as essential to the realization of a more than merely structural purpose. In the one view, Dvořák will appear as a perfected creative mechanism. In the other, he will appear as a man of widened human understanding. His own preference seems obvious.

Four other chamber works might have been included in the "autobiography" implied in those we have studied: the string sextet in A, Op. 48, whose *Dumka* voices its melancholy in a polka rhythm, and which closes with the form, not often chosen by Dvořák, of a theme with variations; a *Terzetto* for two violins and viola, Op. 74 — a considerable structural feat, since you will find, when it is over, that you have hardly missed the 'cello; the string quintet in G, Op. 77, for string quartet and double bass, whose Scherzo seems to us its most distinctive movement; and the string quintet in E flat, Op. 97, written, like the "Negro" quartet, in America, and on themes supposedly taken from American Indian models. They add but little to the portrait.

SCANDINAVIAN
Edvard Grieg (1843–1907)

Like Dvořák, Grieg became the acknowledged musical spokesman of his nation. Awakened by Richard Nordraak, as Dvořák had been by Smetana, to the existence of unmined musical treasure at home, he abandoned the Mendelssohnian ideals he had absorbed at Leipzig and began to explore the national idiom. His musical intuition was perhaps as keen as Dvořák's, but his artistic intelligence was much narrower. The symphony was quite beyond his range. Even the sonata form, whether for solo piano (he left but one early example) or for larger combinations, was seldom attempted. He left four duet sonatas — three with violin, one

with 'cello — none of which has commanding stature. The first two sonatas, in F and G, with violin, have charm but little weight; the two
others have more fat than muscle, and in trying to sustain their own
weight lose their charm. This is because he could not really develop a
musical idea. He could only repeat it — often, indeed, at an unexpected
level or in some new harmonic perspective that lent it true interest.*

Of course, if he cannot make a violin sonata, he cannot make a string
quartet. His one effort, judged as a structure, is an indubitable failure —
precisely because he cannot develop his thought; for development is essential to extended structure. And yet, if you can abandon your prepos-
session with structure, you may find the piece compelling. There is a
good deal of campaign oratory, but even a campaign orator can be in
earnest, and that Grieg is, here.

The orator is in evidence from the start, all four of his "voices" an-
nouncing, *unisono*, the grave thought which may be taken as the main
topic or motto of his address (*Un poco Andante*, G minor, 2-2). His
perturbation over the idea forms the main theme of the *Allegro molto
ed agitato* that follows. Its essence is stated in the first bar, which is literally repeated and then expanded to make a four-bar phrase. Then that
phrase is repeated, a 3rd higher; then its second half comes twice, always
a 3rd higher; then its last bar, now breathless, continues the ascent until
it has covered two full octaves, and here there is frantic insistence for
sixteen bars more before any relaxation of descent is offered. Even that
is not enough. A chromatic crescendo, soon double-stopped in all four
instruments, rises to high G and ends with a two-fisted bang on the lec-
tern. Now the motto returns (93), *Allegro* but *tranquillo*, twice punctuated by the loud bangs. Then (127), twice as fast and repeated in
diminution, it becomes the S.II; but this thought has an unexpected complement — a little upward spurt of eager melody, imitated between violin
and 'cello, and mitigating, for a moment all too brief, the overstrained
tension so far endured. This, too, is built up by diminution; then the S.II
comes back to end the exposition. The development, as argument, really
gets nowhere. Indeed, there is no argument — only assertion, less em-

* Look, for example, at "Åses Tod." The tension, whether rising or falling, never
lets go; yet in that whole piece there are but two brief phrases of melody. I sometimes wonder whether he himself was aware of this, for every repetition sounds as
if it were generated by a new creative tension. At any rate, one who mechanically
constructed a piece on this remarkably obvious plan would appear as ridiculous as
the little man Mozart made fun of in his *musikalischer Spass*.

phatic and with its items differently deployed, but yielding no new illumination.

The slow movement (*Andantino*, B flat, 6-8) begins as a *Romanze* with a gentle, unimpassioned song in the 'cello that is agreeably passed from instrument to instrument. Suddenly it yields to an excited episode (*Allegro agitato*) in which the viola, on a staccato figure derived from the first bar of the *Romanze*, accompanies a rather perfunctorily disturbed melody in the violin. These things are then waywardly alternated, but this romance will hardly outlive a winter of discontent.

A lively Intermezzo (*Allegro molto marcato*, G minor, 3-4) strikes the first really Norwegian note to be heard in the piece. This note is further pursued in the Trio (*più vivo e scherzando*, G major, 2-4). The Finale begins (*Lento*, G minor, 2-2) with the quartet's opening motto theme, descending imitatively. You anticipate a related sequel. Instead there is a light-footed *Saltarello*. There is enough variety in its animation to keep the attention alert, even though a good deal of time is spent in mere foot-stamping. The motto, in G major, returns at the end — portentously approached, but no more relevant than before — and a little snatch of the Scherzo follows; but such recall as this merely illustrates the indigence rather than the wealth of the cyclic form as form.

Little other Scandinavian chamber music has survived in the repertoire. Niels Gade (1817–1890), although almost wholly German in training and sympathy, left two string quintets, an octet, and a piano trio which still retains something of its mild charm. Johann Svendsen (1840–1911), whose Romance for violin and orchestra was long a popular concert number, wrote a quartet, a quintet, and an octet for strings. Christian Sinding, whose *Frühlingsrauschen* captivated every American schoolgirl, left a large number of chamber pieces, remarkable for their sonorous concealment of any true musical interest. Neither Emil Sjögren (1853–1918), of whose five violin sonatas one attained a brief vogue in America, nor Kurt Atterberg (1887–   ), whose Sixth symphony won a large prize offered by the Columbia Phonograph Co. in 1928, and whose output included two string quartets, made any lasting contribution to the literature.

FRENCH

France, in the seventeenth century, attained to a literary and cultural leadership in Europe which was hardly challenged on the continent until the *Sturm und Drang* movement began in Germany, and which was strongly influential in eighteenth-century England in spite of its very different cultural background. A great part of this eminence was attained through the imitation and adaptation of the dramatic masterpieces of ancient Greece. The style-consciousness which was an inevitable by-product of that achievement carried over into the other arts. Music, which had been largely cultivated as a courtly art and which appeared to serve its highest purpose as an adjunct of drama, thus seems to have been regarded as chiefly decorative in value — a sensuous complement of verbal phrase in opera or dance-sequence in ballet, rather than a contributor in its own right to dramatic or poetic meaning. Devoted to so aristocratic a purpose, the art-music of France could neither reflect the commoner aspects of French life nor draw sustenance from the music of the people.*

The national characteristics of French music thus derive, not from the wild-flowers of French folk-song but from the hot-house blooms of the opera. The Revolution, whose moral sap flowed strong in all of Western Europe, both nourished and mutated, in Germany, such vigorous musical plants as Beethoven and his seedlings, the romanticists; but in France it

* It was not so in Germany where the Lutheran faith, encouraging individual interpretation of the Scriptures, encouraged also the individual expression of religious feeling. The naivety of the texts of many Protestant hymns is striking; but the fervor of the tunes (whether borrowed or invented) to which they were sung suggests a very literal and immediate acceptance of Luther's contention that every true believer was a priest of the faith. Neither did this music continue at the folk level. It provided the themes of many instrumental and vocal forms, elaborated by the church organists and their choirs; and the congregations, hearing these elaborations upon melody with which they were already familiar, pursued all but unconsciously what were probably the best courses in music appreciation ever offered. (Imagine a Bach deprived of this resource!)

The French Protestants were Calvinists. Calvin's theology was sterner than Luther's, and while Calvin respected and even enjoyed music, his fear of heresy made him suspicious of any other than Biblical texts for religious song. The Psalms, as paraphrased by Marot and Théodore de Bèze and set to music by Goudimel and Le Jeune, were sung, both in the churches and at home, and even by Catholics as well as Protestants, but neither the texts nor the music had that immediate appeal which was offered by the homely verses and the home-made tunes of the Lutherans.

Thus no direct link existed, in France, between the music of the people and the most cherished of the convictions by which they lived. The link did exist in Germany. And since those convictions were humanistic as well as religious, the link between music and religion, unmistakable on the simple folk-level, was not broken but was rather strengthened as music, growing more "learned" and thus more widely allusive, began to embrace the complexities of life. How far the ultimate superiority of German instrumental music is indebted to this background is a question to which no precise answer could be given; but the debt, in any case, was heavy.

could mature, at best, the wiry but seedless Berlioz. There was thus in France, the hotbed of romanticism in literature and other arts, no true romantic movement in music, and chamber music had no representative composer until the romantic movement was over.

Only three French composers made important contributions to the literature of chamber music during the nineteenth century: César Franck (1822–1890), Camille Saint-Saëns (1835–1921), and Gabriel Fauré (1845–1924). A great preponderance of their chamber music is with piano. From all three there are only four string quartets, and only one — that of Franck — can be accounted its composer's major work. Saint-Saëns, indeed, although his skill cannot but rouse admiration, has so little to say that we shall merely mention his piano quintet (1858 — his earliest chamber work), his two trios, piano quartet, septet for trumpet, strings, and piano (a unique combination, remarkably well written), and his seven duet sonatas — two each with violin and 'cello, one each with oboe, clarinet, and bassoon. He upheld, tenaciously and sometimes with bitterness, the gallic tradition, even though, on occasion, he adopts something of the manner of his more progressive contemporaries.

César Franck (1822–1890)

Franck, although no bearer of the revolutionary banner, was the earliest in time, if not in immediate influence, among the emancipators of France from its withered musical traditions. He was born in Liège, in Belgium, but his ancestry was predominantly German. His father, music-minded but financially astute, wanted him to become a virtuoso pianist and frowned on his efforts in composition. To further this end he was taken at thirteen to Paris where, being too young to enter the Conservatoire, he studied for two fruitful years with Anton Reicha and then, being admitted, won many awards at the Conservatoire. After a not too successful year in Belgium he returned to Paris in 1842, giving most of his time to teaching, but his main interest to composition.

In this field, although already thoroughly grounded in theory, he was essentially self-taught. But he learned from Bach, as did Schumann, the endless fertility which polyphony can contribute to music; from Beethoven something of the technique and the spirituality of quartet-writing; and from his contact with French thought, musical and literary, the virtues of French style — economy, lucidity, verve, the impact of a well-turned, strategically-placed phrase. But his unquestioning religious belief, although it was neither monastic nor dogmatic, colored all his musical thought.*

Franck left but three chamber works of consequence. All three of them exhibit the so-called cyclical structure — that in which themes, or motives generative of themes, recur throughout the movements of a composition. He is often said to have been the first exponent of this structure, but unless the process is redefined so as to accord with Franck's individual procedure, that statement can hardly be true. Beethoven's Fifth will suffice to refute it. Franck's process, however, is both skillful and expressively illuminating. We shall observe it first in the second of his chamber works, the Violin sonata in A.

The sonata was written in 1886 as a wedding present for the great Belgian violinist, Eugène Ysaÿe, whose performance of it was a thing to be remembered. The first movement (*Allegretto ben moderato*, A major, 9-8) has two themes, more contrasted in intensity than in character, the first being allotted to the violin, the second to the piano, which plays its theme solo. The first is a fluid curve on the dominant 9th chord. Its first four notes (D, F♯, D, B) form the germ of many later thematic derivations.† The second theme is a more exuberant strain — really, the outcome and completion of the sense of the first. A brief passage of imitation on the S.I (47) followed by modulatory comment forms what may be called the development, and a slightly altered recapitulation follows, with

* His pupils' favorite adjective for this attitude was "seraphic." Stripped of its hyperbole, this word will serve as well as any for the impression they gained of his personality. He seems hardly to have known what jealousy was, and to have been equally ignorant of the baser passions. These, indeed, he saw, but could not see through; and his portrayal of them — in *Les Djinns*, in *Le Chasseur maudit*, and even in *Les Béatitudes*, where he contrived a sort of backdrop of sin against which to project the virtues which are to make men blessed — is mere fairy-tale horror.

In consequence his tender-minded portrayal of goodness appears, to the tough-minded, fragile to the point of sentimentality. Confronted with evil, the first impulse of the tough-minded (who call themselves realists) is to stamp it out with force — if necessary, lethal; and many are the celebrations, both political and artistic, of such victory. But Franck is not so naive. He sees that the only real cure for evil is to transmute it into good — a difficult process, but one which history, seen in long enough perspective, will somewhat substantiate. In the very realistic perspective of the twentieth century, Franck's theorem appears that of a visionary, and his goodness too good to be true. Music, indeed (as Beethoven found with his Ninth symphony), cannot really argue the theorem. It can only chant its indubitable soundness. Neither has Franck the percipience of a Beethoven. But he is more than a mere visionary.

† Heedless pianists ignore the quarter-rests in the four introductory bars, playing the first note of the accompaniment as if it were a part of the two-note hint of the coming theme.

the S.II of course in A. The pattern is sonata-like; the sense, wholly lyrical.

The second movement (*Allegro*, D minor, 4-4) is a sonata form in both pattern and sense. The main theme, passionately driven by an intertwined figuration, is wholly announced by the piano and then repeated with the violin *unisono*. There is a gentler interlude (24) that ends with a suddenly quiet descent in the violin on the repeated interval of the 3rd from the S.I of the first movement; then a recall of the main theme; then, for transition, an unmistakable recall of the first-movement theme (44). Then the violin soars upward on the wholly appropriate S.II (48) which it has all to itself. Transition to the development is begun on an exquisite parenthesis (67) and completed (*Quasi lento*) by the skeleton of the S.I in half notes, broadly harmonized. These things also begin the development (94), which gives the piano its first chance at the S.II and then briefly combines its second phrase, in the violin, with imitations on the S.I in the piano. The recapitulation is complete, with a deeply agitated Coda.

The third movement is entitled *Recitativo-Fantasia*. It begins with an oblique statement of the opening theme of the first movement, but this, after a short cadenza on the same thought in the violin, reappears with extraordinary gentleness in the piano (11). Extension of this substance leads to the second section — the *Quasi lento* phrase from the second movement in the violin against a delicate accompanying figure, completed by a new strain (59) that will recur in the last movement. Still another (71) follows, in the violin, tense and dramatic, on intervals as affirmative as its rhythm; then the tension abates and the opening theme of the sonata, somewhat broadened against its augmented first phrase in the piano, prepares for the close on the affirmative theme and its dwindling elusive cadence.

The last movement (*Allegretto poco mosso*, A major, 2-2) is really a rondo. Its main theme is a happy little tune begun in the piano and imitated in charmingly lucid canon by the violin. The interstitial themes are cyclic recalls from previous movements: at bar 38, what we may call the S.II — the strain from bar 59 of the *Fantasia*, which recurs again at bar 65; then, after the canon with a new and more brilliant conclusion, the reshaped opening theme of the sonata (99); at bar 117 the canon-theme (now not canonic although the piano's answer is the reversion of five of its six notes), made to lead to the high affirmation from the *Fan-*

tasia; the S.II, now *ff* (170); and finally the canon again with its former brilliant conclusion made still more brilliant.

In its structural skill and in the soundness of its musical substance this music is of an order as high as the general level of the teutonic master-pieces we have studied. In the character of its thought and in its rhetori-cal impact it is not teutonic at all. It is French. To amalgamate these opposed idioms with so little loss of the essentials of either one was no inconsiderable feat.

The sonata was not Franck's first mature essay in chamber music. The piano quintet, seven years earlier, is almost as coherently designed and, as befits its weightier tonal substance, is more deeply imaginative. It be-gins with an Introduction (*Molto moderato, quasi lento*, F minor, 4-4) in which two themes, highly contrasted, are sharply impressed on the ear. The first, in strings alone, is a dramatic, tensely rhythmed descent of the scale to a subdued disquiet on the dominant. The second, in the piano, opposes to it a wholly Franckian gentleness just as, in the slow movement of the Beethoven G major piano concerto, the piano's quie-tude opposes the anger of the orchestra. Both will be transformed.

The main theme of the ensuing *Allegro* has also two essential phrases — a condensation of the opening string-theme, still in the strings, and a stirring hint of elemental energy in the piano. After recitational com-ment in the violin (64) the strings wax lyrical in approach to the S.II in the piano (90). This is patently a transformation of the piano's portion of the S.I. What follows is so intricately derived from these basic themes as to defy verbal description, but the whole design is perfectly lucid. You cannot tell exactly where the development section begins, but you will easily pursue its cumulative approach to a thunderous outburst of the opening string theme (193), the eloquent interjection of the S.II there-after, the still more tense assertion of the opening theme (216) and the long subsidence on the S.II to the recapitulation. This seems really to begin with a fragment of the S.I in the piano (259), but the literal repe-tition comes a little later. The lyrical continuation, however, leads, not to the S.II but to the piano's *quasi lento* reply to the opening. The S.II then follows, growing more assertive and culminating in the real denoue-ment of the drama — the piano's first gentle reply to the strings, now raised to the nth power of intensity. The S.II, similarly heightened, makes the Coda (*Animato* and *Più presto*); but the opening phrase of the move-ment makes the final quiet comment.

[245

The slow movement (*Lento con molto sentimento*, 12-8) is in the distant but strangely relevant key of A minor. The main theme, although cast in disjunct phrases, does not lose melodic continuity. Its repetition (20) is energized by a new rhythmic figure that will reappear in the Finale. The S.II (41) is a long luminous line in the piano to which the cadential phrases of the S.I form the background.* A recall of the S.II of the first movement (58f) precedes and continues to illuminate the climax of the movement (74f), after which there is an enriched but much condensed recapitulation.

No more than you could Franck imagine a Scherzo appropriate to such a scene as this. The quintet thus has but three movements.

The Finale (*Allegro non troppo, ma con fuoco*, F major, 3-4) begins on a note of subdued excitement in the strings against which the militant main theme is generated in the piano. To it succeeds a phrase, still in the piano, that suggests the luminous line from the *Lento*, and this is combined with the rhythmic figure from bar 20 of that movement. That figure presently emerges as the S.II. There is a considerable development and a recapitulation which subsides into momentary obscurity. Then (*Ritenuto un pochettino*) appears a delicately colored version of the S.II of the first movement, and this — really the most pregnant theme in the quintet — soon begins the exciting but by no means meretricious Coda.

The string quartet in D was Franck's last work and, in the estimation of many, his greatest. Although it has less of immediate appeal than the quintet or the sonata, it was the first of his works to receive general acclaim on its first performance — a fact of no mean significance in the history of French musical taste.

The first and last movements show much consideration of the problems of form — a primary consideration when his effort toward the utterance of weightier thought in a manner still accordant with French ideals of lucidity is taken into account. The first movement encloses a sonata structure within the wrappings of a song — a sufficiently novel undertaking. Obviously, this would be impossible without the mechanics of cyclic structure. The themes are shown in Example 38.

It begins (*Poco lento*, D major, 4-4) with the song-theme high in the violin, *ff*, above sonorous double-stopped chords. Its first two phrases

---

* The "scene" is somehow reminiscent of the moment in King Mark's garden when Brangäne warns Tristan and Isolde that day is about to break — a scene often portrayed in the *alba* (morning-song) of the Provençal poets.

EXAMPLE 38. FRANCK QUARTET IN D

(of three bars) show in their harmonization a kind of gentleness very characteristic of Franck. The 'cello takes over the theme (15) with some variation in its line and much in its harmonic texture, but with its character only heightened. After a related episode the theme returns (41) against triplets in second violin and even eighths in 'cello; then it subsides to a quiet cadence in D. The sonata begins (*Allegro*) in D minor on a five-bar theme with a good deal of rhythmic impetus, but still more contemplative than active. A new theme in the 'cello (105) that will reappear in the Finale begins the transition to the S.II (138) — a phrase so quiet that at first all passion seems spent; but this grows into a determined strain (150), essentially in the rhythm of S.I but more vigorous. The exposition ends with a conjoining of first and second themes and a fade-out on S.I. The development follows, with a fugato on the song-theme (again *Poco lento*), the S.I, very intense (*Allegro*), the 'cello theme from bar 105, and the S.II which dwindles into the S.I (271) to begin the recapitulation. The song appropriately ends the movement.

A Scerzo follows (*Vivace*, F sharp minor, 3-8), of a Mendelssohnian lightness but more reminiscent of Franck's *Les Eolides* than of the *Midsummer Night's Dream*. The main theme, in three-bar rhythm, is elusive and nymph-like; the S.II (55) sways alluringly and is presently combined (79) with the antic of S.I. There is a short and very quiet Trio (152), begun in a rocking rhythm but mostly in continuous, fluid eighths, against which (225) the song is intoned in the 'cello. The returning Scherzo is somewhat varied, and the Trio (without the song) makes the Coda. Seen in the perspective of the whole quartet the Scherzo, charming as it is, seems somewhat irrelevant. Something in its vein, however, had to intervene after the first movement, relaxing the attention for the experience to follow.

The *Larghetto* (G sharp minor, 3-4) is probably Franck's most deeply pondered utterance. The intrinsic tensions of the long melody that forms its main theme, if that line is read by itself, will seem slight. (Until its cadence at bar 16, it may well appear to be in B major.) Those tensions are not, indeed, tortured by the harmony, but they are heightened in a way that provides a flood of implications, so that the theme emerges as the portrayal of a very unusual mind, reacting to a highly complex experience. That mental attitude is patently contemplative, lacking any spur to action; but it is not an idle attitude. There is a sense of burdensome weight, borne with submission; but this is not the response to a categorical imperative — to a stern *entbehren sollst du, sollst entbehren* — and the submission is willing since the demand for renunciation comes from above.

The formal design is simple — A–B–A. After the cadence (16) there is much dwelling on the cadential figure of three eighths approaching a dotted quarter; this continues after a brief hint of the theme (29), and is lightened in weight by the triplets which replace the dotted quarter (37f); the theme returns (67), cadencing tentatively in B major (96), but a sudden enharmonic modulation making the diminished 3rd, E♯–G♮, into the major second, F–G, steers the music into C major with a loud song (103) whose fervency cannot be resisted. The main theme returns (151) in high register and *ppp*; so does the climax of the great song; then fragments of the main theme, with *recitando* emphasis on the renunciatory cadence-figure, make an end in B major.

The Finale, in contrast, is long and intricate. It begins with an impatient phrase, *unisono*, whose purpose is that of the opening recitative of the Finale in Beethoven's Ninth symphony. As in that piece, the recitative is made to reject reminiscences of the *Larghetto* and the Scherzo. But when the opening theme of the quartet is proposed (*Poco lento,* 53) it is at once accepted, alternating with the now harmonized recitative and yielding to a broad line (113) that is a transformation of the 'cello theme from bar 105 of the first movement. It so far dominates the movement that we may call it the S.II. Next, the recitative excitedly prefaces and then accompanies what may be called another member of the S.II group—a passionate melodic sweep in both violins (176)—and a third theme (237) follows a return of the S.II and is then combined with it. When the excitement has subsided the key changes to D flat and a sonorous augmentation of the recitative appears, alternating with the S.II. The turbulent recitative generates still another theme (360), akin to that in bar 176. These are the thematic constituents of the piece. The development, whose actual beginning is hard to find, attains to a recapitulation (506) that seems to end with the augmentation of the recitative (705). Thereafter the Scherzo is recalled and is presently combined with the S.I of the first movement; then the theme of the *Larghetto,* augmented in notation but little altered to the ear, seems to sum up the expressive purport of the whole quartet. The recitative, however, *Presto,* rings down a quick curtain.

Like the Finale of Beethoven's Ninth symphony, this movement, at a first hearing, seems disorganized and obscure. It continually disappoints expectations based on more conventional form patterns. Analysis, like repeated hearing, helps somewhat to clarify the total impression, but an awareness of total unity such as those efforts yield, for example with Beethoven's C sharp minor quartet, is hardly attainable. Cyclic structure can help toward, but cannot of itself establish, that unity. Indeed, if the hearer's attention is directed toward that image of experience which is for this commentator the principal objective of structural effort, the mere introduction of a formerly purposeful theme into quite a new context—e.g., the belated appearance of the Scherzo idea in this movement—cannot but seem artificial. Mere recall will not of itself effect actual integration.

Yet, in these three chamber works, Franck managed to embody essential characteristics of French artistry and French thought in musical fabrics of such structural competency as to establish French music on a level comparable to that of German art. It was no small achievement.

Gabriel Fauré (1845–1924)

This judgment will be vigorously disputed in many quarters. It may be argued that the apparent weight of Franck's music is borrowed from alien sources, and that his style is not truly French. Those who uphold this view will give the palm to Gabriel Fauré, whose style is unmistakably gallic, with hardly a trace of foreign influence. He left ten important chamber works: four duet sonatas (two with violin and two with 'cello); one piano trio, Op. 120, in D minor, 1924; two piano quartets, Op. 15 in C minor, 1879, and Op. 45 in G minor, 1886; two piano quintets, Op. 89, in D minor, 1906, and Op. 115, in C minor, 1921; and one string quartet, Op. 121, begun in 1923 and finished on his deathbed. Even the earliest of these, the violin sonata in A, Op. 13, is exquisitely finished; the later works have that virtue in somewhat greater measure, the thicker instrumentation of quartet or quintet still showing a wholly unostentatious polyphony; yet his work has never attained, at any rate abroad, the degree of favor long accorded to Franck's best efforts.

The reason is not hard to find. Fauré's artistic creed — unmistakably reflected in his music — is that of one who, if his heart should appear for a moment on his sleeve, would be painfully embarrassed. The average music-lover, at any rate in America, arms himself as he prepares to listen with a sort of aesthetic stethoscope which he applies to the music pretty constantly; and if he cannot detect a heartbeat is quite likely to think the music — and its composer — as good as dead. He is not, on the other hand, alarmed by rather violent palpitations. Rather, he shows a considerable willingness to suffer with the invalid. But this sort of compassion Fauré never demands of his hearer. He remains aloof from such baser emotional disturbance, and thus may appear to withdraw into a region of "purely" artistic apprehension and sensibility.

To the average listener, in consequence, his music seems unimpassioned and therefore cold. Whether it is really so, and whether the "advanced" music of our own day is to be similarly judged, is a question which will confront us as our study enters the twentieth century. It is hardly a question to be thoroughly explored in such a book as this, but it cannot be wholly ignored, and a beginning may be made in a footnote.*

* The question, pondered, will become an inquiry into legitimate and illegitimate emotional response to experience as it impinges upon us. Illegitimate emotion is that which appears overstrained or inappropriate to its generative experience — as we understand it. The question may thus be simplified by reducing it to the form,

That Fauré stands aloof from the intenser passions is evident in every one of his chamber works. That he is indifferent to them (as Heine thought Mendelssohn to be) cannot be maintained. His melodic lines are gracious rather than stern, but they are never lax or lascivious. His harmony is subtly active, but without the high tensions of frankly subjective utterance. His rhythms, similarly, do not lack energy although they never parade it. His work reflects many essential aspects of what is probably the maturest civilization to be developed in the modern world. Whether it is spiritually the richest civilization is another question — one to which Fauré's music would hardly suggest a competent answer, for his imaginative range is not wide.

For this reason, we shall study but three examples of his work: the violin sonata in A, Op. 13, the piano quartet in C minor, Op. 15, and the

"What is sentimentality?" For sentimentality is only a common name for illegitimate emotion. Sentiment, on the other hand, is legitimate feeling.

The dividing line between the two is not precise. Each of us draws it, satisfactorily to himself; but seldom will any two of us agree as to where it lies. For both of these states of feeling — individual, unpredictable, and often variable even when the experience itself is essentially similar to one which, on another occasion, evoked a different reaction — are "subjective," and thus never quite free of the charge of irrationality.

Critical security can hardly be attained so long as criticism must weigh such imponderables as these. Safety, on the other hand, would appear more nearly assured if the subjective element could be banished. The verbal antithesis to "subjective" is "objective." Objective art, therefore — that in which the artist's individual response to the exciting experience is suppressed, and in which the observer's response may be purely his own — would appear as the only legitimate art.

Yet, if the experience itself is concrete and familiar, objective portrayal, whether of the circumstance itself (as in painting) or of the emotional charge set off by the circumstance (as in music), will appear so merely realistic that the art work itself will have no more than photographic value. The peculiar interest of art itself — of that product of creative imagination which raises objective reality above the merely objective level, and which arouses in the observer awarenesses of meaning which he could never have realized for himself — will be missing.

Can it be, then, that the reality which is the proper "object" of artistic creation is the reality of art itself? — that the realities of ordinary human experience have no essential relation to art? — that the entity of art is an entity apart from life and can hardly make contact with life without becoming smirched?

This, it seems to me, is the essence of the doctrine of "art for art's sake." It views the emotions evoked by ordinary experience as too gross for artistic utterance, and condemns the portrayal of them as sentimental. I have tried to show that the doctrine itself has a certain logic, and this species of art a certain attractiveness. But that very attractiveness, generated out of repulsion *from* the dross of experience, is still as truly related *to* experience as is the most prosaic realism.

That relation may indeed be all but concealed beneath the surface of esoteric artistic design. But the observer's repulsion is still *there*; and repulsion — a highly subjective emotion — may impede objective understanding as fatally as does the sentimentality of a too willing response.

piano quintet in D minor, Op. 85. The sonata was written in 1876 — ten years before Franck's sonata in the same key. How far it served Franck as a model we leave the reader to decide for himself.

It begins (*Allegro molto*, A major, 2-2) with its main theme wholly announced by the piano — a fluid, trippingly syncopated melodic line, activated by sequential lifts of its phrases. The violin does not repeat the theme but heightens its lilt; the S.II (56) appears quite in its proper place and key, showing enough of contrast to keep the attention alert and finally reaching what may be felt as a rather guarded release of passion. This subsides into the development which begins with dialogue on the opening phrase of S.I, on its continuing strain, and finally on the S.II (209) — all without haste and without rest. The recapitulation is quite regular; the Coda (355) begun on the rising scale-figure that closed the exposition, builds up in canon (363f) to a high climax, sinks into meditative reminiscence of the S.I, then makes a moment of brilliance for close.

The *Andante* (D minor, 9-8) has the gentle throb of that rhythm. The succession ♪♩, a little hesitant, is altered to ♩♪ for the S.II — this tiny variant sufficing for a mild but effective contrast. Both themes are delicately drawn. They move suavely over gentle but subtly varied harmonic tensions, portraying a nocturnal moment of great charm.

The Scherzo (*Allegro vivo*, A major, 2-4) shapes its agile little figure into a sometimes three-bar, sometimes two-bar thematic pattern, making it turn intriguing harmonic corners, and never showing an external sign of its high sophistication. The Trio (A major, 3-4) floats airily above a warmly sonorous accompaniment, its one thematic curve proving quite sufficient for interest.

The Finale (*Allegro quasi presto*, A major, 6-8) is a rondo, animated by something more than mere liveliness and showing the same gracious manner as all the rest of the sonata. The S.II (66), like the S.I, is first given to the violin, but the piano amplifies each of them. The S.I returns (141), but briefly; the S.III (175) moves smoothly in duple rhythm against hints of the S.I, still in 6-8, in the piano, and the S.I returns thereafter in C. The rest, although it has been predicted, never grows obvious.

The piano quartet, Op. 15, was written in 1879, three years later than the sonata. The C minor key evidently held for Fauré something of the sternness that Beethoven found in it. The main theme (*Allegro molto moderato*, 3-4) emphasizes the forceful drop of a fifth from dominant to tonic, and its line (*unisono* in the strings) is colored by the modal B♭

instead of the B♮ of conventional tonality. Instead of being insisted upon, the sternness of this four-bar strain is mitigated by a kindred line that veers toward A flat, waxes turbulent for a moment, and then recedes for a harmonized version of the theme. The S.II (38) begins with a timid waver in sixteenths that is continued by a broader ascent in quarter notes. A brief transition on an imitated phrase closes the exposition, which is not repeated. The development (62) begins on the modal figure of the main theme and is continued on the dotted rhythm of its second bar (87). Only a few phrases exhibit the force implicit in the theme, and the addition of the S.II (116) maintains the same reserve until the approach to the recapitulation releases a high energy. This, however, after the *forte* recall of the main theme (159), is again reduced. Neither is there any whipping up of excitement at the end.

The Scherzo (*Allegro vivo*, E flat, 6-8) is wonderfully subtle. Pizzi-cato chords in the strings lay a foundation for the theme — a fragmented pattern in single notes in the piano which ends each of its three-bar phrases with a delightful little click. A 2-4 version of the theme follows in the bowed strings, and these things are then worked out with an art-istry of the first order. A broader line, derived from the opening pizzi-cato, presently appears (100); and this becomes the counterpoint to a slightly contrasted three-bar phrase in the piano. The Trio, in B flat, suggests a new three-bar rhythm in the accompanying piano, but aban-dons it when the more sustained four-bar-rhythmed theme enters. The Scherzo, much abbreviated, returns. The delicate humor of this piece is inimitable.

The *Adagio* (C minor, 2-4), although it avoids the literal portrayal of tramping feet, is still funereal. Its tension, whether stern or compassion-ate, is contained, but this continence only barely disguises its depth. There are but two melodic strains — the rising scale-figure of the opening (whose tension a German composer would have emphasized by a more disjunct phrasing), and a gentler line (27) begun by the violin. This phrase, against a more emollient rhythm in the piano, is presently in-verted (39) and then more freely varied. The movement, conveying its sense by inference rather than by explicit statement, is appropriately short.

The Finale (*Allegro molto*, C minor, 3-4) has as main theme a dotted-rhythmed scale-figure whose one-bar ascent is answered by analogous descent in another instrument. As it goes on, it first becomes more fluid, then (39) more incisive, making transition to a sub-theme in the viola (47) and then to the S.II (95), again in the viola. The piano, hitherto quite subordinate, comes to the fore with a third theme (158). These things, elaborated, make the rest of the piece. It is as skillfully made as the earlier movements, but seems, to this commentator, rather superficially conceived.

The piano quintet in D minor, Op. 89, was finished in 1906 — fifteen years before the second quintet, in C minor, Op. 115, but it had been begun as early as 1890. It is generally regarded as exceptional rather than typical in exemplifying his period of high maturity. (It is the only chamber work of this decade.) Yet it illuminates, more than a typical work would do, facets of his musical mentality and his aloofness (by no means snobbish or consciously intellectual) from the everyday world.

The first movement (*Molto moderato*, D minor — and major — 4-4) is not a sonata-*Allegro*, although its pattern follows in general that classic form. The main theme, begun in the second violin and thickened by *unisono* string additions as new phrases are added, is accompanied by scintillant thirty-second-note arpeggios high in the piano. Its phrases are rhythmically symmetrical and wholly diatonic up to the cadential bar (16); the harmony, although hardly adventurous, is kept inwardly active; and the illumination of the musical image by this increasing tonal light is of compelling interest. A sterner phrase, in strings alone, emerges (30); the piano's scintillant figures are fragmented and blown away, and the S.II appears (45) in the piano — its rhythm decisive, its tonality uncertain, its three-bar design expanded to four by an intercalary pendant in the strings. This phrase is then remodeled by the strings, its tension presently fading, until a new, much gentler melody emerges in the second violin (68) against a thickened accompaniment in the piano. To this the phrase from bar 30 is gradually added, the texture now becoming highly polyphonic. At length the original harp arpeggios return, in lower register and higher intensity against the S.I in the 'cello; the former themes follow; but this is no mere recapitulation but a further development which continues to the end.

The *Adagio* (G major, 12-8) opens with its main theme in the first violin — a cantilena whose suspense (its rhythmic design is that of a single note sustained for ten eighths in the 12-8 measure plus one quarter note) is heightened by very modulatory harmony in the piano. The viola, for counterpoint, has a descending scale-line which seems too much like the second phrase of the main theme of the first movement to be accidental. (Perhaps we misjudge. Fauré did not think highly of cyclic structure.) The syncopation produced by the quarter note appears twice in the measure in the continuing strain (13); the piano has a variant of the S.I (22); and this complex substance is continued to bar 44, where 4-4 time replaces 12-8 and a new theme, ostensibly in B minor, appears in the piano. It is imitated, with enough exactness to appear canonic, in the viola. The S.I returns tentatively (67) and gradually ousts the S.II; but its higher tension affects the S.I, and can be felt to the end.

There is no Scherzo, nor is one imaginable in this context.* The Finale is perhaps intended to suggest something of that character, but its gaiety (if it is that) is of another order. The main theme (*Allegretto moderato*, D major, 2-2), intentionally naive in design, is announced high in the piano, in octaves, with a single harmony-note interjected at the third quarter and in the strings which add another on "four." At bar 25 the piano takes the theme down to the bass. First violin and viola make a countersubject which the other strings enrich without impeding the rhythm. The strings then take over the theme (49), the piano, in high register, enlivening the motion with a figure in eighths; rather daring modulations ensue and the S.I is at last banished by a new motive, *sostenuto*, in the violin (123) to which the piano and 'cello supply a sturdy bass. This rules until the return of the S.I (177) which, with many new details, remains the main topic to the end. Before that happy event the hearer will probably have suspected a struggle against spiritual bankruptcy.

Fauré did not attempt a string quartet until near the end of his life, being "afraid of this form, like everyone else." He was uncertain of its value, and so deaf that a hearing of it could not have helped him even if time had been granted for its revision. No need for that effort is noted by the critics. The work appears "finished," even by Fauré's meticulous definition of that term. Yet it has won little popularity in this country, and we feel that our limited space has been better filled with the works we have chosen.

These men, in the perspective of the present day, appear as the great figures in nineteenth-century French music. Although time may rectify

* Franck's quintet, the first to be written in three movements, may conceivably have been a model; but that is the only similarity.

that estimate in favor of such figures as Florent Schmitt and Albert Roussel, who are seldom heard in America, other late nineteenth-century composers such as d'Indy, Chausson, and Lekeu will probably not emerge as competitors for the first rank. We can merely note here their chamber works, several of which are nevertheless of high interest.

Vincent d'Indy (1851–1931), a pupil and idolater of César Franck, sometimes called the French Brahms, left three string quartets, two piano trios, a piano quintet, and two duet sonatas for piano with violin and 'cello. The intellectuality which made him an important rectifier of musical instruction in France is evident in all these.

Ernest Chausson (1855–1899), likewise a pupil of Franck, shared his master's gentleness of spirit but had far less strength. His conventional chamber works, a piano trio and a piano quartet (his one attempt at a string quartet was left unfinished), are less interesting than his *Chanson perpétuelle* for soprano and piano quintet (also for orchestra).

Guillaume Lekeu (1870–1894), a pupil of d'Indy, in barely twenty-four years of life completed a string quartet, a *Meditation* and *Minuet* for the same, two piano trios, and a violin sonata which, although somewhat Franckish in substance, shows extraordinary promise. A piano quartet and a 'cello sonata, left unfinished, were completed by d'Indy. "He was likely, had he been put on, to have prov'd most royally."

Albert Roussel (1869–1937), after seven years in the navy which put him in touch with oriental culture, began in 1894 to study music seriously. His foreign contacts soon made him impatient with the impressionism of that day, and he came to feel that music should properly be of no nation and of no time. The product of this conviction, a stern, blunt style and a musical substance of great density, yielded little popular acclaim; but he is coming to be recognized as an outstanding figure among the composers of France, even though his work lacks the nationalistic stamp. His chamber works are not numerous. There are two violin sonatas, a piano trio, a string trio, a string quartet, and a Serenade for flute, violin, viola, 'cello, and harp, together with a few smaller chamber pieces. Almost all these date — in time rather than in idiom — from the twentieth century; but while his harmony and rhythm are often daring to the point of obscurity, he was no revolutionist.

Florent Schmitt (1870–1958) is a similar figure, at least in the matter of independence. His chamber music is mostly for unusual combinations such as a *Lied et Scherzo* for double wind quintet, a *Suite en rocaille*

256]

("rock-work") for flute, violin, viola, 'cello, and harp, a quartet for flute, clarinet, bassoon, and piano called *À tours d'anches* (reeds), and quartets for flutes and for saxophones. But there is a big piano quintet (1908), a string trio (1944), and one string quartet (1948).

The two great figures at the turn of the century, Debussy and Ravel, remain to be studied. Both were unmistakably French and proud to maintain their cultural heritage. Neither was primarily a chamber composer, but each left one string quartet which, although they are not representative of their composers' mature style, are highly characteristic of their musical nature.

Claude Debussy (1862–1918)

Debussy, one of the most original musical minds in history, had not that awed respect for the form of the string quartet which kept Fauré from attempting it until his last days. Yet his single essay, written before his style had crystallized, retains a strong attraction for the chamber-music lover. It makes no display of learned devices and is often more pianistic than quartet-like in texture; but it has all the spontaneity of youth, and it pursues with extraordinary facility the cyclic structure of César Franck—a "trick" which all too often appears as a disguise covering imaginative poverty.

The secret of Debussy's success in this work seems to us to lie in the fact that his cyclically recurrent feature, instead of being an unmanageable long theme, is a single brief motive. Its transformations can thus be more varied—may yield either development or brief reminiscence as occasion demands—without the suggestion of pedantry which is not always absent in skillful examples of the device. It is true, on the other hand, that in the pursuit of this variety Debussy's sonata structure suffers. But he shared, whether consciously or not, Poe's belief that the poetic principle could manifest itself only in what may be called a crescendo of lyric excitement: that the musician (for Debussy saw no essential distinction between musical and poetic imagination) might use whatever means were appropriate to that purpose; and, while coherence was of course essential, the shaping of lyrical excitement to fit a pre-established form was to endanger spontaneity—for him the first artistic requisite.

His cyclic motive is announced at the beginning of the first movement (*Animé et très décidé*, G minor, 4-4). Its rhythm is more decisive than its harmony which is interestingly unstable and little concerned to estab-

EXAMPLE 39. DEBUSSY QUARTET

lish the key. (Its principal transformations may be seen in Ex. 39.) A descending sequence on the motive soon exhausts its energy and a colorful interlude follows (13) on a lyrical phrase harmonized by a succession of swift, wind-blown sixteenths — the first inversions of simple triads. The main motive returns thereafter, followed by what you will take to be the S.II of the sonata form (39). Triplets in 6ths (like the former triads) accompany its fluid line and build it to a climax. Development on the main motive follows (61), its statement in the 'cello being answered by another two-bar figure in the violin, remotely derivable from the main motive. These things form the expected development section, which appears to arrive at a recapitulation (138); but after a forceful statement of the main theme the development goes right on. What we took to be the S.II never returns; but the whole piece thus fulfills, far more than a plodding recapitulation and Coda could do, the demand of the poetic principle.

A Scherzo (*Assez vif et bien rhythmé*, G major, 6-8) follows. It is a patent transformation of the opening motive of the quartet, swift and mischievous. For contrast (call it Trio if you like) a broad augmentation of the same motive is played over a murmur of sixteenths in the lower strings. The scherzo theme returns in the viola (85) and is newly worked, as is the Trio. Then, for Coda, the Scherzo theme in a new disguise in

258]

15-8 time is pizzicatoed in all the strings. The end is on the murmur that supported the Trio, but without its theme.

The slow movement (*Andantino, doucement expressif*, D flat, 6-8), although it does not in detail resemble *L'après-midi d'un faune*, does foreshadow its evanescent imagery. Out of a key as remote as Mendelssohn's famous *Fes moll* (F flat minor), hints of the real theme emerge into D flat (5) where, over a tonic pedal, the first violin completes the thought. Its tension, veering toward G flat, is not high, but its burden is by no means trivial. Precise reference to the cyclic motive is hard to detect, yet the music seems haunted by it. Presently, in C sharp minor, 3-8, the viola gives a stronger hint of the motive, and it becomes quite clearly defined at bar 48, where it assumes rank as the main topic of the discourse. The subtlety of the fluid underlying harmony is indescribable. The 6-8 opening briefly returns for the close.

The Finale begins with a sort of Introduction (*Très modéré*, 4-4) that anticipates a new form in which the cyclic motive will appear (15), and makes transition to G minor, in which key still another transformation (*Très mouvementé*, 2-2) will become the main theme of the piece. Its high animation reaches a climax (181) on the broadly augmented theme; the main theme returns, making toward a conclusion (*très animé*) in which the cyclic motive assumes nearly its original form, whipping up at the end a rather conventional excitement.

Debussy entitled this piece *Premier quatuor*, but he never wrote another. He returned to chamber music only in 1915, with a sonata for piano and 'cello and one for flute, viola, and harp, and in 1916–17 wrote a sonata for piano and violin. Of these, the product of the war years when both mind and body were sorely afflicted, only the 'cello sonata persists in public favor. It is unique in form and character. The first movement, very short, has a tense, recitative-like melody for 'cello whose impact would have been weakened if the movement had been longer developed. The middle movement is an ironic Serenade, exploiting the 'cello in many new figures and colors. The last attempts bravely to be gay but fails (probably intentionally) achieving thus a singular intimation of pathos.

Maurice Ravel (1875–1937)

Comparison is inevitable between Debussy and Maurice Ravel, the last composer to exemplify in the late nineteenth-century idiom the national characteristics of French musical thought. Debussy was more conscious of this purpose than Ravel. During the last years he added to his name on the title pages of his works the designation *musicien français*. Ravel let his nationality exhibit itself. But it is no less evident than Debussy's.

There is, however, a difference — difficult to pinpoint but real. Coleridge's distinction between fancy and imagination comes to mind as a basis for the comparison. His distinction is sharp — perhaps too sharp, for the two qualities, in any art, merge indefinably. Yet there is little doubt that Debussy, whether in purely tonal invention or in the association of music with extramusical experience, was the more truly imaginative composer.

In Ravel's music, as in Stravinsky's, conscious artistry is almost constantly evident. In Ravel it appears as a kind of patina or lacquer enhancing the sheen of the substance. In Debussy, the surface — less brilliant — is that of the polished substance itself. This is not to suggest that Ravel's surface is camouflage. The substance is genuine and the surface appropriate; but both are partly chosen and manipulated for effect, while Debussy's effects — in the aftermath not less compelling than Ravel's — originate in the substance itself and exhibit only its native glow.

If this opinion were based only on their quartets it would be precarious. Both are early works, and each shows a native spontaneity that seems to us more precious than artistic skill, acquired and applied as such. French taste dissents from this opinion. So also does a considerable body of contemporary American taste. But a larger body still values character above manner, which seems to us the essence of Coleridge's distinction.

Ravel's quartet was dedicated "to his dear master, Gabriel Fauré." Debussy's, as we have seen, adopts the Franckian technique of cyclic structure, which Fauré did not espouse. So also does Ravel's, but in a much less conspicuous manner. Both Ravel and Debussy, in their later works, largely abandoned the scheme. But it is not unfruitful to apply the Coleridgian distinction to Franck and Fauré.

The main theme of Ravel's quartet (*Allegro moderato — très doux*, F major, 4-4), which will be the chief cyclic feature, appears at first as almost naive. (The themes are shown in Ex. 40.) Its fluid line, which barely touches the tonic, weaves above the rising F scale in 10ths, but the harmony is mildly dissonant. Its complementary strain, rhythmically very similar, is extended in a repetitive figure that enhances the interest of the returning theme (17) in the viola and first violin. An exuberance

EXAMPLE 40. RAVEL QUARTET

implicit in the theme is released (24) in a figure a bar and a half long with a swift sixteenth-note motion for accompaniment. A hint of the main theme recurs and the S.II follows (55) in first violin and viola. The contrast is mild. The development (69) keeps to the implications of the themes, rising to a high climax. The recapitulation (129) is remarkably regular and the Coda gently reminiscent.

The Scherzo (*Assez vif — très rhythmé*, A minor) is rhythmed in a piquant mingling of 6-8 and 3-4 meters — 6-8 for the middle voices, on an angular, hopping figure, and 3-4 for the actual theme which is suggestive of, rather than derived from, the S.I of the first movement. Its continuation (13) is more clearly akin to the S.II. The manipulations are very ingenious. Pizzicato alternates with *arco* for the two strains, but the 'cello is not bowed until the appearance of what may be called the Trio (*Lent*, 3-4), when it finds a new lyric tune and thus initiates a kind of rhapsody, wonderfully colored, on the themes of the Scherzo. The "recapitulation" is again quite regular.

The slow movement (*Très lent*, 4-4) meditates for a little on the intervals of the opening strain of the quartet; then the viola, in G flat, 3-4, initiates the main thought of the movement. Two bars of the cyclic figure are occasionally interjected (19, 26, 45, etc.) into the expansion of this thought to which the first violin contributes (35). The Introduction, amplified, ends the first section. The second violin (65), against an arpeggio figure in the first, now begins a new strain that, heightened and colored, rises to a moment of passionate intensity. As it sinks the cyclic theme is again interjected; a hint of the Introduction follows, and the rest is appropriate peroration.

The Finale begins (*Vif et agité*, F major, 5-8) on a huddled chromatic figure, loud and excited. It dwindles; the 5-8 measure becomes 5-4, and the cyclic motive is interjected (43), but it is soon reshaped into three-bar phrases in 3-4 and extended, forgetting its derivation. The S.II of the first movement follows (74), similarly redesigned; the opening 5-8 measure returns; and all the rest is a manipulation of these things.

Twentieth-Century Trends in Chamber Music

THE word decadent, as the twentieth century opened, was often applied to various current methods or styles in musical composition. It implied a diseased condition, but neither the attacking germ nor the affected region was clearly determined, and since the prognosis did not appear alarming, no intensive research was undertaken toward its cure. Nevertheless, the most violent revolution ever to occur in the history of music was brewing, and, while its relation to World War I is still obscure, several minor "explosions," all but coincident with that event, may one day be shown to be more than merely coincidental.

That war raised many questions (which a second World War has still left unanswered) as to the validity of the code, moral or social, by which the pre-war world, in its inveterately heedless fashion, was living. The musical revolution raised similar questions as to the validity both of the structural process and the expressive purpose (in the last analysis ineluctably moral) of music as the nineteenth century had cultivated it.

Our discussions, thus far, have confidently assumed the existence and the vigorous pursuit of an expressive purpose in the minds of the composers. That purpose, in the relatively few twentieth-century compositions we shall have space (or skill) to study, will prove much more obscure. In many quarters its very existence is denied. If this denial were accepted as sound, not only would our viewpoint, encountering the new music, have to be reoriented; our convictions as to the expressive value of the music we have studied would be vitiated. Being unwilling to abandon those convictions, we shall offer, before we begin to study the new music, a brief account of the structural revolution which, in various aspects, that music exemplifies. Readers unfamiliar with the new techniques may gain therefrom some insight into them. Readers already initiated will of course find the account insufficient and possibly prejudiced. But the question of expression cannot be answered by ignoring it, and some inquiries pertinent thereto will be raised.

The nationalistic trends we have just sketched, although they modified and expanded the common musical idiom in many ways, involved no radical alteration of that idiom. Hardly had the twentieth century reached its 'teens, however, when a radical attack was launched upon the very foundation of the old idiom. That foundation was tonality — the apparently essential awareness of a tonal center or key-note around which, at any moment, the melody and the harmony of the whole musical substance seemed to revolve. They were attracted to that center by a curious, often elusive force, remarkably analogous to the syntactical attraction of the words in a verbal phrase or sentence toward the verb. The harmonic innovations of Wagner and Strauss had enormously widened the possible orbit of the gravitating tones. Strauss, in his later symphonic poems, had combined thematic lines in such aberrant ways that they could not be accounted for on any recognized theoretical principle. But the public, which loves a certain degree of impudence, was delighted, and the purists, who saw no more in these aberrations than a naughty infraction of rule, raged in vain.

They could not imagine, indeed, that the sacrosanct principle of tonality, *as they understood it*, might, under attack, prove to be only a convention instead of the eternal principle which they supposed it to be — that tonic-centrality might be not the principle itself of musical cohesion but (like the modal system which tonality superseded) only another *manifestation* of that principle, while the principle itself still was undefined.

Two notable procedures — the whole-tone scale of Debussy, and the building of chords out of superimposed 4ths, erected into a system by Arnold Schoenberg — opened empirically the path along which the more reasoned revolution was to march. The whole-tone (or six-tone) scale effectively disoriented the ear as to the identity of the tonic.* The per-

* To be seen as a scale, the six-tone series must appear as an orderly succession of alphabetically named notes such as constitutes the diatonic scale. If you begin this succession on C, you will get five patently alphabetic notes: C, D, E, F♯, G♯, to which the alphabetic successor is A♯, for you cannot properly call it a B♭. But the next tone, by the same logic, must be B♯; and your ear will tell you unmistakably that this is not, indeed, the octave of the C with which you started. You have thus quite effectively lost the locus of your tonic.

fect 4th is the only other interval besides the 3rd which, superimposed, will yield chords that will not be assimilated by the ear into the familiar scheme of superimposed 3rds.* It is doubtful that Debussy intended any attack on the principle of tonality, and it is even supposable that Schoenberg, whose attack was to become uncompromising, came only gradually to see that his 4th chords, if admitted as fundamental structures, could lead to nothing else.

By the 1920's, it was apparently agreed among the *avant-garde* that the principle of tonality was unsound. If so, the tonic must somehow be got rid of. France and Germany led the attack. The French method was called polytonality. It operated by combining two or more melodic lines, each in a different key, simultaneously. Tonality is not, in this way, altogether obliterated, but it is so effectively blurred as to be imperceptible.†

The process, as Milhaud argued (citing a Bach *Duetto* in strict canon at the 5th) is not new. But his argument is not convincing, since Bach's two canonic voices, one in C and the other in G, are assimilated at any given moment to one or the other of the two keys. A peculiar intelligibility (or tolerance) will appear after persistent experiment with melodies not assimilable to any one key; and the process is still very much in vogue.

The German method was more startling. Schoenberg's *Drei Klavierstücke*, Op. 11, gave in 1909 the most conspicuous illustration of the new attitude. Melody, often in phrases conformable to convention, was accompanied by "harmony" so strangely constructed and so destructive of ordinary harmonic sense that the implied tonality of the melody was wholly obscured to the conventional ear. Atonality — the absence of tonality — was the naturally acceptable term descriptive of such structure. Whether it was literally a true description is doubtful. Atonal music, upon repeated hearing, makes a kind of sense indistinguishable from the

* If you admit the *augmented* 4th, building the series, C, F, B♮, E, the E will attach itself to C as third of a normal triad, and B–F will appear as a dominant harmony against its resolution — a combination not in the least new to classic harmony. The 5th, superimposed, yields no novelty, even though it is the inversion of the 4th; for C, G, D, A, E is only a 9th chord to which the ear will imagine an added F, bringing it into the orbit of C.

† Play a simple tune like *Ach, du lieber Augustin* in C; accompany it by the appropriate tonic and dominant chords in D flat. You will laugh as you first hear it, but if you persist with the experiment you will begin to tolerate the polytonal combination. Whether your tolerance is merely that or is an expanded understanding of tone-relations is a question you will not easily answer.

sense of tonal music, and its appears that an actual tonic, however obscure, is somehow guiding the ear. Mere charlatanism could not justly be charged against the composer, who had amply demonstrated his musicianship in the string sextet, *Verklärte Nacht*, and other works. Finding that "atonality is like wine; tonality is like water," Schoenberg pursued his new path. He did find, however, that his method could not yield extended movements such as those of the symphony. His search for a solution to that problem led to the invention (which he called a discovery, feeling that the method already existed) of the structural scheme of dodecaphony — the twelve-tone or "serial" technique of composition.* Verbal description of this system, which we must here attempt, will read like the rules for a game of musical chess; but that game is played by many contemporary composers, with modifications of the rules to suit their structural need or capacity, and with a purpose far more significant than the word "game" implies. Our description, intended only for the uninstructed, will be oversimplified.

The twelve notes within an octave — our "chromatic" scale — are also the twelve tones of the dodecaphonic system. But they are understood very differently. For the black keys (the chromatic notes) in the key of C, are alterations — raisings or lowerings — of the white keys. (C♯ is still a C; D♭ is still a D.) The chromatic notes in C still tend toward the tonic or toward E and G, the notes of the tonic chord, which may thus be described as "rest-tones," while all the others, chromatic or diatonic, are "active." (You will find that they tend, in melody, to progress to the nearest rest-tone, although they are often deflected.)

In the twelve-tone system there is no such distinction. Any tone is free to move to any other — i.e., it has no inherent tendency. Atonality is thus a condition in which these tendencies do not operate.† It may be pro-

---

* Gr. *dōdeka* (twelve) + *phōnē* (tone). "Serial" refers to the basic series or row of twelve notes.

† Twelve-tonalists look somewhat pityingly upon what they call the restricted idiom of classic structure. The restriction lies in the tendencies imparted to the twelve notes by their relation to the tonic. In reality, however, the classic scale has thirty-five notes, not twelve. For what is called C *may* be either B♯ or D♭♭ according to its context, and every other note except G♯ (= only A♭) *may* similarly have three letter-names and three tonal identities, each implying a relation to a different tonic.

The twelve-tone scale has but twelve notes, the "black-key" notes being indiscriminately written with sharps or flats. Indeed, the intervals as classic theory sees them barely exist. A minor 3rd in the original tone-row may be written, in the inversion of the row, as an augmented second — the pitch-distance being the only

duced, however, by a contradiction of tendencies, since any two notes, in succession or combined, suffice to suggest to the harmonically experienced ear a chord which will be taken as belonging to the family of chords which define a key; and this intimation of tendency, if atonality is to be attained, should be blunted by the next tone. (This "rule," however, is often broken in twelve-tone compositions).

Proceeding in this way, the twelve-tone composer constructs what is called a "tone-row" or "series," or "basic shape" for his composition. All twelve tones are ordinarily included in the row; but shorter rows are sometimes used, as are segments of the complete twelve-tone row. In a sense, it may appear that the row constitutes the theme of a twelve-tone composition. On the contrary, it is only the basis of the theme or themes; for, in addition to the fact that any note may appear in any octave, the row has no rhythmic implications, and rhythm is still an essential element of twelve-tone composition.

Endless manipulations of the row or its thematic product are possible. The row may be inverted — its original intervals being maintained but taken in the opposite direction (up or down) to that exhibited in the original form. The row may also be reverted (played backwards), and the reversion may be inverted. Transposition to any desired level is of course possible. Neither is the row merely a melodic succession. Its notes may be sounded simultaneously as harmony, and any note may be taken in any octave. The "chords" thus produced out of segments of the row will not, of course, be recognizable as classical triads, 7ths, etc.; yet, since any note may be taken in any octave, they are capable of a sort of inversion, keeping (as inverted triads do) something of their intrinsic character. And since these chords, newly made with each new row, must in some degree be characteristic of the row, the row, thus heard harmonically, may impart a certain character to the composition based upon it. Since the row itself is difficult to remember, and since its inversion and reversion are still more obscure, it would appear that this harmonic peculiarity is of considerable importance for the definition of structural character.

Polytonality and dodecaphony, here sketched in outline, are the two structural methods which have been most conspicuously followed during the twentieth century. Our description, followed literally by a composer,

significant fact. It is arguable that this reduction in interval-significance is itself a restriction.

would yield only rigidity. The actual music is not so. As we shall see, a tone-row may exhibit progressions unmistakably tonal, and yet be manipulated quite strictly according to the prescriptions just described. Tonality, in fact, has proved much harder to eradicate than the enthusiasts of the 'twenties supposed. The new music then, at least in large part, may be seen as a continuation of tradition, and not a complete break with it. It follows that you, still adhering to that tradition, can understand this music if you try to — and keep on trying.

It appears probable that your understanding will rest on the old foundation of tonality — that the newer progressions, instead of being wholly liberated as the word atonality implies, are still bound by, and still obey in their apparently incalculable orbits, the same gravitational force which held classical structures together — the "pull" of an ever-present but not always identifiable central tone or tonic. Yet the difference is so great that the new music must be recognized as having a new syntax.

The classical musical language exhibited phrases and sentences so obviously resembling those of our English language that those words, applied to musical structure, appear wholly appropriate. The new musical language, appearing to reject the cohesions clearly attributable to tonality, exhibits phrases obscure in tonal design and sentences without a discernible end. Since the resemblance of music to language has always been recognized, and since it is not wholly lost in the new music, may it be that there is between tonal music and atonal an analogy with what the philologists call "agglutinative" and "isolating" languages?

Agglutinative tongues divide and classify words as "parts of speech," and the cohesion of their sentences depends upon certain relations between them: relations at least figuratively describable as gravitational — e.g., the "pull" of the noun toward its verb — the subject toward its predicate. Isolating language, such as the Chinese, has no distinguishable parts of speech — no words fixedly classifiable as nouns or verbs or modifiers of these. There is thus no regulated syntactical structure. The speaker makes a substitute for syntax as he goes on, juxtaposing and inflecting (vocally) his words in various ways so as to convey, for example, activity in his word for an object (a word which, in English, would be purely a noun), or to impart objectivity to a word which in English would be purely a verb. It is hard for us even to imagine how thought could be expressed through such a vehicle. We must indeed recognize that men do think, and think profoundly, in Chinese; but to learn to think in a tongue so foreign to our own is a task which would hardly be undertaken on a national scale.

So long as structure only is considered, the similarity between atonal music and isolating language is striking. But the analogy may easily be pursued too far. Both language and music are used for quite another purpose than to exhibit structural interest. They are for communication; that end, however aberrantly pursued, has always proved paramount; and the problem of communication will not be solved by debates over structure considered as an end in itself. So long as men need to communicate, the problem of structure will be subordinated to that need.

The peculiar intimacy which we predicated of chamber music at the beginning of our study seems to this commentator the product of the desire to communicate. A great deal of the chamber music of the twentieth century has been the product of a new fascination with structure. The purpose of expression is often designedly absent. Even where it is discoverable, the intimations conveyed are strongly colored by the new. mode of utterance. How far the result is generated out of the new philosophy bred out of the predominant scientific interest of our day is a question not easily answered. Pope's conclusion, "whatever is is right," apparently will not satisfy the existentialists, for whom the question of right has no meaning. "Whatever is is" is as far as they can go. But even they, unable to find a factual definition of right, still feel the old definition of it to be wrong, and are thus as much bedeviled by the old dichotomy as was John Calvin.

The perplexity, if not the logic, of the new philosophy appears to us to be reflected in the new music. That perplexity is as truly an image of experience — of contemporary experience — as was the abiding faith of Bach or the democratic idealism of Beethoven. It is harder to express effectively, for deep conviction is more persuasive than perplexity. The pure constructionist, of course, escapes the dilemma — only to impale himself on one horn of it. We have chosen (of course out of our own perplexed philosophy) those examples which seem to us to pursue the age-old quest.

It happens that these examples are those most frequently performed. To us, this seems an indication that the musical public is itself still engaged in that quest, and that it recognizes in these examples an effort to illuminate some phase of it. Our "method" of interpretation — the association of tension and motion in music with tension and motion in human behavior — does not work very well here. The new structure is necessarily preoccupied with new structural combinations, interesting as such but of little relativity to the motions of the mind engaged in a search for wider meaning. Yet even here, as we shall try to show, that intimacy which has always been the chiefest charm of chamber music, has been not only sought but found.

Twentieth-Century Chamber Music

THAT the idiom of music, suffering such attacks as we have just described, should emerge as battered and unstable — no longer the "universal language" which Western Europe (considering itself the universe) had laboriously perfected, but a variety of dialects betraying their origin, not only in the polytonal and serial techniques of the main revolutionary movements but also in many nostalgic memories of the once-universal tongue — was to be expected by anyone with the slightest awareness of the incessant shifts essential to the process of human communication. Indeed, whether it was a language at all became a much-debated question.

It is possible, at any rate, to view music wholly as an art and not at all as a language. In that view, what we have called dialects will appear only as varied techniques; and this is the aspect in which contemporary music is seen by the high priests of dodecaphony and their congregations. Even they, however, do not wholly ignore the purpose of communication. Their view postulates an intrinsic, highly esoteric significance in the structured substance of art — a significance ultimately human, but apparent only at so lofty an altitude above everyday experience that none but the most philosophic musical minds can perceive its relation to ordinary human affairs. The path to that summit is still the understanding of structure *per se*; those whose lungs fail as the atmosphere becomes rarer will have learned that music can be pure only when it is disassociated from human experience; and they may even catch a glimpse of the exalted reality envisioned by the priests.

Our dissent from that view will have been apparent from the very beginning of our study. Psychology, which seems to us to reveal consciousness and subconsciousness as interrelated and indivisible, indicates that the views of the purists are extrapolated out of fractions only of that total consciousness, and are thus erected — to be sure, with careful logic — into a theorem which is itself only fractional. More simply, this means that in our view there is no such thing as "pure" music; that the musical experience is far richer than can be accounted for on the basis of structure — unless the word structure is redefined to embrace many nonstructural implications; and that the apprehension of a commanding example of musical structure as pure can yield only a partial awareness of its significance.

The composers we have so far studied have confessedly recognized and striven to illuminate the reference, in music, to experience which is not music. That effort is much less apparent in the music of the twentieth century. We have suggested here, and have argued more explicitly elsewhere,* that the tensions and motor impulses intrinsic in the musical texture resemble and often portray those which the human organism undergoes in its infinity of reactions to extramusical experience. In the musical "vocabulary" of the nineteenth century these tensions, organized relatively to the scheme of tonality and constructed on easily recognizable relations of consonance and dissonance, yielded a palpable gradient from mild to harsh which could be manipulated coincidentally with the accepted processes of syntactical structure. The tensions of the new music, theoretically unregulated, have no intrinsic syntactical function and often appear arbitrary. But the sensory discrimination of harshness will be hard to eradicate from the human nervous system, and one of our elements of musical expression — tone-stress — although less precisely suggestive, will survive until that sensitivity is eradicated.

The other element, rhythm, is essentially unchanged. It is true that the new music, accordantly with its new tonal tensions, sometimes contrives rhythms which might be called synthetic; but the departure of the new rhythm from the old is slight.

Since tonal tension and rhythm appear in all music, the possibility of construction with an expressive purpose still exists in the new art. Expressiveness, however, even in the old music, does not reside in these factors as such. It arises out of those factors if and when the composer so shapes his structural design that the resemblance of the music to an

* In *Music as Metaphor*, University of Minnesota Press, 1960.

actual emotional excitement is recognizable.* To contrive such a design while preserving all the essentials of structural musical syntax is no mean problem. The achievement of the nineteenth century in this direction was considerable. Our study has in some measure illustrated it.

The twentieth century has been preoccupied with the problem of the new musical syntax. Divergent efforts have produced what we called dialects. Commonly intelligible expression demands a common idiom. The amalgamation of the dialects into a common idiom (involving a considerable sloughing of excrescences) has begun. Not only has the syntax begun to be regulated by an evident (although still not precisely definable) principle. Expressive purpose has begun to appear. This is less different from that of former times than one might expect from the high divergence of the new syntax from the old. To weigh the values of expression (in our view, a primary critical problem) is still difficult. Our selection of examples, out of the huge contemporary chamber-music literature — at best a selection dictated by personal preference — will be further narrowed to that in which an expressive purpose is discernible. But we are somewhat reassured by the fact that our choice has already been approved by a large body of critical opinion, and will be fairly representative.

Béla Bartók (1881–1945)

The six string quartets of Béla Bartók appear, not only in the perspective of this writer but in that of the world at large, to be indubitable masterpieces. They date from 1908 to 1939, and illustrate remarkably the trend of significant musical thought during those three decades — and after. Taking them in order, we shall find, first, in a considerably novel idiom, an expressive purpose akin to that of the late nineteenth century; next, a new exploration of technical resource which in the third and fourth quartets seems largely undertaken for its own sake, but is not without expressive purpose; then, in the last two quartets, a fuller realization of that purpose, involving a rejection of some of the experimental techniques of the third and fourth. But since our vision of expressive purpose is less clear, our description will be chiefly concerned with struc-

* To march is to enact intelligibly such an excitement. Music marches — familiarly, in celebration of victory or of death. But it can also march suggestively of a thousand other excitements, too complex for our feet to "utter," for which an imaginary motor act is our only available outlet. But anyone who has ever "walked on air" has the imagination to understand such activity.

EXAMPLE 41. BARTÓK FIRST QUARTET

ture. Some aid will be gained from the illustrations of the themes provided for all six quartets (Ex. 41–46).

The first movement of the First quartet opens (*Lento*, 4-4) with a contemplative theme in the first violin which the second imitates in canon. It soon abandons that device, keeping only to the descending interval with which the theme began. 'Cello and viola at [1] * repeat the canon, the upper voices continuing and creating remarkably euphonious harmony, hardly divergent from the old order. Modulation is incessant, so that there is no tonic identifiable by either ear or eye; but there always seems to be one just around the corner. Two motives are conspicuous in the continuation — the descending 6th with which the quartet began, and a syncopated figure (sixteenth–eighth–sixteenth). The latter will be still more conspicuous in the Finale. Emphasis on the first motive [5 and

* In the first three Bartók quartets passages will be located by reference to the rehearsal numbers in the Boosey & Hawkes scores — the only ones available in this country — instead of, as elsewhere, by reference to bar numbers.

6] gradually yields to a vanishing close of the first section of the movement.

Over a sonorous pedal 5th the viola now recites a new, impassioned phrase which immediately becomes the accompaniment of a broad melody in the first violin, played, strangely, *p* against the impassioned accompaniment (*mf*) in the middle strings. The 'cello [9] has a free inversion of this, and the violin, after a pause, makes on it a two-bar transition back to the opening canon; two bars of insistence on the descending 6th are its outcome; then the first violin makes a brief epilogue. The movement has been more than a moment long; yet, in retrospect, it seems like the climactic moment of a very tense drama.

Without pause, creeping 3rds low in 'cello and viola introduce the next movement. They continue on the same interval in a gracious curve, *accelerando*, that the higher strings repeat. Then the violin, on the descending 6th, announces the motive that will accompany the waltz-like main theme of the movement (*Allegretto*, 3-4). Its first phrases, detached, will become at the end passionately intense. At [3], after the three notes of the A major triad have been sounded *unisono*, the waltz-melody continues with the curve of 3rds for accompaniment (*più quieto*); at [4] a new rhythm appears which presently [5] seems to paraphrase *unisono* the former curve in 3rds, but this figure [6] becomes a murmur accompanying the waltz. The rest — a very considerable development, is on these things, always novel in aspect but always derived. The climax (*Poco sostenuto*) after [28] is on the first detached phrases of the waltz; its scale-accompaniment in the 'cello becomes a whole-tone scale (which doesn't sound like Debussy), and there is a poetic augmentation of the opening figure for close.

A desperately hasty march-rhythm, punctuating recitatives in 'cello and first violin, introduces the Finale (*Allegro vivace*, 2-2). The main motive is that of the first accompanying figure for the waltz in the *Allegretto*. It is now of a furious energy, in actual unison in viola and 'cello beneath an incessant drumming of eighths in the violins. The movement, with some possibly painful adjustments, may be fitted to the Procrustean bed of sonata form. In that view, the S.I will comprise four motives: (1) the drumming eighths; (2) the figure from the *Allegretto*; (3) the syncopated figure from the first movement, there heard as the last half of bar 8 but now comprising that whole bar, and later very conspicuous; and (4) the two-note waver at bars 6 and 10 of [1] — a kind of diminution and inversion of the dotted rhythm of bar 9, or, perhaps more plausibly, the diminution of the first two notes of motive 2. Motive 3 yields the extended passage at [12] which will then function as the S.II. Development will then begin at [14] or, if this is transition, with the S.I *unisono*, at *Meno vivo* thereafter. Motive 2, diminished and suggesting the opening march-rhythm, is lengthened and made into a fugue [17], and motive 4 leads to the recapitulation [27]. This is irregular, but a version of the S.II appears at Tempo I after [35], and the fugue-theme [37] begins the Coda. But all this rigmarole of analysis, if glimpsed through the hectic excitement of the piece, will seem mere logic-chopping.

This quartet seems to us the boldest adventure into new territory to be made in the first decade of the twentieth century.

The Second quartet, which took two years in the making, was finished in 1917. During the intervening years between this and the First, Bartók had almost abandoned composition for the investigation of the folk music, first of Hungary and later of Rumania and other border-lands — monodic music, neither major nor minor, from which appropriate harmony had to be derived, since orthodox, major-minor tonality could not be appropriately applied. The first World War isolated him from the rest

EXAMPLE 42. BARTÓK SECOND QUARTET

of Europe; he had hardly won a hearing at home with his compositions; but a ballet, *The Wooden Prince*, produced at Budapest in 1917, had a remarkable success, and composition rather than research was thereafter the driving force in his life. So far, indeed, had the diverse influences — from Brahms, Liszt, Strauss, Debussy, and the study of native Hungarian music — been assimilated in his mind that, as Halsey Stevens says, "the whole direction of Bartók's later writing might be deduced from this one work" (the Second quartet).

It still bears many earmarks of romantic thought, its first and last movements being slow and often *molto espressivo*. The texture is more linear than in the First, and the tonality accordingly more vague, but the aural impression is hardly more obscure. The structure is really more unified, since fewer motives are used to generate the total substance. The variants of these motives, however, are often pretty remote, and appear newer to the ear than to the analytical eye.

This quartet, like the First, is "on" A, and that tonality is suggested in the opening motive (*Moderato*, 9-8) — two rising 4ths, E–A–D, and a minor 2nd and a 4th, descending. The rhythm will be more stably maintained than these intervals, which are often altered. (Bartók had no scruple against changing the interval of a design, even in a fugue-theme.) The leap of an octave in the 'cello in bar 1 is also motivic, and this interval is also often altered. The 9-8 meter often becomes 6-8, but this never disturbs the quiet rhythmic flow.

The form is quite lucid. The main motive, with an added chromatic descent, and supplemented [2] by the octave-figure, yields an expository section of 19 bars. Resuming, in imitation [3], the main motive is again lengthened by a triplet figure in sixteenths (which pattern the three first notes of the main motive have already assumed). At [5] a new motive on the augmented triad * heightens the tension and mingles with the others, *f*, *appassionato*. If you are looking for a sonata form, this motive may function as an S.II; but it is soon overridden by the triplet sixteenths. One more motive, a scale-wise ascent and descent of three notes, appears in the bar before [9], and may be taken as Cl.S., for what follows (*Poco più mosso*) is development, culminating [14] in a high tension on the octave-motive and subsiding dramatically after a minatory syncopated rhythming of a dissonant chord. Recapitulation follows (more develop-

* H. Stevens shows that this motive derives from the three-note "up-beat" of the main motive.

mental than repetitive), and what we called the Cl.S. now appears definitely in that light.

Many features will stamp the second movement (*Allegro molto capriccioso*, 2-4) as of Magyar origin, but its disposition to kick up its heels is more than merely racial. After a couple of preliminary flourishes on the diminished 5th the second violin begins to thump out a succession of octave D's which it will maintain for forty bars. Against it the first violin hops on F and D; contradicts the D minor impression by a prolonged F♯; and goes on to a crooked figure, ending in a "mordented" descent (F♯, E♯, D, C♯), that seems, today, the spit 'n' image of the Twist. At [10] the opening flourish returns, its peak now a yawing *glissando* in violin and converging 'cello, and all these things are varied, combined, and alternated until a new motive is introduced (*Tranquillo*, in [25]) that gives a moment of respite from the hectic haste. But its eighths become sixteenths and its pace again breathless; in [33] a 2-4 motive is subtly changed to 3-4, and this triple measure (an extraordinarily simple vitalizing of a rhythm that could not have been maintained much longer) will rule to the end. It is established, as was the original 2-4, by persistent knocking on repeated notes, attaining a climax *con gran passione*. Then the 3-4, always hastening, becomes 6-4, *Prestissimo*; wavers on minor 2nds expand their interval and become crooked arpeggio figures; and these, in muted strings, fly through the air so fast the ear cannot follow them. The end is a little broader and, in contrast, very loud. You will think you have orbited the earth and come safely down. (If you must have a form-pattern, you can call the piece a sort of rondo.)

The third movement (*Lento*, 4-4), begun in muted stillness and on fragmentary phrases, seems at first wholly "atmospheric." At bar 3 of [1], however, the shape of the main motive of the first movement emerges broadly in the first violin; is aped in smaller intervals three bars later; and appears in the 'cello at the end of the section, followed by two long bars of the minor 3rd, A–C—a sort of tonal anchorage "on" A minor. At [2] another motive appears (*Un poco più andante*), its downward curve being that of the last three notes of the other motive. (As it ends, the 'cello's version of the first is repeated.) This new motive rules the whole section. At [4] a simple, chorale-like melody appears, harmonized homophonically but in 4th chords; the violin [5] paraphrases it two octaves higher, merging into the second motive; and the 'cello [6] interjects a variant of the first motive. To this the two violins reply, with notable gentleness, in a rising succession of two major 3rds; the dialogue rises to high intensity; then follows, *sotto voce*, a new section, in only two real parts, on intervals which, presently expanded, become suggestive of the main motive. That motive, with its intervals contracted, emerges (*Lento assai* in [8]) and is followed by intense ejaculations; then the main motive is suggested [10]; the quiet 3rds answer; over the sustained A–C the second motive descends, and the 3rds, very low, approach to final, pizzicato A's.

The form is often described as "chain-like"—i.e., one thing after another. But the impression it leaves is not one of loose diversity, but rather of one underlying mood, side-lit by the chorale but still returning upon itself.

The Third quartet was composed ten years after the Second. These ten years show the farthest excursion Bartók made into the region of what may be called atonality. But he never erected the discoveries he made into any theoretical system such as that of dodecaphony, and he seems, later, to have felt that the outposts of the atonal region were un-

EXAMPLE 43. BARTÓK THIRD QUARTET

fertile, for the last two quartets as well as other late works mark a perceptible retreat.

He was not striving to found a system, but to discover a workable amalgamation of occidental and oriental idioms. Heredity and early environment had given him an immediate understanding of the oriental, and his exhaustive studies of folk-music had enlarged and intellectualized that understanding. On the other hand, his severe training in the Western idiom, which incidentally made him a pianist of the first rank, contributed equally to his musical intuition; and he felt that the possibility of the amalgamation must be tested to its limit. Basically, his linear harmony, apparently wholly atonal, was really a product of the characteristics of his "polyglot" melody. But the texture, to attain to vividness, had to be elaborated; and since he was, as performer, a virtuoso for whom difficulties hardly existed, this elaboration often takes the form of virtuosity. In the two violin sonatas of this period, that virtuosity so far dominates that they can hardly be considered as chamber music. The quartets, however, adventurous as they are, remain within the boundary of that genre.

The Third quartet is the shortest and the most highly condensed of all, and the most obscure to the ear. It is played without pause and thus appears as one movement, which it really is in spite of the high contrast between its two opposed characters, for as Bartók himself indicated, the four divisions of the piece are to be seen as *Prima parte*, *Seconda parte*, *Ricapitulazione della prima parte*, and *Coda* (which is a recapitulation of the second part). The first and third divisions are slow; the second and fourth, fast — a distinction which hardly needs explanation. But the thematic structure is not so simple.

Over a chord made of C♯ + d (harmonic) in 'cello, e in viola, and d♯' in second violin — really four consecutive semitones — the first violin plays a tortuous melodic line, eventually comprising all the other eight notes of the chromatic scale (but this is no twelve-tone scheme, for A♯ is returned to before the series is complete). The chord, muted, sounds wholly vague — a background, rather than a harmony; the melody, in consequence, tortuous as it is, stands apart from the harmony and is not in the least interpretable in its light. Its five bars, indeed, are really introductory, for the actual "theme," whose germ is a three-note figure of rising 4th and falling 3rd, begins only thereafter. It is imitated in free canon between the violins, then at [1] by viola and 'cello. At [3] viola and first violin have it at the 4th (it was formerly at the 3rd); and the 'cello — after a cadence on the open 5ths, G–D and A–E (very strange-sounding after all the dissonance), which is followed by a pause of a whole bar — starts on the three basic notes an ostinato figure which, at [4] is doubled in speed in the viola and imitated, one eighth later, by the 'cello. Above this the violins begin to suggest the rhythm of a new subject — thirty-second twitching into double-dotted eighth, *sul ponticello*. The function of this motive, however, is subordinate. It merely generates a straining sonority [6] on an inversion of the basic figure (descending 5th in place of rising 4th) which, returning to the original form of the figure, generates [7] such a rhythming of double- and triple-stopped chords as no four-stringed instruments had ever produced. A sort of interlude on the basic figure (still canonic), and brief insistence on the twitching motive (in [10]), brings a kind of clarification. The basic motive is turned into a long melody, in octaves in second violin and viola, that spins itself to a quiet close.

The *Seconda Parte* (*Allegro*) is much more "visible" to the ear. Its rhythmic unit is the eighth note, and while there are frequent shifts from the basic 2-4 (= 4-8) to 3-8, 5-8, and 6-8 in the notation, the eighth-note throb is pretty evident throughout. The theme is a diatonic, scale-wise line plucked by the 'cellist on simple triads spanning the 10th. Its dance-impulse is manifest. The first violin, *arco*, scampers over the same curve in sixteenths — a pattern that will by and by yield a little fugue. The process, however, is variation on these two things (really, one), and the first new shape to be evolved is a lithe, dotted rhythm [3] in first violin, with the triads below. Heavy rhythmic stomping marks a transition, and what may be seen as the S.II of a sonata form appears in viola and 'cello [10] — really the triad-theme again, beneath double-stopped rhythmed chords in the violins. At [13] (*Più mosso*) the theme is in canon, ultimately four-voiced, with viola and 'cello [16] having the inversion of the line. Motion in sixteenths, sporadic during the canons, begins to rule at [19] and the exposition of the sonata form ends with a *rallentando* which introduces the development [23]. This presents the theme in various new rhythmic shapes, finally arriving [31] at the fugue mentioned above. The recapitulation [36] begins with the plucked triads in canon between 'cello and first violin. It is really, thereafter, further development, culminating in wild *glissando* swoops in contrary motion [44] and hammered chords, reminiscent of a similar passage in the *Prima Parte* (in [10]) and thus anticipating the Recapitulation of that part which follows.

This is a very recondite recapitulation. The curve of the basic figure (rising 4th–falling 3rd) is barely discoverable in the deliberate motion and the unadorned texture; the *martellato* passage from [10] is recognizable by ear; but even close study leaves this commentator uncertain of the derivation of most of the section. The aural impression, on the other hand, is grateful.

The Coda is quite evidently a further development of the running variant of the main theme of the *Seconda Parte*. The thin, whistling tone (*sul ponticello*) of its beginning becomes "ordinary" at [3], and the derivations (e.g., the extension of the upward scale at [10]) will not be difficult to recognize.

This quartet was submitted in a competition offered by the Musical Fund Society of Philadelphia. In 1928 the first prize ($6,000) was divided between Casella and Bartók. He had returned to Budapest after an American tour when the award reached him. The award created a great sensation there, and probably helped toward that freedom of mind which enabled him to compose the Fourth string quartet.

Written only a year after the Third, the Fourth quartet naturally displays many of that work's characteristics. The tonal devices, *sul ponticello* and *glissando*, unusual in chamber music, are amplified by a pizzicato so forceful that the string snaps against the fingerboard with a sound like a tap on a snare drum. Rhythms are reinforced by double stops, and the sonority thus often appears orchestral. Yet the ideas themselves are so unusual, and these devices so appropriate to them, that the boundary of chamber music does not seem to have been crossed.

The quartet has five movements, of which the first and fifth, and also the second and fourth, are linked by derivation from two motives, one of which is common to each pair. The middle movement (slow) may thus be seen as the peak of an arch. As in the Third quartet, the purpose of expression, although in our view it clearly exists, is subordinated to that of design. (The common indications, *espr.*, *appassionato*, etc., frequent in the first two quartets, are almost wholly absent in the Third and Fourth — a sign that the particular sort of expressiveness intended by those marks is not wanted here.)

The basic motive of the first and fifth movements is a brief, closely

EXAMPLE 44. BARTÓK FOURTH QUARTET

chromatic figure that rises a diminished 3rd and falls a semitone below its first note. It first appears (7)* in the 'cello; it is inverted (12) as counterpoint to its original form; and its intervals are expanded (15f). Thereafter it is fragmented into little pieces or kept intact as the progress of the texture dictates — the design being that of the sonata form. At bar 58 a little figure of thirty-seconds on half tones begins to form the accompaniment for the expanded form of the main motive in the 'cello; and this motive, combined with its inversion and otherwise elaborated, forms the S.II of the sonata pattern.† A syncopated see-saw of diverging *glissandi* (79) precedes its hoarse, low-registered conclusion. Then

* The numbers in parentheses, from now on, are again bar-numbers, not rehearsal-numbers.

† Mosco Carner conceives the exposition to extend only to bar 49, where a halt occurs preparatory to what we have called the S.II. He sees this "subject" as development (which it obviously is, being derived from the basic figure); and sees the movement as monothematic, with its recapitulation at bar 92. The high contrast of this section (58–92) appears to us to function as S.II, with continuous development thereafter, including the Coda (*Più mosso*, 126). Since Bartók's recapitulations are always developmental, we prefer to dispense with that feature and gain the interest of a second subject.

the main motive, *unisono* but combined with the open G's and D's of the three lower strings, reasserts itself. After another wild *glissando* the smoother form of the motive, subdued but in cumulative imitation, begins a tortuous climb to the Coda (*Più mosso*).

What might justly have been labeled *Scherzo* follows (*Prestissimo, con sordino*, 6-8). Its theme, a chromatic rise and descent covering a 5th, seems like a liberation of the main motive of the first movement from the cramped register in which that figure was confined. The always muted strings give it a peculiar color and also mollify the dissonances. After bar 70 the streaking motion (but not the speed) is halted, and a new motive on the diminished 3rd, D–f♭, and its intervening E♭ appears (79). These things, along with the *glissandi* already heard, form the substance of all the rest.

The slow movement (*Non troppo lento*, 4-4) is mostly given over to a long rhapsodic 'cello solo against which there are only sustained chords in the other strings. These begin *non vibrato*, then adopt that device. The difference is striking. As the 'cello ceases the first violin begins to twitter above the continuing chords (35); second violin and viola, on individual figures, each contribute bird-notes; they join for a moment in a duet; so do first violin and 'cello; then distant twitters bring the end.

The fourth movement (*Allegretto pizzicato*) is plucked throughout, mostly quite delicately, but on occasion with the startling snap of the string on the fingerboard. The thematic line, begun in the viola (6), is clearly the diatonic counterpart of the chromatic rise and fall in the second movement. At bar 48 the figure of the diminished 3rd gives contrast. The texture thickens as the scale-theme returns, and the snaps punctuate it. As an imaginative contribution to the varied "scenes" portrayed by the quartet, it is equal to the singularly suggestive slow movement.

The Finale (*Allegro molto*, 2-4) is powerfully rhythmic. Its thematic substance, first appearing after fifteen bars of double-stopped stomps, is almost precisely that begun in bar 15 of the first movement. Its intervals will be altered as the exhilaration increases, but there is no obscurity. A high contrast is offered (151) by a curious accompaniment-figure, all on the arpeggiated open strings of the 'cello and the second violin, against which first violin and viola dance a dainty *pas de deux* (*leggero, grazioso*), its theme a paraphrase of the main motive which soon returns (163). The variety attained by the expansions of interval and by inversion and fragmentation of the theme is inexhaustible. The abstractness suggested by analytical observation of these things is wholly banished when they strike the ear as living sound. Remote as it is in implication from our ordinary contacts, this music offers the hearer an experience to be shared.

The Fifth quartet was commissioned by the Elizabeth Sprague Coolidge Foundation, and is dedicated to her. It is the longest of the quartets; yet it was written, surely at white heat, in the space of a month, in August–September, 1934. While its structure is not less integrated than that of the Third and Fourth, it is less radical in its dissonance, and is thus much easier for the ear to apprehend. The first and second themes of the sonata structure are plainly differentiated both in contour and rhythm, and the whole design is spacious enough so that a lesser concentration is required of the hearer.

The quartet is "on" B flat, and that fact is announced at the outset by three bars of rhythming, essentially on that one note. The outline of the main theme grows out of this rhythming (4) in viola and 'cello, and its definitive shape emerges in the same instruments (8) against hopping 4ths that were the product of the simpler outline of the theme. (Its upbeat is a quintolet of narrow intervals that suggests, and will often become, a simple chromatic figure; its peak a sustained note; its end a quiet eighth-note descent. It is clearly exposed in four bars.) Transition begins (14) on a figure from the hopping 4ths; the opening rhythms are interjected; then (45) the S.II emerges — a rise and fall, mostly in fluid triplets and scale-wise, in 6-4 time or 8-4 (3 + 2 + 3) or 5-4. The development begins with the opening rhythm on E (59), a tritone from B♭, instead of on F, the classical dominant. Its evolutions are not abstruse. The recapitulation (126), after the initial rhythming, presents the S.II with its curve inverted (but easily recognizable) before, instead of after, the S.I, which has now lost its descending "tail" and is combined with the opening rhythm (167). The Coda (*Allegro molto*) mingles both subjects, and ends with the quintolet figure against its mirrored inversion.

The Fourth quartet had two Scherzi surrounding the slow movement. The Fifth has two slow movements surrounding the Scherzo. The first of the two (*Adagio molto*, 4-4) is "on" D, but is so "atmospheric" that neither tonal center nor theme is clearly evident. Nine bars of detached phrase-snippets over a bass that descends from D to D vaguely suggest that tone-center. Then (10), over a plain C major chord, the first violin

EXAMPLE 45. BARTÓK FIFTH QUARTET

begins to interject slightly longer but still tentative phrases. But the C major chord is really the beginning of a chorale — or a part of one — against whose final D major harmony the violin's line makes a long cadential descent. Now, over a pedal G, tremolando in the second violin, detached gruppetti in the first violin punctuate, somewhat as in the opening, three-note melodic phrases in viola and 'cello against a pizzicato appoggiatura A♭ which slides down to the same pedal G. The 4th, direct or inverted, is the characteristic interval of these phrases, and out of them the first violin (31) builds an expressive melodic line that will be paraphrased in the *Andante*. On that same interval (*Più lento*, 35) longer curves are then canonically drawn which culminate in the three-note form, *espressivo*. Then comes a hint of the chorale (46) and a return to the atmosphere of the beginning, now considerably rarefied.

286]

TWENTIETH-CENTURY CHAMBER MUSIC

The second Scherzo (*Alla bulgarese, vivace*) groups the nine eighths of its measure as $4 + 2 + 3$, giving a curious irregularity that is soon accepted as regularity. Over this Bulgarian rhythm, and in agreement with it, the thematic figure (often the arpeggio of a classically-built chord) undulates — sometimes canonic, sometimes inverted — forming the whole Scherzo proper. The Trio adds an eighth note to the measure, grouping the ten notes primarily as $3 + 2 + 2 + 3$, but occasionally as $2 + 3 + 2 + 3$, or $2 + 3 + 3 + 2$. The first violin is the soloist for forty bars, accelerating its speed to *vivacissimo*; the second violin then mirrors (inverts) its melody as a second to it; and at bar 44 the viola reinforces the first violin, but at the 9th below. The impression, with all the melodic strings muted, sometimes *forte*, is weird, for the redistributions of the ten eighth notes often contradict the accent-pattern of the melody. The Scherzo returns, greatly altered as to distribution (the violin is no longer solo) and also as to design, building toward a Coda (*Agitato*) in which a long sequence of tiny intervals, blurred by canonic imitation and inversion, yields a colorful scale-wise version of the theme, *espressivo*. But the end is evanescent.

The second slow movement (*Andante*, 3-4) is on a larger scale than the *Adagio* but has the same A–B–A plan and a somewhat similar atmosphere. It begins on a rhythmic motive (quarter plus four eighths), pizzicato, *espressivo* — high B's, ending in a glissando gruppetto. The other strings imitate. The viola (7) begins to bow pedal G's, and the violins little trills; presently (13) a melodic phrase emerges, *molto espressivo*. A new rhythm appears (*Più andante*); the 'cello interjects what a lawyer would call leading questions (three quarter notes), and at last the first violin (*Più lento*) remembers the theme from bar 31 of the *Adagio* and paraphrases it, somewhat freely and at greater length than the original thought. This "night-scene" is more extended and more colorful than the other, the melody being made to reach what, in "modern" music, is almost an anachronistic ecstasy of lyricism. The softly surging figures in thirty-seconds that underlie it die away; the *Più andante* rhythm is thrice struck (the third time, *col legno*); and beneath the first violin's B *natural* the 'cello, pizzicato and glissando, plays a succession of 10th chords that comes to rest on the triad of G *minor*.

The Finale is probably the swiftest piece in chamber-music literature. It flies so fast that the hearer can identify only the most unmistakable formal landmarks; yet he will never feel wholly disoriented. If he plods over the score on a surveyor's slow two feet, he will discover many more of those marks, and will thus see how it was that he did not get lost. Only a few results of that effort can be set down here, but they may suffice to show how sensitive was the composer's electronic intuition in charting the flight.

Rhythmic consciousness is first stimulated in a brief Introduction. Then the main theme, *Presto*, emerges out of reiterated E's to which viola and 'cello add a characteristic ictus. The theme's tonal line derives from the more tortuous S.I of the first movement by straightening that line into a nearly scale-wise progression.* Inversions and other manipulations are many; the rhythmic organization — mostly in two-bar groups but sometimes in three — is complex; but while you will not have time to observe a tithe of these things you will still keep your bearings.

The rhythmic ictus that underlay the theme emerges alone (109) as a sign that something new will presently appear. At first you will see only the Introduction (150); but this too is expectant and the S.II finally appears (202). Its speed (*Più presto*) and its delicacy (*scorrevole* —"flowing"— and *leggerissimo*) make it difficult to recognize as a derivation from the tortuous quintolet in the S.I of the first movement, especially since the concluding upward minor 2nd there becomes a downward major 7th here. The motion and the general character of that design, rather than its actual pattern, rule until bar 250 where the S.I in the viola combines with the S.II in the first violin. Diverging scales (330) hint at another landmark; the Introduction returns again (360); there is thumping, *col legno*, on the ictus, *Prestissimo*; and this accompanies a fugato, begun by the viola (373) on the S.I and carried through all the voices as the main feature of the development section of the sonata form although each entrance is marked *oscuro* and may thus be missed. At bar 480 the S.II appears; the speed slows to *Allegretto capriccioso*, and the falling 7th of that theme is featured against the simplification of the S.I to a mere chromatic scale. The insistent E's of the opening (546) announce the recapitulation.† This, as is usual with Bartók, is no mere restatement, but

* This scale includes many notes that, in our notation, appear chromatic but are really integral in the oriental idiom which Bartók is trying to amalgamate with the occidental. For example, Bb and B♮ may occur indifferently in a G-mode without suggesting either G minor or G major.

† Halsey Stevens sees the S.II (480) as beginning the recapitulation, with the main subjects thus appearing in reverse order. To us the altered character of the S.II stamps it as developmental.

its variants from the exposition need not be rehearsed. Quite unusual, however, and in a vein of sardonic humor, is the interpolation of a silly little tune out of some imaginary book of nursery rhymes, *Allegretto, con indifferenza*, harmonized on the plain tonic and dominant of A major.* The polytonal repetition of the tune in B flat over the A major harmony, which ought to sound even more ironic, has the contrary effect (at any rate to our ear) of a return to the general idiom of the quartet. The Coda, on always distorted scales, rushes to its hilarious close.

Pascal remarks somewhere that a reader who takes up a book expecting to find an accomplished writer will be surprised and delighted if he finds also a man. Although the man, Bartók, is evident in all the quartets we have examined, he is far more in evidence in the Sixth. Written five years after the Fifth, it seems to flow from the pen without restraint, in an idiom not really altered, yet somehow mellowed — and mellowed by the association of music with that which is not music.

EXAMPLE 46. BARTÓK SIXTH QUARTET

* It sounds as grotesque in its context as would our naive experiment in polytonality, suggested in the footnote to p. 265. But the comparison, if the rule is allowed to work both ways, reveals that irony is a dangerous weapon in an argument.

That association must of course be revealed through the process of musical structure. But the structural unit in the Third quartet was so far the tiny motive that themes, in their ordinary aspect, hardly seemed to exist, or, if built up out of the motive, became so altered (as in the recapitulation of the First part in the Third) as to be all but unrecognizable. In the Sixth quartet the thematic contours are retained — to be sure, with alterations — so clearly that their purport is readily apparent. The obscurer motivic structure might have been called cyclic. That of the Sixth is definitely so.

It begins (*Mesto*, 6-8) with an unaccompanied melody of thirteen bars in the viola, its first three bars in particular forming a sort of "motto" which, in various aspects, will introduce each of the four movements, and will form the actual theme of the last. Following this solo, all the strings, *unisono*, heavily propound in measured, detached phrases, what will become the actual theme of the movement. This is somewhat obscure, since the first three notes (G–Ab–Eb, rising) are reverted to form the second phrase (A–D–C♯) — the actual beginning of the theme. This phrase, repeated an octave lower, is followed by C–E–F–G–F♯–A — the rest of the theme; and this brief *pesante* section thus forms a sort of "table of contents" for the theme itself, and for the whole quartet.

The first violin plays the line, *Vivace*, to start the real movement; the second repeats it a half-step higher; the others harmonize its final A♯ with the first three notes, in inversion or *recto*; the first violin (31) gives it a new twist by inverting its first three notes, and with this impetus the exposition of the theme is started. The theme, intact or in fragments, seems to be everywhere at once, since the whole texture is derived from it. The resultant harmony is remarkably euphonious. Many chords in the vocabulary of the nineteenth century appear — often enough to give a more positive impression of tonality than in any other quartet except the First.

The outline of the sonata form is likewise more visible. The first phrase of the theme, squarely emphasized as in the "table," becomes (68f) patently preparatory. What it introduces is the S.II (81) — a theme whose warmth (it is marked *con calore*) is wholly appropriate to the image thus far formed. As it descends, continued in second violin and viola, the first violin finds a sequential accompanying strain which (*vivacissimo, agitato*) becomes the whole substance of the thought. The development — again introduced by the *pesante* table — begins with the main theme in viola and 'cello (166). A repetitive figure, clearly on the dominant of C, surrounds (180f) the fragmented theme in viola and second violin. The S.II does not appear in its original form, but its second phrase does emerge out of the first theme (237f), making approach to the recapitulation. Some take this to begin with the S.I in the viola (268). We see it as beginning with the S.I in its original register in the first violin (278). The reprise is much compacted, the S.II appearing (312) in the second violin and the brief Coda at bar 355.

The second movement begins with the motto theme in the 'cello, newly harmonized by *tremolando* chords in the inner voices and a contemplative counterpoint above, in the first violin. But this is only an Introduction. The main movement is a march whose jerky dotted rhythm at once galvanizes our imaginations into action. Its climax is a heavy canonic tramping (43f). The volume subsides and the second violin, on his G string, has a stentorian second theme (58) which the first presently imitates. The Trio begins on a high, rhythmed Ab in the 'cello which launches into a rhetorical theme against tremolando shakes in the violins and the 'cello's rhythm strummed pizzicato in the viola. The first violin's G string plays a strident continuation (99); then all the instruments, on a sort of Alberti-bass figure but each in a different key, make a tiny cadenza. The march, colorfully reworked, returns.

The motto, now in the first violin, again forms the Introduction to the third movement. What it introduces is called *Burletta* — as impudent a little piece as was ever penned. The rhythm is vital enough to satisfy the veriest jazz-hound; the tone (at first scraped *au talon*) is rough and all but savage; the violins interject glissando slides on quarter tones; and the only discernible "melodic" line is all but submerged in the uproar. The hurly-burly subsides and a gentle Trio-interlude ensues (*Andantino*, 6-8, 9-8, etc.) on curves reminiscent of the first movement. The March returns, more impudently scored than ever, hastening its pace in expectation of a rousing climax. Instead, the *Andantino* thrice tries to enter, but the rhythmic drive repels it.

The Finale (*Mesto*, 6-8) is all made on (rather than of) the motto, in a texture largely resembling that of the Introduction to the *Burletta*. Dissonance is again reduced to that intensity which ruled in the first movement, and the direction, *espressivo*, is wholly appropriate to the melodic line, which is mainly in first violin and 'cello. But these two have a subdued variant of the main theme which they are directed to play *senza colore* (in effect, without vibrato). This dull hue is painfully suggestive. It does not last, however, and a new sense is now given to the theme by turning the major 2nd (D♭–E♭) of its bar 2 into a diminished 3rd (e.g., E♮–G♭, bar 18). The implications of this contractile interval are wonderfully brought out. At length the theme is greatly augmented (*Più andante*, and again *senza colore*); but the sequel is now a reminiscence of the main theme of the first movement (46), followed by its inversion; next, the S.II of that movement is recalled (*dolce, lontano*) also with its inversion; then, after a kind of cadenza figure, *unisono* (67), the diminished-3rd version of the motto theme ascends, over shivering harmonies; the rising 4th of the main theme, broadened more widely than in the "table" and softly punctuated by the D minor chord, is stridently asserted (it is harmonized by the diminished 3rd); a contracted version of the motto theme is quietly eloquent, and the end is made on a mingling of D minor and F major.

Here, indeed, is a man.

Paul Hindemith (1895–1963)

Paul Hindemith, probably the most prolific of contemporary composers except Darius Milhaud, has made voluminous contributions to the literature of chamber music. Being a virtuoso of the first rank on the viola, his writing for strings is always practical, however difficult it may be. But he knows at first hand the capabilities of every other orchestral instrument, and has written for many unusual instrumental combinations with equal facility. There are sonatas for violin, viola, 'cello, flute, oboe, English horn, clarinet, bassoon, horn, trumpet, and trombone with piano; trios, not only for strings but for such odd combinations as viola, heckelphone, and piano (Op. 47). Seven string quartets have been listed, but the first has been withdrawn.

Even his earliest works show a considerable impatience with convention, and in maintaining that attitude he has thought out both a basic theory of music that derives from the old art (the triad remains for him the primary harmonic unit), and a system of composition as thoroughly reasoned as that of the twelve-tonalists. His system rationalizes extremes of dissonance as great as those of dodecaphony, but he has never adopted or even countenanced the idea of atonality. His textures range from occasional monophony to intricate polyphony, but his adherence to the older forms of musical discourse is manifest.

His fertility in manipulating the substance of music and the abounding energy of his temperament have doubtless overdriven his creative imagination. His style is patently teutonic, which means that he cannot abandon a thought until he has brought its structural possibilities into clear view. He falls, in consequence, into that error which the French deplore — *il dit tout*: he says everything, leaving little to the imagination of his hearer. But this does not imply that he has no imagination. Both his music and his critical writings * show a profound sense of music as a cultural possession rather than as an esoteric delight for the initiated. Yet for reasons beyond our grasp but in some measure related to those we have suggested, the appeal of his music is seldom immediate — which is to be expected, and stops short of being final — which is more important.

Any selection from so large a body of work would appear random. Ours, which must be limited to two examples, may appear wholly so. They will serve, at any rate, to illustrate the nature of Hindemith's artistic growth.

The violin sonata in D, Op. 11, No. 2,† dates from 1920. It is so "conservative" as hardly to represent his current manner; yet it reveals much of his maturer personality. Its first movement begins with a vigorous *unisono* theme (*Lebhaft, mit starrem Trotz* —"Lively, with stern defiance"— D, more minor than major, 4-4). The defiance is bold, but begins to appear, on longer acquaintance, somewhat shallow. Its continuation is a sweeping upward arpeggio (12-8) on the G flat chord, making transition to the S.II (*Fliessend* —"flowing"— 3-4): a quiet line whose romantic intensity grows and wanes agreeably. The development (*Lebhaft* — "lively") begins on a transformation into 3-4 of the S.I. It is interestingly harmonized and whipped up to a stormy climax. The recapitulation begins with the S.I an augmented 4th higher than at first, but it rehearses the former matter quite faithfully. In the Coda the S.I becomes a swift 12-8 figure. The slow movement ("Quiet and measured," D minor, 2-4) has as main theme a three-bar pattern quite classic in outline and implication. The middle section is faster, in alternate 3-4 and 2-4 time, with all the insistence and much of the warmth of romanticism. It gradually

---

* *A Composer's World: Horizons and Limitations*, Cambridge, Mass., 1952, will give a purview of his theory and his musical philosophy.

† No. 1 is also for piano and violin; No. 3 is for 'cello and piano; No. 4 is for viola and piano; Nos. 5 and 6 are for unaccompanied viola and violin.

increases its tempo to *Lebhaft* and its import to passion. Then the opening returns, at first a half-step lower than it began but soon rising to its original pitch. The Finale, "In the measure and character of a fast dance," begins as a thoroughly teutonic, refreshingly plebeian Waltz. This theme alternates with a more fluid strain, accompanied by scintillant (and incidentally very difficult) triplet figures in the piano. There is naturally no display of contrapuntal learning. Neither (to our apprehension) is there here any clear relevancy to what has gone before.

The other example we have chosen is often counted as the Sixth of Hindemith's string quartets, but if (as appears to be the fact) his First has been withdrawn, this is the Fifth. It is the first of two written for the Budapest Quartet, and performed by that group in Washington in 1944 and 1945.

It begins with a slow movement (*Very quiet and expressive*, 4-4) that is really an Introduction. Its main theme, announced by the viola solo, displays at once the peculiar relation of the triads of a key which, if we understand it aright, is basic to Hindemith's theory. Three notes (D–E♭–C) suggest tonic and subdominant in G minor; E♮–B♮–G♯–G♮ substitute the E triad (major, then minor) for the submediant triad (E♭–G–B♭), and E♭–D–F♯ re-establish with its dominant the G minor tonality. The theme is then exposed fugally by the other instruments, similar and often more obscure harmonic relations being exhibited; yet, with repeated playing (even on the piano), the tenuous connection between extremely dissonant notes becomes reasonably clear. (The rationale of longer progressions is harder to perceive, but unless such perception can be effected by an attentive ear it will remain an unknown value.) A new motive (*Broad*, bar 17) gives momentary contrast and is later repeated, but the main idea supervenes and rules to the end.

After an outline of G major and minor in the 'cello, the main movement (*Lively and very energetic*, 2-2) follows without pause. Its vigorous theme is sounded *unisono*, cadences on B♭, and is thereafter manipulated in all the voices in turn, forming thus the S.I of a sonata exposition. At bar 83 (after I) the S.II appears in the first violin — its rhythmic pattern somewhat resembling that of the S.II of the Introduction. Development begins at M (119) with the S.I again *unisono*. This presently subsides on its inversion in the 'cello; the S.II appears in the first violin; then, combined with that inversion, the S.II is broadly augmented in the viola. This tactic is pursued for some time, perhaps with too much persistence, the S.II being also augmented (at R) with the S.I for counterpoint. There is no formal recapitulation. The Coda (V) begins with the S.I, again *unisono* but ending on an octave leap whose dotted rhythm persists against that of the main theme. The cadence on E flat major, preceded by A major with its added 6th, has the rationale we noted in the Introduction.

The third movement is headed, *Quiet, Variations.* The nine-bar strain, set forth by the first violin in B minor, 3-4, is repeated by the viola with a new counterpoint in the violin to form the first section of a quite conventional variation-theme. The second section, after a six-bar intensification of the same thought, returns to the opening strain, finds a new continuation, and ends with the opening strain in the 'cello (C) with the same continuation. The first variation is on bits and pieces of the theme, contracting its design into twenty-four bars. The second, *L'istesso tempo*, reshapes the thematic line into a light dotted figure which fills out the original longer design. The third smooths the dotted rhythm into murmuring sixteenths, again contracting the design. The last (*Lively, gay*, essentially in 6-4) figurates the theme in a florid pattern of running eighths, first in violin, then in viola, and at last turns the figuration into an accompaniment for the theme itself (as in the final section), first in the violin, then in the 'cello. The quiet end is in B major.

The last movement (*Broad and energetic*, 4-4) has as main theme a vigorous march whose clear thematic line is first repeated in the second violin (A) and then fragmented and syncopated. A broader second theme (C) likewise in the first violin, is accompanied by the dotted rhythm that accompanied the S.I, and this tune is repeated in the viola. Thereafter, a few bars of lighter motion bring a cadence in E and a third theme (F), much more fanciful, that is exposed fugally and developed in a great variety of *stretti.* Against this tripping figure the S.I, somewhat altered, appears in the first violin (H) and is repeated in stretto by viola and second violin and then by the 'cello. The figuration becomes more excited; the S.I (altered) comes in the first violin, high above (K); the viola takes it over, then the first violin; and in this way approach is made to a *Very broad* version of the main theme, apparently final. It is not so. A Coda follows (*Allegretto grazioso*, 3-8), in the vein of, and possibly derived from, the lighter episode at (F), and the end is made on this playful note.

Hindemith's chamber music, although voluminous, varied, and (as this quartet will show) constructed with a skill so apt that structure seems to present no problem, finds slighter favor with audiences than it apparently deserves. In this commentator's view, one reason for this is the lack of a dominating expressive purpose — not in individual movements (the first movement of this quartet is patently so ruled), but in the concept of the whole work. He does not particularly favor the cyclic scheme, which we have found Bartók to employ; but that scheme does not guarantee even an audible thematic cohesion (to say nothing of an expressive); for a given sequence of notes, wholly re-rhythmed and re-harmonized, yields a visible rather than an audible cohesion.*

Alban Berg (1885–1935)

To those for whom the interest of structure is the chief (and since in their vocabulary structure and expression are synonymous, apparently the only) musical interest, the craftsmanship of dodecaphony — more methodical than any other contemporary manner — has a high attraction. But that method is also capable of relaxation and adjustment — of adjustment to the purpose of expression as we have understood that word in this study.† Our next example — the *Lyric Suite* by Alban Berg, will illustrate that adjustment.

Berg discovered the depth of his interest in music rather late, having

* The descent of a minor 3rd plus a half-step (dotted quarter and eighth) appears in bar 2 of the main themes of the first and last movements. A descending minor 3rd appears also in the first bar of each theme. It naturally occurs elsewhere (e.g., in the imitative passage before O in the first movement). Although the symmetry is patent, I do not think it structurally cyclic.

† Seen purely as method, dodecaphony is repellent. Few but craftsmen delight in pure craftsmanship, and the musical public, whose delight in music which reflects its more general, extramusical interests is great, can hardly be expected to cultivate that minute analytical observation upon which full appreciation of craftsmanship depends. Yet the public ear *is* attracted to atonal music: at first with a kind of incredulous interest in its novelty; next (as it learns to follow one or two of the contrapuntal lines out of which the texture is woven), by the intimation of new character which these lines convey; and when it has learned to accept these, along with their inevitable umbra of unfocused dissonance (for not even the acutest ears can attend to the whole detail of a complex musical structure, tonal or atonal, as it passes), it may accept that umbra as equivalent to — and possibly more stimulating than — the umbra of polyphony attendant on the main melodic line in a Wagner opera or a Mahler symphony.

Now, assuming that an expressive purpose has guided the invention of a twelve-tone row (as will be the fact in our next example), the question as to whether the complex manipulations of that row, and the total musical texture resultant, have really illuminated that expressive purpose or have provided it with an umbra possibly only adventitious as regards the expressive purpose — this question will remain dreamed of being either a poet or a painter. Songs he had written attracted Schoenberg's attention, and in 1904 he became that master's idolatrous pupil. His formal studies ended in 1910. The twelve-tone technique was still far in the future; yet in the last of his five Altenberg songs, Op. 4, written in 1912, a strictly developed twelve-tone row is combined with a passacaglia theme and another consisting of rising 4ths. He appears to have been for some time in doubt whether to follow the lead of Mahler or of Schoenberg, and the first World War, during which his health kept him at desk-service, did not help him toward a decision. Both influences are visible in the opera, *Wozzeck*, whose libretto Berg himself contrived out of Büchner's drama of almost a hundred years before; but that of Schoenberg is paramount. Both in the opera and the *Lyric Suite*, "atonality" of course is apparent – but it is only apparent, for even in those parts which are twelve-tonal, his row is so made that frequent hints of tonality are inevitable.

There are six movements: I *Allegretto giovale*; II *Andante amoroso*; III *Allegro misterioso* (a Scherzo with a *Trio estatico*); IV *Adagio appassionato*; V *Presto delirando* (another Scherzo with a *Tenebroso* Trio); and the Finale, *Largo desolato*. The movements are linked together by the recurrence in each of a feature of the preceding movement. Movements I and VI are wholly in twelve-tone structure. The exposition and recapitulation of Movement III and the *Tenebroso* Trio in V are also twelve-tone, but in these the original tone-row is altered. The others are "free." The original tone-row is shown in Example 47, along with the beginning of a song which Berg set to the notes of the row before the suite was begun.* Taken in pairs (as 1–2, 3–4, etc.) the

unanswered until a more reasoned criticism of total musical value than we at present possess has been established.

The question may easily be dismissed by assuming, as much contemporary criticism does, that extramusical reference (expression) does not and ought not to exist. But that dismissal is only a denial – precarious indeed – that the public ear is a fact of high import in the history of music.

* O (= Original form), I (= Inversion of the original), R (= Retrograde form of O), and RI (= Retrograde Inversion) are the conventional abbreviations for the four forms of the row.

Berg, in a letter to Webern (1925) calls the song "my first attempt at strict twelve-tone composition." Not only is the row precisely followed in the quoted phrase. It is pursued (beginning at *Händen zu*) *seriatim* and without transposition save at the octave throughout the voice part for the two four-line stanzas of the text. In the Suite, the treatment of the row is vastly freer; yet, far more than does the theme of the first movement of Bartók's Sixth quartet, the row in twelve-tone composition provides a "table of contents" for the work.

Schlies - se mir die Augen bei - de   mit den lie-   ben Händen zu

EXAMPLE 47. BERG LYRIC SUITE — ORIGINAL TONE-ROW AND SONG
WRITTEN BEFORE THE SUITE

notes yield successively the intervals 2nd, 3rd, etc. to major 7th (written
as diminished 8ve), all descending. Also, the first six notes are all "white"
(on the piano); the next five are "black." And since any note may be
taken in any octave, the unmelodic-looking line of the row may assume
the form shown in the top line of Example 48, in which each half is the
inversion of the other. The two triads, A minor (2–3–4) and E flat minor
(9–10–11), help to give this form of the row its unmistakable "feel" of
tonality.

EXAMPLE 48. BERG LYRIC SUITE FOR STRING QUARTET

The introductory bar compacts into three chords all twelve notes of
the row: 1–3–5–6; 10–12–11–2; 9–8–7–4; and ends with a six-note chord
built of superimposed 5ths; 3–5–6–4–2–12 — as expectant a dissonance, in
this idiom, as a dominant 13th (which it almost is) in the old idiom. Then
follows the rhythmed form of the original row, *literatim*, in the first
violin — a theme whose "joviality" is self-evident. The second part of
Example 48 shows the theme of the *Allegretto giovale* — obviously made
on the row — and also the "free" theme of the *Adagio appassionato*.

The next three bars allow the theme to subside. The 'cello continues
the theme (bar 4); then violin and 'cello (bars 5–6) reiterate the "consequent" strain, G♭, F, E (10, 1, 2). At bar 7 the rhythm of the main

298]

theme is begun on E♭ (9) and continued *seriatim* to 8; and this version is canonically imitated in viola and second violin. At bar 11 melodic progress becomes stationary in obvious preparation for something new, and this something is a "bridge-passage" leading to the second theme (*Poco più tranquillo*, 23). This is made of 8, 9, 11, 12 (D♭, E♭, B♭, B♮), the missing 10 (A♭) being taken in the viola. Against the thematic lines the other notes of the row appear in contrapuntal or harmonic combinations. These cannot be verbally described, but it will be evident that a sonata form is in process. At bar 33 a three-bar Cl.S. appears, ending the exposition. But what follows, although it is much altered, is a developmental recapitulation, so that there is no development-section proper. The whole movement is only sixty-nine bars long.

The *Andante amoroso*, beginning in 6-8, is not in the twelve-tone technique, although its main theme, set forth at once by the first violin, comprises precisely the twelve notes of the chromatic scale. It is gracefully accompanied by the second violin and is freely continued (remarkably euphoniously) for fifteen bars, when the time becomes a livelier 3-8, and the new theme is derived from the second theme from the first movement. (The A♮ is the counterpart of the viola's "missing note.") The first theme returns (41) and a third theme in 2-8 time appears (56), yielding the essential pattern of the Rondo. The beginning of the recapitulation at bar 81 is obvious, but the continuation, involving some reversions, is more obscure.

In the *Allegro misterioso*, 3-4, the row from the *Allegretto* is begun a 4th higher in the first violin, but its fourth note is No. 10 in the original series. These four notes reappear in second violin and viola before the complete row (its former order now changed to 1, 2, 3, 10, 5, 6, 7, 8, 9, 4, 11, 12) is set forth in full (bar 2). The form is that of the Scherzo (A–B–A — B being the *Trio estatico*). All the strings are muted throughout, even in the *ff* Trio, and the ordinary hearer is not likely to recognize that the Scherzo, on its return, is precisely itself played backwards.

The *Adagio appassionato* (4-4) begins with the intense and somber theme in the 'cello shown at the end of Example 48.* It is imitated in stretto by the higher voices and developed intricately to bar 14, where a phrase in triplets forms a second theme. (A thematic relation can be

---

* Since there will be an unmistakable quotation from *Tristan* in the final movement, I may not be wholly fanciful in seeing here a hint of Tristan's terrible "Ich selbst ich hab' ihn gebraut" in the third act.

descried to the previous *Trio estatico*.) A swirling climax builds up, the main theme in viola and first violin (from 24) being conspicuous on the way to its crisis (34). It subsides, but a lesser one develops from bar 45, and the Coda (59) paraphrases a new theme which the 'cello (with the viola a 7th above) had introduced at bar 40. The tensions created in this movement are high; yet they yield an image of experience so vivid as to evoke from almost any doubting Thomas the ejaculation, "Here is poetry!"

The *Presto delirando* (3-8), like the *Andante amoroso*, begins with a theme of twelve different notes, although these are not treated as a row. Its swift motion carries on for fifty bars without a divided beat, and although the manipulations of the theme are hard for the ear to follow, the rhythm has such impetus that that effort seems needless. It is suddenly broken off for the *Tenebroso* Trio which may properly be so called if the beginning is called a Scherzo. This section is dodecaphonic. Its row is another alteration of the one first illustrated, those notes being now arranged in the order, E, F, A; E♭, C, G♯, C♯; G, F♯, D; B, B♭, and set forth as chords, successively of 3, 4, 3, and 2 notes as our semicolons indicate. E and F (1 and 2) are added to B♮ and B♭ to begin a new series of chords. They are blended (*flautando, ppp*) so that each new chord begins inaudibly against the slight crescendo of the former one, and by and by they begin to shiver (*tremolando*). The Scherzo returns and is much extended; the darkness also falls again; then a chord, ultimately of eight notes of the row (5, 8, 9, and 11 are missing), raps out five bars of a threatening duple rhythm and the Scherzo-theme returns *unisono*, pizzicato, *ff*, to begin the recapitulation. This is of course a further development of the theme. Still more is offered by its wild leaps in the Coda.

The Finale (*Largo desolato*, 3-2) has the same row as the *Tenebroso*, except that it begins on F and its seventh note (D) is taken in the lower octave. (The 'cello's C string is tuned down a half-step to reach the final B.) It is plucked out four times in the 'cello with gradually added counterpoints in the upper strings, but when the bows are resumed (7) the serial technique is abandoned. Impassioned phrases in the first violin begin a rhapsodic discourse, continued (10) by the 'cello and (13) by the viola. It is perhaps going too far to say that a kind of Tristan-mood governs the piece, but at any rate the curiously divided quotation (26-27) of the opening motive of that opera does not sound like an interpolation.

The end is a remarkable vanishing. Second violin, 'cello, and first violin in turn disappear from the score and the viola wavers to extinction on the low 3rd, D♭–F, leaving F, the first note of the opening row, as the last note to be heard.*

Anton Webern (1883–1945)

Since we have spoken of one pupil of Schoenberg's before attempting to deal with that prime revolutionary, we shall also speak of another — Berg's fellow student, Anton Webern. Their work under Schoenberg was continuous from 1904 to 1910; the idea of atonality was germinating; teacher and pupils were deeply interested in its possibilities; but Schoenberg seems to have viewed his students' efforts with understanding and encouragement of their own individuality rather than with any desire to mold them after his own pattern. The system of dodecaphony was still far in the future, and Webern was to adopt that system only after long efforts to realize the most unusual tonal images his fancy bred.

Those images, as seen in his earlier works, seem to have originated in the heart rather than in the head. Yet his was a more consistently logical mind than Berg's, and when he did at last adopt that system he pursued it more relentlessly than Berg ever did. But his was a mind also intent upon the obscure implications which musical tones as such may convey; and the logic of such obscurities (for the force of implication is lost when its reference becomes explicit) cannot be systematized into conceptual clarity. He conveys these implications, in his earlier works, by such a me-

* To one with an inquiring mind as to the total validity of the twelve-tone system, this Suite raises many questions. That its purport was intentionally expressive in the ordinary sense of that word the whole sequence of movements (and incidentally their superscriptions) bears witness. Many commentators accept the piece as a "latent" drama. The twelve-tone structure was abandoned at the most dramatic moments of that "story." Was this because Berg found it unsuited to amorous or impassioned or desolate feeling? The last movement is generally said to be wholly dodecaphonic, but prodigies of analytical acumen would be required to account for most of it as in that style, and H. F. Redlich (*Alban Berg, the Man and His Music*, New York, 1957), after stating categorically that Movement VI is twelve-tone in its entirety (p. 145), says (p. 153), "The movement is dodecaphonic, but by no means exclusively so." René Leibowitz (*Schoenberg and His School*, New York, 1949), who also recognizes the dramatic import of the work, ends his comment on it (p. 160) with the statement: "Thus in the *Lyric Suite* the genius of Berg becomes definitely aware of that culmination of contemporary polyphony which is the twelve-tone technique." Is this awareness of technical process really Berg's most significant attainment? Or, in an earnest endeavor to widen the resources of the musical language, did he discover the system of dodecaphony to be only a partial contributor to that end? The ramifications of this question are endless.

ticulous choice of instrumental color that it is hard to tell whether the structural or the coloristic impulse was the original creative stimulus.*

Many more color-implications can be suggested by the variety of orchestral tone than can be conveyed by four strings. Yet in Webern's *Five Movements for String Quartet*, Op. 5, an extraordinary variety of such suggestion is offered. I do not pretend to "understand" this work, although most of it seems to me to make sense. I shall merely describe a few of the impressions, whether of structure or color, that I get from it. That effort however will serve, better than a necessarily much longer study of the one string quartet (Op. 28) that Webern left, to give at least a notion of his style.† It is only with the string trio, Op. 20, that he adopts the twelve-tone technique; but this serves, not so much for the shaping of a new style as for the achievement of musical movements of normal dimensions.

The first of the Five Pieces is the longest of them. It has fifty-five bars. Two sharply dissonant chords, combining the two-note motives C–C♯ and F–E that precede them, introduce the main theme (*Heftig bewegt*, 3-4). It has eight sixteenths of different pitch, like a tone-row. It is repeated at once, but is now accompanied by itself, a 7th lower and at the time-interval of one sixteenth, which completely changes its rhythmic accentuation. It vanishes in bar 4 and the next two bars, on detached chords like those of the opening, lead to a new theme (7) in the 'cello, very quiet and huddled within the diminished 4th. It has a continuing strain, much expanded as to interval, in the duetting violins. Pizzicato sixteenths, on a figure analogous to the S.I are similarly imitated. Against a similar texture the S.II appears (19), but the S.I, imitated a beat later, takes the forefront. It dwindles, however, and the quieter tempo of the S.II, as well as rather obscure variants of that theme, will rule for seventeen bars. From bar 44 there is a kind of recapitulation.

The second movement (*Sehr langsam*, 4-4) has its theme at first in the

* He shifts his color not merely phrase by phrase but note by note within the phrase. For example, the first of his *Five Orchestral Pieces*, Op. 10, begins with the unaccompanied two-note motive, B–C. Harp and muted trumpet play the B; harp, celesta, and a harmonic on the viola play the C. Schoenberg, in his *Harmonielehre*, had suggested the possibility of *Klangfarbenmelodie* (tone-color melody). Webern hardly attains it, but his is the nearest approach to that objective.

† Besides the two works here mentioned, there are the following: *Six Bagatelles for String Quartet*, Op. 9 (1913); a string trio, Op. 20 (1927); a quartet for piano, violin, clarinet, and saxophone, Op. 22 (1930); and a *Concerto for Nine Instruments*, Op. 24 (1935).

viola, *with tender expression*. Its intervals, in ruminant motion, expand from the major 3rd to the diminished 8ve and contract again; the second violin (5) takes the lead for a moment but returns it to the first (7) which it then accompanies. The piece is thirteen bars long. Its implications, actually expressed, would have filled ten times that number.

The third movement (*Sehr bewegt*, 2-2) has a basic rhythm of four quarter notes plucked by the 'cello on C♯ for six bars. Its theme adopts (4) the imitative process of that in the first movement. A descent on major 3rds, accompanied by its inversion in the 'cello (7) makes transition to a second theme (9), on contractile 3rds which suddenly plunge downward. This theme really rules to the end, resuming (*molto rit.*) at bar 12 and again (against an *ostinato* bass) at bar 18 (*accel.*). The end is on the first form of this theme, *unisono* and *fff*. This piece has twenty-three bars.

The fourth movement (*Sehr langsam*, 3-4) is the least perplexing to the ear of the five. Its tiny theme (F♯–B–F♮–C, descending) appears after two mysterious bars on detached tremolando chords, *sul ponticello*. After imitation in second violin and 'cello, the second violin rises on the intervals that formed the introductory chords; the viola begins an *ostinato* figure on the augmented triad, and the first violin fades into silence on a variant of its pendant (5) of the four-note theme. There are four bars of epilogue, giving the whole movement the length of thirteen bars.

The fifth movement (*In zarter Bewegung*, 6-8) first establishes an undulant motion in the 'cello; interjects chords that generate little melodic figures; and manipulates these without repetition but with palpable continuity for the twenty-six bars of the piece.

More otherworldly music than this strange group of pieces offers has never found tangible form. Schoenberg, commenting on the not dissimilar *Six Bagatelles*, Op. 9, found that "every glance is a poem, every sigh a novel." René Leibowitz quotes a friend of his as saying, "When you have learned to appreciate a melody of Webern, all others, beautiful though they may be, are just so much marshmallow-whip in comparison." Looked at with the objectivity so strongly favored by twentieth-century thought, the aesthetic attitude here implied has its perils. Pursued to its logical extreme it would narrow musical appreciation to an almost microscopic area. Its vehemence, also, smacks strongly of that exaggeration of sentiment which, in the estimation of the *avant-garde*, afflicted the romanticists. Indeed, it seems legitimate to question whether "modernism" (which romanticism once was) is not itself that same attitude — perhaps in retrograde inversion.

Arnold Schoenberg (1874–1951)

We have left until the last the commanding figure of Arnold Schoenberg who has probably exerted the profoundest influence on contemporary musical thought of any twentieth-century composer. Yet his music is far less frequently performed — at any rate is less widely heard — in America than that of Stravinsky or Hindemith or many another notable figure. The fact of his influence is thus an anomaly. Only one work of Schoenberg is at all familiar to concert audiences — *Verklärte Nacht*, originally a sextet for strings, but more frequently heard in orchestral dress. And that work shows almost none of those characteristics of Schoenberg's thought which have changed the face of contemporary music.

Since he is so little heard, it might be argued that his work is, after all, that of a theorist rather than a composer. But that argument will not hold. His compositions did not come out of his theory. His theory came out of his effort as composer, and no one who reads the tale of his devotion to musical art can suppose him — however preoccupied he may seem with the problems of structure — to have been indifferent to its power of reflecting the workings of a mind disturbed by human emotion. His frequent adaptations of music to words of considerable poetic import are further evidence.

Dodecaphony however, if looked at merely as a structural system, is forbiddingly intellectual. It is difficult to apprehend as more than a structural system, and its apologists, of whom Josef Rufer and René Leibowitz are the most competent, are so absorbed with it as a system that they do not greatly aid the student who wishes to find in it what he finds in more familiar music. The adoption of that system — e.g., by Stravinsky in his seventies and by many others long devoted to the old order — is a strong proof of its validity, as method. But it does not prove the validity of that system for the purpose which the world has always held to be the ultimate objective of all artistic creation. That objective is the recognizable portrayal of human impulse.

Art, that is, talks to us about ourselves, and compels our interest in proportion as we recognize in it the reflection of our own desires. It can flatter our ego by portraying its tenderness in such fashion as to disguise its weakness. It can repel us by portraying strength in the rough (but possibly tonic) guise of hardness. So repelled, we turn away, refusing to learn the hard lesson. Having learned it the hard way — by experience — we return, find our wiser selves in the art we rejected, and embrace it, praising its intellectuality. Very likely, we shall now call the tenderness we once loved, and which we now see as exaggerated, sentimentality. We are not so likely to see hardness, in the guise of intellectuality, as exaggerated; but it may ultimately appear as only an inversion of the same weakness.

Hardness and intellectuality characterize both the system of dodeca-phony and Schoenberg's musical idiom. (The same charge was leveled, by many music-lovers, against the idiom of Brahms and of Beethoven, and even of Mozart.) The incessant dissonance of twelve-tone music * seems more repellent in Schoenberg than in Alban Berg, or even Webern, who largely veils his dissonances in such diaphanous tonal colors that we "see" rather than hear them. That a valid expressive purpose may have demanded Schoenberg's dissonance will be recognized only when that purpose is perceived. This commentator makes no claim to a sound dis-crimination in this matter. Pieces have been chosen for illustration, not of his manner of pursuing the twelve-tone technique, but rather of his way of fulfilling expressive purpose. His contribution to the literature of chamber music is as follows: String quartets: No. 1, in D minor, Op. 7 (1904); No. 2, in F sharp minor, Op. 10 (1907) — its last two movements with soprano voice, set to two poems of Stefan George; No. 3, Op. 30 (1927); No. 4, Op. 37 (1936). (There is also an earlier quartet than Op. 7, now in the Library of Congress.) The string sextet, *Verklärte Nacht* (1899, rev. 1943); a Serenade, Op. 24, for clarinet, bass clarinet, mando-lin, guitar, violin, viola, and 'cello — its last movement on a sonnet of Petrarch, for baritone voice (1923); quintet for winds, Op. 26 (1924); Suite for 2 clarinets, bass clarinet, violin, viola, 'cello, and piano, Op. 29 (1927); *Ode to Napoleon*, after Byron, for speaking voice, strings, and piano, Op. 41 (1942); string trio, Op. 45 (1946).

To these should be added *Pierrot lunaire*, Op. 21, which we shall ex-amine in some detail. First, however, a glance at the string quartets.

The First, Op. 7, long antecedent to dodecaphony, now seems only mildly adventurous, for its day, in melody, harmony, or rhythm. There

* The mind accepts more readily than the ear the Schoenbergian theorem that there is no true dissonance.

are strong evidences, however, of the passion that animated *Verklärte Nacht*, and its formal organization is provocative. It is cast in one huge movement which contains the four divisions of the conventional form, but organizes them somewhat unexpectedly. The main theme (*Nicht zu rasch*, D minor, 4-4) appears to be exposed quite normally, in the first violin, with a figure of accompaniment in the viola and a melodic line in the 'cello. These are elaborated in triple counterpoint (30) and a transition is made on them to the S.II (somewhat slower, A, bar 97) which is similarly structured. Other thematic lines appear, so that this is properly a "second-subject group." These things are then somewhat developed. What follows, however, is not the recapitulation but the Scherzo (B, p. 17). The pattern of its theme is not unusual, but its tempo fluctuates capriciously. A contrasting dotted rhythm appears (39) and this is developed with the main theme. Now, however, comes, not the Trio of the Scherzo, but the recapitulation of the opening first-theme group, the S.I being combined with the dotted rhythm from the Scherzo, and other motives being so altered as to be at first unrecognizable. This is far more than a mere recapitulation. Even in the aspect of a development it is so varied that one loses one's bearings; yet it is the recapitulation of the first theme-group only. It ends with a long manipulation of bar 5 of the main theme which took its present form at bar 9 as that theme was first exposed. It disappears in a long series of augmentations and the slow movement follows (K) — at first ejaculatory in the first violin then smoothed to broader phrases, all in muted strings. As it ends, after a second strain in 12-8 time, 'cello and first violin return to the opening theme — the 'cello on its inversion, the violin on its truncated original form; then follows the theme from bar 57 of the second subject group; and these and other things make a sort of rondo-finale. Our description is sorely contracted and confused, but it will at least suggest the perplexity of the listener at his first hearing of the piece. The effort was toward a higher organization — obviously on the cyclic plan — of the whole movement-sequence of the sonata. With many hearings the design becomes clear, and one's admiration for the really coherent presentation grows. But the work sets a model of structure which it would be dangerous for any but the most experienced to follow.

The Second quartet, Op. 10, in F sharp minor, is much more adventurous harmonically than the first, but is much more clear in formal organization. Stirrings of atonal thought become more evident as the work proceeds. Key-signatures appear in the first three movements but not in the last. This, however, closes on the chord of F sharp major, and a harmonic analysis would probably show a general gravitation — as remote as that which our outer planets obey — around the F♯ as tone-center. The expressive import of the first two movements, competently analyzed, would similarly show relativity to the two poems whose setting for soprano voice form the last two movements. These poems of Stefan George,* are entitled *Litany* and *Entrückung* which here means Transport. Each suggests a mental image, obscure and distant, of ultramundane being as the poet's ultimate desire. The Litany is essentially a prayer for deliverance from the tortures of passion. It ends:

> Kill this fond yearning, close up the heart-wound!
> Take from me loving, give me thy peace!

The vocal line is tortuous as melody but its prosody respects that of the verse. One is inclined to question, however, the enormous drop from high C to low B on the word *Liebe* (loving, in the translation). It is possible that the fleeting presence of tonal centers makes the atonality of most of the fabric sound extravagant, as this interval certainly does.

The second poem is enacted, if one may use the term without a baser implication than was intended, in the stratosphere. The journey is a search for the Master — still invisible — and the "action" may perhaps be suggested in the stanza:

> I free myself, and weave in tonal spirals
> Of endless gratitude and wordless praises,
> And, undesirous, yield to the vast aether.

The Third quartet, Op. 30, twenty years later than the Second, is of course written in the twelve-tone technique. The texture is much more transparent than that of the earlier works, and the whole pattern approximates closely the classic scheme of the four-movement sonata: I, *Moderato*, 2-2, in almost incessant eighth-note motion; II, *Adagio*, 4-8 — a set of extremely intricate variations on an apparently simple theme; III, an Intermezzo, *Allegro*, 9-8, which diversifies its originally normal rhythm by grouping the eighths as 2 + 3 + 4 and in other ways; and a final Rondo (*Molto moderato*, 4-4). The whole work is based on the tone-row shown here with its inversion, begun on C (Ex. 49).

The *Moderato* begins with an *ostinato* figure made on Nos. 1–5, re-

* Three syllables, the accent on the second. Both G's hard.

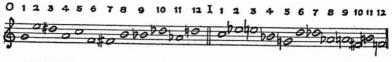

EXAMPLE 49. SCHOENBERG THIRD QUARTET, OP. 30 — TONE-ROW

peated in the octave in second violin and viola for twelve bars and then persisting in transposition and other alterations. Against this (5) the first violin makes the S.I out of Nos. 8–12. Nos. 6 and 7 are delayed, appearing in the 'cello bars 8 and 9. The violin extends its melody on the Retrograde Inversion of the row, the 'cello supplying Nos. 8 and 7 (as G♯ and C♯). The S.II (62) begins on the Inversion of the row in very wide intervals and continues on the Retrograde of the Original form. But in the recapitulation the S.II (now in the 'cello, 174) is made on O, followed by R.

Obviously, to extend this analysis to cover the whole detail of a single movement would be a thankless task. No one is apparently expected to be able to discern the row itself of a twelve-tone composition from the music as it proceeds; to hear its inversion would be more difficult; and the retrograde form will yield about as much of its original sense as would a sentence of English pronounced backwards. The whole quartet is built on the row exhibited above, and that fact will be discoverable — at first with ease and later with difficulty — by anyone who cares to examine the score. One who brings to the music only his ears must remain in ignorance of many of the feats of structure in which the work abounds. For the tone-row, although it provides for the eye a compact "table of contents," is for the ear an extremely obscure index.

If the only reward of such a listener were indeed a clearer awareness of these feats, it is unlikely that he would find many hearers to share his effort. Strangely, although our analogy between atonality and isolating language seems to be strengthened when so esoteric a syntax as that offered by the twelve-tone system is applied to an atonal fabric, the unaided ear — unaided, that is, by anything more than repeated hearing — begins to make a not wholly unfamiliar kind of sense out of the fabric. The rhythmic designs, in this quartet, are not obscure; and it is possibly on the basis of its readily apprehensible rhythm that the ear is enabled to clarify the tonal tangles. Rhythm is also, in our view, one of the elements of musical expression; and while the defenders of dodecaphony seldom take note of expressive purpose, we suspect that even their enthusiasm is in some measure kindled by the rhythmic (and sometimes even the melodic) portrayal of impulses ranging far beyond the region of "pure-ly" musical stimulation.

The Fourth quartet, Op. 37, nine years later than the Third, has also the conventional four movements — an *Allegro* in discernible sonata form, a *Commodo* which bears similar resemblance to the Minuet, an *Adagio* whose most striking feature is a recitative for all four instruments in uni-son, later repeated in inversion, and a Finale approximating to the Rondo. René Leibowitz speaks of it as "a flood of the most limpid music, a suc-cession of melodies each more beautiful than the next,* of rich and varied harmonies and rhythms — all in all, a musical discourse of the most ex-ceptional quality. There is not a single figure . . . which does not have its precise function in the musical structure. . . . All this is explicitly made possible through the use of the new technique, for tonal technique could not always fulfill those needs for the satisfaction of which the form of the string quartet was expressly created. . . . It seems almost impos-sible at the present time to make any new contributions to the string quartet."

We shall not attempt a detailed analysis of this piece. It would be no more helpful than our meager description of the Third quartet. The last sentence of our quotation from Leibowitz suggests the conclusion which Anton Rubinstein drew from the music of Chopin — that its implication was essentially *finis musicae*. The literal implication of Leibowitz's words is palpably *finis dodecaphoniae*. But his admiration is so exclusively re-served for structure that he appears indifferent to that association of music with non-musical experience which we think of in this book as expression. Instead of that analysis, then, we shall revert to Schoenberg's pre-dodecaphonic period and offer some comment on another innovation of his, the *Sprechstimme*, as it is employed in one of his most character-istic works, *Pierrot lunaire*, Op. 21. The device had been anticipated in *Die glückliche Hand*, but is here used systematically.

Schoenberg calls the pieces *Melodramen*. As in Beethoven's day, the word implies a dramatic scene recited to the background of music — a kind of substitute for recitative such as Mozart had used in *Zaïde* and Beethoven in the grave-digging scene in *Fidelio*. (There is no implication of such blood-and-thunder exaggeration as our English equivalent for the word suggests.) Schoenberg all but invariably indicates for his "speaking

* I am afraid this phrase was inadvertently written (*Schoenberg and His School*, tr. Dika Newlin, p. 125).

voice" precise musical pitch; but this is not to be maintained for the whole duration of the note. It does "state" the pitch, but abandons it at once by falling or rising.* The composer expressly warns the reciter both against lapsing into a singing manner of speech and against striving for realistically natural utterance.

The "interpretation" of the work, whether by the performers or the critical listener, is thus of extreme difficulty. (Albertine Zehme, the first interpreter, to whom the work is dedicated, devoted a full year of study to the problem.) If — as one must suppose — the *Sprechstimme* and the words it utters are to predominate in the hearer's attention, a vast deal of the background music will be beyond the grasp of any but an ear long prepared. Even so, the sense in which the text is to be taken — if the music is supposed to illuminate its character — is a problem to which merely analytical listening gives hardly a clue. For Schoenberg expressly cautions the reciter against reading anything into his text which is not already in the music. He provides explicit dynamic and rhythmic indications for the utterance of almost every phrase, but these, if obeyed only literally, will convey (as often happens with classical music) the impression that the music is not "in" the performer.

The background of actual music is provided by five instruments — piano, flute (or piccolo), clarinet (or bass clarinet), violin (or viola), and 'cello — at their full strength forming a piano quintet. This strength, however, is seldom employed, and one piece (No. 7) is accompanied only by the flute. The tonal texture is extremely dissonant, but since the music was written before the twelve-tone system was evolved it is cast in definite figures and manipulated after relatively conventional structural patterns. Each number thus possesses a distinctive musical character, outlined by these figures in what are often remarkable ingenuities of rhythm.

The text is very "artistic" in structure. There are twenty-one poems, all of thirteen lines with from two to five stresses; the first two lines complete the second quatrain, and the first line recurs to complete the poem. This design, however, does not dictate the musical structure, which goes its own way but is often artistic to the point of preciosity. A few only of the twenty-one numbers can be described here, but we have made a translation of the text which corresponds (except in a few cases where

* *Der Sprechton gibt sie [die Tonhöhe] zwar an, verlässt sie aber durch Fallen oder Steigen sofort wieder* (From the Introduction).

Schoenberg, repeating phrases, has made rhythmic alterations) precisely
to the rhythms of the words as set to music, and the listener, substituting
the English syllables for the German as he hears them, should gain therefrom a fairly clear idea both of the verbal meaning and the musical manipulation of the text. (To this commentator, Schoenberg's setting seems
far more macabre than does the text. Of this we leave the reader to
judge for himself.)

In No. 1 ("Moondrunk") the piano has a little repetitive figure which
is basic to the florid passages in the other instruments also, and will appear as the "theme" of the whole piece. It will probably be audible only
as a general contour, for its pattern is often obscured by self-imitation
(see bar 8, in canon at the distance of a sixteenth) or by other devices.
Yet, if the ear does not strain too much to catch detail, there is conveyed
an over-all impression of both continuity and character. The *Sprechstimme* (labeled *Rezitation*) shows, when its suggested pitch-line is scrutinized as melodic, far less of what might be called musical organization;
but both its inflection and its rhythm are clearly patterned on verbal
utterance, even though the inflection sometimes far exceeds the intervals
of even rhetorical speech.

The composer acknowledges some essays in "tone-painting," one of
which is visible in the shimmer of chromatic chords at the end of No. 2
("Columbine"); and many instrumental effects, such as that produced
by drawing the wood of the bow across the strings (in No. 10) and the
piano's chords in harmonics (really, sympathetic vibration) in No. 11,
bar 18, No. 14, bar 10, and elsewhere, appear similarly suggestive.

In No. 18 ("The Moon-Streak") the elaborateness of the texture can
hardly escape the charge of preciosity. A five-note phrase, anticipated
in the transition from No. 17 and now extended, is begun in clarinet and
imitated in canon two beats later by piccolo at the 12th. At the same
time, the piano has the augmentation of this line, an octave above the
clarinet, in the right hand, with the augmentation of the piccolo in the
left, four beats later, and two octaves below. Concurrently also, violin
and 'cello, rhythmically activating a slowly descending pitch-line, move
in canon at the octave at the interval of three beats. When winds and
strings reach the middle of bar 10 (exactly half the length of the whole
piece) they make an about-face and play backwards what they played
"forwards" up to this point, while the piano continues its augmentations
to the end!

[311

Only a more than Nietzschean super-musician could detect by the ear alone the features of design we have just described. There are, indeed, more of these in almost every number, presented simultaneously, than can be attended to by the most agile observer. But so are there more things in a Wagnerian scene or a Brahms symphony than can be simultaneously perceived, even by a listener familiar with the score. For we *attend* to one thing at a time, no matter how rapidly we shift our attention from one to the other, and no matter how full the receding periphery around the focus of our attention. But to take account of any one thing, and to register it on that screen of memory on which we similarly record related things, we must know what that thing *is*. If we know what it is, we can dismiss it from our sharpest attention while we similarly identify a related thing; and when that next thing has been identified, we can bring the first one back into focus, thus making sure that it was there all the time, even though we let it out of sight for a moment. This is the way in which we "keep track" of a Bach Fugue or a Brahms symphony.

The difficulty of identification with *Pierrot* is much greater. Schoenberg's phrases have so strange a melodic shape that we can hardly grasp — and much less remember — their pattern. Their tonal contour, to the unaccustomed ear especially, seems wholly irrational. Since we get a great share of our musical pleasure from melody *as* tonal contour, we may soon give up and cease to listen. We forget that melody has a rhythmic as well as a tonal contour, and that this rhythm may well serve for identification if the tonal contour fails.

The rhythms in almost every number of *Pierrot*, examined apart from the tonal contours, show a high appropriateness to the implication and the mood of the poem (rather than to its meter); and if we attend to the rhythm of the music and the sense of the text, allowing the tones to go their way almost unobserved, we shall find that these two factors make sense. Indeed, there is here nothing really unfamiliar, even though the detail is often so complex as to be confusing.

The "Three Times Seven Poems" from Albert Giraud's *Pierrot lunaire*, which Schoenberg set to a German translation by Otto Erich Hartleben, follow. Read merely as poems they convey an impression of rather overstrained nineteenth-century romanticism. Their twentieth-century musical dress greatly enhances the strain but does not — to our ears — alter their romantic character.

TWENTIETH-CENTURY CHAMBER MUSIC

I. MOONDRUNK

That wine that with our eyes we drink
The moon, at night, pours down in torrents.
Its freshets overrun entire
    The far horizon's rim.

Desires, then, terrible and sweet,
Flow numberless amid its streaming!
That wine that with our eyes we drink
The moon, at night, pours down in torrents.

The Poet, whom devotion spurs,
Grows drunken from the blessed beaker,
Toward Heaven then he turns enraptured
Gaze and, reeling, sucks and gulps down
That wine that with our eyes we drink.

II. COLUMBINE

The milky flowers of moonlight,
Those white and wondrous roses
Bloom in the July evenings —
Oh, could I pluck but one!

To heal my troubled sorrow
I seek at that dark river
The milky flowers of moonlight,
Those white and wondrous roses.

My yearning all were silenced
Could I in fairy fashion,
With gentlest touch, unpetal
Upon thy tawny tresses
The milky flowers of moonlight.

III. THE DANDY

And now, with fantastical light-beam
The moon doth illume all the crystalline flasks
On that black and most holy of wash-stands —
The unspeaking Dandy's of Bergamo.

Within its resounding bronze vessel
Laughs clearly the fountain's metallical ring.
And now, with fantastical light-beam
The moon doth illume all the crystalline flasks.

Pierrot, with countenance waxen,
Stands dreaming and thinks, "How to make up today?"

He puts aside red and the orient's green
And then covers his face, in the true artist's style,
With nought but a fantastic light-beam.

IV. A PALLID LAUNDRESS

There's a pallid laundress there
In the evening washing white things;
Naked arms, as white as silver
Stretching downward through the flood.

Through the light-beam winds are seeping:
Lightly they bestir its stream.
There's a pallid laundress there
In the evening washing white things.

And the gentle Maid of Heaven,
Sweetly flattered by the branches,
Scatters on the darkling meadows
Her light-woven, spotless linens.
There's a pallid laundress there.

V. VALSE DE CHOPIN

As a faded drop of blood
Stains the lips of one who's dying,
Just so rests upon these tones
A charm that seeks for nothingness.

Chords of wild abandon tangle
Desperation's icy dream
As a faded drop of blood
Stains the lips of one who's dying.

Hot-exultant, sweetly-yearning,
Melancholy-gloomy waltzing
Never leaves in peace my senses —
Clings to each thought that arises
Like a faded drop of blood!

VI. MADONNA

Rise, O Mother of all sorrows,
On the altar of my verses!
Blood from out thy withered bosom
Hath been spilled by raging sword-strokes.

And thy never-healing flesh-wounds
Are like eyeballs, red and open.

Rise, O Mother of all sorrows
On the altar of my verses!

In thy wasted hands upheld
The body of thy first-born lieth
To be shown to all mankind;
But mankind's eyes are still avoiding
Thee, O Mother of all sorrows!

VII. THE AILING MOON

Thou night-like, death-diseasèd moon
There on Heav'n's ebon pillow laid,
Thy glance, with fever overgrown,
Grips me like alien melody.

Of quenchless lover's woe dost thou
Now die, by yearning quite through-pierced —
Thou night-like, death-diseasèd moon
There on Heav'n's ebon pillow laid.

Thy lover who with wine-blank'd mind
Creeps toward his love, all thought erased,
Feels joy to see thy rays at play —
Thy death-pale, woe-engender'd blood —
Thou night-like, death-diseasèd moon.

(END OF PART I.)

VIII. NIGHT (PASSACAGLIA)

Sinister black butterflies
Have done to death the sun's bright light.
An unopen'd magic-book,
The horizon lies, all silent.

Out of mists from deeps unmeasured
Rises scent that murders mem'ry!
Sinister black butterflies
Have done to death the sun's bright light.

And from Heaven, earthward bound,
Sinking down with leaden swaying,
Unseen fall the monstrous creatures
On the hearts of men descending —
Sinister black butterflies.

IX. PRAYER TO PIERROT

Pierrot, all laughter
Have I forgot!

[315

Its form, its brilliance
Is gone — is gone!

Black waves the banner
Now from my mast.
Pierrot, all laughter
Have I forgot!

O give me back,
Thou vet. of the spirit,
Snow-man of lyric,
Marquis of moonshine,
Pierrot, my laughter!

X. THEFT

Red aristocratic rubies —
Bleeding drops of former glory —
Slumber in the shrines of dead men
Down there in the vaulted graveyards.

Nights, with all his boon companions,
Down Pierrot will go, to steal there
Red aristocratic rubies —
Bleeding drops of former glory.

But, there, ev'ry hair will stiffen,
Pallid fear freezing their muscles:
Through the darkness there — like eyeballs! —
Stare out from the shrines of dead men
Red aristocratic rubies.

XI. BLACK MASS

At fearsome ev'n-communion,
'Mid blinding glare of monstrance
And flick'ring light of candles,
Comes to the altar — Pierrot!

His hand, all god-devoted,
Rips down the priestly garments
At fearsome ev'n-communion
'Mid blinding glare of monstrance.

With benedictive gesture
Shows he, to fear-blanched * spirits
The dripping, blood-red Hostia —
His heart — in bloody fingers,
At fearsome ev'n communion.

* Schoenberg repeats this word (*bangen*).

XII. GALLOWS-SONG

That wither'd hussy,
That long-necked creature,
Will be his final
    Belovèd one.

In his sick mem'ry
Sticks, like a bent nail,
That withered hussy,
That long-necked creature.

Scrawny as stone-pine,
On neck a pigtail,
Madly she'll throw lean
Arms 'round the rascal —
That wither'd hussy.

XIII. BEHEADING

The moon, a shining scimitar
Upon a black and silken cushion,
Grown ghostly big, sends down dire threats
    Through sorrow-darkened night.

Pierrot, frantic, runs here and there
And gazes up in deadly fear at
The moon, a shining scimitar
Upon a black and silken cushion.

'Neath him his knees go loose and shiver;
Pow'rless, he suddenly collapses
And feels it swoop, all vengefully
Upon his sinful neck descending —
The moon, that shining scimitar.

XIV. THE CROSSES

Holy crosses are the verses
On which poets, mute, are bleeding,
Stricken blind by flocks of eagles
Fluttering like evil spirits.

On those bodies swords were gorging,
Glorying in the bloody scarlet!
Holy crosses are the verses
On which poets, mute, are bleeding.

Dead, the head; all stiff, the hair-locks —
Far away, the shouting rabble.

Slowly sinks the sun beneath them
Like a red and regal diadem.
Holy crosses are the verses.

(END OF PART II.)

XV. HOMESICKNESS

Gentle mourning, crystalline complaining
Like old-time Italian pantomiming
Sounds far distant: like Pierrot, so wooden,
Now become so modern-sentimental.

And it rings throughout his heart's dry desert —
Echoes, muted, throughout all his senses —
Gentle mourning, crystalline complaining
Like old-time Italian pantomiming.

Now forsakes Pierrot the mien of sadness!
Through the paling firelight of the moonshine,
Through the light-sea's tide a heartfelt yearning
Rises up, right up to Heaven's homeland —
Gentle mourning, crystalline complaining.

XVI. A SCURVY TRICK

In Cassander's shiny head-piece,
In that dome where air goes whistling,
Bores Pierrot, his eyes a-twinkle,
Gently, with trepanning-cutter,

And then packs in, with his big thumb,
Wads of priceless Turkish 'baccy
In Cassander's shiny headpiece,
In that dome where air goes whistling,

Then pushes a tube of cherry
Back there in the shiny bald spot
And, complacent, smokes and blows out
Puffs of priceless Turkish 'baccy
From Cassander's shiny head-piece.

XVII. PARODY

Hair-curlers glinting, shining,
Stuck in her graying hair,
Sits the Duenna, crooning
There in her jacket red.

Awaiting him in the arbor
She loves Pierrot to madness,

Hair-curlers glinting, shining,
Stuck in her graying hair.

Suddenly — hear — a whisper!
A breath that titters softly:
The moon, the spying rascal,
Is aping with his white rays
Hair-curlers' glint and shine.

XVIII. THE MOON-STREAK

With a whitened streak of brilliant moonshine
On the shoulder of his coal-black topcoat,
So Pierrot walks out in the mild evening —
Out to hunt for luck and new adventure.

Something suddenly shows on his topcoat.
He inspects himself and finds, precisely
There, a whitened streak of brilliant moonshine
On the shoulder of his coal-black topcoat.

"What now?" thinks he, "that's a streak of gypsum!"
Wipes and swipes, yet he cannot erase it.
So he goes, all poison-swollen, onward —
Rubs and scrubs until the early morning
At the whitened streak of brilliant moonshine.

XIX. SERENADE

With grotesque and giant bow-stick
Pierrot scrapes on his viola.
Like a stork on one foot standing
Sadly plucks a pizzicato.

Now here comes Cassander, raging
At this night-time virtuoso.
With grotesque and giant bow-stick
Pierrot scrapes on his viola.

Now he throws down his viola
And with delicate left fingers
Wrapped round the neck of the bald-head
Dreaming plays upon his bald spot
With grotesque and monstrous bow-stick.

XX. HOMEWARD JOURNEY (BARCAROLLE)

The moonbeam is his paddle,
Water-lily serves as boat
Whereon Pierrot sails southward
With fair propitious winds.

The stream hums low scales softly
And rocks the tiny craft.
The moonbeam is his paddle,
Water-lily serves as boat.

To Bergamo, his homeland
Will Pierrot now return;
Soft-gleaming, there to Eastward
The green horizon glows.
A moonbeam is his paddle.

XXI. O LONG-LOST SCENT

O long-lost scent from fairy-time,
Again dost thou bedew my senses!
A crazy lord of knavery
Flies through the lightsome air.

A lucky wish has made me gay
With joys that I have long neglected.
A long-lost scent from fairy-time,
    Again bedews my sense.

Now all my antics I give o'er:
From out my sunlight-flooded window
I watch in peace the well-loved world
And dream of blessed distant regions.
O long-lost scent from fairy-time!

Chamber Music in the
United States

IN THAT general perspective which we have so far tried to maintain, chamber music in the United States (which we shall hereafter call Ãmerican) doubtless belongs in the nationalistic category. But while Russian or Bohemian or Scandinavian nationalism connoted a distinctive background of mental attitude and custom, the notion of American nationalism evokes a cultural image so confused as to be all but indefinable. There is, however, one similarity. We found the characteristics of the European nations most distinctively portrayed in their dance-music, and that seems to be true also of America.

We have seen that the simple dance-form — of course with many cross-fertilizations — flowered in Europe (but chiefly in Germany) into the sonata form which underlies both symphony and chamber music of the classic order. In America, the one really fertile contribution to the flora of music has been Jazz. Appearing only after the symphony, even in Europe, had begun to decline, it has seldom been assimilable into modern examples of that form; but its influence, even on European music, has been extensive and healthy.

Its parent — the rag-time of the gay nineties — was generally viewed as a sort of musical weed, to be vigilantly uprooted from respectable musical gardens. But the virility of the plant exceeded the vigilance of the gardeners; its offspring, Jazz, sprouting in New Orleans, came at length to the attention of what one might call the musical horticulturists, European as well as American; and further pruning and cross-fertilization have established its status as a flowering plant of no mean value. For its true creative impulse is a sort of naive, bubbling excitement which, at its best, is immediately improvisatory; and that image of experience which we recognize in learned as well as in naive music as true is most convincing when, along with the learned structure which widens the range of the composer's imaginative vision, the perfected utterance still shows traces of its essentially improvisatory origin.

The formal musical education of America (and of England as well) in the nineteenth century emanated from what might be called the cloisters which German musical culture had instituted. American music students went to Europe expecting to be cloistered, and found within those walls such wealth of musical nourishment that they felt no sense of confinement. Returning to America, they naturally tried to shape the rawer American listener after the pattern (essentially German) to which they had all but unconsciously shaped themselves. America, that is, became a musical colony of Germany. Few indeed were the conspicuous American musicians who had not been trained in Germany, and many were the German emigrants who, after the revolution of 1848, helped to perpetuate America's colonial status.

Among the most conspicuous American composers of the nineteenth century — John Knowles Paine (1839–1906); Arthur Foote (1853–1937); George W. Chadwick (1854–1931); Edgar Stillman Kelley (1857–1944); Edward MacDowell (1861–1908) and Horatio Parker (1863–1919) — only Arthur Foote had no European training. All these save Edward MacDowell wrote chamber music, some of them in considerable volume; but none of their efforts has survived in the contemporary repertoire. Two notable performing groups — a piano trio founded by Theodore Thomas and William Mason, and the outstanding Kneisel quartet — brought the intimate beauty of chamber music to select audiences, and stimulated many similar organizations, amateur and professional, to the exploration of its literature; but the still small voice of chamber music was largely unheeded by the average music-lover.

France, after the first World War, emerged as a strong claimant for leadership in the musical world. Many young American composers were thus attracted to Paris, a large number of whom sought the instruction of Nadia Boulanger. How large her share was in the emancipation of America from its colonial status is a question we cannot pretend to answer. The emancipation, at any rate, was extensive. But another force, even stronger, was also at work — the emancipation (as it was then understood) from the tyranny of the tonic in the whole scheme of musical thought; and this revolution in the musical language itself was more far-reaching than any mere escape from a European tradition could have been.

It entailed endless experiment, much of which was all but fruitless, and it naturally shifted the emphasis in creative effort from the expressive aspect of that problem to the structural. Results of that experiment in Europe were indicated, as far as the scope of this book would permit, in the previous chapter. They have been not less varied in America. Partly because of our heterogeneous population, which cannot but retain highly diverse and all but unconscious traces of ancestral attitude, we have shown a considerable distrust of theory in art, and have formed a more eclectic taste than that of the more homogeneous European communities from which our art derives.

That grouping which gave at least the semblance of a classification in our study of nationalistic chamber music is thus not applicable in our sketch of American effort in this field. Neither is there any definite grouping into schools. The influence of Nadia Boulanger is doubtless great, but she has never sought to tag her pupils with her mark. Neither, for that matter, did Schoenberg, who has many followers in America. Even his system, now mostly called the "serial" technique, has been adopted in modified form by many composers who find its rigidity, when strictly pursued, repellent. And the contemporary musical idiom, shunning the directness of diatonic phraseology, is almost certain to make the use of "native" themes (which, anyhow, are more familiar than native, and whose connotations cannot but be narrow) sound "dated." * For these and many other reasons our selection of examples, necessarily limited, will appear haphazard and our discussion indefinite in aim.

A beginning may be made with Charles Ives (1874–1954) the most consciously American of all our composers. Although he studied composition with Horatio Parker at Yale, his musical imagination was far ahead of that instruction and pursued its independent course to the end of his effort as composer, brought about around 1930 by a diabetic condition. Recognition of his work came almost wholly after its completion, but his last twenty-four years were thus much brightened. His first string quartet (1896) is subtitled *A Revival Service*; there is a "Pre-Second String Quartet" (1905) and a Second (1913); a piece called *Space and Duration* for string quartet and a mechanical piano; another called *All*

---

* How soon the contemporary idiom itself may become dated is a question which only the future can answer. It is nevertheless a question of some import.

the Way Around and Back for piano, violin, flute, bugle, and bells; *The Innate* for string quartet and piano; a trio (not subtitled and somewhat more conventional) for piano, violin, and 'cello; and four sonatas for violin and piano, the last of which is subtitled *Children's Day at the Camp Meeting*.

These titles suggest a merely naive imagination. But the implied hymn-tunes and popular songs, although quoted recognizably, are backgrounded by music far from naive — music which illuminates the emotional context of the camp meeting, for instance, as that of a significant event for the participants. The method is naive. The intended image of experience is not. Such a constructive process could hardly be successful, to the rhetorical ear. But the image, if you can catch it, is compelling.

A not dissimilar imagination is that of Henry Cowell (1897–   ). Unlike Ives, he had European training; like him, he devoted it to the realization of considerably unconventional images, less autochthonous than Ives's, but no more European than those. He is an enormously prolific writer, over a thousand works having come from his pen. (He and his wife have also given us a significant biography of Ives.) His first chamber work, called *Ensemble*, is for string quintet (two 'celli) and two "thundersticks"— somewhat concave wooden blades, attached to strings, which the "performers" whirl and whirr about their heads, with increasing speed yielding gradations from a murmur to a roar. Their contribution to the rather straightforward music of the strings is somewhat like that of his "tone clusters" to the rather diatonic piano pieces in which they appear.* This piece has four movements, the first, *Larghetto*, 6-4; the second a Scherzo; the third, *Adagio*, for 'cello alone but with a thunderstick solo; the fourth a brief *Allegro* for strings only. Cowell's chamber pieces are mostly for unusual combinations and seem to this commentator largely experimental. His book, *New Musical Resources* (1930), reveals the bent of his mind; but that mind, as both book and music will testify, is highly original.

Hardly less versatile but more attuned to the current of American mu-

* In isolation, tone clusters are mere noise. In their musical context they contribute a strange blurred amplification of the harmony (often very appropriate) suggested by Cowell's tune and its bass — these two voices being usually clearly defined. The thundersticks yield no definable tones; yet they appear to amplify similarly the harmonic sense of the strings. To inexperienced ears, even the complex polyphonic harmony of Bach or Brahms, and certainly the irrational harmony of atonal linear counterpoint, may offer little more. But that little is a value not to be ignored. For it is capable of expansion.

sical endeavor, Aaron Copland (1900–   ) has been relatively little concerned with chamber music. Two works only seem to have enlisted his full constructive energy: the sextet for clarinet, piano, and string quartet, and the piano quartet first performed at the Coolidge Festival in Washington in 1950. Both show a highly developed skill; neither one, to our mind, offers that invitation to intimacy which is the most precious of chamber music's many virtues. The piano quartet, rather unexpectedly from the composer of *Appalachian Spring* and *Billy the Kid*, is largely based on an eleven-note "row" predominantly in whole-tone intervals. As an essay in this structural manner, the work is highly finished; its appeal, however, is to the structural rather than the poetic imagination.

Because of his wide influence on American composition — an influence based on indubitable achievement — Ernest Bloch (1880–   ), of Swiss origin but since 1917 (except for a nine-year sojourn in Switzerland) resident in America, seems to fall into the next place in our hasty sketch. His Jewish sympathy has yielded many works of high expressive intensity (the 'cello rhapsody, *Schelomo*, and the three *Poèmes juifs* are examples), and that manner, somewhat restrained, governs also his chamber music, all of which seems to have been written in America. Intensity is the impression chiefly conveyed by the first string quartet (1916), although this is mitigated by the pastoral second movement. The next chamber work is a piano quintet (1923) in which the unusual color of quarter tones gives to the second theme a peculiar character somewhat out of accord, to our ears, with that of the whole movement. The slow movement is superscribed *Andante mistico*; the third, *Allegro energico*, with a second theme *barbarico*, but the end is calm. The second string quartet (1946) is all but atonal. It is unified by a motto theme that points the way to the passacaglia and fugue of the finale. This quartet won the Critics Circle award for chamber music (1947). The third (1951–52) is gentler in dissonance but not less purposive. Its main theme features a succession of sturdy downward 5ths that form a cyclic unit for the whole work. The fourth quartet (1954) is generally similar.

We may also speak of Ernst Krenek (1900–   ), who came to America at the same age as Ernest Bloch, and who has wielded a comparable influence — considerably different in direction — on our musical thought. Beginning as a disciple of Mahler, he turned in 1933 to the dodecaphony of Schoenberg which for some time he pursued exclusively but by no means slavishly. But his earlier training with Franz Schrecker was not eradicated, and the twelve-tone system was often forsaken, as in the Third piano concerto (1946). He is a very prolific composer. His chamber music includes eight string quartets, several duet sonatas and suites, and a string trio. His earlier manner is well exemplified in his Fifth string quartet (1930) whose three movements are entitled *Sonate*, *Tema und Variationen*, and *Phantasie Adagio*. The sonata movement is remarkably conventional in design, even to the marked repetition of the exposition section. The technique is nowhere extravagant, and the music reveals an expressive purpose of significant weight. His later manner seems to us well illustrated in the string trio (1948) which is in the twelve-tone technique. The row — F, B, G, A♭, D♭, C, B♭, E, D, A, E♭, F♯ — is manipulated with high ingenuity.

Externally, Bloch's chamber music displays no conscious Americanism. (His one effort in this direction, the "epic rhapsody," *America* (1927), was hardly successful.) He speaks of an America which he has in some measure assimilated out of his long residence here — a nation too complex to be represented by mere nationalistic labels. And his influence has been of that nature.

It is visible not in the detail but in the general purport of the work of Roger Sessions (1896–   ) who was first Bloch's pupil and later his assistant and successor at the Cleveland Institute of Music. Of all our contemporary composers, he is probably the most deeply conscious of the problems of meaning and structure in music — problems which he has considerably illuminated in a little book, *The Musical Experience of Composer, Performer, Listener* (1950). He is in no sense a mere stylist, since he shapes his musical thought to accord with "the inner gestures which embody our deepest and most intimate responses" to experience; and tricks of style are but a feeble counterpart of those responses. In consequence his style is austere and often obscure; but even though you seldom feel that you have fully understood his speech, you are convinced that his is no idle utterance. His total output is not large. It includes three stage works, four symphonies, and concertos for violin (1935) and piano (1956), and his chamber pieces are correspondingly few — two string quartets, one string quintet, and a duo for violin and piano. The second quartet begins with a fugal *Lento* (4-4), quite searching in its intensity; there follow an *Allegro appassionato* whose passion seems to us rather intellectual, an *Andante tranquillo* (4-8) with five variations, all rather remote in their derivation but individually clearly characterized, and for finale a lively *Presto* (3-4). In all these, although technical difficulties demand skilled performers, the problems of interpretation are far more severe. But the intimacy of chamber music is there for those who seek it.

Like the music of Roger Sessions, that of Wallingford Riegger (1885–   ) betrays a considerable teutonic influence. (He studied in Berlin after graduation from the Institute of Musical Art in New York, and conducted opera in Würzburg and Königsberg.) His musical manner seems to us more abstract in constructive purpose, but less obscure in expressive import, than that of Sessions. A remarkable example is his *Study in Sonority* for ten violins (1927); others, not dissimilar in purpose, are a *Divertissement* for flute, harp, and 'cello; three canons for flute, oboe, clarinet, and bassoon; *Music for Brass Choir*, and a nonet for brass (1951). There are two string quartets – the first, Op. 30, being rather ostentatiously in the twelve-tone technique. (The tone-row, direct, is vigorously rhythmed to form the main theme of the first movement; in retrograde it forms the *Molto Adagio* introduction to the following Scherzo; in inversion it is the basis of the slow movement, alternately *Adagio* and *Andante*; and in retrograde inversion it yields the finale, *Vivo*.) The second quartet is not in the twelve-tone manner but is to our ears an equally ingenious study in rhythmic complexities. Both quartets were published in 1949, and a piano quintet followed in 1950. His music seems at first to command, rather forbiddingly. On closer acquaintance it invites, sometimes with a wry smile.

Walter Piston (1894–   ) first chose painting as his medium of artistic utterance, and one is inclined to wonder how far his sense of color and design in music (which he began to pursue after graduation from the Massachusetts Normal Art School in 1916) has been affected by that study. His chamber music includes, along with four string quartets, a quintet for flute and strings, a *Partita* for violin, viola, and organ, a Sonatina for violin and harpsichord, a *Divertimento* for nine instruments, and a quintet for horn and woodwinds. His first European training was with Nadia Boulanger (1924–1926) after graduation from Harvard. A Guggenheim fellowship (1934) widened his horizon, and almost all his compositions were written thereafter. His eminence as teacher almost equals that as composer as his textbooks on harmony, counterpoint, and orchestration, as well as his many eminent pupils, will testify. The quintet for horn and wood shows high skill in handling the combination of not very variable colors. The first movement (*Animato*, 4-4) is in sonata form with well-contrasted subjects; the second (*Con tenerezza*, 6-8), led off by the oboe, finds quietly appealing melody for every member of the group; the *Scherzando* has a piquantly irregular rhythm, and the finale (*Allegro comodo*, 2-4) is a remarkably effortless rondo. The Fourth string quartet (1953) progresses from a sober sonata-movement (*Soave*, 2-2) to an *Adagio* (9-8) with an elegiac theme in the 'cello; real animation begins with the Scherzo (*Leggero vivace*, 2-4) whose sprightly theme is well developed, and the finale (*Con fuoco*, 6-8) has a vital rhythmic energy which never really weakens.

With the exception of Charles Ives, Roy Harris (1898–   ) seems to us the most characteristically American of all our composers. He turned seriously to composition only after returning from service in the first World War, and only "found his voice" (as he put it) when he went to Paris for study with Nadia Boulanger. It was his voice, however, not hers, which he found, and it spoke so appealingly to his countrymen that in the middle 'forties he became the most frequently performed of all our composers. A decline in popularity followed, almost as notable as the rise – a fact variously interpretable in its critical implications, but in any light somewhat disturbing. Chamber music turns up frequently in the long catalogue of his compositions, but only his piano quintet (1936) seems to have enduring interest. He seems to us to have a notable intuition for musical imagery but an insufficient awareness of the function of structure toward making that imagery convincing.

Samuel Barber (1910–   ) has written little chamber music – an early *Serenade* for string quartet (1929), a rather classical quartet, Op. 11, from which the slow movement has been widely heard as *Adagio for Strings*, a 'cello sonata (1932), *Dover Beach* – Matthew Arnold's poem, set for baritone voice and string quartet (1931), and *Summer Music* for woodwind quintet (1956). His style is conservative – probably because he has a distinctive gift for melody and little disposition to distort his melodic line beyond recognition through ingenious manipulation. But his imagination is predominantly dramatic, so that full realization of his image demands larger media of performance than chamber music offers.

In high contrast is the Second string quartet of Elliott Carter (1908–   ), which is a remarkable essay in structual virtuosity. It rivals in difficulty the *Lyric Suite* of Alban Berg, and presents both to eye and ear formidable obstacles to immediate understanding. Yet the drive of a musical purpose is evident throughout. It is unique in specifying a distinctive character for each of the four instruments: the first violin often playing in a bravura style, the second in regular rhythms; the viola is predominantly expressive, and the 'cello has many *rubato* passages to which the accompanying parts must of course be adjusted. An Introduction of 34 bars leads to the main movement, *Allegro fantastico*, led by the first violin as solo up to the Coda which is an accompanied Cadenza for viola. The "subjects" are fragmentary and considerably dominated by the interval of the 4th, with complex rhythms often in quintuplets against triplets or capriciously syncopated accompanying voices. The second movement, *Presto scherzando*, is mostly in 5-4 time, with the second violin leading and a Cadenza for 'cello at the end. The third, *Andante espressivo*, 3-4, is led by the viola solo, but ends with an unaccompanied Cadenza for the first violin which recalls matter from the first movement. The last, *Allegro*, becomes extremely complex, with the actual notes of its motives, often distributed among several voices, indicated on an extra staff. For sheer virtuosity this quartet should be given the palm, certainly among American chamber music, and possibly among the whole literature.

Two more important figures, shunted to America by the war, must be included as contributors to our slowly crystallizing American musical idiom: Ernst Toch (1887–   ) and Darius Milhaud (1892–   ). Each has been deeply interested in chamber music. Toch has written at least nine string quartets, one of which, in the serial technique (which he does *not* espouse), is really a satirical effort. There are also many chamber pieces for various combinations, with or without piano. His textures are highly polyphonic and often sharply dissonant; his structure is involved, but as lucid as his by no means commonplace thought will permit. Milhaud, one of the famous "Six" in the burgeoning France of the 'twenties, was the most articulate spokesman for polytonality. His chamber music forms but a fraction of his enormous output; yet there are at least sixteen string quartets, of which Nos. 14 and 15 are so constructed that they may be performed simultaneously. His manner is almost always charmingly lucid, and though his matter does not lack weight, one can hardly resist the conclusion that composition has become for him a diversion.

Those so far named are the most conspicuous of our older native or naturalized composers. Neither they nor any of the younger men to whom we now briefly turn has been able to steer the current of American musical thought in any single or determined direction. Many figures of evident significance are emerging, in whose work skill is always evident and imaginative purpose beyond the boundary of skill often discernible. Among these the following, whom we select out of personal preference rather than critical judgment, and whom we list alphabetically for lack of any precise classification, are notable:

Marc Blitzstein (1905–   ), a pupil of Nadia Boulanger but also of Schoenberg, is mainly interested in the stage, but has written one string quartet and a *Serenade* for the four strings as well as some smaller pieces. Norman Dello Joio (1913–   ) writes mostly in a lighter vein, and his chamber pieces are for unusual combinations such as his sextet for three recorders and three strings. David Diamond, likewise a pupil of Boulanger, has four string quartets and a dozen or so of chamber pieces with piano and strings or winds or for winds alone. His idiom, at first very aggressive, softens notably in his later works. Herbert Elwell (1898–   ), whose *Happy Hypocrite* has been widely performed, is another Boulanger pupil. His two string quartets and his violin sonata seem notable efforts toward expanding the contemporary idiom without defying tradition. Irving Fine (1914–   ) is a more consciously intellectual composer. Piston and Boulanger were his earlier teachers, but his style, remarkably concise, shows many other influences. There is a very impressive string quartet (1950), a violin sonata (1946), and a *Partita* for wind quintet (1948). Ross Lee Finney (1906–   ), who worked with Nadia Boulanger and Alban Berg, seems to find in chamber music his most natural expressive outlet. He has written seven string quartets, sonatas for viola and 'cello with piano, and a piano trio, and has set — to our mind notably — the *Chamber Music* cycle of poems by James Joyce. The serial technique is often ingeniously interpolated.

Romeo Eugene Gutsché (1907–   ), who has just been awarded a Guggenheim fellowship for the completion of his opera, *Judith*, a modern adaptation of the biblical tale, has written four string quartets, of which one is a notable experiment in quarter tones. Two quartet-groups, tuned a quarter-tone apart, make that interval an integral instead of a merely incidental factor in the texture. He has also devised his own twelve-tone technique, after Schoenberg, but employs it with a singular mildness. Howard Hanson (1897–   ), the most familiar figure to the general public among all our serious composers, included among the brilliant works that first established his reputation three chamber pieces: a piano quintet, a *Concerto da camera* for piano and string quartet, and one quartet for strings. Thereafter there is only the *Fantasia on a Theme of Youth* (1951). He has recently put forth a plausible reconciliation of twentieth-century harmony with that of the preceding era. How far that structural scheme may prove to interpret or guide the still uncharted effort of the future only a bolder mind than ours would dare to say. But that such a generally accepted musical idiom as he there envisages must exist before we can achieve a generally intelligible musical literature seems to us indubitable.

Opposed to that assumption are the recent experiments in music based on electronic tone-production: music as remote from all the extant literature, tribal or civilized, as are our adventures in outer space from travel whether by horse and buggy or jet plane. No real literature in this idiom has as yet emerged; but that a musician of such solid attainments as Otto Luening (1900–) pursues the experiments is a provocative fact. He has written three string quartets and six duet sonatas, is a skilled pianist, flautist, and conductor, and has written extensively for orchestra. I have neither heard nor seen (nor could I read) his *Suite from King Lear* for tape recorder alone; but his vision and that of his colleague Vladimir Ussachevsky may well be longer than mine.

Quincy Porter (1897–), educated at Yale and in Paris (with V. d'Indy) and also with Bloch at Cleveland, is an experienced chamber-music player (violin and viola). His output in this field is large — eight quartets and many other works for more or fewer instruments. His idiom is pretty bold, but his thought is such as to demand it. William Schuman (1910–) is much more an orchestral than a chamber-music composer, but has managed to produce four string quartets and a curious *Quartettino* for four bassoons. He seems to us to follow rather than lead the still largely uncharted course of American music. John Verrall (1908–), a competent 'cellist and pianist, has a large list of chamber works, headed by six string quartets and including many others for a great variety of combinations. He has lately turned to quartet composition addressed to less experienced performers — an effort to be highly commended since it glimpses a purpose all but lost from sight in the conflicting hurly-burly of present-day aims.

A similar purpose guided — perhaps by remote control — first the imagination and thereafter the structural effort of the acknowledged masters of chamber music. It was an offering of intimacy, originating in an image, not of factual experience but of the perceptual and emotional awareness awakened in us by factual experience.

That image is fragile. To be communicated — to be evoked in the mind of a communicant — it must be shaped with exquisite skill. That skill is hard to distinguish from the technique of construction which analytical theory expounds, and which can be learned by assiduous study. The practitioner of that technique can indeed make music in its own structural image — can worship it, and can assemble admiring congregations to enact the ritual of worship. But admiration is not intimacy, which is evoked by a kind of "real presence" unrecognized in the ritual of skilled construction.

That presence, toward which we have often fumblingly tried to point, is evident in many of the older masterpieces we have studied. It is possible, if the "unrestricted" musical idiom of our day learns to obey the restrictions which true imagination must impose, that it may reveal that presence more clearly than did the older musical language. But that very desirable end will not be attained out of faith in the gods of structure, nor by sacrifice on their altars.

INDEX

Index